VITRUVIUS

WRITING THE BODY OF ARCHITECTURE

THE MIT PRESS CAMBRIDGE, MASSACHUSETTS LONDON, ENGLAND

VITRUVIUS

WRITING THE BODY OF ARCHITECTURE

INDRA KAGIS McEWEN

This book was set in FFScala and Scala Sans by Graphic Composition, Inc., and was printed and bound in the United States of America.

Library of Congress Cataloging-in-Publication Data
McEwen, Indra Kagis.
    Vitruvius : writing the body of architecture / Indra Kagis McEwen.
        p. cm.
    Includes bibliographical references and index.
    ISBN 0-262-13415-2 (hc. : alk. paper)
      1. Vitruvius Pollio. De architectura. 2. Architecture—Early works
    to 1800. I. Title.
  NA2515 .M38 2002
  720—dc21

                                                        2002075356

À la mémoire de Jean

CONTENTS

Preface   viii

Introduction   1

I   THE ANGELIC BODY   15

Commentaries.
Auctoritas.
A Perfect Ten.
Unified Bodies.
Signification.

2   THE HERCULEAN BODY   91

The King's Double.
The Once and Future King.
Benefiting the World.

3   THE BODY BEAUTIFUL   155

Vitruvian Man.
Religio.
Venus, *venustas.*
Corinthia.

4   THE BODY OF THE KING   225

Gnomonice.
The Prima Porta Statue of Augustus.
Corpus imperii.

Conclusion   299

Notes   305

Bibliography   407

Illustration Sources   477

Index   480

PREFACE

It is admittedly a bold venture to take on Vitruvius. More than twenty centuries have elapsed since he wrote. The language he wrote in is long dead. Iconic classical status has petrified *De architectura* and added further to its remoteness. If I have succeeded in traversing even a part of the great distance that separates Vitruvius's work from mine, it has been in no small measure thanks to the critical attention and support of the following.

Richard Brilliant and Joseph Rykwert read and commented on early drafts. Professor Brilliant's observations were invariably bracing and salutary, and Professor Rykwert's unfailing encouragement kept me optimistic. Their generosity has been truly extraordinary.

Others who have assisted me in important ways include Hans Böker, Jane Francis, George Hersey, Alberto Pérez-Gómez, Christine Ross, Belgin Turan, Bronwen Wilson, and Mark Wilson Jones. I am grateful to them, particularly to Professor Böker, and also to all those who made helpful remarks and suggestions when I presented parts of this book in lectures and conference papers. Its remaining flaws are, of course, my sole responsibility.

Research was initially funded by the Graham Foundation for Advanced Studies in the Fine Arts, and subsequently by the Social Sciences and Humanities Research Council of Canada. I am grateful to both these institutions for their support.

Friendly assistance was always forthcoming at the library of the Canadian Centre for Architecture. The librarians in the Interlibrary Loans department of the McLennan Library of McGill University cheerfully made even the most obscure material accessible. Dottore Paolo Liverani at the Vatican Museums was especially gracious when I went there to photograph the Prima Porta statue of Augustus. Sarah Balleux was a great help with the drawings.

Once again, it has been a pleasure to work with the MIT Press. My thanks to Roger Conover for his commitment to the project, to Matthew Abbate for editing the manuscript with rigor, discretion, and good judgment, and to Patrick Ciano for designing it with sensitivity. Lisa Reeve at all times kept the lines of communication open. I am particularly grateful to Betty Goodwin and René Blouin for kindly letting me use *Pieces of Time IX* as a cover image, and also to Judith Terry for her expert help with proofreading.

My daughter Marianne supplied invaluable photographic assistance. For her and for her brothers Jean-Sabin and Jérémie, I give thanks above all. Their love has been my lifeline. This book is dedicated to the memory of their father, my husband Jean McEwen, who died while I was writing it.

Montreal, August 2002

A NOTE ON TEXT AND TRANSLATION

For books 1, 2, 3, 4, 7, 8, 9, and 10 of *De architectura,* I have followed the Latin text of the eight volumes of the new ten-volume Budé edition so far published by the Presses Universitaires de France. For the other two books (5 and 6), I have followed the text of the Fensterbusch Vitruvius of 1964. All translations of Vitruvius are my own, with the Latin cited in the notes for reference. Unless otherwise noted, translations of other classical authors follow the Loeb Classical Library.

VITRUVIUS
WRITING THE BODY OF ARCHITECTURE

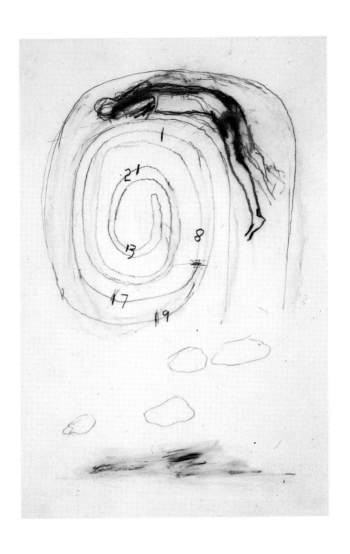

Betty Goodwin, *Pieces of Time IX,* 1996. Oil, graphite, and charcoal on mylar, 43.2 x 28 cm. Private collection. © Betty Goodwin. Photo by Richard-Max Tremblay.

INTRODUCTION

Autrefois les sçavans n'avoient pour but dans leurs études que les recherches des opinions des Anciens, se faisant beaucoup plus d'honneur d'avoir trouvé le vray sens du texte d'Aristote que d'avoir découvert la vérité de la chose dont il s'agit dans le texte.

Claude Perrault, *Ordonnance des cinq espèces de colonnes*[1]

In the mid 20s B.C., an aging military architect about whom little is known presented Augustus Caesar, new ruler of the Roman world, with ten books on architecture.[2] The only major work on architecture to survive from classical antiquity, and the first self-consciously comprehensive account of the subject, Vitruvius's *De architectura* in time became *the* text on architecture to which, at least until the eighteenth century, all other texts referred.[3]

   The best known of such texts appeared in the Renaissance, after the legendary discovery of the ninth-century Vitruvius manuscript now known as the Harleianus by the humanist Poggio Bracciolini at St. Gall in 1414 and, more importantly, after the invention of printing.[4] Not only were there editions of *De architectura* itself, in Latin or in translation, many with commentaries and sumptuous illustrations.[5] Beginning with Alberti's *De re aedificatoria libri decem* of the mid fifteenth century, Vitruvius was also the principal, if not always explicit, referent for architectural treatises that took him as their point of departure.[6] For Renaissance theorists, Vitruvius's authoritative voice from the past both raised for the first time and defined for all time what the important issues in architecture were, laying down essential terms of reference not only for architects and their patrons but for all educated people.

The authority of *De architectura* did not escape the wholesale demotion of ancient texts that accompanied the scientific revolution in the seventeenth century, however, and by the end of the eighteenth the work had become less a source of architectural truth than a text to be investigated for information about the architecture of antiquity—and, more often than not, to be censured for misinformation about it. The historiographical ground rules underlying the recent resurgence of Vitruvian studies among classicists and classical archaeologists in continental Europe continue to fall within such essentially positivist guidelines, initially laid out before a hostile audience by Claude Perrault near the end of the seventeenth century.[7] Legitimate study of ancient texts like that of Vitruvius, Perrault claimed, should entail less an attempt to discover the "true sense" of the text than to verify "the truth of that with which the text deals."[8]

Bracketed by this fundamentally modern premise, the scholarly investigations of classicists during the past three and a half decades have indeed resulted in a much more detailed assessment than ever before of the truth of that with which *De ar-*

chitectura deals.[9] Although it is still little, we know more about the author himself.[10] The nature, operability, and Hellenistic origins of his proportional schemata are better understood, thanks largely to the work of German scholars, especially Burkhardt Wesenberg.[11] Elisa Romano has explored his literary influences and cultural milieu in her *La capanna e il tempio*.[12] His language has been examined by Louis Callebat;[13] his mechanics, the subject of book 10, by Philippe Fleury in a recent monograph.[14] Each of the volumes of the new French translation being published in the Budé edition has appeared with a newly established Latin text, full critical apparatus, lengthy introduction, extensive commentary, and up-to-date bibliography.[15] Also recent among modern translations is the handsome two-volume Italian one by Antonio Corso and Elisa Romano, extensively commented and annotated like the Budé volumes, and conducted under the direction of Pierre Gros, acknowledged leader in current Vitruvius studies.[16]

Gros's work on Vitruvius has ranged widely, but his chief preoccupation as a classical archaeologist has been to read *De architectura* in terms of the specifics of Roman building practice in the late republic and early empire.[17] Contrasting the variety and inventiveness of the built work of the period with the generally unitary prescriptions set out in the treatise, he concluded early on that Vitruvius's project was a normative one, motivated by the desire for rational systematization;[18] not with a view to establishing a systematic handbook for practitioners, nor entirely with the aim of dignifying the architectural profession by making architecture a proper liberal art like rhetoric, as Frank E. Brown argued over thirty-five years ago.[19] Neither a *Fachbuch* for practitioners nor a *Sachbuch* for educated laymen, *De architectura* and its evidently normative *parti*, Gros has maintained, must be understood in terms of values specific to the time and place of its writing.[20] What Romans valued above all were the *honores* that were the reward for public service.

Although less methodically circumscribed than the Vitruvius scholarship of classical scholars in continental Europe, there has been a corresponding renewal of interest in Vitruvius among English-speaking scholars, though not among classicists, who tend to ignore him or at best to diminish his importance.[21] Significantly, Ingrid Rowland, author of the just-published new English translation of *De architectura*, is not primarily a classicist, and her collaborator, Thomas Noble Howe, is an architect.[22] The only monograph on Vitruvius in English is a very brief study, first published twenty years ago.[23] English-speaking scholars, moreover, almost never participate in European colloquia on Vitruvius.[24]

Today, anglophone Vitruvians are to be found less among classicists than among architects and architectural historians working under the rubric of what is taught in professional schools as "history and theory." Whereas European classicists have concentrated primarily on reconstructing "the truth of that with which the text deals," in terms that aim to be rigorously *scientifiques*, architectural Vitruvians, among whom Joseph Rykwert has figured as a chief and very influential exponent, are less concerned with *De architectura* as a repository of facts that are either true or false than in reading the work as the entry point into the (pressing, it is claimed) question of architectural meaning.[25] If these scholars read the text historically, which many do not, they tend to treat it either as the beginning of the architectural tradition that ended with the scientific revolution or as the end of the one that began with the Greeks, to whose understanding of architecture Vitruvius, who worked almost entirely from Greek sources, serves primarily as a kind of window. Either way, the Roman Vitruvius of ca. 25 B.C. slips through cracks, as it were, and with him the historicity of his work. The ahistorical remnant tends to be read as part of a continuum, a source of metaphors and insights that are, or should be—for architects—perennially informative. Of these, the metaphor of architecture as a reflection of the human body is fundamental.[26]

But what is "body" and what is "architecture"? And why, leaving aside for the moment important distinctions between architecture and building, as well as those between human and nonhuman bodies, is architecture a metaphorical body? Questions like these are indeed beyond history. My aim is to broach them, if at all, indirectly by targeting as closely as possible the historical specificity of the work. It seems just possible that the transhistorical voice many English-speaking historians continue to hear in Vitruvius may *sound* universal precisely *because* it is Roman. Which, as I shall argue, is precisely what apologists for the imperial Roman order, Vitruvius among them, intended.

Literary evidence for the reception of Vitruvius in antiquity is rare. He is not mentioned at all in the surviving work of any of his Augustan contemporaries. Pliny, in the mid first century A.D., refers to him as a source three times in his lists of *auctores*.[27] Frontinus mentions him in his late first-century A.D. work on aqueducts.[28] The abridgement of *De architectura* written by Cetius Faventius in the early third century was the first of many works to reduce the treatise to a *Fachbuch*.[29] Servius evokes him as a writer "de architectonica" in his commentary on the *Aeneid* written in the fourth century A.D.[30] Sidonius Apollinaris writing in Gaul in the mid fifth century elevates him to something like mythical stature, anticipating in this his virtual apotheosis in the Renaissance. For Sidonius, Vitruvius is to the plumb line as Orpheus is to the plectrum.[31]

Although a number of inscriptions name a Vitruvius who may or may not be the author of *De architectura,* they are not especially informative.[32] Archaeological evidence is, to say the least, equivocal, with the thrust of much scholarship since the Renaissance being that Vitruvius's rules were rarely, if ever, followed.

Insofar as the "real" or historically specific Vitruvius is the focus of this study, I might be said to be allying myself with the continental European classicists. My interest, however, is primarily architectural, and unlike theirs my aim is less to establish the "truth of that with which the text deals" than, so to speak, to take a great leap backward and adopt the very methodological principle Claude Perrault dismissed over three hundred years ago: to try to discover *le vray sens du texte,* the "true sense of the text." What, to put it simply, was Vitruvius trying to *say*? And why?

As a tactic, this means respecting the text's opacity— allowing what in contemporary critical discourse would be termed its "otherness." An opaque text is, obviously, not a window: neither to the transhistorical truth of architecture (whatever that may be) nor to objects, facts, or events that are in principle verifiable. Such a text has its own identity, is itself an object, fact, or event. Vitruvius thought of his text as a body. This is the focus of my study.

Vitruvius claims, repeatedly, that he was "writing the body of architecture"—the *perfect* body of architecture (*emendatum,* without a flaw), he insists at one point.[33] This is how he begins the preface to book 4.

When I noticed, Imperator, that many who have provided rules and scrolls of commentaries on architecture have not left orderly works but only incomplete drafts, scattered like fragments, I decided it would be a worthy and most useful thing to bring the whole body of this great discipline to complete order and, in separate scrolls, develop a register of conditions for each of its different subjects.[34]

Pierre Gros has singled out this preface as crucial for understanding Vitruvius's intentions, stressing that the project of bringing together a written *corpus* of architectural knowledge from scattered sources is the very hallmark of his originality.[35] That Vitruvius should have done so, or thought he had, is also what underwrites his hope for renown.

"Little celebrity has come my way," laments Vitruvius, who does not appear to have enjoyed much success as an architect.[36] Moreover, avenues to fame were open chiefly to aristocrats who participated in Roman public life—to generals who led victorious armies in battle, above all.[37] The inscriptions that petrified the short-lived apotheosis of the triumph awarded to such *imperatores* recorded *their* names on the *monumenta* they paid for from the spoils of war, not the names of the architects charged with their construction.[38]

Not particularly successful professionally, nor as a *scriba armamentarius* in the service of prominent men himself a prominent figure, nor even, by his own diffident avowal, a writer of great talent, Vitruvius nevertheless hopes, in the preface to book 6, "that once these scrolls have been published [he] will be known even to posterity," adding a little later that he "decided to write the whole body of architecture and its principles with the greatest of care, thinking it would be a not unwelcome service to all peoples."[39]

Written compilations as such did not constitute a claim to fame, however. Nor did originality for that matter, at a time when in Rome truly original undertakings—revolutionary ones, such as Augustus's seizure of command for instance—tended to be presented (and accepted) as a return to the *mos maiorum,* the customs of the ancestors that Cicero said were the foundation of the Roman commonwealth.[40] Pierre Gros sees the notion of service as central to Vitruvius's undertaking, and in this, he claims, *De architectura* as *corpus* plays a key role. Public service, he says, meant providing Augustus, who would famously leave Rome a city of marble, with a kind of brief or complete catalogue on what was to be done.[41] The theme of utility or service has also been the focus of Antoinette Novara's work on Vitruvius.[42] She claims that Vitruvius views his project not only as a service to builders like Augustus who, thanks to *De architectura,* will be able to judge and appreciate what they have undertaken to build, but beyond as a humanistic service *omnibus gentibus,* to all peoples, and even to posterity.[43] The most beneficial thing of all in this regard, she points out, concurring with Pierre Gros, is his having assembled all architectural knowledge into a single well-ordered *corpus.*[44] Why this *corpus* is to be of such great benefit is one of the questions I hope to answer in this book.

Does *corpus* simply mean a compilation? None of the modern translators who render Vitruvius's written *corpus* variously as *Gesamtwerk* in German, *système accompli* or *ouvrage d'ensemble* in French, *sistema organico* in Italian, and "comprehensive treatise" in English seem to have recognized what I have called the opacity of the metaphor.[45] Nor, for that matter, its novelty. It is common enough to speak of a "body" of written work today, but in Latin the use of *corpus* to refer to written work does not predate Cicero, who uses it only twice in family letters, and then with no suggestion of encyclopedic totality.[46] And although the age of Cicero, which was the age of Vitruvius's cultural formation, was full of compilers, none of Vitruvius's older contemporaries such as Varro or indeed Cicero himself, both named by Vitruvius as mentors, appear to have used the term *corpus* to refer to their *Gesamtwerke*.[47] This is very curious. For if, as Claudia Moatti has argued, *rassembler la matière dispersée*—exactly what Vitruvius says he is doing for architecture in the preface to book 4 just cited—was indeed the *mot d'ordre* among writers of the late Roman republic, one would expect the literature of the period to be rife with references to written *corpora,* and this is simply not the case.[48] The first writer to use the term *corpus* in the *Gesamtwerk* sense that scholars assume to be conventional and transparent is Vitruvius himself, who indeed uses it more often and more insistently, even, than any later writer.[49]

This suggests three things. First of all, that the usage was in fact *not* conventional among Latin writers. Second, that *corpus* for Vitruvius, to whom the locution *corpus architecturae* ("the body of architecture") is unique, bears a special relation to his topic—to the matter (taking him at his word) that he is *writing,* not to what he is writing *about.* And last, that his calling his work a *corpus* also bears a special relation to the time of its appearance, which was not in the late republic, when the encyclopedists just mentioned were writing, but at the beginning of the reign of Octavian-Augustus, Julius Caesar's adoptive son and heir.[50]

In the service first of Julius Caesar and later of Augustus himself, Vitruvius was active during the tumultuous years of almost uninterrupted civil strife that marked the transition from republic to empire—the transition from an oligarchy, where power passed yearly from one set of magistrates to another, to the de facto monarchy of a single all-powerful man.[51] *De architectura* appeared in the triumphal period that followed the return of peace, zealously (and not without justification) credited in both the art and literature of the period, not least by Vitruvius himself, to the new ruler.

"When your divine mind and power, Imperator Caesar, were seizing command of the world and all your enemies had been crushed by your invincible strength" is how he begins the preface to book I, addressing Augustus in terms one Roman historian has called "the most complete statement of the concept of empire outside the *Res gestae* [Augustus's autobiography]."[52] In January of 27 B.C., the Roman senate rewarded Octavian with unprecedented *honores* that included the bestowal of the name Augustus, a name never before given to any human, and whose multiple evocations covered a range of meanings all pointing to a special relation with the gods and the god-given power to set the world to rights.[53]

De architectura appeared at the beginning of the Augustan building boom that would not only transform Rome from brick to marble, but would also leave its indelible mark on Roman territories stretching from Cappadocia in the east to the farthest reaches of western Spain, fashioning the scattered lands ruled by Rome into what Ovid, writing near the end of Augustus's long reign of over forty years, would call *corpus imperii,* the body of empire.[54] But when Vitruvius wrote his *corpus* at the beginning of Augustus's reign, the phrase *corpus imperii* was not yet current, and another thing I hope to show is how the specifically architectural *corpus* he wrote provides a framework for understanding the *corpus* the Roman world would become during the reign of the autocrat for whom it was written.[55] Grasping the "true sense" of this written *corpus* depends on grasping what the *corpus* of *imperium* entailed, and vice versa.

Arguing the plausibility of such an intricate web of connections defies a linear approach. My intention is to unravel it piecemeal, in four separate chapters, each dealing with a single aspect of the Vitruvian *corpus.* In the first chapter, "The Angelic Body," I discuss how Vitruvius appears to have understood the task he describes so strangely as "writing the body of architecture." This chapter deals with the book as a book, with the corporeal identity of Vitruvius's written messenger, the *angelos* he constitutes as a unified body of ten *volumina* or scrolls, whose signification I explore in terms of contemporary events and currents of thought, Stoicism and Stoic theories of language in particular.[56p]

In the second chapter, "The Herculean Body," I address the book's and its author's relation to Augustus, Vitruvius's dedicatee, taking into specific account the notion of service that scholars have recently viewed as key in understanding the intent of *De architectura.* The benefits to be conferred by this Herculean body are nothing less than those of civilization itself whose dissemination was Rome's self-appointed "Herculean" task, which Vitruvius presents as unrealizable without his own *corpus.* The argument is developed from an exegesis of the preface to book 2 where the architect Dinocrates impersonates Hercules in order to attract the attention of Alexander the Great.

A close reading of book 3, chapter 1, where Vitruvius articulates the celebrated links between architecture—temples specifically—and the human body, is the point of departure for my third chapter, "The Body Beautiful." This chapter discusses the role of proportion, the role of the circle-and-square geometry bodied forth in Vitruvian Man, so called, and the connection of both to the architectural beauty Vitruvius invariably, and with pointedly deliberate intent, calls *venustas*. Beauty was to play a decisive role in forging the new world order.

Chapter 4, "The Body of the King," explores the nature and unprecedented extent of the Augustan building programs that consolidated Roman rule in the palpable extent of an architectural world-body made congruent with the king's. Included is a close examination of the latter's representation in the famous statue of Augustus from Prima Porta, sculpted not long after the appearance of Vitruvius's treatise. The argument of this final chapter is that in *De architectura* the world-body the Prima Porta Augustus presents as an image becomes a real possibility.

Angelic, Herculean, beautiful, and kingly bodies together constitute Vitruvius's complete body of architecture. That there *was* no "body" of architecture before Vitruvius wrote it, and that its appearance in the early Augustan principate is rooted in the imperial circumstances that brought it to light, leads to the unsettling conclusion that the body of architecture is the body of empire. The birth of *architectura* as a clearly defined discipline appears to be codependent with the Roman project of world dominion. Vindicating its part in that project was Vitruvius's principal aim. Is architecture, now, a discipline unrelated to the imperial body in which Vitruvius rooted it? Has it ever been? In provoking such questions, the historically specific Vitruvius of ca. 25 B.C. acquires more than antiquarian interest.

THE ANGELIC BODY

Commentaries.

Auctoritas.

A Perfect Ten.

Unified Bodies.

Signification.

Writing alone can assemble scattered fragments of written knowledge into what Vitruvius calls a "perfectly ordered *corpus*."[1] There is no imaginable alternative. And, with its own field of operations, its own material and spatial presence, writing inevitably shapes the "what" it is ostensibly about. The bearing of this truism on the quiddity of *De architectura* is worth exploring.

In the hierarchy of the known—at least for Vitruvius and his contemporaries—what was written took precedence over what was not. A person was not known until his name was recorded on a census roll, or better still (and better known) chiseled on a public inscription, preferably in large letters at the top.[2]

In 45 B.C., after the appearance of Varro's 41-volume compendium of Roman custom, *Antiquitates rerum humanarum et divinarum,* Cicero paid tribute to its author. "In our own city we were like foreigners wandering and drifting, but your books brought us home so that we might know who and where we were."[3] For intellectuals like Cicero, true knowledge of who and where you were lay in a written record of *mores,* many far from current, not in changeable collective memory and customary behavior.

The information (market days, feast days, anniversaries, foundation dates of temples, etc.) compiled and publicly posted on calendars in the late republic and early empire similarly supplanted the lived and mutable with the written and ostensibly fixed.[4] Indeed if, as Jack Goody has argued, it is through writing that hierarchies of knowledge become established in the first place, it should not be surprising to find writing itself at the top of a list that does not (cannot, *as a list*) exist prior to its writing.[5] For that is where Vitruvius puts it on his list of what he says an architect should know. An architect, he writes, should be educated in nine *disciplinae*. Writing comes first.

He [the architect] should know writing, be skilled in drawing and trained in geometry. He should be able to recall many histories, listen carefully to the philosophers, not be ignorant of medicine, know music, remember the responses of jurisconsults, and be well acquainted with astrology and the order of the heavens.[6]

"An architect should know writing [*litteras*]," he continues, "so that he can produce a stronger memory in commentaries."[7] Vitruvius does not specify who or what is to achieve a "stronger memory" through such writings (the architect or his work?) or whose memory is at issue (the architect's? public memory? the memory of posterity?).[8] But the essential point is clear. Writing nails memory down, makes it *firmior,* more steadfast, longer lasting, more powerful.[9]

Echoing precisely this view and confirming that, in this context, *litterae* does indeed refer to writing, Vitruvius's contemporary Livy called *litterae* "the only faithful guardian of the memory of achievements." The events of early Roman history set forth in his first five books, writes Livy at the beginning of his sixth, are dim because they are far off, and also because "in those days there was very little use of writing, the only faithful guardian of the memory of achievements, and even what existed in the commentaries [*commentariis*] of pontiffs and other private and public documents, nearly all perished in the conflagration of the city."[10] Although, unlike Vitruvius, Livy does specify what the memory guarded by writing is *of*—memory of achievements (*res gestae,* things done)—Livy does not seem to feel compelled to specify in whose memory they are guarded, any more than Vitruvius does. Both writers appear to understand memory as something "out there," a shared *topos* or common ground, which for Livy was the topography of Rome itself.

COMMENTARIES

Both Livy and Vitruvius name commentaries in connection with the role of writing in producing stronger memory. Livy says their disappearance contributes to the obscurity of the events he related in his first pentad. What was a *commentarius*?

Vitruvius seems to understand *commentarii* as the kind of writing architects normally engage in. In his remarks on the purpose of writing at the beginning of book 1, and elsewhere too, he refers both to his own writings and to his architectural sources as *commentarii*.[11] Commentaries also include other writings besides architectural ones. Through commentaries, he writes in the preface to book 7, the wisdom of the ancestors is handed down from generation to generation, building up step by step to reach the highest degree of subtlety.[12] Without such writings nothing would be known of the exploits at Troy, for instance, or of the thoughts of philosophers, or of the achievements of kings like Croesus, Alexander, and Darius. Writings on architecture, philosophical works, and annals of great deeds, all apparently for Vitruvius *commentarii* like his own, guard the memory of all men.[13]

A common view among modern scholars is that *commentarii*—literally "reminders" or "aide-mémoire" and the Latin equivalent, more or less, of what were called *hypomnêmata* in

Greek—were succinct records in which public officials set down their experiences in order to provide guides for people engaged in practical occupations.[14] Whatever their more exalted role, and certainly not excluding it, the missing *commentarii* of pontiffs regretted by Livy in the opening lines of his sixth book may have fallen into such a category, although they could have been just lists, with no advice-giving component. A bronze tablet from Banasa in Morocco discovered some thirty years ago refers to a *commentarius* that was in fact a list, one in which Augustus Caesar recorded the names and details of every person to whom he granted Roman citizenship.[15]

When Pompey was elected consul for the first time in 70 B.C., he asked his friend Varro to write him a *commentarius* on the *officium*, or office, of Senate performance, because "due to his extended time in the military he was not privy to matters of Senate conduct nor to city affairs in general."[16] Varro obliged with a work he called an *eisagôgikon* or "introductory guide" from which Pompey "might learn what he ought to do and say when he consulted the Senate."[17] The little book recorded not especially Varro's own experiences but what practices had been established by the *mos maiorum*, the custom of the ancestors.[18] That architecture also had an *officium* (according to Vitruvius) suggests a possible parallel between the "introductory guide" Varro wrote for Pompey and the kind of commentary *De architectura* was meant to be.[19]

Frontinus, the late first-century A.D. author of a work on aqueducts and one of the few ancient authors to mention Vitruvius, calls his own work a *commentarius* in which, like Vitruvius, he claims to have gathered hitherto scattered facts "into a body so to speak"—a work meant, he says, to serve as a *formula ad-*

ministrationis to guide him as newly appointed curator of Rome's water supply.[20] It would not be unreasonable to infer that the ostensibly practical subject matter of Vitruvius's treatise, which might even have provided a model for Frontinus's *De aquis,* made *De architectura* a similar kind of work.[21]

The general Marcus Agrippa, Augustus's principal minister and son-in-law, was closer in time to Vitruvius and almost certainly known to him.[22] Agrippa also wrote a commentary on aqueducts.[23] Another commentary he wrote was meant to accompany, or provide statistics for drawing, the world map completed by Augustus after Agrippa's death in 11 B.C. and displayed in the Porticus Vipsania in the Campus Martius, in order, Pliny writes, "to set the world before the eyes of the City."[24]

Like many Augustan projects, the map project originated with Julius Caesar, who appears to have initiated it shortly before his assassination in 44 B.C. Two late antique sources tell of four Greek geometers Caesar sent out east, west, north, and south to measure the world, in an undertaking that had linked geography to conquest since the time of Alexander the Great, tabulating its extent in lengths of rivers traversed and lists of mountain ranges overrun.[25] Augustus, who extended the limits of the Roman world beyond those established by his adoptive father, continued Caesar's cartographic enterprise under the direction of Agrippa, who compiled the four geometers' statistics in his *commentarius*—a work of geography, certainly, but also a record of the achievements of Caesar, of Augustus, and of Rome.[26]

One of the sources on the map project may even bear traces of Agrippa's original preface to that commentary.[27] "I have discovered by careful and vigilant reading," wrote the anonymous author known as Aethicus in the late fourth or early fifth century,

that the Senate and People of Rome, masters of the whole world,
conquerors and rulers of the globe, at the time when their triumphs
reached everything that lies under heaven . . . having subjugated
the world by their prowess, marked everything with their own bound-
ary, wherever the earth extends. And lest anything should escape
their divine mind, which is master of all things, they traced out
what they had conquered according to the four cardinal points of
the sky, and by their celestial wisdom announced that everything
that is surrounded by ocean consists of three parts, meaning Asia,
Europe and Africa.[28]

The resonance of this with the opening of *De architectura*
is uncanny, with one telling difference. The subjections, triumphs, and "divine mind" the later text credits to the Roman
people are credited by Vitruvius to Augustus alone.[29] Vitruvius
may have known Agrippa's work. Not the map itself, only installed in the Porticus Vipsania about forty years after *De architectura* appeared, but Agrippa's commentaries which may well
be the *orbis terrarum . . . scripta,* the "written world," that Vitruvius refers to in connection with the sources of various rivers in
book 8.[30] In this geographical context, the ground covered by
commentarii was the worldwide arena of Roman achievement.

Although, in keeping with the four parts of the sky, Caesar
sent out four geometers in four different directions to measure
the earth, the earth they measured was tripartite, as indeed it
had been since the time of Herodotus.[31] Agrippa himself appears
to have said so. "The world is divided by three names," one

source cites him as having written, using what sounds to the modern ear like a strange turn of phrase, "Europe, Asia, and Libya or Africa."[32] "The three parts of the world are called Europe, Asia and Libya or Africa" would sound better, but in the odd phrasing actually used the three parts of the world do not pre-exist their naming. In the text, three names divide the world and, by implication, bring its three parts into existence—or at least into the realm of the known. Unnamed, they would remain unknown; and known because written, not drawn. Map commentaries, with their lists of names and numbers, carried greater epistemological weight than their graphic renderings. The size, scale, and overall configuration of graphic representations could vary considerably.[33] The names and numbers, "faithful guardians of the memory of achievements," in principle at least did not.

As every beginning student of Latin knows, "Gaul as a whole is divided into three parts."[34] For so wrote Julius Caesar at the beginning of his commentary on his conquest of Gaul.[35] Caesar's Gallic campaign lasted seven years, from 58 to 51 B.C. His commentaries describing it, unusually, were written in the third person, and the seven books that comprise them appeared at the end of the period in question.[36] An ostensibly objective third-person record of achievements, Caesar's *Bellum gallicum* is also geographical, as indeed its opening words attest.[37]

Strabo, who wrote his geography in the latter part of Augustus's reign, saw a parallel between the generals' methods and those of geographers who put together "an image of the whole inhabited world" from scattered fragments. Like geographers, Strabo writes, generals "are not present everywhere, but carry out successfully most of their measures through others, trusting the reports of messengers, and sending their orders around in conformity with the reports they hear."[38]

As a general Caesar worked through messengers; as a writer he worked from military dispatches, assembling in his commentaries the *litterae* (as they were called) sent to him by legates in the field and those he in turn sent to the Senate at Rome, where bulletins of success in battle were greeted as *litterae laureatae,* laureate letters—messengers of victory.[39] The award of a triumph could depend on such reports.[40]

Latin students begin with Caesar's commentaries because his writing is so clear and concise. "Naked, upright and beautiful," wrote Cicero admiringly.[41] What could be clearer than "Gaul as a whole is divided into three parts, one inhabited by the Belgae, another by the Aquitani, and a third by . . . the Celtae or Galli"? But why, if Gaul is a "whole," does it not include (for example) Gallia Narbonensis, which had been a Roman province since the mid-second century B.C.? Because, one suspects, as a province it was no longer foreign and conquerable. "The whole of Gaul was now subdued," writes Hirtius at the beginning of the eighth book he wrote as an appendix to Caesar's seven.[42] The assertion certainly has a finer and more final ring than "the parts of Gaul not previously subdued now were." For Hirtius to be able to make the claim on Caesar's behalf, the "whole of Gaul" had to preexist its conquest—which Caesar made sure of in the very first line of his commentary.

And why do the Galli give their name to the whole of Gallia even though their own territory is only one of its three parts? Above all, why three parts? The Helvetii, whose alleged ambition to take over the rest of Gaul made them Caesar's initial target, were "closely confined by the nature of their territory," bounded by the Rhine, the Jura mountains, and Lake Geneva.[43] Then why is Helvetic territory part of the whole from which it is so emphatically cut off, yet not itself a "part" like the territories inhabited by the Belgae, Aquitani, and Galli?

A whole, wrote Aristotle, is that which has a beginning, a middle, and an end.[44] Three, for Pythagoreans, was the number of completion and fulfillment.[45] Commenting on the perfect numbers of Pythagorean arithmetic, Theon of Smyrna wrote, "the number three is also perfect, since it is the first number which has a beginning and middle and end . . . and it is the first bond and power of the solid, for in three dimensions is the solid conceived."[46] Mathematically, three originated the possibility of palpable extent and projected it onto the world.

At Rome, high on the Capitol, the Temple of Jupiter Capitolinus, shrine of *the* supreme Roman deity and named for him alone, had a triple cella that housed a triad of divinities, Jupiter himself of course, but also Juno and Minerva. In Varro's allegorizing account, Jupiter was to be understood as the sky, Juno as the earth, and Minerva as "ideas," a tripartite (Roman) scheme which for Varro "embraced the totality of existence."[47] The world itself was tripartite. So, for Plato, was the soul.[48]

A whole by definition had three parts. So too *as a whole* had Caesar's Gaul. The map the modern reader longs for would only confuse an assertion whose verbal clarity and force lie beyond the possibility of cartographic elucidation.[49]

While retaining the authority of official records like the ones kept by pontiffs, Caesar's commentaries altered what Jörg Rüpke calls the *commentarius* "genre," of which the tripartite division, he claims, was to become a constitutive signal.[50] Certainly Caesar's commentaries, as well as those of Agrippa and Frontinus which came later, did profess totality in a way that earlier *commentarii* do not appear to have done. Frontinus's *De aquis* was *all* about aqueducts, beginning "ab urbe condita," from the foundation of the city.[51] Agrippa's commentary covered the whole world. Caesar's seven books of commentaries made a unit, both territorial and temporal, of the seven years he says it took him to conquer the whole of Gaul. Vitruvius, who recalls his attachment to Caesar in his first preface, would have been a young man in his twenties at the time, and was almost certainly with him during the period in question.[52]

Architecture too is a whole. "Architecture itself has three parts, building, the construction of clocks [*gnomonice*], and mechanics," Vitruvius writes.[53] Books 1 to 7 of *De architectura* deal with building, book 9 deals with *gnomonice,* and book 10 with machines, which include the machinery of war.[54] A little like the Helvetic territory of Caesar's *Bellum gallicum,* book 8, on water, is ambiguously situated, a separate part of *De architectura* but not a "part" of architecture, even though the construction of aqueducts was a major aspect of Roman building practice, and even though Vitruvius probably participated in their construction.[55]

The encyclopedic ambitions Vitruvius shared with Varro, Cicero, and other writers of the late Roman republic he also, as a writer of commentaries, shared with Caesar, his first patron, with whom he shared camp life and a professional interest in weaponry as well.[56] This last area of common experience was absent from his relations, if any, with other writers, and bound his discipline to the very center and agent of Roman conquest.

Writers equip men with so many benefits, declares Vitruvius in the preface to book 9, that "not only should they be awarded palms and crowns, but they should even be voted triumphs and proclaimed to have consecrated seats among the gods."[57] The contrast between athletes (who exercise only their own bodies and win *honores*) and authors (who exercise both their own minds and those of others, but are not rewarded) that Vitruvius evokes was a *topos* among Greek authors.[58] But the mention of triumphs projects it into the Roman context.

In the paragraph immediately preceding this declaration Vitruvius praised the benefits conferred on all peoples by the writings of wise men like Pythagoras, Democritus, Plato, and Aristotle. In Roman experience, however—that of Vitruvius in particular—triumphs were the prerogative of victorious generals, not athletes. One thinks of Augustus, of course, and of other *imperatores,* but especially of Caesar, whose achievements, unforgettably conveyed in lapidary *litterae,* won him the vote of a triumph which culminated, as did all such processions, in his solemn ascent to the Temple of Jupiter on the Capitol.[59] Caesar, moreover, had recently joined the council of the immortal gods, as indeed Vitruvius recalls in his first preface.[60] The transfer of the athlete/author *topos* to late first-century Rome gives writing the spatial dimension of conquest and transforms the mental athlete into a *triumphator.*[61]

While crossing the Alps to join his troops in Gaul in 54 B.C.,[62] Caesar wrote a short work on grammar called *De analogia,* which he dedicated to Cicero: "You have won greater laurels than the triumphal wreath, for it is a greater achievement to have extended the frontiers of Roman genius than those of Rome's empire."[63] In a similar vein, Vitruvius's contemporary the philosopher Quintus Sextius developed a specifically Roman branch of Stoicism which Seneca later admired. For Sextius, the Stoic sage was to exercise the *imperium* of reason in imitation of a

Monument to Victor Emmanuel II, Rome, inaugurated in 1911.

good general. Always ready for combat, he is to march his virtues through enemy territory *agmine quadrato,* in square formation, armed against attack from any side.[64]

At the opening of book I, Vitruvius's well-educated architect is to master knowledge consisting of both *fabrica* and *ratiocinatio* if, "fully armed," he is to reach his goal "speedily and with authority."[65] Swift attack seems to be the watchword here, reminding one of the speed and authority for which Caesar made himself known.[66]

Further along, the disciplines that "arm" the architect are the steps (*gradus*) by which the architect ascends to the *summum templum architecturae,* the highest temple of architecture, the summation for Vitruvius of all learning.[67] As no Roman could help knowing, and as unavoidably conspicuous no doubt as the Victor Emmanuel monument is today, the highest temple in Rome was the huge, golden-roofed Temple of Jupiter on the Capitol whose steps the laurel-wreathed victor solemnly ascended on the day of his triumph[68]—Caesar (so Dio Cassius) on his knees.[69] Tacitus called it *pignus imperii,* the guarantee of empire.[70]

Scholars do not usually connect "summum templum architecturae" with the Capitol.[71] They usually take Vitruvius to mean that architecture occupies a high and holy ground, with *templum* taken not as a building but in the augural sense evoked by the late second-century A.D. scholar Festus. A *summum templum* in this sense would be the place from which one "contemplates" or views on all sides and which in turn, being prominent, is visible from all sides.[72]

But augural and Capitoline *templa* are far from being mutually exclusive. It was axiomatic in Vitruvius's day that correct

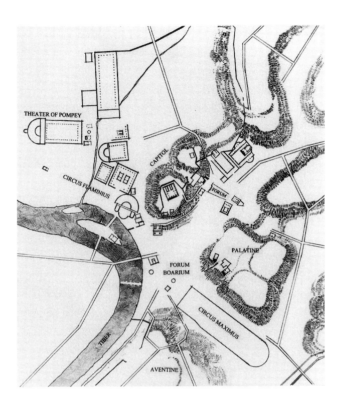

The monumental center of republican Rome.

interpretation of divine will through augury was what, above all, underwrote Roman might.[73] The metonymic "guarantee" of this might was the Temple of Jupiter on the Capitol, where the *augurium* (place from which auguries were taken) also stood.[74] Standing at the top of the steps of all the other disciplines, "summum templum architecturae" writes architecture into the equation.[75]

Knowledge of history should be included in an architect's arsenal of disciplines in order to enable him to justify the use of certain ornaments, writes Vitruvius.[76] The story he selects to illustrate his point is a story of conquest and triumph—the capture and destruction of a city, the slaughter of its male citizens, and the enslavement and public humiliation of its female ones. As Vitruvius tells it, Carya, the Peloponnesian city in question, was sacked by the Greeks for collaborating against them with the Persian invaders—in the early fifth century B.C., one naturally assumes, when Xerxes overran much of Greece. Permanent admonitory chastisement of the Caryans' treachery is the reason caryatids, statues of widowed Caryan women wearing their finest clothes, are put in the place of columns to support entablatures. "So that they might be led in triumph not just once, but enslaved forever as a lesson."[77]

But the Persian advance was arrested at Salamis in 480 B.C., and Xerxes' armies never reached the Peloponnese. Although the genesis of the fifth-century monuments of the Athenian Acropolis can indeed be traced to that Athenian victory, the Erechtheion caryatids which used, traditionally, to be taken as the ones referred to in Vitruvius's story were in fact called *korai* by the classical Greeks—"maidens"—not "caryatids."[78] The term itself originates with Vitruvius, who seems to have been wrong or at least seriously confused on this point.[79]

The issue of Vitruvius's historical accuracy is far less interesting here than his choice of this particular story as exemplary.[80] It operates in the same triumphalist arena as the *litterae* that Caesar no doubt tailored to his specific purpose, and which, compiled in his commentaries, were subsequently read as history.[81] The context in which Vitruvius wrote his caryatid story is the same as that in which the plan for the Forum of Augustus was formulated, a project initially vowed in 42 B.C. to celebrate the avenging of Caesar's murder and the defeat of the treacherous citizens who murdered him.[82] In the Corinthian porticos that flanked the Temple of Mars Ultor (the Avenger), which was the monumental focus of the Forum and which, for the first time, brought the god of war inside the sacred boundary of the city, were deployed images of the great men through whom Augustus traced his and Rome's divine ancestry: on one side, Aeneas son of Venus, and Aeneas's descendants, the Julii; on the other, Romulus son of Mars and the great military men who descended from him.[83] In the second story of these porticos, caryatids, copies of the Erechtheion *korai* whose story Vitruvius chooses to illustrate the use of history, took the place of columns. The whole complex justified the Augustan present through a reconstruction of Rome's past. The "stronger memory" produced by Vitruvius's commentary, whatever its factual shortcomings, secured the caryatids in the golden age of Pericles, and made them part of the legitimating Augustan narrative.[84]

Writing tops Vitruvius's list of the nine disciplines meant to constitute an architect's education. It comes before drawing, which, for the author of *De architectura,* was indeed secondary. Only ten drawings, none of which have survived, appear to have been originally included in the work.[85] Pierre Gros has shown recently that, although much scholarship since the Renaissance has been directed toward devising graphic renderings of Vitruvius's text as the surest means to understanding what he was trying to say, Vitruvius himself deliberately shunned drawing and resorted to graphic methods with much reluctance only when words completely failed him.[86] For him, writing explains better than drawing—whatever the frustrated modern architectural reader may think.[87] Writing, not drawing, is the basis for all reasonable discussion and constitutes the field in which *De architectura* is to operate.

The knowledge of the architect is furnished with many disciplines and various kinds of learning. Judiciously exercised, it demonstrates everything the other arts achieve. It is brought into being by fabrica *and* ratiocinatio. Fabrica *is the continuous and routine practice of the activity the hands accomplish out of matter; its offspring is a work whose form is in keeping with its intended purpose.* Ratiocinatio *is what can show how, and explain to what degree, things have been made with skill and calculation.*[88]

Ratiocinatio explains, and the word for "explain" here is

explicare, literally to unfold, or unroll, as in to unroll a book roll. *Ratiocinatio* is not equivalent to writing; but without writing, *ratiocinatio*—the "discussion" which Vitruvius says is to complement and complete the knowledge of hands-on practice—is all but inconceivable to him.[89] Moreover, like the victory without the dispatch to record it or the map without its accompanying commentary, *fabrica* without writing has no *auctoritas,* no authority.

Architects who aim at employing themselves with their hands without the aid of writing will never be able to achieve authority equal to their labors. Those who rely only on discussion and writing will look as if they have chased a shadow and not the thing itself. But those who have mastered both, like men fully armed, will attain their goal speedily and with authority.[90]

Auctoritas was an endemically Roman notion.[91] Originally a legal term related to vouchsafing and guaranteeing, authority was the security offered by an *auctor* who underwrote an action undertaken by someone else.[92] A contractual matter in the legal sphere and, analogously, in the politico-religious one, *auctoritas* entailed trust, mutual obligation, and good faith: what the Romans called *fides.*[93] The shrine of Fides stood next to the Temple of Jupiter on the Capitol—itself, as noted, a "guarantee of empire"—and was surrounded by bronze tablets inscribed with laws and treaties.[94]

Auctoritas was held by an *auctor.* The term is derived from the verb *augeo:* increase, magnify, augment. *Auctores* included artists and builders and, J. J. Pollitt has suggested, were people who "had the power to bring something into existence and/or insure that its existence continued."[95] "Augustus," a profoundly religious epithet connected with augury, belongs to the same semantic field as *augeo/auctor/auctoritas.*[96] Augustus had more authority than anyone.[97] "After this time [after 27 B.C., when the Senate gave him his new name], I excelled all in *auctoritas,* although I possessed no more power [*potestas*] than others who were my colleagues," he wrote near the end of his autobiography.[98]

Writing seems to have had a good deal to do with it.[99] The phenomenon known as the Roman "epigraphic habit" first took serious hold in the early empire, under Augustus.[100] Augustus himself was obsessed with writing, never speaking extempore and even reading prepared texts to his wife Livia when he had something particularly important to say to her.[101] In order to discourage absenteeism in the Senate "he had the names of all the senators entered on a tablet and posted."[102] For the first time and at his initiative, laws to be considered were similarly inscribed and posted ahead of time.[103] The bronze tablet from Banasa mentioned earlier that refers to a *commentarius* in which Augustus recorded the names and details of everyone to whom he granted Roman citizenship is further evidence of what Fergus Millar has called his "obsession with documentation."[104] Much (all?) of Augustus's correspondence with Aphrodisias, the Carian "city of Venus" in Asia Minor in which he took particularly keen interest because Venus was supposed to be his ancestress, survives because it was chiseled onto the walls of the theater there.[105] This last was probably not at his initiative, of course, but the Aphrodisians obviously considered it the appropriate thing to do.[106]

This is how Vitruvius addresses Augustus in the second paragraph of the preface to book 1.

When I realized that you had care not only for the common life of all men and the regulation of the commonwealth but also for the fitness of public buildings—that even as, through you, the city was increased [aucta] *with provinces, so public buildings were to provide eminent guarantees* [auctoritates] *for the majesty of empire— I decided not to hesitate and took the first opportunity to set out for you my writings on these matters* [his rebus], *for it was concerning this* [de eo] *that I was known to your father [Caesar] and this is what first attached me to his might.*[107]

Commentators tend to assume that the "matters" (*his rebus*) with which Vitruvius says his writings deal and the infuriatingly vague "this" concerning which (*de eo*) he says he was first attached to Caesar refer, respectively, to architecture and to his activities as an architect.[108] His meaning is at once more subtle and more pointed.

The preface to book 1 began, "When your divine mind and power, Imperator Caesar, were seizing command of the world." Vitruvius invariably addresses Augustus as "Imperator" or "Caesar," or both, in all ten prefaces except one.[109] Although other writers use "Caesar" to address him, no other writer ever uses "Imperator" or "Imperator Caesar."[110] Epigraphic and numismatic parallels are frequent, however. "Imperator Caesar," the official name that appeared, usually abbreviated, on public buildings and on coins, belongs to the language of inscriptions, not that of literature.[111]

Vitruvius could not confer authority on his work by "amplifying" his themes the way poets and historians do, he stresses in the preface to book 5.[112] A writer on architecture must, he says, be brief.[113] And so, resorting to lapidary measures, he inscribes "Imperator Caesar" on *De architectura* the way a stonecutter might chisel IMP. CAESAR onto the entablature of a public monument, or a moneyer stamp it on a coin to guarantee its value. Vitruvius never addresses Augustus as such—neither does any other prose writer—but the "aucta" and the "auctoritates" of the passage from the preface to book 1 just cited implicitly invoke the authority of the new name.[114]

Initially, the passage in question sets up a parallel between, on the one hand, Augustus's concern for the regulation of life in common in a restored *res publica* and, on the other, his concern for the fitness of public buildings.[115] Next, just as Augustus had "increased" the city (*civitas*) with provinces, so public buildings, as eminent *auctoritates,* would secure the majesty of empire.[116] *Auctoritates* in the plural were, specifically, duly witnessed *written* records or "guarantees" that transcribed official resolutions.[117] Strictly speaking, public buildings did not "represent" power, any more than a dispatch "represented" a victory. Equivalent or at the very least analogous to writing, the *auctoritas* of public buildings made power a matter of public record.

What, besides the inscriptions that invariably appeared on them, made buildings authoritative? In what way did they record power? Essentially, according to Vitruvius, by increase. *Auctoritas* in buildings is a concomitant, variously, of increased spending, of greater richness of materials, of grander spaces, of

Restored inscription on the base of the gnomon-obelisk of the
Horologium Augusti, Augustus's giant sun clock in the Campus Martius,
Rome, inaugurated in 9 B.C.

heightened contrast in the light and shadow of a peristyle, of bigger columns and more of them.[118] The *magnificentia* taken as the cause or consequence or both of *auctoritas* has to do, literally, with magnification. *Magnus facio,* "I make big."

The late republican *imperatores* were, of course, no strangers to displays of architectural magnificence.[119] But what these fiercely competitive men had not thought about and Vitruvius had (for some time, apparently, and with great deliberation: *magnis cogitationibus*) was *why* architecture would "increase" the commonwealth and *how* it would record Roman greatness.[120] And this, as the ensuing chapters of this book will attempt to demonstrate, not locally or piecemeal but comprehensively, worldwide. *Fabrica* alone, to recall Vitruvius's own term, is necessarily local and specific. It has, he asserts, no authority. *Ratiocinatio,* on the other hand, systematizes. Its scope is universal. Like writing, *ratiocinatio* secures *fabrica* the way IMP. CAESAR secured the value of a coin or the authority of a public monument. And *ratiocinatio* without *fabrica,* like IMP. CAESAR without a coin, a monument, a book—or a man—to bear the name, is just a shadow, not the real thing.

Thus, it was not architecture as such that initially "attached" Vitruvius to Julius Caesar's might. It was, rather, the connection of architecture to *imperium.* Augustus's ambitions took up where Caesar's left off. It was for Augustus then that Vitruvius duly recorded the "matters" that had initially forged the bond between Caesar and himself.[121] And so he writes, concluding the first chapter of book 1: "What I hope to present in these scrolls is proof of the real power of the art and of the *ratiocinationes* in it, beyond question and with the greatest authority— not only to builders but to all learned men."[122]

De architectura consisted of ten *volumina,* or scrolls. Although for Vitruvius the work is, insistently, a *corpus,* the first and only mention of its consisting of ten books occurs at the very end of book 10, on mechanics. Vitruvius may not have intended ten books initially, but there is no question that ten scrolls constituted the finished *corpus* he presented to Augustus.[123]

In this scroll I have given as complete an account as I could of the principles of the machines I consider most useful in times of peace and war. Now in the previous nine I brought together the ones for the other different subjects and parts, so that the whole body of architecture might have all its members developed in ten scrolls.[124]

The ten separate *volumina* that divided up *De architectura* at its completion were not like the contiguous, sequential books of medieval codices and modern editions.[125] Book 2 of the Fensterbusch translation, for instance, ends on page 131 and book 3 begins on its verso, page 132.[126] The "books" of modern editions are not discrete tactile units,[127] unlike the *singula volumina,* separate scrolls, to which Vitruvius consigned his individual subjects.[128] Separate scrolls with a different subject in each are his means for bringing the body of architecture to *perfectam ordinationem,* complete order, he says.[129] The *ordinatio* of his compilation is again vindicated in virtually identical terms in the preface to book 5.[130] *Ordinatio* heads his list of the six things on which he says architecture depends, enumerated in the second chapter of book 1.[131] "*Ordinatio* is the proper relation of parts of a work taken separately and the provision of proportions for over-all symmetry. It is constituted from quantity—*posotês* in Greek."[132] As for architecture, so for *De architectura?*

Quantities certainly played an important role in constituting the works of Varro, whom Vitruvius admired and who especially favored four, the number of cosmic order.[133] The quadripartite structure of people, place, time, and thing was his preferred framework for systematizing the vast quantities of information contained in his enormous literary output.[134] St. Augustine explains how four governed the division of the 25 books of Varro's *Antiquitates rerum humanarum* as well as that of the 16 books of the accompanying *Antiquitates rerum divinarum* on Roman religion, which was dedicated to Caesar as *pontifex maximus*.[135] Varro's *Hebdomades*, a collection of portraits of 700 eminent men, was governed by seven, just like (so Varro) the organization of the heavenly bodies and the birth and growth of humans, and indeed of Varro himself who had, he says in his preface, entered the twelfth hebdomad of his age and had written 70 hebdomads of books.[136]

Insistence on a connection between number and nature was part of the Pythagorean doctrine, which had many adherents among Roman intellectuals of the late republic.[137] Because the sect initially flourished in southern Italy, where Pythagoras lived for much of his life, there was a tendency to consider him something of a native son, and his philosophy as being at least as Roman as it was Greek.[138] In the preface to book 5, Vitruvius invokes Pythagorean maxims for ordering literary composition "by cubical principles," which, he notes, arose from things originally "observed by our ancestors in the order of nature."[139] Varro's point in "numbering" his books would have been to affirm their

Plaster, wood, and surgical gauze model of *De architectura*, by author.

participation in that same order. Because, like dice, when a cube is thrown it remains immobile on whatever side it rests, works written according to "cubical principles" stay put in the memory.[140] As far as one can tell, Vitruvius did not follow these principles, which prescribed that no more than three 216-line "cubes" constitute one *conscriptio,* although it is far from certain what exactly he means by a *conscriptio.*

One thing is certain, though: *De architectura* was constituted by ten scrolls. Book rolls, nine to eleven inches long, consisted of sticks (*umbilici*) to which one end of the papyrus roll was attached and around which it was rolled.[141] The lines of text, written in columns, ran parallel to the long edge of the roll. Unrolled, a papyrus scroll averaged between 20 and 30 feet in length. An open codex is limited to the display, usually, of only two columns of text at a time. A continuous, virtually endless colonnade unfurled before the eyes of an ancient reader who unrolled a scroll. Rolled up, tied with strings or straps called *lora,* and, if particularly precious, wrapped in parchment jackets rubbed with cedar oil to preserve them from decay, *volumina* were neat short rods, physical units that could be counted the way beads on an abacus are counted, with the fingers. The units of *De architectura,* while remaining single and separate—something Vitruvius seems to have set some store by—added up to ten.

The ten-book division is far from inherent in the thematic organization of *De architectura,* however, and indeed bears a rather strained relation to it. Book 8, on water, fits uncomfortably into the schema and, as already discussed, cannot be classified under any of the three so-called "parts" of architecture (building, clock construction, and machinery).[142] Books 3 and 4, both very short and both on temples, could easily have constituted a single book. Together their length is about the same as that of book 10 alone.[143] The division between them is awkward. Book 3 breaks off abruptly after dealing with the proportions of the Ionic order, whose origins are not accounted for until the opening chapter of book 4, along with the origins of the Doric and the Corinthian, whose proportions book 4 subsequently deals with. Seven books (another heavily loaded number) are devoted to building, and only one each to the other two "parts" of architecture, making, diagrammatically at least, for a rather lopsided structure in which the book on water does not figure at all.[144] Ten books were clearly not the spontaneous or accidental concomitant of the compilation. Ten was an artifice, deliberately assigned to it. But this is not to say that the ten-part division was artificial or arbitrary.

Ten, Vitruvius knew, was *perfectus*—complete, finished.

Moreover they [the ancients] deduced the standards of measure that all works obviously require from the parts of the human body: finger, palm, foot, cubit. And they arranged these into the perfect number the Greeks call teleon. *The ancients determined ten to be the perfect number; for it was, in fact, discovered from the hands and the number of fingers. Indeed if nature completes both palms with ten fingers, it was also Plato's opinion that the number ten is perfect because individual units, called* monades *in Greek, complete the decade. But as soon as these go over to make eleven or twelve, they cannot be perfect until they reach another decade. For units are fragments of ten.[145]*

Ten is *perfectus,* complete, because nature revealed its perfection through the fingers of two hands. Fingers not only supply the basic unit of measurement for building (the other units, also body parts, are multiples of it); hands—"completed" here by ten fingers—are, Vitruvius affirms elsewhere, the *means* of building as well.[146] *Fabrica* is the "routine practice of the activity *the hands* accomplish out of matter."[147] Primitive humans began to build, says Vitruvius in the first chapter of book 2, because, besides upright posture, "they, unlike other animals, had this prize from nature . . . that they easily handled any thing they liked *with their hands and fingers.*"[148] Ten originates in nature (fingers reveal this) and is mediated from nature to building through measurements supplied by fingers to palms, feet, and forearms; to the whole body, in fact, whose "number," Vitruvius claims, the ancients said was ten—*teleon* in Greek, "that which has been brought to fulfillment." *Perfectus* is its Latin equivalent. The purpose of this somewhat redundant argument is clear: to bind building to nature through the body, with ten fingers playing the key role both of making that body specifically human and revealing it as "perfect." This obvious (to Vitruvius) truth about ten is not only revealed via fingers in *fabrica,* but also affirmed in the *ratiocinatio* of men like Plato. *Fabrica* and *ratiocinatio* together bring architecture into being.[149]

Only one surviving source on the mathematical perfection of ten has anything explicit to say about fingers.[150] Another view is that the notion of the body's "number" being ten may originate in the pebble diagrams of one Eurytus, a fifth-century B.C. Greek mathematician known only through secondary sources, who assigned numbers to natural phenomena such as "man" and "horse" by picking out their salient points with pebbles.[151]

On this hypothesis, the pebbles for "man" would, presumably, have added up to ten in some way.[152]

Pebble diagrams, not usually of men or horses, played a key role in ancient mathematics. Ancient mathematicians, particularly those of Pythagorean stripe, understood numbers geometrically, in spatial terms. Indeed, in Vitruvius's opening account of the nine disciplines, arithmetic is not listed as a separate discipline but falls under the rubric of geometry, which is third on the list, after writing and drawing.[153] Thus the number one was a point; two was a line (two points); and three was a plane (three points). Inasmuch as a minimum of four points are needed to construct a solid, four *contained* the first three numbers and was the geometrical number for body, if one understands "body" as the Stoics did, which is to say as anything material, and encompassing, for them, all that could be said to exist.

Pebblewise, four expanded into its constituents is • (one pebble), and • • (two pebbles), and • • • (three pebbles), and • • • • (four pebbles). Plato understood that ten was perfect, says Vitruvius, because these *singulara res,* individual units, add up to or "complete" ten. Units as units only exist as fragments of ten, which is to say as parts of a whole. Unless they are parts of a whole, fragments have, strictly speaking, no identity. Individually, they are not bodies, and so not really real.

The figure that demonstrates the point about ten is the *tetractys,* ten pebbles arrayed in triangular formation, like this.

Thus, says Pythagoras in an essay by Lucian, "what you think is four is ten, a perfect triangle and our oath."[154] The "oath" in question was the *tetractys* itself, by which the Pythagoreans swore as the "fount and root of everflowing nature."[155] Spatially deployed in a "perfect triangle," ten was a tripartite whole, like Gaul, the world, the soul—and architecture. The sum or "fulfillment" of four, ten (like four, only more so) was also the number of cosmic order.[156] It was, again according to Lucian, "the principle of health," insofar as health depended in ancient western medicine on the proper balance of the four elements (earth, air, fire, and water) in the body.[157] As the tetrad, it was the ultimate source of all possible musical harmonies in ancient musical theory.[158] The Pythagoreans also called ten *mnêmê,* memory.[159]

One of the best-known texts on the magnitude and power of ten survives in Iamblichus's third-century A.D. report on a short work called *On the Pythagorean Numbers* by Speusippus, Plato's nephew and successor at the Academy in fourth-century B.C. Athens.

He [Speusippus] devotes the other half of the book to the decad, showing it to be the most natural and most initiative of realities, inasmuch as it is in itself (and not because we have made it so or by chance) an organizing idea of cosmic events, being the foundation stone and lying before God the Creator of the universe as a pattern complete in all respects. He speaks about it in this way.

"Ten is a perfect number [teleios] *and it is both right and according to nature that we Greeks and all men arrive at this number in all kinds of ways when we count."*[160]

De mensibus, a work on the Roman calendar by John Lydus, a Byzantine antiquarian who wrote under Justinian in the sixth century A.D., contains two lesser-known passages on the perfection of ten, both based on earlier sources.[161] Ten, the agent both of individuation and of unity, encompasses all the "forms, calculations, proportions, and harmonies of the other numbers."[162] It is the key, John Lydus writes, citing both Parmenides and Philolaus, to the whole order of nature. Later in the same work he begins his account of the Roman months (originally ten of them) with a similar encomium in which the decad, the "circle and limit of all the numbers," bounds the unlimited, holds all the numbers together, and is nature's special stamp on humans to whom, uniquely, it has given ten fingers.[163] And because the decad, as he puts it, "fills up" the yearly cycle of nature by causing the universe to revolve, ten is both the container and the content of time itself.

Throughout *De architectura,* Vitruvius is at all points concerned to demonstrate the necessary connection of his topic to *natura,* the cosmic totality Pythagoreans thought was ruled by ten. In chapter 4 of book 1, for example, the choice of a healthy site for a city and its proper orientation entails understanding that all bodies are composed of four elements, heat, moisture, earth, and air.[164] The same physics is repeatedly invoked in book 2 to account for the proper choice of building materials.[165] The overriding point of the opening chapter of book 3, which is the context of the paragraph on ten under discussion, is to show that temples, especially, must be built following the same *ratio* that nature follows in "building" a man's body.[166] Laying out the plan of a Roman theater in book 5 entails inscribing four equilateral triangles in a circle, "just as astrologers calculate the twelve celestial signs from the musical harmony of the stars."[167]

In book 8, Vitruvius is not at all surprised by all the different kinds of water the earth contains. If the human body, composed mainly of earth, can contain juices as varied as blood, milk, urine, sweat, and tears, how much more variety is to be expected in the far greater body of the earth, of which the human body is but a small fragment?[168] Fully two-thirds of book 9, on the construction of clocks, is an account of ancient astronomy—the order of the heavens that supplies the "numbers of time" as Plato put it in the *Timaeus,* a work that particularly fascinated Vitruvius's contemporaries.[169] In the opening chapter of book 10, on mechanics, Vitruvius writes, "Now all machinery is brought forth from the nature of things and founded on the teaching and guidance of the revolution of the universe."[170]

The necessary connection between architecture and nature—between architecture and universal order—is in part Pythagorean, but above all grounded in Stoicism. The Stoic system's coherence for the younger Cato, its fervent apologist in Cicero's *De finibus,* was as perfect and complete as that of the natural order it accounted for.[171] Even *more* coherent than the natural order.

Nothing is more finished, more nicely ordered, than nature; but what has nature, what have works made by hand to show that is so well constructed, so firmly jointed and welded into one [as the Stoic philosophy]? Where do you find a conclusion inconsistent with its premise, or a discrepancy between an earlier and a later statement?

Where is lacking such close interconnection of the parts that, if you alter a single letter the whole thing falls apart? Though indeed there is nothing that it would be possible to alter.[172]

Stoicism and Pythagoreanism both belonged to what Varro called "natural theology" in the *Antiquitates rerum divinarum,* his now lost work on Roman religion whose essentials St. Augustine transmits in his *City of God.*[173] Natural theology was the second of the three parts of the *ratio*—theology as a whole—whereby the gods are "explained."[174] The first, "mythical" part was poetic and "particularly suited to the theater," the third belonged to the city, and the second, the special domain of philosophers, concerned the *mundus* (universe), "the most important of all existing things."[175]

Mathematically, the perfection of ten is perfection of the perfect Stoic world and of *De architectura* as well. At the level of *fabrica,* just as the Stoic sage was to live "according to nature," so, in effect, says Vitruvius in book 2 where Stoic physics governs the choice of materials, the architect must build according to nature.[176] But if he is to have *auctoritas,* he will understand *architectura* as a *ratio* that accounts for the world in the same way the "natural theology" of the philosophers does, as a perfectly coherent whole. The ten scrolls in which Vitruvius develops it make *architectura* a discipline as perfect as the decad was for Speusippus: the "organizing idea of cosmic events," the "most natural and most initiative of realities"; a reality—being "initiative"— that allowed for "increase."

Indeed, for Vitruvius ten initiates an even more elaborate numerology. For all its cosmic force, ten was not the only perfect number. Six, according to the mathematicians (as opposed to the "ancients" who favored ten), was also perfect, although the mathematical reasons for its perfection seem to have escaped Vitruvius.[177]

Greek currency was based on six, with six obols making a drachma. Romans, however, preferred the "ancient" number ten, Vitruvius says, and made the denarius ("tenner"), consisting of ten asses, the basis of their currency.[178] In time, however (in 141 B.C., actually, when Roman bronze coinage was devalued), the denarius, while remaining in name a "tenner," was valued at sixteen asses.[179] Vitruvius says that this was because the Romans

recognized that both numbers are perfect, both six and ten, and joined both into one and made the supremely perfect number sixteen. They found the rationale for this in the foot. That is, if you subtract two palms from the cubit you are left with a foot of four palms, and a palm has four fingers. So a foot has sixteen fingers and a bronze denarius as many asses.[180]

As already demonstrated, ten, geometrically, is a triangular number—spatially, a tripartite whole. So is six.

To add ten and six geometrically is to add two triangles and "complete" the square of four (sixteen), creating a double *tetractys,* as it were, with the four pebbles on the diagonal acting as the base of both sixes.[181]

"Squaring" and squares were, supremely, the agents and evidence of Roman order.[182]

If ten can be said to belong to what Varro called "natural theology," sixteen would have belonged to his theology of the city. The Etruscans, from whom Cicero says the Romans had learned the art of divination "in its entirety"—an art maintained in spite of the logical shortcomings intellectuals saw in it, owing to its great service to the commonwealth—divided the sky into sixteen parts for the purposes of divination, a number obtained by doubling the four cardinal points, and then doubling them again; four squared, in other words.[183] Vitruvius does not say this, but then he did not have to. In a context where interpretation of prodigies and portents was a daily occurrence, this kind of thing would have been common knowledge—if not among the general populace, then certainly among the members of Vitruvius's intended readership who had read their Varro.

There is another thing Vitruvius does not mention and did not need to. This is the nature of the new Roman coinage of which both he (as the recipient of stipends from Augustus, whose generosity he gratefully acknowledges in his first preface) and his patron (who issued many of the new coins that constituted these stipends) would have had common, firsthand knowledge.[184] Fergus Millar has pointed out that "from 31 B.C. onwards almost every single issue of official Roman coinage, in gold, in silver and bronze portrays Octavian-Augustus."[185] This was revolutionary. Until the last year of Julius Caesar's life (44 B.C.) no Roman coin appears ever to have portrayed a living Roman, and then, until 31, they did so relatively rarely.[186] Denarii worth sixteen asses were preponderant among the coins in circulation, whose authority as legal tender throughout the world was, from the time of Augustus, guaranteed by the ruler's head on the obverse.[187] It is unlikely that the numerology Vitruvius invokes shaped the denominations of Roman coinage in quite the straightforward and direct way he claims, but recording facts was not in any event his primary aim. The appeal was rhetorical, an appeal to assent underwritten by universal consensus as to the worth of Roman (now almost exclusively Augustan) currency, and by the theology, both civil and natural, that "explained" it.

The same theology explains Roman feet. Coins gave known numerical measure to value; feet to distance and size.[188] Arrian, writing in the second century A.D., tells the following story about Alexander the Great's arrival in India.

Some Indian sophists, the story goes, were found by Alexander in the open air in a meadow, where they used to have their disputations; when they saw Alexander and his army, they did nothing more than beat with their feet on the ground they stood on. When Alexander enquired through interpreters what their action meant, they replied: "King Alexander, each man possesses no more of this earth than the patch we stand on."[189]

The futility of conquest. But what if the transitory relation between feet and ground were a quantifiable matter of known and lasting record? Not the feet of any single mortal, but the immortal, theologically correct feet of an entire nation?[190] Among Alexander's followers were writers to record for posterity his every heroic move.[191] Romans like Caesar and Augustus recorded their own achievements, and then went on to measure them, presumably in perfect sixteen-finger Roman feet.[192]

According to Vitruvius, one of the three "ideas" or forms of a building's arrangement is its *ichnographia,* the Greek word he uses for what is usually understood as the ground plan.[193] *Ichnographia,* literally the "drawing of a footstep," is "the properly related use of compass and ruler that renders how figures are marked out on the grounds of areas."[194] Varro corroborates, if a little cryptically. "The base for standing is a foot [*pes*], from which in buildings the ground is called a great foot [*pes magnus*]," he writes in *De lingua latina,* in a context that invokes etymological evidence for a connection between *pes* and *pecunia* (money).[195]

The paragraph on ten and the ones on supremely perfect sixteen-part Roman measurement, both monetary and linear, appear in the chapter that introduces the two books (3 and 4) Vitruvius devotes to temples. Among built works of architecture, temples above all simultaneously propitiated and testified to the correct relation with the gods that was understood to guarantee Roman supremacy.[196] Temple building and temple restoration, which Augustus saw as particularly important and took special pains to record in some detail, were a major aspect of the worldwide building boom that followed his seizure of command.[197] It would be difficult to prove the precise extent of the role played by the Roman foot in imperial building programs in the provinces, although there are scholars who suggest it was considerable.[198]

But once again, the theology implicit in the Roman foot is the same as the theology implicit in the buildings—temples in particular, and especially those dedicated to the imperial cult—whose ubiquitous "footprints" marked the grounds of areas all over the world they thus made Roman. Theology for the Romans included the theology of victory.[199]

UNIFIED BODIES

Vitruvius assumes a connection between money and linear measurement. Connected by the same "reckoning, account, calculation, computation," money and measurement have the same *ratio*,[200] a word Vitruvius does not actually use in this context, which is surprising for someone who uses it virtually everywhere else. *De architectura,* in which the noun appears more often than any other (a total of 331 times), is shot through with *ratio*.[201]

Ratio is not limited to numerical calculation of course, neither in Vitruvius nor in general. Nor are numbers excluded by the qualitative relations that are the province of speculative *ratio* (reason), as Pythagoreanism and Vitruvius's own adaptation of it attest.[202] Indeed, if *architectura* depends on *ordinatio* "which is constituted from quantity, called *posotês* in Greek,"[203] it also depends, among other things, on arrangement: "the suitable assembly of things and their fitting execution in works that are put together with quality [*cum qualitate*]."[204]

At the time Vitruvius wrote, *qualitas* was a fairly new word in Latin. It first appears in Cicero's *Academica* as a neologism coined by Varro to provide a Latin equivalent for the Greek *poiotês:* how things are put together or made (*poiô*, I make), which is what determines qualitatively what they are *like (qualis* in Latin), and indeed that they be like anything at all, the assumption being that existence rules out the possibility of formlessness.[205] As Varro is said to have put it, when active force combines with passive matter, "they called [the product] 'body' [*corpus*], and, if I may use the term, 'quality.'"[206]

Ratio, in this context, was the immanent soul of the world that brought bodies into being and ensured their continued existence. It would not be very difficult to see in the action of *ratio,* thus expressed, a cosmic parallel with the action of a Roman *auctor* who, in the human sphere, brought something into being and guaranteed its continued existence.[207] Elsewhere Cicero calls this world soul a *divina mens*—the providential divine mind that organizes the universe and presides over its destiny.[208] So too in Vitruvius, where *divina mens* is not only the mind that presides over cosmic phenomena in books 8 and 9 but also the one that, in the first chapter of book 6, has placed the Roman people in the ideal position at the center to "seize command of the world."[209]

De architectura begins by invoking a divine mind. "When your divine mind and power, Imperator Caesar, were seizing command of the world," Vitruvius writes, using for Augustus in the very first words of the treatise terms that are virtually interchangeable with those he uses in book 6 when writing of the Roman people as a whole.[210] In a man's body, the equivalent of the *divina mens* that ruled the world was what the Stoics called its *hêgemonikon,* its soul or "ruling principle," which was located in the chest.[211]

Bodies were wholes whose wholeness as qualified matter was, above all, a question of coherence.[212] The agent of coherence—in the body of the world and in all the bodies in it—was *ratio*. Different levels or concentrations of *ratio* made for varying degrees of coherence, which in turn made for different kinds of bodies. The Stoics distinguished three of these, depending on how well they held together.[213] Writing in Greek, Sextus Empiricus, an important third-century A.D. source on Stoic thought, explains.

Of bodies, some are unified [henômena], *some made up of things joined together* [synaptomenôn], *some of separate things* [diestôtôn]. *Unified bodies are ruled by a single bond* [hexis], *such as plants and animals; those made of things that are joined are put together of adjacent elements which tend to combine in a single principal entity such as chains and buildings and ships; those formed of separate things, like armies, flocks and choruses, are the sum of parts which are disjoined, and isolated and which exist by themselves.*[214]

That the *kosmos* is a unified body of the first kind, Sextus continues, is proven by "sympathies"—between the moon and the tides, for instance. The elements that form jointed bodies or those made up of separate parts do not "sympathize" with one another, as they do in a unified body where "when the finger is cut, the whole body shares in its condition." Obviously, the paradigm of unified bodies is human.

Seneca's late first-century A.D. account in Latin is similar. Some *corpora*, like man, are *continua*, joined in uninterrupted succession, he writes. Others, such as ships and houses, are *com-*

posita, put together; and others, like an army, a people, or the Senate, are made up of *membra separata,* which cohere through law or office. No good comes of things that are discontinuous or disparate, Seneca observes.[215]

For Pomponius, a Roman lawyer of the second century A.D., the first kind of body is contained by a "single spirit" (*uno spirito*) and includes not only men but also building materials—timbers, stones, and "similar things." The second kind depends on connections of physical proximity to establish coherence between many things and includes buildings, ships, and armaments. The third kind is constituted when many separate bodies "are not dispersed, but are subordinated under a single name such as a people, a legion, a flock."[216]

Although Vitruvius himself draws no attention to such distinctions, they do throw light on the kind of coherent and unified body he meant his "body of architecture" to be. Vitruvius understood architecture in terms of a purposeful universe, a world-body shot through with same cohesive *ratio* that made, for Cato, the Stoic system which reflected it "so well constructed, so firmly jointed and welded into one."[217] It is especially in its unquestioning assumption of the cardinal value of coherence that *De architectura* belongs to Stoicism.[218] And being first and foremost a *value,* coherence is not the same as consistency, uniformity, or even accuracy.

For Stoics, coherence was the touchstone of truth, and truth (*alêtheia*) was a body, "a collection of several elements, consisting in knowledge," and to a certain degree equivalent to reality itself.[219] From truth, they distinguished "the true" (*to alêthes*), which was hardly real at all. As a judgment or expression that was either true or false, the true was not a body. It belonged to the class of incorporeals the Stoics called *lekta*.[220] To illustrate the difference between truth and the true, Sextus Empiricus explains that when a doctor says something false for the good of his patient, or a general relays a false message in order to encourage his men, truth persists and indeed is enhanced. The doctor's or the general's assertions are not true, but "the true" has no value. Truth does.

That coherence should be a value in building is obvious. Buildings are expected not to fall apart. The materials used to build them are expected to be solid and durable. But for Vitruvius, coherence is also a value in *architectura*, which, he is careful to point out, is not the same thing as building.[221] Equivalent to the "knowledge of the architect," *architectura* is a form of knowledge whose coherence makes it a body.[222] Like all bodies, *architectura* coheres through *rationes*—the same that Cicero claimed in *De oratore* were the prerequisite for the formation of any *ars* (geometry, oratory, grammar, etc.) in order to cement fragmentary knowledge, formerly "diffuse and all in pieces," and bind it together.[223]

Architectura, knowledge constituted as a compound, also has what Vitruvius calls an *officium*.[224] So too the third kind of Stoic body—essentially political—which coheres through law or *officium*. An *officium* mainly had to do, simultaneously, with moral obligation and public office or position, for one's position was what determined one's obligations.[225] Cicero's *De officiis* (usually translated as *On Duties*) was written in 43 B.C., the last year of his life, and exerted considerable influence on Vitruvius.[226] The work is less about the duty prescribed by categorical imperatives than about the appropriate behavior dictated by situation and circumstance. *Officium* for Cicero approximated the

Greek *kathêkon,* a key term of Stoic ethics which meant, roughly, "fitting behavior."[227] Like the corporeality of bodies, the fitness of fitting behavior was also assessed by its coherence, as the third-century A.D. doxographer Diogenes Laertius explains: "The term *kathêkon* is applied to that for which, when done, a reasonable defense can be adduced, such as coherence in the course of life, which indeed pervades the growth of plants and animals. For even in plants and animals, they [the Stoics] hold, you may discern fitness of behaviour."[228]

The body constituted when many separate bodies "are not dispersed, but are subordinated under a single name" coheres through law or *officium,* the behavior befitting one's place in the collectivity.[229] Cicero, for whom law was the bond of civil society, called the *res publica,* the Roman commonwealth, a body.[230] The *corpus rei publicae* was sick, he wrote in the hectic year that followed Caesar's assassination, a diseased body whose pestiferous members were to be amputated so that the whole might survive.[231] In the language of people like Cicero, the body politic in its ideal state was clearly of the first kind—living, unified, and human.

Caesar, whose philosophical affiliations, if any, are alleged to have tended to Epicureanism, had the insolence (so Suetonius, citing a contemporary of Caesar's) to proclaim publicly that the *res publica* was nothing but a name, without body or visible form.[232] That the pronouncement should have been considered insolent obviously assumes an antithetical consensus about the true nature and value of the relation between the designation "res publica" and the reality it referred to.

At the end of his account of the nine disciplines an architect should know, Vitruvius writes:

Inexperienced men might find it astonishing that a person, as a matter of course, should be able to master so many subjects and contain them in his memory. But they will easily believe it possible once they realize that all disciplines are joined to each other by the things they have in common. For the whole of learning is put together just like a single body, from its members.[233]

The "things" the various disciplines have in common can be summed up in a single word: *ratio,* the not entirely adequate Latin equivalent of the Greek *logos.* The knowledge of the architect "is brought into being by *fabrica* and *ratiocinatio,*" Vitruvius wrote at the beginning of book 1, chapter 1.[234] Every *ars,* he elaborates near the end of the same chapter,

is made up of two things: the work and its ratiocinatio. *The first of these belongs to those who are trained in particular things: that is, the execution of a work. The second is common to all learned men: that is,* ratio. *For instance, the* ratio *concerning the rhythm of the pulse and movement of the feet is common to both musicians and doctors. . . . Similarly, between astrologers and musicians there is common discourse concerning the sympathy of the stars and musical harmonies . . . and in all the other subjects many, even all things are held in common for the purposes of discussion* [ad disputandum].[235]

   Ratio here has specifically to do with language. The

learned men who held nearly all things in common "for the purposes of discussion" were men whose ratiocination took linguistic form.[236] The Stoics held that without language there *was* no reasoning. Not necessarily the capacity to speak, but rather the capacity for internal speech, what A. A. Long has called "articulate thought," which depended on humans having an idea of connection or sequence.[237] According to the Stoics, it is precisely because of the capacity for articulate thought, which entails the mutually dependent abilities to infer, connect, and use language, that humans, uniquely among all living creatures, are able to mirror the world-ordering activity of the cosmic *logos.* If *ratio*-as-language is understood as the privileged channel of communication with the order of the cosmos, it is not surprising that Vitruvius, determined as he was to demonstrate the connection of *architectura* to that order, should have favored writing over drawing.[238]

Vitruvius makes *fabrica* as much a parent of the architect's knowledge as *ratiocinatio.*[239] How, within the framework set out here, might one understand the contribution of *fabrica* to the body of *architectura?*

Fabrica, Vitruvius insists, is a question of repeated manual activity, a habit acquired from long experience: "the continuous and routine practice of the activity the hands accomplish out of matter; its offspring is a work whose form is in keeping with its intended purpose."[240] *Fabrica* thus described is the Latin equivalent for what the Greeks called *technê,* the purposeful activity that depended on the trained ability Aristotle called *hexis.*[241] For Aristotle, *hexis* was also the acquired habit of ethical conduct.[242] Because of their shared condition of *hexis* (trained ability), both the craftsman and the moral person perform in ways that are at once coherent and appropriate to the specific task at hand.

The notion is also present in Stoic ethics.[243] The Stoics called the cohesive bond of unified bodies *hexis*.[244] Diogenes Laertius adds an important refinement to this in a distinction that highlights the respective contributions to *architectura* of *fabrica* and *ratiocinatio*. Citing Chrysippus and Posidonius, Stoics respectively of the third and early first centuries B.C., Diogenes writes that in the Stoic view mind (*nous*) pervades every part of the cosmos, just as the soul (*psychê*) pervades us, but that through some parts it is more pervasive, through some less. "For through some parts it passes as *hexis*, as through the bones and sinews; but through others it passes as *nous*, as through the ruling part [*hêgemonikon*]."[245] Thus, to summarize a rather complex matter, world-pervasive *pneuma* would appear to behave in two different ways.[246] As *hexis*, it binds human and animal bodies *qua* bones and sinews, as well as those of plants. In a different form, *hexis* also binds the lifeless bodies of stones and timbers. This *hexis*, common to all unified bodies including those of men, is sometimes, following Aristotle, called the "vegetative" soul. It is as *nous* or *logos*, however—as articulate thought bound up in language—that *pneuma* permeates the *hêgemonikon* or "ruling part" unique to human beings.

Fabrica, to follow this line of reasoning, contributes to the body of *architectura* as *hexis* does to the "vegetative" coherence of unified bodies; those which, even in their mute bone-and-sinew aspect, were emphatically not without soul (since nothing Stoic was). *Fabrica*, the *hexis* of hands and fingers, gives *architectura* its vegetative soul in the palpable world of qualified matter. Of course, once *fabrica* and *ratiocinatio* have brought *architectura* into being as a discourse and once it has been circumscribed in a written body, its connection to the bones and sinews of hands-on practice runs the risk of becoming increasingly tenuous.

It is generally agreed that the cosmic physics of the Stoics, first developed by Chrysippus in the third century B.C., is based on contemporary medical theory.[247] In the complete coherence or perfect blending of unified bodies, *pneuma* (active divine breath made up of fire and air) entirely permeates matter (passive earth and water) to constitute not only the bodies of stones and men, but also the living body of the entire world.[248] The natural state of all animal bodies, including those of humans, is health, and is maintained by a proper balance of these same four elements, Vitruvius writes in his chapter on choosing a healthy site for a city.

For just as all bodies are put together from the elements the Greeks call stoicheia *(that is, heat and moisture, earth and air), so too, through their natural tempering by mixtures, the attributes of all the animals in the world are fashioned, each according to its kind.*[249]

A healthy body is maintained by the "natural tempering" of elements. A healthy body is a *unified* body. The terms Vitruvius repeatedly uses to describe the result of an unhealthy imbalance of elements all invoke the dissolving, weakening, or loosening of bonds. Too much heat "cooks out" firmness, for example; cold strengthens.[250] "If moisture occupies the pores of bodies and unbalances them, the other elements, as though spoiled by the liquid, are washed away, and the strength in their bonds is undone."[251] Bodies are not autonomous, moreover, and the "natural tempering by mixtures" in fish—a little heat, mainly air and earth, no water because they live in it—is not the same as in land animals or in birds, whose habitats supplement, in each case, a different element.[252]

Therefore, if these things are indeed as we have said, and if we agree that the bodies of animals are put together from elements by whose excesses or shortfalls, we conclude, their bodies are afflicted and dissolved, we have no doubt that we must take great care to try to choose the most temperate regions of the sky when seeking healthfulness in the positioning of city walls.[253]

Among humans, people of Italic race, being at the center, are the best tempered (*temperatissimae*) of all, both in mind and in limb, writes Vitruvius in the first chapter of book 6. Placing them at the center is how the divine mind has made them particularly suited for seizing command of the world.[254]

The *rationes*, or principles, invoked for the proper choice of building materials in book 2 are virtually identical to those invoked for health, with *temperatura* called on repeatedly to account for their internal coherence as *corpora* and for their enduring coherence with one another when assembled on a building site. Alder, a poor wood for building above ground, is, on the other hand, excellent for pile foundations in marshy areas because it is *temperata* with much fire and air, leaving room for the penetration of water into its *corpus,* where a perfect balance of elements makes alder piles "imperishable for all eternity."[255]

Two things are to be stressed. The first is that, as Vitruvius tells it, the bonds of unified bodies consist in the relationship (*ratio*) between their constituent elements, which in turn depends on the situation of the body in question. Second, the good bonds so constituted make for bodies that *last*.

Architecture, as we have seen, depends on *ordinatio*, "the proper relation of parts of a work taken separately and the provision of proportions for overall symmetry," which was constituted from quantity; it also depends on arrangement, "the suitable assembly of things . . . that are put together with quality."[256] Third on Vitruvius's list of the things on which architecture depends is eurythmy, "the beautiful appearance and fitting aspect of the parts once they have been put together."[257] Fourth comes symmetry, already mentioned in connection with *ordinatio* which helps provide for it.

Symmetry is the fitting concord of members of the work to each other and the correspondence of individual elements to the form of the whole figure by means of a fixed part. Just as in a man's body the symmetrical quality of eurythmy is achieved from the cubit, foot, palm, finger, and other small parts, so too in bringing works to their proper completion.[258]

There was, as Pliny the Elder later affirmed, no word for *symmetria* in Latin.[259] Vitruvius sometimes approximates with *commodulatio, commensus,* or, adjectivally, with *commodus.*[260] Commensurability—that each part bear a measurable relation to every other part as well as to the configuration of the whole— is its constitutive principle. The means to it is the choice of a *rata pars,* a fixed or calculated part, taken, in a temple, from the thickness of a column or a triglyph, for example; in artillery, from the size of the hole through which the projectile is shot.[261] "Symmetries" are the bonds achieved through *compositio,* "putting together," by means of a fixed part. Although the symmetrical quality of such jointed bodies as temples and catapults is not identical with the *temperatura* that makes for healthy, longlasting bonds in the unified bodies of men, animals, and building materials, for Vitruvius *symmetria* and *temperatura* are clearly analogous, as Chrysippus (who understood both as *symmetria*) had affirmed.[262] Vitruvius sees them as complementary, for "tempering" must supplement *symmetria* by ensuring that good bonds have visibility in beautiful appearance and fitting aspect (eurythmy) "once the parts have been put together."[263] It was not enough that good bonds exist: they must be *seen* to exist.

Tempering, says Vitruvius, is to supplement *symmetria* when proportions are to be adjusted "by additions or diminutions" to the specific circumstances of site, situation, and use—the practice later literature usually refers to, a little reductively, as "optical correction."[264] Writing about theaters in book 5, Vitruvius says that symmetries "cannot answer to all conditions and purposes in all theaters, but an architect must consider in which proportions it is necessary to follow symmetry and which ones to temper to the nature of the site or the size of the work."[265]

Whether calculation, reason, money, measurement, language, or a condition of ineffable "tempering," *ratio* was a question of relation, a bond.

Vitruvius was active professionally during the war-torn years of the dying Roman republic. Claudia Moatti has argued that the reason people like Cicero took such an interest in philosophy, and the reason for Varro's huge systematizing compilations, was to *rationalize* in written remedies alternatives to the disintegration of traditional *mores* perceived to be at the core of the rotting *res publica*.[266] It was rather as if these authors of what Moatti has called a literature of crisis imagined that coherence in books could stand in for the discordant realities of public life.

Cicero died in 43 B.C., Varro in 27 at the age of 90. By 27 B.C. the situation had been saved, so everyone agreed, by Augustus, whose victory over Mark Antony and Cleopatra at Actium four years earlier had brought the civil wars to an end. *De architectura* was completed when the literature of crisis was being replaced by works such as those of Virgil and Horace which celebrated the dawning of a new age.[267]

In one of his early odes, written in 29 or 28 B.C., Horace asks to which of the gods Jupiter should assign the task of restoring the right relation with the gods to whose rupture recent civil discord has testified.[268] Apollo? Venus? Mars? No, not to these—the gods who had presided over the conflicts that were now over—but rather, writes Horace, "to you, winged son of gentle Maia who, reshaped in a young man here on earth, would accept being called Caesar's avenger."[269] Caesar's avenger is the young Octavian, soon to be named Augustus. The winged son of Maia, whom Horace's poem would have doubled by Octavian, is Mercury.

"Provider of profit and giver of speech," it was Mercury who more than any other Roman god conveyed the relational quality of *ratio* in the Roman marketplace.[270] At once Hermes, Greek god of world-pervading *logos,* and Mercurius, Roman god of the *mercator* who mediated commerce by fixing a negotiated value on the object of a transaction, the winged Mercury of Augustan Rome—moneybag in one hand, herald's caduceus, a sign

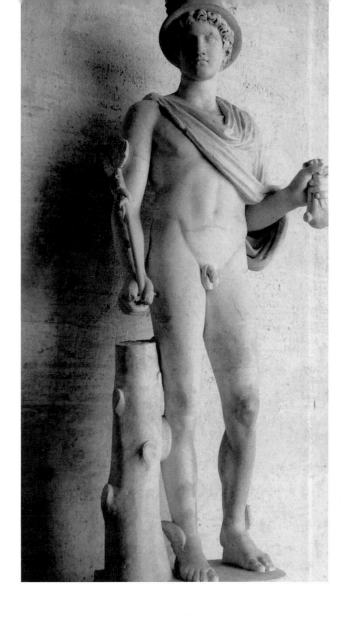

Mercury with moneybag and caduceus, late first century A.D. Musei
Capitolini, Rome (inv. 60).

of peace, in the other—was the ubiquitous power inherent in good bonds and measurable relations.[271] In Horace's ode and in the coins that from 30 B.C. almost never circulated without Octavian-Augustus's image on them, this power now belonged to Rome's new ruler.[272] There are even coins, *denarii* issued at or around the time the poem was written, on which Octavian appears in the guise of Hermes-Mercury, making the *mercurius* of negotiated value which inhered in all coins visibly identifiable as a single, living person.[273] Reciprocally, all Augustan coins—and those with Mercury on them with particular point—showed that the new ruler's person inhered in the negotiated value of currency, whose habitual use (currency) throughout the Roman world was one way of transfiguring hegemony as *hexis*.[274]

Architecture was another. Indeed, Augustus's imperial head on coins was sometimes complemented by a building, often a temple, as its reverse type, joining all three—the coin, the building, and the builder—in a single world-pervasive *ratio*.[275]

With the coming of the principate, almost all major building activity (like most coins) was bound to the person of the new ruler. Beginning about 29 or 28 B.C., every major new project in Rome and many away from it referred directly to him and/or to his immediate family, even if someone else had initiated the project.[276] The *divina mens* Vitruvius invokes at the opening of his first preface is the *ratio* of the conqueror who has brought peace, of the negotiated value of currency, and, in *De architectura*, of a builder. *The* builder, as Vitruvius fulsomely acknowledges.[277] That is why, he concludes, "I have delineated a complete set of rules so that by considering them you yourself can take account both of what finished works are like and of how future ones will be; for in these scrolls I have laid out all the *rationes* of the discipline."[278]

The first preface begins with the words *divina mens,* the divine mind or *logos* that belongs to Vitruvius's dedicatee. It ends with the word *rationes.* Regularly reinvoked as "Imperator" or "Caesar" or both in each of the subsequent prefaces, the *divina mens* of Rome's new ruler adds the final, authoritative layer to the pervasive *rationes* that make *De architectura* a unified body.[279]

St. Augustine, almost certainly citing Varro, writes,

Now it may be said that it is language itself that is Mercury. This is suggested by the interpretation they give of him; for they derive the name Mercury from medius currens *"running in between," because speech "runs between" men. His name in Greek is Hermes, because speech, or rather interpretation—which is clearly connected with speech—is called* hermeneia. *The reason why Mercury presides over commerce is that speech is the means of communication between sellers and buyers. The wings on his head and feet symbolize the swift flight of speech through the air; he is called a messenger because it is through speech that thoughts are conveyed.*[280]

If the relational quality of Mercury is to be understood as a "running in between" ("currency," after all, comes from *currens,* "running"), that quality does not inhere in any etymological link between *Mercurius* and *medius currens,* as Varro would have one believe.[281] To point out that Varro, here as elsewhere, was almost certainly mistaken does not, however, elucidate his purpose. What his compulsive etymologizing signals is a preoccupation with defining the relation or *ratio* that secured the forms of words to their meanings. Varro seems to see this relation as consisting in certain resemblances, which suggests one way of understanding the relation between the body of architecture that Vitruvius wrote and what he meant it to signify.

SIGNIFICATION

Julius Caesar, who so insolently dismissed the *res publica* as nothing but a name, without body or visible form, wrote a work on grammar called *De analogia* which he dedicated to Cicero.[282] The work was his contribution to the dispute among late republican intellectuals about whether language was a natural or a conventional phenomenon.[283] Caesar—predictably, given his pronouncement on *res publica*—took what was known as the analogist position: that language was conventional, independent of nature, and ought to be governed by strict rules of regularity, which is to say by *analogia* (*ana-logon*, "according to *logos*").[284] The opposite view, which was Stoic in origin, was that language was a natural growth, reflected in the linguistic irregularity ("anomaly") justified by common usage.

Varro gives a complete account of both positions in books 8 to 10 of his *De lingua latina*, a work Vitruvius names in his encomium on the universal benefits of writing in the preface to book 9.[285] Varro's own conclusion is a compromise position. Linguistic regularity exists in nature; common usage imitates this, while allowing for variants.

Those who give us advice in the matter of speaking, some saying to follow usage and others to follow ratio, *are not so much at variance, because usage and regularity* [analogia] *are more closely connected with each other than those people think. For* analogia *is sprung from a certain usage in speech, and from this usage likewise is sprung* anomalia. *Therefore, since usage consists of unlike and like words . . . neither* anomalia *nor* analogia *is to be cast aside, unless man is not of soul because he is of body and soul.*[286]

The final, rather startling leap from the coexistence in language of both anomaly and analogy to the assertion obviously meant to clinch the argument—"unless man is not of soul because he is of body and soul"—is the most intriguing part of the passage.[287] In the gap lies Varro's unspoken appeal to an assumption about the perfect coherence of body and soul in men and, even more interestingly, the intimation that language is like that. Admitting the anomalies attending individual bodies does not allow the denial of soul (= *ratio*), which is "regularity" itself in men, for, Varro implies, the order of nature is reflected in the order of words, *as in the order of the human body.*

Further along, where he discusses the irregular nominative cases of certain nouns, he once more invokes the specifically corporeal order of words.[288] An anomalous nominative like *Hercules* or *homo*—he calls the nominative a "head," *caput*—is nevertheless followed by oblique cases (genitive, dative, accusative, etc.) which, unlike the nominatives, do exhibit regularity (*analogia*) in their inflections. "Is it not a fact," he continues, again assuming common knowledge, "that, if you should put the head of

Philip on a statue of Alexander and the limbs should conform to *ratio* [*membra conveniant ad rationem*], so too would the head [Philip's] that corresponds to the limbs of Alexander's likeness?" The point of this rather cryptic pronouncement seems to be that if a statue's limbs are properly proportioned, you can put an "anomalous" head on it and still end up with a perfectly satisfactory overall *ratio*. So with *Hercules, homo,* and their inflections.[289] Once again, the order of words resembles the order of a man's body, ultimately to be valued in the totality of its overall coherence. Like the units of ten discussed earlier, fragments, be they words or body parts, only take on their proper identity as parts of wholes.

Moreover, if there is a *ratio* that connects the meaning of *pes* to that of *pecunia* (both are measurements), or the meaning of *Mercurius* to the *medius currens* of both money and language, then that *ratio* must—allowing for variants—be embedded in the particular shapes of the words themselves.[290] Otherwise body and soul would not really be connected and coherence would founder. Factual evidence is adduced by the etymologies, so many of them spurious by modern standards, that Varro brings to bear.[291] Similarly, for Vitruvius, the perfect *ratio* of ten was embedded in, and proven by, the corporeal *fact* that men have ten fingers and further that, through measurement, these fingers modulate the overall shapes both of men and of temples. The cosmic order of *De architectura* is a linguistic order, which is also the order of a man's body or of a temple, whose symmetry "arises from proportion, which is called *analogia* in Greek."[292]

This still does not answer the question of signification, however: the question of what *De architectura* was meant to signify, and how. Vitruvius himself raises the issue very near the beginning of his first book.

These two things are contained in all matters, but above all in architecture: that which is signified and that which signifies. What is signified is the matter set forth by what is said. What signifies this is a demonstration developed through the principles of learning.[293]

Scholars usually take the "signified" of this passage to refer to *fabrica* or construction, the "signifier" to *ratiocinatio.*[294] *Ratiocinatio,* in this bipolar view, "signifies" or represents *fabrica.* By the same token, *De architectura* would represent architecture. This has led to some frustration among modern readers who find in Roman ruins a reality that the treatise often *mis*represents; many things considered quintessentially Roman in architecture—amphitheaters for example, and especially vaulted construction—are not represented in *De architectura* at all. One fairly common conclusion is that Vitruvius, who favored Hellenistic precedents, was a *laudator temporis acti,* a eulogist of times gone by, and more than a little out of date.[295] The operative assumption here is that something called architecture was already there, and that Vitruvius, through his conservatism, failed to do it justice; that architecture preexisted *De architectura,* in other words. But did it? This chapter has explored a number of areas in which the indications point in quite the opposite direction.

Another approach to the question of signification suggests an alternative way of understanding what Vitruvius meant when he claimed to be writing the body of architecture; two approaches, in fact, which are mutually illuminating and are both firmly anchored in the immediate context of its writing. One of these is suggested by John Scheid's account of ritual significa- tion.[296] The Stoic theory of language, specifically the theory of what Stoics called the *lekton,* points toward the other.

It is important, first of all, to understand that *significare* in Latin means to "show by signs," not "represent." Scheid's essay deals with three instances of Roman ritual practice that involve such signification—the case of the *flamen,* or priest of Jupiter, that of the triumphant general, and that of the vestal virgins. The conventional view has been that each of these is an instance where the person in question, unusually costumed and bound by strict ritual constraints, somehow "represents" a god in a liv- ing image. For the lifelong duration of his office, the *flamen* rep- resented Jupiter. So did the triumphant general, but only for the day of his triumph when, with his face painted red like Jupiter's statue, he climbed to the god's temple on the Capitol in Rome. For the 40 or so years they were bound by their vows, vestals rep- resented Vesta, goddess of Rome's public hearth.

Scheid's contention is that these people were not the living image of the god or goddess. They performed rather as the god's double, in the same way that, according to Jean-Pierre Vernant, the archaic Greek *kolossos* "doubled" a dead man or woman, and fixed the power of death in the world of the living by giving it a visible form.[297] The *flamen* did not *represent* the god but, as double, *signified* the god's power—showed it by signs—and made it visible. Scheid points out that St. Augustine uses the verb *significare* to describe precisely this kind of ritual activity.[298] The signifier in the ritual context would be a man or woman who wore certain clothes and performed certain gestures. The signi- fied was not another being, but the ephemeral *power* or meaning of another being, which mediated between the signifying cele-brant and the absent god he or she celebrated. The arrest of the prescribed behavior would mean the evanescence of that power and the disappearance of the god. The triumphant general only mediated the god's power for a day. The *flamen,* who was never al-lowed to be absent from Rome and who, moreover, could never sleep away from his home where the legs of his bed were coated with the mud of Roman soil, fixed the signified power perma-nently, or as permanently as humanly possible, in a specific place—Rome. This does not imply that the gods were "con-structed," for their existence was never in question.[299] But it does imply that their presence in human communities was a fragile affair and coexisted with human action.

The notion of signifier-signified, first developed by Greek sophists in the fifth century B.C., was a key aspect of Stoic lan-guage theory.[300] Words bore a special relation to things, and a well-formed locution could even at times surpass the thing re-ferred to.[301] A striking case in point is Cato's claim that the co-herence and beauty of the Stoic system surpasses even the coherence of the natural order it is meant to account for.[302] But signifier-signified is a truncation of the full Stoic formulation which has three terms, not just two: signifier, signified, and the thing referred to. This means, of course, that the signified and the thing referred to are not the same.

Sextus Empiricus explained the theory this way.

The stoics . . . [say] that three things are linked together, what is sig-nified [to sêmainomenon], *that which signifies* [to sêmainon], *and the existing thing* [to tynchanon]. *That which signifies is the utter-*

ance . . . what is signified is the specific state of affairs [to pragma]
indicated by the spoken word . . . the existing thing is the external
reality. . . . Of these, two are bodies, the utterance and the existing
thing. But the state of affairs signified is not a body but a lekton.[303]

Lekta are not bodies. Like void, place, and time, *lekta* are what the
Stoics called "incorporeals."[304] *Lekta,* things signified, mediate
between the words of significant utterances and existing
things.[305] They have no independent existence, but are temporally dependent on the duration of thoughts and sentences.[306]
Signs or signifiers say something *about* something. Although
lekta are not themselves bodies, and indeed do not create them,
they can affect the appearance of what the Stoics called the "representations" (*phantasia*) of bodies—how people perceive
things—by determining what they may be seen to be like.[307]

　　De architectura is *about* architecture, a ten-scroll written
work which, if one follows this line of reasoning, did not so
much bring architecture into being as shape its representation
into a body that had to be written if it were not to evanesce with
the thought or utterance with which it coexisted. If, in other
words, what it signified were to last. "An architect should know
writing so as to be able to produce a stronger memory in commentaries."[308]

　　Seneca reports the use of three Latin equivalents for the
Greek word *lekton: effatum* "pronouncement," *enuntiatum* "dec-
laration," and *dictum* "thing said."[309] Another Latin counterpart
seems to have been *res,* the "matter" of utterances, for, wrote
Quintilian in his *Institutio oratoria* at the end of the first century
A.D., "Every speech [*oratio*] consists of those things which are

signified [*ex iis quae significantur*] and those which signify [*quae significant*], that is, of matter and words [*ex rebus et verbis*]."[310]

Silvio Ferri, among others, claims that Vitruvius's *quod significatur* (signified) is *fabrica*—construction. Vitruvius continues his paragraph on the question by asserting that whoever would call himself an architect should be trained (*exercitatus*) "in each part," that is, both in signifiers and in what they signify. The obvious conclusion, for Ferri and others, is the equation *ratiocinatio* = signifier, *fabrica* = signified.

This is understandable enough, given that Vitruvius has just written (paragraph 1) that *fabrica* and *ratiocinatio* together bring the knowledge of the architect into being, and further (paragraph 2) that they jointly constitute the arms that allow the architect to attain his goal.[311] Would he be saying more or less the same thing yet again in paragraph 3? Vitruvius was no stranger to redundancy, and the paragraph in question may indeed be another instance of his tendency to repeat himself. But he concludes the signifier-signified paragraph by listing the nine disciplines he considers to be the means to the architect's attaining expertise "in each part"—what the architect needs to know to become a *perfectum artificem,* an accomplished master of the art.[312] And there is not a single reference to *fabrica* or construction in the list that follows, nor in the ensuing paragraphs (4 to 10) which explain why each of the disciplines is needed.

This should come as no surprise, if one recalls that *fabrica,* "the continuous and routine practice of the activity the hands accomplish out of matter," is the habit or *hexis* of hands-on practice that, as argued earlier, gives architecture its vegetative soul. Clearly, *disciplinae* cannot have a great deal to do with *fabrica* so defined. Writing, drawing, and geometry are the first three disciplines Vitruvius lists and would appear, rather, to furnish signifying skills. The next six (history, philosophy, music, medicine, law, and the *rationes* of the sky) contribute to the stock of "matter" which may be signified. In paragraph 3, while still obviously writing about *architectura*, Vitruvius seems no longer to be concerned with *fabrica* and *ratiocinatio* but to have broached another, related topic.

Vitruvius says that the signifiers and signifieds contained in all matters inhere *tum maxime*, to the highest degree, in architecture.[313] Why in architecture above all?

If one may, with Quintilian, understand that every *oratio* consists of signifying *verba* (words) and signified *res* (matter), then signifier and signified, while belonging in general to language, belong in this context specifically to the discipline of rhetoric. So too, as a number of scholars have shown, in its method and structure at least, does *De architectura*, whose author cites Cicero's *De oratore*, along with Varro's *De lingua latina*, as a work he particularly admires.[314] For instance, many of the words Vitruvius uses for the things on which architecture depends—*ordinatio, dispositio* (arrangement), *eurythmia*—are also rhetorical terms which, Louis Callebat has suggested, signal an author with some rhetorical training who was thus able to formulate an architectural discourse using terms that were familiar to his audience: members of the Roman elite who were virtually all trained, practicing orators, but who were unlikely to know a great deal about architecture.[315] Also part of this rhetorical vocabulary were "signifier" and "signified," *verba* and *res,* which indeed were an orator's stock in trade.

Naturally, there was more to the art of rhetoric than just matter and words. Through *inventio* they had to be thought up;

through *distributio,* properly arranged; through *elocutio,* well said; and through *actio,* delivered. They also had to be stored for ready recall, which was where *memoria* came in.[316] Not natural memory but artificial memory, the "art" of memory, so called, on which two of the three surviving ancient sources date from the first century B.C., one of these being at the end of book 2 of Cicero's *De oratore.*[317] "Rerum memoria propria est oratoris," Cicero wrote, "the memory of things is proper to the orator."[318]

To review the now familiar procedure, the practitioner of the art of memory "deposited" *res* or *verba,* represented by images (*imagines*), into a series of ordered locations (*loci*) in his mind and had only to revisit these locations for the matter or words to be recalled in their proper order. Order is the crucial operative. Cicero says that it is order above all (*maxime*) that lights up the memory, an order that in this context is clearly more spatial than temporal.[319] Further, fixing *res* in the memory was more expeditious than fixing *verba,* for if one were able to recall one's "matter," words would follow of their own accord.[320] *Loci* were required to lodge the *imagines* that signified *res* because, said Cicero, voicing what was a commonplace of ancient thought, "a body without a *locus* is unintelligible."[321]

But as Jocelyn Penny Small has claimed, the Greeks never confounded the places (*chôrai,* or *chôroi*) without which bodies were unintelligible, with the rhetorical *topoi* of mnemonic systems, as Cicero does in the passage just cited.[322] *Topoi,* for Aristotle and the Greeks, were "purely mental constructs with no physical aspects."[323] The transfiguration of the Greek orator's mnemonic *topoi* into *loci* imagined as real (in principle, measurable) places appears to have occurred in late republican Rome.

According to the anonymous, first-century B.C. author of

the *Rhetorica ad Herennium,* these *loci* were constituted as houses, intercolumnar spaces, recesses, arches, and the like.[324] Quintilian, a century and a half later, elaborates on the use of houses but adds that one can also use public buildings, a long road, the ramparts of a city, or pictures.[325] None of these, of course, exists without building: one of the three parts of architecture in which, says Vitruvius, *tum maxime* signifiers and signifieds are contained. He would appear to have meant this quite literally, if indeed signifiers and signifieds are for Vitruvius as for Quintilian *verba* and *res,* although of course the orator's "artificial" memory locations, even if drawn from the real world, were rebuilt, as it were, inside his mind.

The role of the hut of Romulus on the Capitol, says Vitruvius, was to "signify [*significare*] the *mores* of ancient times and impress them on the mind."[326] The image here is of a primitive hut; but primitive construction methods are not its signified matter. For an educated Roman, the *mores vetustatis* signified by the hut of Rome's founder would have been the same as the customs of ancient times that Cicero claimed were the foundation of the Roman commonwealth.[327] Given its *locus* on the Capitol next to the Temple of Jupiter Capitolinus, it also signified the first beginnings of Rome's greatness.[328]

Placing images in such locations is just like writing, according to the Roman sources, "for the *loci* are very much like wax tablets or papyrus, the images like letters, the arrangement and disposition of the images like the script, and the delivery is like reading."[329] Indeed, Quintilian's personal mnemonic favored writing itself over the place-and-image system.[330] For him written words, which acted like *imagines,* while impressing "matter" on the places of the wax tablet on the writer's knees simultaneously impressed it onto the tables of his memory, from whose *loci* he could, as in the more traditional system, then draw it forth at will.[331]

Mary Jaeger claims that Livy wrote his *Ab urbe condita* as a *monumentum,* reminder, in which the "achievements of the Roman people" Livy records are so fused to the places of Rome's collective memory as to be unintelligible without them.[332] Jaeger brings the art of memory to bear on her discussion. One suggestion is that Livy's division of his work into pentads of five books each reflects the prescription that each fifth *locus* of the artificial memory be clearly marked.[333] Another is that his selectivity in choosing Roman monuments is not so much reductive as the necessary concomitant of mnemonic schematization: a Rome tailored, one might say, for writing on the mind.

Ann Vasaly has shown that Cicero consistently made the city and its monuments "an integral part of the perceptible proof that formed the chief subject matter of [an] oration."[334] In one of his last speeches, addressed to Julius Caesar in 44 B.C., Cicero complains about having to speak indoors where he could no longer invoke the incontestable material presence of these potent signifiers.[335] One can use words to reply to an argument made with words. But how does one answer to the self-evident *fact* of a building? Particularly one about whose signification (the hut of Romulus or the Temple of Jupiter, for instance) there is, or should be, no collective doubt? Cicero's frustration on this occasion leads one to believe that he would have agreed with, or at least understood, Vitruvius's claim that architecture above all is the repository of signifiers and of signified matter. "So great a power of suggestion resides in places," wrote Cicero, "that it is no wonder the discipline of memory is based on it."[336]

Virgil too makes monumental Rome an integral part of his narrative in the *Aeneid,* to the degree that, according to T. P. Wiseman, to miss such allusions is to miss the poet's intent.[337] Being implicit rather than explicit, such evocations (principally of Augustan monuments) often elude the modern reader, but would have been obvious to the ancient Roman one. In Virgil, as in Cicero and Livy, the signifying power of words is made to depend upon the far greater signifying power of built works and their topographical *loci;* on architecture, in other words.

"To write about architecture is not like writing history or poetry," writes Vitruvius in the preface to book 5, a preface whose text is developed between the "Imperator" he opens with and the "Caesar" he addresses at its close.[338] The theme of the preface is the difficulty of transmitting architectural knowledge.[339]

Histories hold the reader's attention through suspense, says Vitruvius; poems by meter and the "choice arrangement of words." Neither of these is at the disposition of the writer on architecture. The amplification orators rely on to lend authority to their themes is no help either, for amplification would only further confuse architectural writings where both the terms and the procedures described are already unfamiliar.[340] "Therefore, in pronouncing strange terms and giving the proportions of the members of works, my explanations will be brief so that they may enter into memory; for in this way, minds will be able to receive them easily."[341]

There follows the discussion of writing according to Pythagorean "cubical principles" already alluded to. When thrown, a cube, like a die, remains immobile on whatever side it rests. Similarly, cubical writing "will produce motionless stability of the memory there [*ibi*]"—presumably in the place where it lands.[342] As mentioned earlier, Vitruvius does not appear to have followed such principles. Rather, what he seems to be doing is (memorably) marking this, his fifth preface—*ibi*, there—as a memory *locus*, with an *imago* that is the stablest of all the geometrical solids, halfway between the "Imperator" of his opening address and the "Caesar" of his concluding one, and—if one imagines the ten scrolls stacked up in the form of the *tetractys*—anchoring the entire work at the spatial center of its triangular deployment.

I

II   III

IV   V   VI

VII   VIII   IX   X

Although he does not seem to have actually written "cubically," Vitruvius does appear to understand that his recourse to brevity serves a similar "cubical" purpose.[343] At least as important mnemonically, if not more so, is his recourse to order—what Cicero called the light of memory. In his fifth preface, Vitruvius says that he has written a single body of architecture, with a separate scroll for each different subject, which, by implication, may be recalled at will because its *locus* is part of an ordered sequence.[344]

Vitruvius clearly understood the efficacy of this tactic. In the preface to book 7, he tells the story of Aristophanes of Byzantium, one of the judges of a literary competition held at the Library in Alexandria, who was able to identify six of the seven contestants as plagiarists because "every day, with supreme application and the greatest diligence, he [Aristophanes] would read through all the books *in their proper order.*[345] Thus, after all the poets had made their presentations, Aristophanes "trusting in his memory" was able to go directly to the right shelves, pull out the appropriate scrolls, and, by comparing the texts in the library to those that had just been read, force the spurious poets to acknowledge their guilt.[346] The question of fraud would not even have arisen had neither the fraudulent poems nor their sources been written down. More importantly, Aristophanes was able to unmask the deception because his memory was spatially ordered in the same way as the library shelves.

The same ordering principle governs Vitruvius's insistent and repeated identification of the relative position of each of his own scrolls, whereby every book begins and ends with a connective paragraph that clearly defines its location with respect to the others.[347] Given its spatial coordinates within the framework of the whole ten-scroll *corpus,* the "matter" in each scroll is properly placed for ready recall.

The two short paragraphs of the preface to book 4 constitute the very briefest (most "cubical") of Vitruvius's ten prefaces. It is the only preface besides the clearly marked fifth one to address both "Imperator" and "Caesar" and separate them with a block of text. Moreover, it is within this strategically placed block of text that the stress on order occurs—an emphasis that recurs, similarly located and almost verbatim, in the following preface.

When I noticed, Imperator, *that many who have provided rules and scrolls of commentaries on architecture have not left orderly works but only incomplete drafts, scattered like fragments, I decided it would be a worthy and most useful thing to bring the whole body of this great discipline to complete order and, in separate scrolls, to develop a register of conditions for each of its different subjects. Therefore, Caesar, in the first scroll I set out for you what its* officium *is. . . .* [348]

Between the "Imperator" and the "Caesar" of this, the preface to book 4 (and also, later, of book 5), is where Vitruvius locates the *order* of the work or, more precisely, where he locates the sentence that *describes* that order. Words (*verba*, signifiers) are positioned between "Imperator" and "Caesar," which are other words, but these last, being in the vocative case, address a particular person. The words that describe the order of *De architectura* are not "just" words, of course. They are *about* something. As signifiers, they say something about architecture. Since what these words signify—the *lekta* or schematized matter of the whole work—coexists with the signifying words, where Vitruvius puts them is also, obviously, where he puts their signified matter. The order they signify is lodged inside the person addressed by "Imperator" and "Caesar," their enframing architectural *locus*, who here and again in the preface to book 5 becomes the mnemonic house of *architectura*.

The trope, moreover, works both ways. In the single, long and particularly dense sentence that concludes his first preface, Vitruvius summarizes his reasons for writing *De architectura* for Augustus. Memory is one of them. He began to write for him because he was bound to his patron by benefits received, he starts out. Also, he continues, because he has noticed how much Augustus has been, is, and is planning to build . . .

both public and private buildings in keeping with the greatness of your achievements so that these might be transmitted to the memory of posterity and abide in its care, I have delineated complete and detailed rules so that by considering them you yourself can take account both of what finished works are like and of how future ones will be; for in these scrolls I have laid out all the principles of the discipline.[349]

On the one hand, the buildings built by Augustus—architecture in its narrow sense—provide the places of posterity's memory into whose abiding care his *res gestae,* achievements, are consigned.[350] On the other hand, the *praescriptiones terminatas,* complete and detailed rules, that Vitruvius claims to provide in his treatise circumscribe and delimit in writing the knowledge (*architectura*) Augustus needs in order to grasp for himself what these places are or will be like.

Two complementary memories are at work here. One, posterity's, is to be furnished with buildings that locate the builder's achievements, which, without such *loci* to give them substance, would drift into oblivion, evanescent as *lekta* or the forgotten matter of a public address. The other memory belongs to the builder himself—Augustus. The first, the memory of posterity, Vitruvius implies, needs the second, whose mnemonic frame is the spatial scheme of a perfect body of ten discrete scrolls. Common to both is the person of the new ruler, repeatedly invoked as Imperator or Caesar or both in all ten prefaces except one.

Book 8, as intimated earlier, is an anomaly. Although

necessary for completing Vitruvius's perfect decad, its subject matter, water, does not fit into the tripartite whole of architecture (building, the construction of clocks, mechanics). It is also the only book not overtly addressed to Augustus. It has been suggested that the absence of an "Imperator" or a "Caesar" in the eighth preface may simply be an accident of transcription.[351] On the other hand, the omission may have something to do with what book 8 is *about*.

Romans certainly made every effort to contain, channel, direct, and control water, whose flow Heraclitus made the phenomenal analogue for the ever-changing flux of lived experience.[352] Water, Vitruvius stresses, is the source of life itself.[353] But in book 2 where he discusses how the elements combine in bodies and in building materials, it is water, the enemy of coherence, that more than any of the other elements dissolves good bonds. Profoundly ambiguous archetype of preliterate, mythical memory and forgetfulness,[354] water is also the enemy of mnemonic schematization. You cannot chisel IMP. CAESAR onto water.

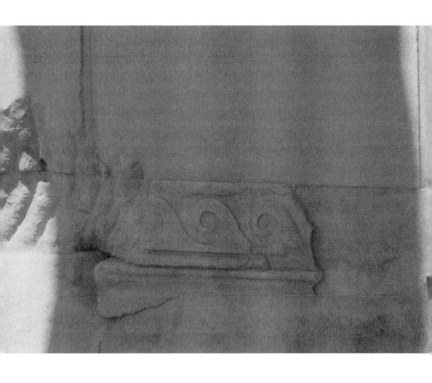

Wave motive at the base of the cella wall of the Temple of Mars Ultor, Rome, dedicated 2 B.C.

2

THE HERCULEAN BODY

The King's Double.

The Once and Future King.

Benefiting the World.

When Alexander was taking mastery of the world, the architect Dinocrates, confident in skill and the power of thought, came out of Macedonia to the royal encampment eager for recognition. From his homeland he brought letters from friends and relations to the king's courtiers and highest ranking officers so as to gain easier admission.[1]

Unable to obtain the speedy access he desired, Dinocrates impatiently took up his own defense.

He had towering stature, appealing good looks, and a majestic build. Putting his trust in these gifts of nature, he left his clothes at his lodging, anointed his body with oil, placed a crown of poplar leaves on his head, covered his left shoulder with a lion skin, and, grasping a club in his right hand, came into the tribunal where the king was giving justice. The stir his appearance caused made Alexander catch sight of him. Struck with admiration, he commanded the people to make way so that the man could approach and asked him who he was.

"Dinocrates," he answered, "the Macedonian architect who brings to you ideas and designs worthy of your renown. For I have formed Mount Athos into the shape of the statue of a man in whose left hand I have traced the walls of a most spacious city. In his right, there is a bowl to draw out all the rivers in the mountain, water that from there pours out into the sea."

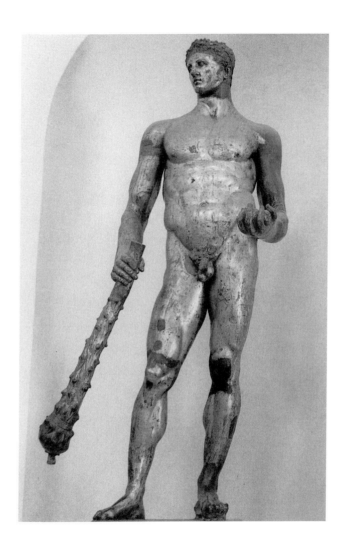

Gilded bronze statue of Hercules from the Forum Boarium, Rome, first century B.C. Musei Capitolini, Rome (inv. 1265).

The theme of the project delighted Alexander, who straight-away asked if there were fields around that could maintain the city with supplies of grain. When he learned that this was not possible without transport from beyond the sea, he said, "Dinocrates, I appreciate what a magnificent achievement this design is, and am delighted by it. But I note that if someone were to lead a colony there, his choice of site would be condemned."[2]

In such a location, a city, like a baby without a nurse's milk, would be unable to grow or thrive without a ready supply of grain.

"Therefore, much as I think your design is to be esteemed, I consider the place unacceptable. Yet I want you to stay with me so that I can put your works to use." From then on Dinocrates never left the king and followed him into Egypt. There, when Alexander noticed the safe natural harbor, the excellent market, the grain-bearing fields throughout the whole of Egypt, and the many advantages of the great river Nile, he commanded Dinocrates to establish the city of Alexandria in his name. And so, commended by his appearance and the stateliness of his body, Dinocrates attained his fame. As for me, Imperator, nature has not given me stature, age has spoiled my appearance, and bad health has sapped my strength. Deserted by these defenses, it is therefore with the help of knowledge and writings that I hope to attain recognition.[3]

The story of Dinocrates and Alexander forms the sum and substance of Vitruvius's preface to book 2, the one on building materials.[4] In no other preface is an anecdote, if there is one, given such exclusive prominence.[5] Although Varro has been named as the source for the story, and although there are other ancient authors who mention Dinocrates, Vitruvius's is the earliest version of the story that survives.[6] His account, moreover, is more elaborate than any of the others and its details, for the most part, are tellingly unique.

At a time when architects had trouble gaining recognition, Dinocrates seems indeed to have succeeded. As "Dinochares," he is the fifth on the list of five architects whom Pliny considers to have excelled in their craft; Pliny also names him twice in connection with the foundation of Alexandria.[7] In Ausonius's fourth-century A.D. poem on the Moselle, "Dinochares" again appears, this time as seventh of seven great architects in a list headed by the legendary Daedalus and credited by Ausonius to the tenth book of Varro's *Hebdomades*.[8] Ausonius, presumably following Varro, makes "Dinochares" the builder of Ptolemy I's palace at Alexandria, of a four-sided pyramid which "devours its own shadow," and of a miraculous levitating statue of Arsinoë in her temple at Pharos.[9]

"Dinochares" is not the only variation. For Strabo, who mentions only the involvement of unnamed, plural architects in connection with the foundation of Alexandria, and (following Strabo) for the third-century A.D. grammarian Solinus, a "Cheirocrates," from Rhodes (not Macedonia), collaborated in the rebuilding, under Alexander's patronage, of the colossal

Temple of Artemis at Ephesus in the latter part of the fourth century B.C.[10] The surviving manuscripts of Pseudo-Callisthenes' third-century A.D. Alexander romance hesitate between "Hermocrates" and "Hippocrates," again from Rhodes, as Alexander's architect at Alexandria.[11] Plutarch discusses the Mount Athos project twice, but its perpetrator is one "Stasicrates" who also, according to Plutarch, designed a magnificent funerary monument for Hephaestion, Alexander's inseparable companion.[12]

Three authors besides Vitruvius name "Dinocrates" in connection with Alexandria: Valerius Maximus, Ammianus Marcellinus, and Julius Valerius, a Roman historian of the late third century A.D.[13] Like Pseudo-Callisthenes, Strabo, and Solinus, Julius Valerius also gives Rhodes as the architect's place of origin.

All these names converge less on a single identifiable personage than on a persona who emerges from a nexus of constants—grand architectural projects (real or imagined), architect, and king—all related in a gloss on power for which the name "Dinocrates," most frequent of the aliases, can be read as a kind of epitome.[14]

Kratos, of course, is power or might itself, particularly mastery through bodily strength.[15] *Kratos* was also the name the Pythagoreans gave to the number ten.[16] The masculine noun *ho dinos* has to do with circularity or circular motion—whirlpools, eddies, circular threshing floors, the whirling of a sling.[17] Like the feminine *hê dinê, dinos* can also be the rotation of the heavens: the whirling that the pre-Socratic philosopher Anaxagoras said was how *nous* (mind) regulated the universe, a creative force of nature that resonates with the natural power Vitruvius says was constructed (*architectata*) to govern the revolutions of the universe—the same cosmic spin he says brings the principles of machinery into being.[18]

The adjective *deinos* means fearful, terrible, clever, skillful—boldly or dangerously skillful as often as not.[19] In Sophocles' *Philoctetes,* wily Odysseus speaks with skill and wisdom (*deinou kai sophou*); in Plato, Socrates tells the sophist Protagoras, more with censure than approval, that he is *sophos kai deinos.*[20]

Confident in *sollertia* and *cogitationes*—in the skill and power of thought that are cognates, respectively, of the *fabrica* and *ratiocinatio* that together bring *architectura* into being—Vitruvius's Dinocrates comes out of Macedonia, the homeland this version uniquely makes him share with Alexander.[21] Alexander of Macedon and "Dinocrates, *architectus Macedo*" are countrymen. Vitruvius insists on this. Yet agreement among the other sources makes it almost certain that the "real" Dinocrates came from Rhodes. Why would Vitruvius claim otherwise?

Here as elsewhere, Vitruvius appears to be more concerned with the concrete coherence and value of the whole "body" Stoics understood as truth (*alêtheia*) than with the particulars they called the true (*to alêthês*), which they judged insubstantial and of no value.[22] The common origin Vitruvius assigns to architect and king means that they are operating from the same center. The shared purpose—the shared values—that this implies contributes infinitely more to the coherent body of *De architectura* than would any accurate reference to Dinocrates' true place of origin.[23] Shared values are essential in an architect who is to double his king.

The man who announces himself to Alexander as Dinocrates *architectus Macedo* is immensely tall, superbly built, and—except for the freshly applied coat of oil, the poplar leaf crown, the lion skin, and the club—stark naked. The reader is meant to recognize him, of course. So is Alexander. The spectacularly nude man who calls himself Dinocrates looks like Hercules. Or at least like the Hercules Roman audiences instantly recognized in paintings, sculpture, coins, and written descriptions, thanks to the standard code of attributes Vitruvius so carefully details here: nudity, inordinate size, muscular build, lion skin, and club. Even Dinocrates' well-oiled skin resonates curiously with two well-known larger-than-life bronzes which also glisten, not with oil but with gold.[24] (The crown of poplar leaves will be dealt with in due course.) In no other version of the story does Dinocrates impersonate Hercules. No other source even mentions the architect's appearance.

It was normally Alexander's own prerogative to appear as Hercules, from whom the Macedonian kings, and Alexander himself with particular insistence, claimed descent.[25] Alexander's extraordinary exploits were regularly identified with the hero's twelve labors, both by others and by himself.[26] Sacrifices to Hercules were often part of Alexander's religious observances.[27] Hercules also appeared to Alexander in dreams to encourage him when an especially challenging conquest lay ahead.[28]

In Vitruvius's story, the glistening colossus with his club and lion skin thus doubles the king's own preferred persona. Moreover, the man wearing as it were the mask of Hercules is an architect. Dinocrates' ruse—which is really Vitruvius's ploy, of course, since he has set it up—is far more than just a courtly compliment, or even a bid for attention, although there is no denying it is these too. On the face of it, there is considerable slippage between what the signifying *verba*, "Dinocrates *architectus Macedo*," signify (*architectura*, the knowledge of the architect)

Alexander the Great wearing a lion skin helmet. Marble relief on the Alexander Sarcophagus from Sidon, late fourth century B.C. Istanbul Archaeological Museum (inv. 370).

and what the massive physical presence unmistakably shows by signs ("Hercules," but named otherwise). There is a space between the two. In this space, which is the space of signified rhetorical matter, the contours of *architectura* merge with those of Hercules. Or, to put it another way, situated in the same rhetorical *locus,* the matter signified by "Dinocrates *architectus Macedo*" and the matter represented in the unforgettable image Vitruvius sets before the king and the reader are one and the same. The terms bracket architecture with the king's own Herculean persona. Moreover, the "knowledge of the architect" (Dinocrates' *sollertia* and *cogitationes*) now appears wholly palpable in the body of Hercules, as incontrovertible a physical fact as Mount Athos itself. "I am you, Alexander," Dinocrates is saying, "both 'Hercules' and *architectura*—which together double your true self":

"Dinocrates . . . the Macedonian architect who brings to you ideas and designs worthy of your renown. For I have formed Mount Athos into the shape of the statue of a man in whose left hand I have traced the walls of a most spacious city. In his right, there is a bowl to draw out all the rivers that are in that mountain, water which from there pours out into the sea."[29]

In Plutarch's *Moralia* of the second century A.D., Mount Athos from a distance already has something like the shape of a man, with projections that look like limbs, joints, and human proportions.[30] "Stasicrates," who points this out in Plutarch's version, has followed Alexander into Asia and, finding the work of

Alexander's usual portraitists unequal to the king's true majesty, proposes fixing the king's image in the mountain's immovable bulk. As in Vitruvius, the statue is to have a city in one hand (10,000 inhabitants are specified, although which hand is not) and in the other an urn out of which a river flows down to the sea. Besides his precision about left and right hands, Vitruvius also differs in his stipulation that the projected statue is of an unspecified man (*statuae virilis figura*) not, at least not overtly, of Alexander.[31] In Vitruvius, the subject to be represented in the architect's grandiose memorial is left open.

In both versions Alexander is delighted. In both he declines. In Plutarch, where there is no intervening Hercules, Alexander loftily replies that he can do without such a monument to vanity, because the mountain ranges of Asia already bear the imprint of his exploits. In Vitruvius, Alexander rejects the project because the city is badly located and the people in it would starve.

Vitruvius has the king enter gladly into the Herculean dialogue Dinocrates has set in motion, with a response that makes Alexander even more Herculean than the Hercules look-alike who stands before him. For the club-wielding slayer of monsters was also traditionally *philanthropos,* friend of men, city founder and benefactor.[32] It had been above all in *philanthropia* that the Athenian orator Isocrates had enjoined Alexander's father, Philip of Macedon, to be like his mythical ancestor.[33]

Prefiguring the Everyman of medieval allegories, when the Hercules of a fifth-century B.C. fable by Prodicus meets Vice and Virtue (*Kakia* and *Arêtê*) at the crossroads of his life, he chooses the hard road signposted by *Arêtê,* who trains his nature in the ways of goodness.[34] This Hercules' great strength is moral strength. The mythographers said that performance of his labors was his path to immortality.[35] Romans said it was his service to mankind.[36]

Vitruvius's second preface is not just about Dinocrates and Alexander, of course. If Dinocrates doubles the king, he is in turn doubled by Vitruvius, who himself doubles the "Imperator Caesar" to whom he addresses *De architectura*. But Vitruvius is nothing like Dinocrates, at least not physically.

As for me, Imperator, nature has not given me stature, age has spoiled my appearance, and bad health has sapped my strength. Deserted by these defenses, it is therefore with the help of knowledge and writings that I hope to attain recognition.[37]

Nature, age, and bad health have robbed Vitruvius of the very three defenses—towering stature, appealing good looks, majestic build—in which Dinocrates put his trust. Or so Vitruvius says. It is all too easy to be taken in by the artful disclaimer that has furnished many Vitruvius scholars not only with otherwise scanty biographical evidence but also with support for the view that Vitruvius was hopelessly conservative and, understandably given his advanced years, out of touch with the realities of current architectural practice.[38] If his age was really such a disadvantage, why, apart from false modesty and the demands of rhetorical symmetry, would he draw attention to it? One imagines he had his reasons.

Ruled by the Senate, the Romans, who derived *senatus* from *senex* (old man), were in fact ruled by old men, or at least by men who were over forty-six which, by Roman reckoning, marked the beginning of old age and of the years during which public honors accrued.[39] And the crowning glory of old age, writes Cicero, is *auctoritas*.[40] Greater than the sensual pleasures of youth and invulnerable to wrinkles and gray hair, *auctoritas* he says brings honor and distinction, "the morning visit, being sought after, being made way for, having people rise at one's approach, being escorted to and from the forum, being asked for advice."[41]

Writing, Vitruvius claims, gives an architect *auctoritas*, that specifically Roman measure of worth already discussed in some detail. How much more authoritative, then, an architect/author who is old.[42] Or better still, dead.

It will be, Vitruvius writes in his ninth preface, "as if face to face" with Lucretius that those born in later times will be able to discuss the nature of things; the art of rhetoric with Cicero himself; the Latin language with Varro. The opinions of the Greek philosophers and of wise writers like these, "their bodies absent, will flower in old age . . . and have greater authority than all those who are present."[43] Books are the missing bodies of writers consecrated by old age.

Hercules himself was not always young either. Bearded representations make him if not exactly old, at least visibly mature. Most famous among these is the Farnese Hercules, Lysippus's celebrated mountain of a man who slumps tiredly over his club after completing his labors.[44] A curious story, told in Greek by the second-century writer Lucian, tells of a very aged Gallic Hercules, who went by the name of Ogmios.

In their pictures . . . they make him out as old as can be: the few hairs he has left (he is quite bald in front) are dead white and his

skin is wrinkled and tanned as black as any old salt's. . . . Such
as he is, however, he has all the proper attributes of that God:
the lion's-skin hangs over his shoulder, his right hand grasps the
club . . . nothing is wanting to the Heraclean equipment.[45]

The strangest thing of all about this Gallic Hercules is his following, for he drags along with him a willing crowd of men
whose ears are attached by delicate chains of gold and amber to
his tongue. Lucian is flummoxed until his Gallic interlocutor en-
lightens him.

"We Gauls connect eloquence not with Hermes, as you do, but with
the mightier Heracles. Nor need it surprise you to see him repre-
sented as an old man. It is the prerogative of eloquence, that it
reaches perfection in old age. . . . Hence if you will consider the re-
lation that exists between tongue and ear, you will find nothing
more natural than the way in which our Heracles, who is Elo-
quence personified, draws men along with their ears tied to his
tongue."[46]

This Hercules is not Lucian's invention. There really was
an Ogmios in Gallic religion, one whose head, filling the center
of a Gallic gold coin of the first century B.C., is chained with
what appear to be strings of beads to the other smaller heads
around the edge.[47] Ogmios does indeed appear to have com-
bined Herculean attributes, notably the club, with those of Mercury (the Gauls' chief god, according to Julius Caesar) when, in

the first century B.C., the Gauls began to give their gods images drawn from the repertoire of Greco-Roman culture.[48]

The fusion or pairing of Hercules and Mercury described by Lucian was not unique to northern barbarians. On the obverse of a Roman coin of 87 B.C., the faces of Hercules and Mercury appear back to back as the two faces of Janus.[49] Spatially the gate, temporally the beginning, existentially the point of transition that is all points—with some points of course more importantly transitional than others—Janus, an indigenous Roman god, had no equivalent in Greek mythology.[50] His two faces, usually identical but here not, clearly signaled an identity of Hercules and Mercury, whose pairing gave precision to the generic meaning of gates and beginnings.[51] To the left of Hercules, who faces left, is the ubiquitous club; to the right of Mercury's winged head is his caduceus, sign of peace, of negotiated relations, and of a herald's right to speak.[52]

A hundred years later, the two gods were again paired, this time on either side of the entrance to the Temple of Augustan Concord in the Forum Romanum. The reverse of a sestertius of Tiberius, issued in 35–36 A.D., shows its main elevation.[53] On the right of the broad stair leading to the temple platform stands a statue of Hercules, cradling his club on his left arm. His right hand is lifted up behind his head. On the left of the stair stands Mercury holding his caduceus aloft with his right hand. His moneybag hangs from his left.

Tiberius, Augustus's stepson and designated heir, dedicated the temple in his own and his dead brother Drusus's name on January 16 of 10 A.D., anniversary of the day Augustus had received his new name in 27 B.C., the day that was celebrated as the birthday of the Augustan principate.[54] The T-shaped

Reverse of a sestertius of Tiberius of 35–36 A.D.,
with the front of the Temple of Augustan Concord.
Mercury is on the left and Hercules on the right.
British Museum, London (BMC Tib. 116).

Corinthian hexastyle temple, faced with Luna marble, was the last and by far most dominant Augustan work in the Forum Romanum, and completed its transformation into a dynastic monument that had begun when Augustus dedicated the temple of his deified father, directly opposite, nearly forty years earlier.[55] The Temple of Concord was situated at the foot of the Capitol, at the western end of the Sacra Via, just below the Tabularium, where the Roman archives were kept. A caduceus was carved into the marble threshold of the temple cella, a little to the left of center. The corresponding slab to the right is missing, but it is assumed that its surface was cut with the image of a club.[56]

Projected outward into the Forum by their prominent position on the front ends of the high balustrades that framed the entrance stair, the statues of Mercury and Hercules together constituted the gate through which anyone approaching the temple necessarily passed, joint custodians of Augustan *concordia:* of peace, cosmic harmony, a unified empire, civic concord, the reconciliation of opposites, all inescapably bound up with the person of Augustus, his family, and his succession.[57] Further inward at the precise point of entry, the emblems of club and caduceus cut Hercules and Mercury into the cella threshold with signs whose signified matter converged with the spatiotemporal matter of this and every Roman door. The Aedes Concordiae Augustae celebrated the Augustan peace that was rooted in the Roman past (at least two earlier temples of Concord had stood on the site); that had begun on January 16, 27 B.C.; and that would continue through Augustus's heirs of whom Tiberius, who dedicated the temple on another January 16, was to be the first.[58] Its context fixed this particular Roman door—the point of entry to

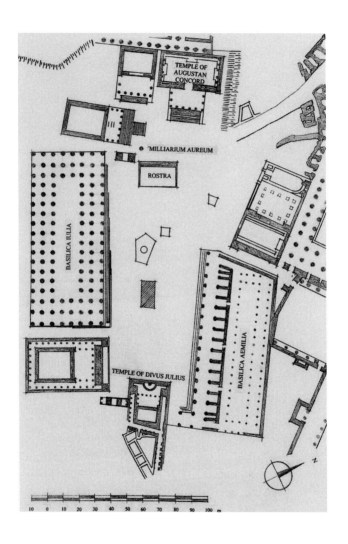

Plan of the Forum Romanum in the second century A.D.

the cella of a temple whose *dies natalis* was January 16—as the enduring instant of that insistently repeated beginning.

What did Hercules and Mercury have to do with it? Most obviously, the club and the caduceus were the dual aspects of Roman power: brute force and *logos*, the power of reasoned speech, with the latter tied to commerce on which the peaceful unity of the empire also depended.[59] Pliny mentions a "two faced Janus" dedicated by Numa "which is worshipped as indicating war and peace" and who is also, he says, the god of the duration of time.[60] The mighty Hercules (war) and rational Mercury (peace) fit quite neatly, but there is more.

Zeno, founder of the Stoic school in the fourth century B.C., is reported to have claimed in his now lost *Republic* that "Eros is a god who stands ready to help in furthering the safety of the city." Others who preceded Zeno, the report continues, knew "Eros as a god far from anything ignoble . . . [for] in the public gymnasia he is enshrined along with Hermes and Heracles, the first presiding over eloquence, the second over physical strength; when these are united, friendship and concord are born."[61] Cornutus, a Stoic who wrote in the first century A.D., concludes his allegorized account of Hermes-*logos* thus: "People also give him homage at the palaestra along with Herakles because it is necessary to employ strength with reasoning. For to the person who places his trust only in the power of the body, but disregards Reason, which introduced skills into life, a person might properly respond, 'Dearest, your own great strength will be your death.'"[62]

Beyond this, Hercules, as noted earlier, was *philanthropos*, a model of virtue among philosophers. Indeed, for the Stoic allegorists, Hercules was himself a philosopher. According to Heraclitus Homericus, a near contemporary of Cornutus, the three heads of Cerberus, whom Hercules brings up from Hades into the light of day, are the three parts of philosophy: logic, physics, and ethics.[63] As the light of divine reason, Hercules dispels the fog of ignorance.[64] Plutarch writes that when he grew old Hercules became a philosopher, an expert in both dialectic and divination.[65]

For Cornutus, "Herakles is the universal *logos* in its aspect of making Nature strong, in control and indomitable."[66] The Pythagoreans, much earlier, had called him *dynamis tês physeôs,* the force of nature, a notion further developed by the Stoic Cleanthes in the fourth century B.C.[67] Pythagoras himself is reported to have concluded an address which dealt with concord, among other moral issues, by evoking Hercules and reminding his audience that Hercules had founded Croton, Pythagoras's adopted city in southern Italy where his sect first flourished in the sixth century B.C.[68]

In the natural theology of the philosophers, Hercules was not simply the brawn that complemented Mercury's brain.[69] Divine reason was a single, world-pervasive *pneuma,* but it permeated the world-body in two different ways, to recall Diogenes Laertius's report on the question.[70] As a natural, vegetative, "Herculean" force, it was the tension that bonded bodies in their bones-and-sinews aspect. As Mercurial *nous,* it was the articulate thought unique to human beings—the eloquence that, in Lucian's story, bound the Gallic Hercules to his willing following. On this view, and like the two faces of Janus whom Varro called *mundus,* the world, Hercules and Mercury form a single head, at once the key to the coherent totality of things and the specific point in time at which, in the temple in the Forum, Augustan *concordia* repeatedly begins.[71]

Manilius's *Astronomica,* begun at the end of Augustus's reign, has provided Barbara Kellum with the key to the temple's astrological program, in which the signs of the zodiac are all linked together in a single narrative by statues emblematically deployed inside the cella.[72] Manilius himself relates these same zodiacal signs both to the parts of the body and to the parts of the world.[73] The coherence of the temple's cosmic/dynastic narrative, literally *built* into its fabric, is profoundly Stoic and, like the building, ultimately corporeal.

Like many Augustan authors, Manilius was a Stoic.[74] So were Livy and Virgil, who wrote at the beginning of Augustus's reign.[75] Pierre Grimal has suggested that the strong Stoic orientation of Augustan literature took its cue, or at least drew support, from Augustus himself. From early adolescence until about 30 B.C. his tutor was the Stoic Athenodorus of Tarsus, whom he admired greatly.[76] For the next twenty years after the conquest of Egypt, the Alexandrian Stoic Arius Didymus was philosophical intimate and advisor to the mature world ruler.[77] Arius was the author of a work known as the *Epitome,* an abridgment of mainly Stoic philosophy which survives only in fragmentary form, and which he may have written for Augustus as a philosophical résumé similar in schematizing intent to that of *De architectura.*[78]

C. Julius Theon of Alexandria, another Stoic, succeeded Arius Didymus as Augustus's philosophical advisor.[79] Among Augustus's written works, Suetonius mentions an "Exhortations to Philosophy."[80] A number of Roman historians have studied the advent of the principate itself in terms of the "slow but steady flow of Greek philosophical ideas into Roman political life."[81] The Stoicism that was a common ground between Augustan authors and their patron was also a shared *topos* through which Vitruvius, clearly addressing a *lecteur averti,* presented Augustus with his case for architecture.

Hercules and Mercury together constitute the gateway to the cosmic/dynastic narrative of the Temple of Concord, built at the end of Augustus's reign. From Hercules and Mercury, Athenaeus reports, friendship and concord are born.[82] Of this, the Temple of Concord stood as a palpable demonstration, incontrovertible built proof. At the beginning of Augustus's reign, Vitruvius made these gods' Stoicized selves, immanent in *fabrica* and *ratiocinatio,* the point at which both *architectura* and *De architectura* began.[83]

THE ONCE AND FUTURE KING

The Hercules in front of the Aedes Concordia Augustae has his right hand raised behind his head. He is crowning himself, although with what exactly it is difficult to decipher from the small, rather fuzzy image on the Tiberian coin.[84] Crowns or wreaths belonged to winners. Triumphant generals wore laurel, as Hercules also did at times. Victorious Olympic athletes were crowned with olive, as is the gilded bronze Hercules in the Conservatori museum.[85] In the preface to book 9, Vitruvius complains that such crowns really belong to writers, not to athletes.[86] The Dinocrates-Hercules of Vitruvius's story crowns himself with poplar leaves.[87] Why poplar? The white poplar is sacred to Hercules, say Virgil, Ovid, and Pliny the Elder.[88] Pausanias, in his second-century A.D. *Description of Greece,* reports that the Eleans use white poplar wood in their sacrifices to Zeus because Hercules brought the tree to Elis from the banks of Acheron, the river of Hades—a holy provenance bound up with intimations of immortality for anyone who could go there and get back.[89] Virgil, insistently, makes poplar and so too Hercules native to Rome.

On the eve of Aeneas's first arrival at Rome in book 8 of Virgil's epic, just as he is about to fall asleep on the riverbank, the river god appears before him "raising his aged head among the poplar leaves" to prophesy the city's foundation.[90] Except that, as old Tiberinus foretells, there is already a city there, or at least a settlement, ruled by the Arcadian king Evander.[91] When Aeneas arrives at the site with his fleet, Evander and his Arcadians are in the middle of celebrating the rite of the *ara maxima,* the annual feast of Hercules, at this his "greatest altar." The scene is set in the place that was to become the Forum Boarium, the market beside the river where the cult of Hercules was indeed historically concentrated, and near which a late republican round Temple of Hercules still stands.[92] Evander interrupts the celebrations to greet the new arrival, whom he recognizes as the hero from Troy, and invites Aeneas to sit down on a lion's skin to hear the story of the ritual's origin.[93]

When Hercules "glorying in the spoils of triple Geryon"— his tenth labor, in the course of which he slew the three-bodied monster in question and stole his magnificent herd of red cattle—arrived with his stolen herd at the very place where Aeneas and Evander are sitting, the valley between the Aventine, the Palatine, and the Capitol was being terrorized by Cacus, the fire-breathing monster who lived there. Cacus, whose name (*kakos,* bad man) makes him as unmistakably evil as Evander's (*eu-andros,* good man) makes him good, steals four of the herd's best bulls and as many heifers.[94] To make Virgil's rather long story short, Hercules discovers the theft, throttles Cacus with his bare

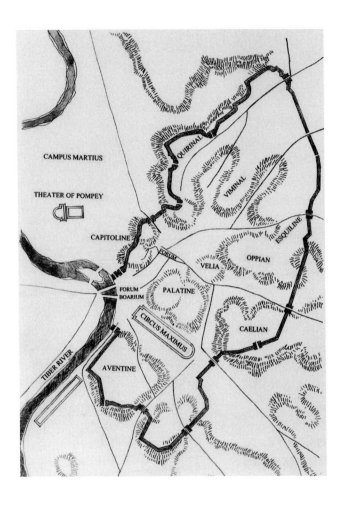

Plan of republican Rome.

hands, and retrieves his booty from the cavern where Cacus has hidden it.[95] "From that time this service has been solemnized," concludes Evander, "and joyous posterity has kept the day."[96] All—Aeneas's men, Evander himself, and the Salii who dance around the altar singing of Hercules' deeds—wreath their hair with poplar, "the shade dear to Hercules," and resume feasting.[97]

As in Prodicus's fable, the Hercules of Virgil's story is once again "at the crossroads," with Cacus and Evander standing in for the *Kakia* and *Arêtê,* the vice and virtue of the earlier version.[98] But Prodicus's "crossroads" was geographically nonspecific, and *Kakia* was not killed but simply bypassed in favor of *Arêtê*. In Virgil, good triumphs on the left bank of the Tiber in the cattle market between the Aventine, the Palatine, and the Capitol, where Virgil situates the temporal beginning of Rome. Literally at the crossroads between the land road that connected central Italy to Etruria in the north and the Tiber, which was the water road inland from the sea, the riverbank site was also Rome's geographical point of entry.[99] In the Roman context, Hercules' defeat of Cacus, the monster who personifies evil, is the original lustration of the swampy, uninhabitable *place* of arrival that prepares it for all the arrivals that are to follow.[100]

A force for good, Hercules also brought to Rome *humanitas* in its specifically cultural or learned aspects. North of the Forum Boarium, in the Circus Flaminius, where the spoils of war were traditionally displayed during the days that preceded the triumphs that set out from there, were two more temples of Hercules. One of them, built by Fulvius Nobilior from the spoils of his victory at Ambracia in western Greece in 189 B.C., was the round Temple of Hercules Musarum, which contained statues of the Muses along with one of Hercules playing the lyre.[101] The temple was

The Forum Boarium, Rome, with the late republican temples of Hercules Victor (left) and Portunus (right).

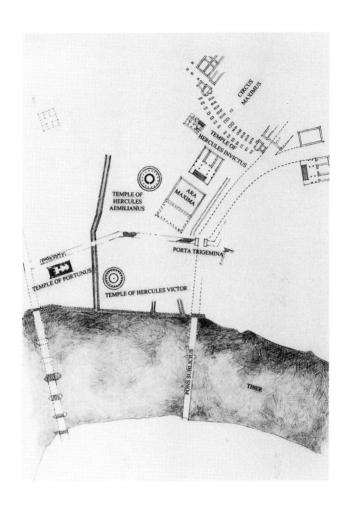

CIRCUS MAXIMUS

TEMPLE OF HERCULES INVICTUS

TEMPLE OF HERCULES AEMILIANUS

ARA MAXIMA

PORTA TRIGEMINA

TEMPLE OF PORTUNUS

TEMPLE OF HERCULES VICTOR

PONS SUBLICIUS

TIBER

Plan of the Forum Boarium in the late republic.

dedicated to a Hercules scholars have identified as Pythagorean: a lyre-playing *musagetes* (leader of the Muses), set up in Fulvius's victory monument as patron of the arts and orchestrator of universal harmony.[102] Cicero points appreciatively to the temple's simultaneous celebration of culture and conquest when defending *humanitas* in his oration on behalf of the poet Archias.[103]

"Why had Hercules and the Muses an altar in common?" asks Plutarch in one of his *Roman Questions*. "Is it because Hercules taught Evander how to read, as Juba records?"[104] In another passage in Plutarch, for which no source is given, Hercules' knowledge of letters enables him to read an ancient inscription urging "the Greeks to live . . . in peace, by always taking philosophy as their field of contention . . . and settling their disputes by an appeal to the Muses and discussion."[105] Writing around the same time as the Temple of Hercules Musarum was built, Fabius Pictor, Rome's earliest historian, attributed to Evander the introduction of the alphabet to Rome; Livy later credited him with the same "miraculous" invention.[106] The Hercules who made the future site of Rome hospitable to Evander's small Greek colony, and so to goodness itself, was perhaps the same who "as Juba records" taught the good king how to read.

The Hercules-Cacus episode in the *Aeneid* is made part of Hercules' tenth labor, the one that should have marked their accomplishment, according to some mythographers.[107] Following this tradition, the Augustan poet Propertius has Hercules address his stolen herd as "the final labor of [his] club."[108] The hymn of the Salii in Virgil's story is an enumeration of all the monsters Hercules has killed, beginning with the snakes he strangled in his cradle and ending with the slaughter of Cacus— his crowning achievement, as Virgil tells it, and tenth on Virgil's

Hercules Musarum, reverse of a denarius of
Q. Pomponius Musa, 66 B.C. British Museum,
London (BMC RR Rome 3602).

list.[109] Those who took oaths and made agreements at the *ara maxima* owed a tithe, or tenth part of their profits, including war booty, to Hercules.[110]

Almost every surviving Augustan author of note tells the story of Hercules' arrival at Rome, although only Virgil lays such stress on the poplar.[111] In historical times, celebrants of the rite of the *ara maxima* wore laurel, but when the ritual first began, before the founding of the city, at the very first celebration of its initial lustration, this was not yet the case.[112] So Virgil tells it at any rate, establishing the autochthony both of Hercules and his cult, celebrated in his epic by men who, like the river itself since time immemorial, are poplar-crowned.[113]

Hercules purified the future site of Rome in a struggle that was accomplished at the Forum Boarium. When? In mythical time, before the arrival of Aeneas at the time of Evander, long before the time of Romulus, Aeneas's descendant and Rome's eponymous founder for whose divinization that of Hercules, according to Livy, served as a model.[114] But in historical time too. The rite of the *ara maxima* is generally agreed to have been celebrated annually on August 12 or 13.[115] Augustus's triple triumph, celebrating his victories in Dalmatia, at Actium, and at Alexandria—the three-day triumph that marked the end of the civil wars and the dawn of a new era—began on August 13 of 29 B.C.[116] This meant that every year, from that time forward, when Romans celebrated Hercules and his victory over evil, they would also have been celebrating Augustus.[117]

The eighth book of the *Aeneid* opens in the mythical past with Aeneas, a new Hercules, arriving at Rome on the same day as had Hercules, "glorying in the spoils of triple Geryon."[118] It concludes historically with Augustus "entering the walls of Rome in triple triumph," the event Virgil enshrines as the culmination of all of Roman history at the end of his long description of Aeneas's shield.[119] Pierre Grimal has shown that the whole point of Virgil's making Aeneas arrive at Rome on the day he does is to have the Augustan present fulfill that mythical beginning.[120]

Virgil was not the only Augustan writer to affirm an identity of Hercules and Augustus. The association was almost canonical, with particular stress laid on Augustus's Herculean *virtus* as well as on his *humanitas.*[121] There is little evidence that Augustus himself actively promoted the identification (one supposes he did not have to), although Suetonius says that when he was at Tibur, "he very often gave justice in the porticoes of the Temple of Hercules," where the epigraphical evidence directly links the cult of Augustus to that of Hercules.[122]

Near the end of the sixth book of the *Aeneid,* Virgil had already prophesied Augustus's reign, which was to surpass in greatness even the most glorious of Hercules' exploits.[123] The panegyric is a Latin rendering of traditional encomia of Alexander the Great.[124] If Hercules mediates between Dinocrates and Alexander in Vitruvius's second preface, he also, in Virgil, mediated between Augustus and Alexander. Indeed, it has been argued that, historically, the old Italic Hercules of the Forum Boarium, patron originally of merchants and traders, only became the Hercules Victor and Invictus who championed Roman generals when, from the time of Scipio Africanus in the third century B.C., Alexander himself became their envied model and inspiration.[125] Roman generals, in other words, were seen or saw themselves as Herculean *through* the paradigm of Alexander, which was primary.[126]

On the third day of the triple triumph of 29 B.C., Augustus celebrated his conquest of Egypt the year before. When he was in Alexandria, he visited the tomb of its founder where

he had the sarcophagus and body of Alexander the Great brought forth from its shrine, and after gazing on it, showed his respect by placing upon it a golden crown and strewing it with flowers; and being then asked if he wished to see the tomb of the Ptolemies as well, he replied, "My wish was to see a king, not corpses."[127]

That year, or possibly the following one, Augustus adopted a new official seal.[128] After Caesar's murder, he had used Caesar's seal ring with Venus Victrix on it.[129] A seal with the image of a sphinx on it soon replaced it. Afterward, from his Alexandrian conquest in 30 B.C. most probably until 23, Augustus sealed all his official and personal documents with the head of Alexander the Great, including, one assumes, any communication he might have addressed to Vitruvius who completed *De architectura* during the period in question. There is no record of how Alexander was portrayed on this seal ring, but the majority of Hellenistic and Roman coins, medals, and indeed rings with his head on them make him a Hercules, helmeted with a lion skin.[130]

The earliest possible date for the completion of *De architectura* is thought to be 29 B.C. The key piece of evidence for this is the opening of Vitruvius's first preface.

When your divine mind and power, Imperator Caesar, were seizing command of the world, and all your enemies had been crushed by

Glass paste cameo of Alexander-Hercules,
probably early Augustan. Musée du
Cinquantenaire, Brussels.

your invincible strength and citizens were glorying in your triumph
and victory and all subjected peoples awaited your nod . . . in the
midst of such great preoccupations, and fearing to vex you by in-
truding at a bad time, I did not dare to bring forth the writings on
architecture I had developed with much deliberation.[131]

The time referred to is the triumphal period that followed Augustus's conquest of Egypt, specifically the triple triumph of August 13–15 in 29 B.C., celebrated with processions that, after their departure from the Circus Flaminius, entered the walls of Rome at the Forum Boarium where a very ancient statue of Hercules *triumphalis,* alleged to have been dedicated by Evander, was dressed for the occasion in the same triumphal garb as the *triumphator* himself.[132] The Imperator Vitruvius addresses whose enemies have been laid low by his *invictus virtus* is clearly Herculean. Herculean too is the *cura,* care that Vitruvius says he noticed in Augustus "not only for the common life of all men and the regulation of the commonwealth but also for the fitness of public buildings."[133]

One of the *curae* Augustus undertook in his early career as *princeps,* and one which involved him directly with the "common life of all men," was the *cura annonae* that put him in charge of the *frumentationes* (distributions of free grain) that took place either in or near the Forum Boarium.[134] After the Alexandrian conquest, at least a third of Rome's grain supply came from Egypt, whose grain-bearing fields, Vitruvius says, were one of the reasons why Alexander "ordered Dinocrates to establish the city of Alexandria in his name." Thanks to Augustus, Alexandria and the grain-bearing fields that surrounded it now belonged to Rome.[135]

Among the eight large reliefs on the emperor Trajan's early second-century A.D. arch at Beneventum, one has him at Rome engaged in a *frumentatio*.[136] The activity can be located with some precision because in the background, presiding over the scene, are the statues of three gods: Portunus on the left, Apollo Caelispex on the right, and in the middle Hercules. Filippo Coarelli has shown that each represents the cult statue of his respective temple near the Forum Boarium. Portunus is the tutelary deity of the small surviving Ionic temple near the Tiber, traditionally known as the Temple of Fortuna Virilis; Apollo Caelispex of his, no longer extant small temple further to the south; and Hercules of the still extant Corinthian round Temple of Hercules Victor that stood between them.[137] The cult statue of Hercules Victor represented on Trajan's arch was made late in the second century B.C. by the Greek sculptor C. Scopas *minor*, about the same time as the temple itself was built.[138] Both the temple and its statue were part of the city Vitruvius knew at first hand.[139] The Hercules in question has a lion skin on his left shoulder, grasps a club in his right hand, and wears a crown of poplar leaves.[140]

Unlike any other surviving representation of him, this Hercules is outfitted in exactly the same way as the Dinocrates-Hercules who doubles Alexander in Vitruvius's second preface.[141] (Except, of course, for the head which, even crowned with poplar leaves, would have remained recognizably Dinocrates' own.) When, in Vitruvius's story, the king objects to the Mount Athos project because it has failed to take the crucial question of grain supplies into account, it is not the voice of Alexander

The *annona* relief from Trajan's arch at Beneventum with Hercules at the center on the upper left. Early second century A.D.

speaking. Indeed Plutarch's Alexander makes no such objection. Rather, as if Vitruvius had suddenly substituted Augustus's head for that of Alexander, the thoroughly Augustan reply affirms at once Augustus's own *cura* and its reflection in the philanthropic avocation of a Hercules, also Victor and Invictus, who is specifically sited at the place of Rome's mythical first foundation. If you can change the head on a statue, as Romans often did, how much more easily in a piece of writing.

When Julius Caesar had an equestrian statue of Alexander by Lysippus set up in his forum, he had the head removed and replaced with his own.[142] Later, in the first century A.D. under Claudius, the head of Alexander in two paintings by Apelles in the Forum Augustum was replaced with that of Augustus.[143] Varro assumes common knowledge of such practices in the late republic when he asks in *De lingua latina*, "Is it not a fact that, if you should put the head of Philip on a statue of Alexander and the limbs should conform to *ratio*, so too would the head [Philip's] that corresponds to the limbs of Alexander's likeness?"[144] The same principle would apply to the head of Caesar or Augustus placed on Alexander's body or, for that matter, to the head of Dinocrates on the body of Hercules.

Given this Varronian line of reasoning, and provided that the overall *ratio* of their bodies conforms to regularity, could you not likewise change the head of the world—or a book? Vitruvius, who admired Varro, seems to have thought so.[145] His first preface, which many believe was written last as an introduction to the entire work, heads both the highly theoretical book 1 and all of *De architectura*. It begins with a ruler preoccupied with "seizing command of the world" and with an architect wondering if he can approach him to present him with his work. In the second preface, which begins the body proper of the work, the architect has found in Hercules a way to do just that. As architect and world ruler respectively, the Vitruvius and Augustus of the first preface replace the Dinocrates and Alexander of the second. The persons named ("heads" or "nominatives") have changed, but the overall *ratio* has not. Vitruvius even provides the reader with a numerically precise point of reference against which to test this.

The second preface begins, "Dinocrates architectus cogitationibus et sollertia fretus, cum Alexander rerum potiretur." The first preface opens with, "Cum divina tua mens et numen, Imperator Caesar, imperio potiretur orbis terrarum." The tenth word in both prefaces is *potiretur*. Twice Vitruvius uses the same person, tense, and mood (third person singular, imperfect subjunctive) of the deponent verb *potior*, "take possession of," "become master of," and gives it the same relative position in his text. In the second preface, Alexander "rerum potiretur." *Rerum potior* means to have "complete" or "supreme" mastery of things.[146] In the first preface, Augustus "imperio potiretur orbis terrarum." *Imperio potior* means to take possession of with *imperium*, in Rome the legally vested power of supreme command.[147] *Potior* is a very strong verb. In his first two prefaces—surely no accidental symmetry—Vitruvius gives *potior* exactly the same powerful tenth position. But the first preface, being first, takes precedence. It sits, if one imagines Vitruvius's ten scrolls deployed in the triangular form of a *tetractys,* at the top of the heap.[148] So too Imperator Caesar.

In this context, Vitruvius's vagueness about who is to be represented in the architect's project of shaping Mount Athos into the form of man ("statuae virilis figura") begins to seem deliberate.[149] The *ratio* or "theme" that so delights Alexander in the story remains coherent, even if the person the architect proposes thus to wed to the power of nature is now a different one.

The same maneuver substitutes Vitruvius for Dinocrates, whose body, as already discussed, is that of Hercules, the king's double. In pointedly disclaiming any similarity between that body and his own, Vitruvius in fact affirms the opposite, so as to present his knowledge and writings as rhetorically identical with the Herculean body that commands Alexander's attention.

After their initial encounter, Dinocrates never leaves Alexander's side.[150] Alexander and Dinocrates may have been an inseparable team, but they were still two different people. In *De architectura,* Vitruvius obviates that difference by writing, as it were, Augustus's head onto his own ten-scroll body of architecture, which is something Varro says you can do both with statues and words and still remain coherent.

Before *De architectura* was written, Vitruvius and Augustus, like Dinocrates and Alexander, were two separate people, occasionally brought together by the services Vitruvius performed and the *beneficia* he says he received for them.[151] Mary Beard's insights concerning writing and religion show that when, in *De architectura,* Vitruvius seals his relationship to his patron with repeated written invocations of "Imperator" and "Caesar," he turns theirs into a permanent, indissoluble connection.[152] Without the emperor, the body of architecture is headless. Without *De architectura* the emperor has no body.

Dionysius of Halicarnassus was a Greek writing, like Vitruvius, in Rome in the early years of Augustus's reign. Dionysius tells the same story as Virgil about Hercules' arrival at the future site of Rome, except that in his account the celebrants of the initial rite of the *ara maxima* wear laurel, not poplar.[153] Dionysius, however, follows this "mythical" account with a so-called "true" one, in which a pointedly philanthropic Hercules,

the greatest commander of his age, marched at the head of a large force through all the country that lies on this side of the Ocean, destroying any despotisms that were grievous and oppressive to their subjects . . . establishing lawful monarchies, well-ordered governments and humane and sociable modes of life. Furthermore, he mingled barbarians with Greeks . . . groups which hitherto had been distrustful and unsocial in their dealings with each other; he also built cities in desert places, turned the course of rivers that overflowed the fields, cut roads through inaccessible mountains, and contrived other means by which every land and sea might lie open to the use of all mankind.[154]

The *philanthropia* of Dionysius's Hercules, clearly not without its architectural dimension, is an apology for world conquest. Indeed, this Hercules would be lost without architecture, particularly without the machinery to which Vitruvius devotes the last and longest of his ten books, the third part of architecture which includes the machinery of war as well as the very engines such a Hercules would need for cutting roads through mountains and changing the courses of rivers.[155] So too the Hercules who rescues Prometheus near the beginning of Diodorus Siculus's "Library of History." As Diodorus, a near contemporary of Dionysius, tells it, Prometheus was a governor of Egypt; when the Nile, called "eagle" because of its strong current, flooded excessively, Hercules turned the river back to its former course and thus saved Prometheus.[156]

Both Dionysius's and Diodorus's accounts of Hercules reflect the mythography of Euhemerus of Messene, whose *Hiera anagraphê*, written some twenty years after Alexander's death, asserts that the gods were all originally great human rulers, later deified through posterity's grateful recognition of their services.[157] In the early part of the second century B.C. the Roman epic poet Ennius, whom Vitruvius singles out as a personal favorite, translated Euhemerus's work as *Historia sacra*, the earliest Greek work to be translated into Latin.[158]

Vitruvius thinks that *De architectura* will be of service.[159] In the preface to book 6, he expresses the hope "that once these scrolls have been published [he] will be known even to posterity," adding a little later that he "decided to write the whole body of architecture and its principles with the greatest of care, thinking it would be a not unwelcome service to all peoples [*omnibus gentibus*]."[160]

The last phrase reappears in a similar context in the preface to book 9, where Vitruvius writes about the honors that ought to be bestowed on writers "who perform unlimited services to all peoples [*omnibus gentibus*] for all time," rather than on athletes (who do not).[161] He names Pythagoras, Democritus, Plato,

Aristotle, and "other wise men" as examples of such writers, men whose precepts bear fruit "not only among their fellow citizens but among all peoples [*omnibus gentibus*]."[162] Who are all these "peoples"?

According to Seneca, the Stoic Athenodorus of Tarsus, the first of Augustus's many philosophical advisors, used similar terms when he likewise compared the fairly useless cultivation of an athlete's body to the philosophical cultivation of a political leader's soul—the liberal education, pursued from boyhood on, whose purpose was to make such a leader useful to his "fellow citizens and to all mortals." "Civibus mortalibusque" is the phrase that appears in Seneca's Latin report of a passage Athenodorus would originally have written in Greek.[163] "Mortals"— *thnêtoi* in Greek—are everyone who is not *athanatos*, immortal; all humans, in other words. The background in Athenodorus's case is the common humanity and brotherhood of man, a key notion of Stoic ethics, grounded in the unique relation to the cosmic order all humans share.[164] It would not be unreasonable to suppose a similar background in Vitruvius's hope to be of service to "all peoples," who thus constitute mankind. But the expression he uses is *omnes gentes*, not *mortales*, and if his sentiments are Stoic, this *omnes gentes* gives them a pointedly Roman spin.

Omnes gentes also appears at the opening of Vitruvius's first preface: "When your divine mind and power, Imperator Caesar, were seizing command of the world, and . . . all subjected peoples [*gentes omnes subactae*] awaited your nod . . .".[165] When other Roman authors write *omnes gentes* (rather than just *gentes*) the context is almost invariably identical.[166] For instance, when the anonymous author of the early first-century B.C. rhetorical treatise *Rhetorica ad Herennium* gives an example of a standard "middle style" speech, it concerns traitorous allies who would "attempt to usurp that sovereignty over the whole world— the command all peoples [*omnes gentes*] . . . have accepted, when conquered either by the arms of Rome or by her generosity."[167] Pompey, whose achievements "crowned by glorious victory on land and sea encompassed all peoples [*omnes gentes*]" in one of Cicero's elogia of him, is *victor omnium gentium,* conqueror of all peoples, in another.[168] In the *Philippics,* Cicero writes that the Roman people are not meant to be slaves, since the immortal gods have decreed their command of "all peoples."[169] In his fourth Catalinarian oration, he calls the *curia,* the Senate house in the Forum Romanum, their ultimate refuge.[170] Another speech names the Capitol as their citadel.[171]

At the end of the first century A.D., Martial, in one of his epigrams, says that he is "acclaimed and read through the whole world" and that he is "spread out over all the peoples held by Rome."[172] Martial's phrasing (poetic license, no doubt) allows the possibility of peoples *not* held by Rome, but in general the Roman representation of mankind ignored that possibility. To properly qualify as mankind, you had to be civilized, and being civilized meant being ruled by Rome, the city placed by the "divine mind" at the center, "in an excellent and temperate region so that it might seize command of the world."[173] So Vitruvius in the chapter immediately following his sixth preface with its declaration about hoping to be of service to "all peoples."

In a similar vein, and sounding very much like Dionysius of Halicarnassus on the subject of the philanthropic Hercules in the passage cited earlier, Pliny the Elder writes of Italy as

a land which is at once the nursling and mother of all other lands,
chosen by the providence of the gods to make heaven itself more
glorious, to unite scattered empires, to temper manners, to draw
together in mutual comprehension by community of language the
jarring and uncouth tongues of so many nations, to give mankind
humanitas *and in a word to become throughout the world the*
single fatherland of all peoples.[174]

The *omnes gentes* to whom Vitruvius says he hopes to be of
service can be none other than the subjected peoples who await
the nod of Imperator Caesar in the preface to book 1. You cannot
disengage them, any more than you can disentangle the philanthropic Hercules from Hercules Victor and Invictus. The world
community of which Romans saw themselves as custodians
did not extend beyond—indeed depended upon—the reach of
Roman *imperium*. It was not so much that the Romans imple-
mented the Stoic ideal, as that its universal scope gave imperialism its *ratio*.

An Olympic athlete like Milo of Croton may be *invictus,*
writes Vitruvius, without mentioning that, curiously enough,
this same Milo disguised himself as Hercules when he led an attack on Sybaris in 510 B.C.[175] But such a man bequeaths nothing
to other men except the short-lived honor of victory among his
fellow citizens. The benefits bestowed by wise men like Plato
and Pythagoras are universal and longer lasting. These are not
bestowed directly on all peoples, however. Rather, says Vitruvius,
it is through the learning of such men that others are able to acquire the necessary wisdom to institute "the ways of *humanitas,*

the equitable justice and laws without which no city can be safe and whole."[176]

He follows this with examples of the kind of learning which, one must assume, he understands as paving the way for the spread of *humanitas:* Plato's method for doubling the square; Pythagoras's discovery (by *ratio* and not by *ars*) of the theorem that bears his name, and permits the accurate construction of 3-4-5 set squares which bypass the trial-and-error methods of artisans.[177] These are the two geometrical operations essential in centuriation, the process whereby Romans "squared" the territories they conquered and inscribed on them the geometrical order of the cosmos and of Rome.[178] Vitruvius sums up these and other mathematical discoveries as having been directed not only to the "correction" of *mores* but also, everlastingly, toward the service of all.[179]

Geometry, writes Vitruvius in his sixth preface, is the very footprint of man.

When the Socratic philosopher Aristippus was cast upon the shore of Rhodes by a shipwreck, he noticed drawings of geometrical shapes and, they say, shouted out to his companions, "Be of good cheer! I see the footprints of men." He then proceeded to the town of Rhodes and went straight to the gymnasium, where he was given gifts because of his philosophical discourse—enough not only to outfit himself, but also to supply those who were with him with clothing and other vital necessities. When his companions wanted to return to their homeland and asked him what they should report there, this is what he told them to say: that children should be equipped only with such possessions and travelling supplies as could swim ashore with them from a shipwreck.[180]

Learning alone, of which geometrical figures are the *vestigia,* "footprints," Vitruvius continues, makes a man a citizen in every city, and able to withstand the vicissitudes of fortune.[181] Further along, in one of his rare autobiographical interpolations, he expresses gratitude to his parents for his own education, and for the care they took in having him instructed in an art "which cannot be demonstrated without knowledge of letters and all the learned disciplines."[182]

A story about a shipwrecked philosopher, virtually identical to the one Vitruvius tells, appears in the first book of Cicero's *De republica,* where the younger Scipio tells it in order to illustrate the point that "though others may be called men, only those are men who are perfected in the arts of *humanitas.*"[183] Although Cicero's philosopher—"Plato, or perhaps someone else" in his version—also notices cultivated fields, only the geometrical figures in the sand are taken as evidence of the presence of men, *educated* men being the only real men in the view he presents.[184] In Cicero's account, the purpose of education is to form men who serve the commonwealth. But *De republica,* on the best form of government, written in the mid fifties B.C. and set much earlier in 129, is confined to the specifically Roman context. There is no talk of education making one a "citizen of every city." To be a leading citizen of Rome was enough for Cicero's Scipio who, moreover, considered the precepts and examples of one's Roman elders more important than liberal education ("Greek" learning) for the formation of the ideal statesman.[185] Men of Cicero's day had already begun to claim that Rome ruled "the whole world," but world citizenship was not yet part of the agenda.[186]

Writing thirty years later in the early principate, Vitruvius takes a rather broader view. The Aristippus story appears in the preface to book 6, his book on private construction. He begins the first chapter with the assertion that, because of differences in climate, the kinds of buildings built in Egypt must be different from those in Spain, in Pontus (on the Black Sea), and in Rome, surveying in his short list the outermost limits of the territories inhabited by *omnes gentes,* and concluding it with Rome—the center from which, he argues at the end of the same chapter, the divine mind has ordained that they be ruled.[187]

The course of the sun that "tempers" all these different climates (along with the constitutions of the men who inhabit them) is the same "tempering power" that determines all the different kinds of water in the world, listed with evident relish and amazement in a particularly long chapter of book 8.[188] Without such variety in the earth's juices there would be no incense-bearing trees, or peppercorns, or myrrh, or silphium, and everything the earth brought forth would be the same.[189]

After another discussion of "geometrical footprints"—for so might one call the discoveries of Plato and Pythagoras reviewed earlier—book 9, on clock construction, opens with the observation that the divine mind has so constituted matters that "the shadow of the gnomon at the equinox has a certain length in Athens, another in Alexandria, and yet another in Rome."[190] The lengthening and diminution of the shadows of gnomons determine the configuration of the analemma, or "face" of a sun clock, which itself is the pattern (another geometrical footprint) of the order of the universe which Vitruvius says is discovered through "architectural principles and the tracings of the compass."[191]

Ichnographia, the plan of a building—the "drawing" (*graphia*) of its "footprint" (*ichnos*)—is, according to Vitruvius, "the properly related use of compass and ruler that renders how figures are marked out on the grounds of areas."[192] Plans cannot be drawn without geometry, which "teaches the use of straight lines and the compass (especially important for readily delineating the way buildings are marked out in areas) as well as the use of set squares, levels, and lines," providing also the means for resolving "the difficult questions of symmetries."[193]

Properly orienting a new city entails geometrical methods similar to those involved in laying out the analemma of a sun clock, with a bronze gnomon playing the crucial role of determining the cardinal points, and hence the directions of the prevailing winds to be avoided in laying out the streets of new cities.[194] Vitruvius must have thought the procedure particularly important since he describes it twice, once as a surveying operation conducted on the ground, and again at the end of the chapter as a diagrammatic geometrical operation, referring to two no longer extant *schemata* at the end of his first scroll.[195] This "geometrical footprint" appears in one of the four chapters of book 1 devoted to the essentials of founding new cities, a matter of considerable immediate concern in the 20s B.C., at the very peak of what Fergus Millar has called "the first and only period (that of Caesar, the Triumvirs and Augustus) in Roman history which saw the state engaged in active and large-scale settlement of citizens outside Italy," with colonial foundations bearing initially Caesar's and later (far more frequently) Augustus's name in all the territories held by Rome.[196] It is, ultimately, in terms of its potential as the site of a future colony that the Herculean king of Vitruvius's second preface assesses Dinocrates' proposal to shape Mount Athos into the figure of a man.[197] Detailed plans and land grants for Augustan colonial settlements were recorded in a document called the *liber beneficiorum,* the book of benefits, which was kept in the imperial archives.[198] *Architectura,* the art above all of the geometrical footprint, was the purveyor of these benefits.

True riches are what you can save from a shipwreck; to put your trust in fortune is to travel on slippery roads; learning is the one stable center that also, as in the case of Aristippus, ultimately provides all the necessities of life.[199] On these points Vitruvius's sixth preface is particularly long-winded and redundant, with corroborative citations not only from philosophers but also from poets and playwrights, all of them Greek like Aristippus. Of this learning, which makes a man at home anywhere in the world, the geometrical footprint is both the evidence and the emblem. Euclidean geometry, Luciano Canfora has observed in a different context, was the common language of the learned world whose chief center, from the third century B.C. on, was Alexandria, with its international community of Greek scholars, its museum, and its great library.[200] The shift of that center to Rome had begun in the late republic. Augustus's Alexandrian conquest marked its definitive accomplishment.

In the old days when the Romans waged war on savage tribes, wrote the geographer Strabo at the end of Augustus's reign, there was no need of education, for "force is stronger than reason in dealing with barbarians."[201] Boeotia, he says, although perfectly situated climatically for hegemony, lost its natural advantage because its leaders belittled discourse (*logos*) and neglected training and education (*agôgê kai paideia*): things that are "particularly useful in dealing with the Greeks."[202] The Romans knew better, says Strabo, and "from the time that they began to have dealings with more civilized tribes and races, applied themselves to *paideia,* and so established themselves as lords of all."[203]

"Only when the Republic was crumbling could *paideia* properly take root [in Rome]," Andrew Wallace-Hadrill has noted.[204] Claudia Moatti has explored the reasons for this, concluding that for intellectuals of the late republic, Greek learning provided rational alternatives to the disintegration of traditional *mores* seen to be at the core of the rotting *res publica*.[205] That the commonwealth was "shipwrecked" was a common way of referring to the crisis.[206]

Destruction threatens the Roman ship of state at its mythical beginning when Aeneas sets out from Troy in the first book of the *Aeneid* and a violent storm imperils his fleet. Neptune intervenes to calm the waves with his words just as, writes Virgil, when violence breaks out in a great nation, a man "honored for noble character and service" intervenes to calm the insurgents with his speech.[207] That the Neptune of the passage is also Augustus, who saved Rome from the incipient shipwreck of the civil wars, has been widely recognized and need not be dwelt on here.[208] What is worth stressing is the power of *speech* to put an end to conflict.

Vis dicendi is the power of speaking that belongs to the orator.[209] The purpose of Cicero's *De oratore,* one of Vitruvius's acknowledged sources, was to shape that power into an *ars,* a communicable body of knowledge, by giving it a *ratio* drawn for the most part from Greek teaching.[210] A number of scholars have noted that *De architectura* has a similar purpose, and that it draws heavily on Cicero, especially *De oratore,* for its method.[211] In a frequently cited article written over thirty years ago, Frank E. Brown argued that Vitruvius's aim in so doing was to dignify the architect's profession by turning what was looked down on as a manual trade into a liberal art for which rhetoric was the model.[212] Pierre Gros has questioned Brown's view on the grounds that Vitruvius's primary purpose was to attain distinction (*honores*) by serving the commonwealth, which is to say, by serving the men who ruled it.[213] Such men include those Vitruvius calls *aedificantes*—the magistrates traditionally charged with public building—and the *patres familiarum,* heads of households, to whom he hopes his sixth book, on domestic construction, will be of particular use, as well as to "all learned men"; but above all to the man who by 29 B.C. had supplanted them to become, in the public sphere at least, sole builder: Augustus, for whom, Gros argues, *De architectura* was to serve as a kind of brief.[214] What does the art of the orator have to do with such service?

Speech is unique to humans, insists Cicero's Crassus in *De oratore.*[215] As discussed earlier, speech as *logos* was the privileged channel of communication with the order of the Stoic cosmos.[216] For Crassus, the speech of an educated man is the hallmark of *humanitas.*[217] Most important of all, Crassus says, there is no other power strong enough to have gathered "scattered humanity into one place [*unum in locum*], or to lead it out of its brutish existence in the wilderness [*a fera agrestique vita*] up to our present state of civilization as men and as citizens or, once cities were established, to give shape to laws, tribunals and civic rights."[218] This power, Cicero wrote in his early *De inventione,* was first discovered at "a time when men wandered at large in the fields like animals and lived on wild fare," unguided by reason and relying chiefly on bodily strength. It was the articulate force of a "great and wise man"—the first orator—that persuaded this scattered multitude of savages, mutinous and rebarbative at first, to come together into one place (*unum in locum*) and, with speech and reason (*rationem atque orationem*), eventually tamed them to gentleness.[219]

Immediately following the anecdote about Dinocrates and Alexander, and its point that the book is to replace the body, comes Vitruvius's account of how, as he puts it, the *rationes* of building arose: the origins of building, or the history of the primitive hut, as it became known in later literature.[220] The unnamed writers on matters concerning the beginning of *humanitas* to whom Vitruvius refers include Lucretius, as has often been noted, possibly Varro, and also, certainly, Cicero.[221]

"In their old way of life, men were begotten like animals in forests, caves, and groves and spent their lives feeding on wild food," Vitruvius begins.[222] When, as a result of a violent storm, the trees in a certain place caught fire, the people nearby were terrified at first and fled. In time, however, realizing how beneficial the fire was to their bodies, they came closer, maintained it with more fuel and, through repeated attempts to communicate with one another, eventually acquired the faculty of speech.

Thus, because of the discovery of fire, the first assembly, deliberation, and society among men were brought into being. And as more came together into one place—people who, unlike other animals, had this prize from nature, that they walked not face down but up-

right so as to look at the magnificence of the world and of the stars,
and also that they easily handled any thing they liked with their
hands and fingers—together they began to build shelters.[223]

Vitruvius follows this with a catalogue of huts and their
methods of construction, describing those still observable in foreign nations, circling first the least civilized, outermost reaches
of the Roman *orbis*—Gaul, Hispania Lusitania, Aquitania, Pontus—then progressing inward through Phrygia, Marseilles, and
Athens to conclude with what (as any educated Roman would
have instantly recognized) was the foreordained nexus of civilization's origin: the hut of Romulus on the Capitol and the
thatched shrines on the citadel next to it.[224] *Arx omnium gentium,*
the citadel of all peoples, Cicero once called it.[225] There was another, probably older and certainly much better documented hut
of Romulus on the Palatine.[226] Of the two huts, whose primitive
construction methods would have been virtually identical, Vitruvius chooses to evoke the one at the head of the world.

In Lucretius, lawless brutes become civilized (a mitigated
good, as he presents it) for no apparent reason and to no apparent purpose. Lucretius, after all, was an Epicurean. After his
vivid account of the savage state, he goes on, "next, when they
had got themselves huts and skins and fire . . . the human race
first began to grow soft."[227]

The fire in Lucretius is almost incidental, as are the
huts.[228] In Cicero there are neither huts nor fire. But for Cicero
there is *ratio,* and its mouthpiece the original orator who, like the
fire in Vitruvius's story, brings the scattered multitude together

into one place (*in unum locum:* both Cicero and Vitruvius use the same key phrase) to form the first human community.[229]

For the early Stoics, as it had been for the pre-Socratic Heraclitus, *logos* was fire; nature, the coherent totality of things, was a *pyr technikon,* a craftsmanlike fire.[230] Stoics thought the cyclical renewal of the world, its *renovatio,* was brought about by fire, "a living being and a god."[231] Arius Didymus, Augustus's philosophical advisor from 30 B.C. on, wrote that fire was the "seed" that contained the *logoi* of all things—the causes of everything that has been, is, and will be.[232] Varro called fire the soul of the world, and derived the word *ignis* from *gnasci,* to be born, "because from fire there is birth, and everything which is born the fire enkindles."[233]

At the center of the world in the Forum Romanum, the Temple of Vesta sheltered the public hearth of Rome—and of *omnes gentes.* Two months after Augustus became *pontifex maximus* in 12 B.C., Rome acquired a new, second public hearth in the shrine Augustus built for Vesta next to his house on the Palatine.[234]

According to Posidonius, the Stoic who perhaps more than any other shaped Roman Stoicism in the early part of the first century B.C., man's ultimate purpose was to live in contemplation of the order of the universe, cooperating as far as possible in bringing it about.[235] If Cicero's orator is the persuasive voice of this order, its *hands* are Vitruvius's hut builders, who "unlike other animals" walk upright, can contemplate "the magnificence of the world and of the stars," and are uniquely endowed not with speech, as in Cicero, but with hands and fingers. Ten of them, to be precise, a number, as Vitruvius writes later in book 3, that reveals the human body's perfection.[236] The power of fire to renew the world works through the hands and fingers of builders.

For both Cicero and Vitruvius the ultimate good, unrecognized by Epicureans like Lucretius who shunned political engagement, is to come together into one place, which is the fundamental prerequisite for the formation of political communities.[237] To serve that community—a community indistinguishable, for Cicero, from the Roman *res publica*—was the very highest *officium,* epitomized in the art of the orator.[238] Like Hercules, Cicero writes elsewhere, those who perform such services to "this great *res publica*" obtain immortal glory.[239] The service Vitruvius sees himself as performing has the same beneficent purpose as the orator's art. But being worldwide in scope, it operates through the persuasive force of *architectura.*

Huts, of course, are just the beginning. Nature not only furnished people with senses like other animals, Vitruvius continues; she also armed their minds with the power of thought and deliberation, which subjected the other animals to their power. And so, step by step, advancing from the construction of buildings to the other arts and disciplines, they were led from their brutish existence in the wilderness (*e fera agrestique vita*— precisely Cicero's phrase) to gentle *humanitas.*[240] From huts people advanced to houses with foundations, tiled roofs, and walls of brick or stone, and finally, Vitruvius concludes, "by applying themselves to their studies, were led from wayward and uncertain opinions to the certain calculations [*rationes*] of symmetries."[241]

Humanitas, for Vitruvius, begins with building. *Architectura* is its summation. The disciplines that arm the architect in book I—the steps (*gradus*) by which he ascends to the *summum templum architecturae,* the highest temple of architecture—are the same as those through which the hut builders of Vitruvius's story advance *gradatim,* step by step, from building to gentle *humanitas,* eventually reaching the "certain *rationes* of symmetries."[242] As every Roman knew, the Capitol was where the highest temple in Rome, the Temple of Jupiter, stood.[243] So too does the hut of Romulus that concludes Vitruvius's catalogue of primitive huts.

Vitruvius's near contemporary, the elder Seneca, also evokes the hut on the Capitol, explicitly connecting it with the great gleaming temple by whose "gables of pure gold" he says the hut is "illuminated." For the Romans, Seneca continues, do not "conceal their humble origins but instead make a display of them and consider nothing great unless it is made obvious that it rose from a small beginning."[244] Greatness, being relative, needs smallness to give it its proper scale; a smallness which greatness in turn illuminates. The huts in Gaul, Pontus, and Aquitania that Vitruvius lists did not stand in the same light.

It is Vulcan, god of the forge—*Ignipotens,* "powerful in fire," as Virgil names him repeatedly and with some insistence—who fashions Aeneas's shield in the eighth book of the *Aeneid.*[245] Virgil's description, overtly concerned with the summation of Roman destiny, locates the Capitoline hut directly in front of the Temple of Jupiter, placing both hut and temple at the top (*in summo*) of the shield itself.[246] The victory at Actium is located at the center, celebrated on the second day of Augustus's triple triumph of 29 B.C., which Virgil also describes, as discussed earlier.[247] In the concluding scene, Augustus reviews the parade of captives: "conquered peoples [who] move in long array, as diverse in fashion of dress and arms as in tongues."[248] The "Nomad race," the "ungirt Africans," the Leleges and Carians and "quivered Gelonians": *gentes omnes subactae,* to recall Vitru-

The Gemma Augustea, sardonyx cameo of ca. 10 A.D. In the upper register Augustus, flanked by the goddess Roma, holds an augur's *lituus* in his right hand; in the lower register, *gentes omnes subactae*. Kunsthistorisches Museum, Vienna (AS IX A 79).

vius's phrase, all assembled within the confines of the shield's circumference which Virgil bounds not with the mythical river Ocean as Homer, Virgil's model, did the shield of Achilles, but with the Euphrates, the Rhine, and the Araxes—rivers at the limits of the Roman world.[249]

If the great golden Temple of Jupiter Capitolinus became all the more magnificent with the rustic little thatched hut as its foil, "summum templum architecturae" is similarly enhanced. In the hut of Romulus on the Capitol, the "body of the great discipline" that Vitruvius elsewhere says he has assembled in *De architectura* acquires the same scale-giving humble origin—and present greatness—as the city of Rome to whose destiny *architectura* is thereby inextricably bound.[250]

Building can only begin after the fire has gathered Vitruvius's scattered multitude into one place. Architecture can only begin when, by an analogous process, wayward and uncertain opinions coalesce into the certain *rationes* of symmetries, the very process that, by Vitruvius's own account, attended his compilation of incomplete drafts and scattered fragments in the "whole body" of *De architectura*.[251] The first hut villages are the germs of future cities. *In summo* stands *architectura*, the knowledge of the architect—the city of the mind.

"The knowledge of the architect is furnished with many disciplines and various kinds of learning," writes Vitruvius at the opening of his first book. "Judiciously exercised, it demonstrates everything the other arts achieve."[252] For Cicero the art of the orator, with its power to assemble the vagrant multitude, had been the *summum* of learning.[253] Huts are the initial *demonstration* of that same power. *Architectura*, the art of the geometrical footprint, is metonymic evidence both of universal order and of the learning possessed by the cultivated man who has knowledge of it. The "proving" of all the other arts, it is a *demonstration* of learning and a passport to ubiquity. To understand the scale, as it were, of this intention, it is worth recalling that in the archaic Greek world it had been the craftsman, not the learned man, who found a home "in every city."[254]

The shipwrecked philosopher in Cicero's version of the Aristippus story does not recognize cultivated fields as human footprints. As an educated man, he only recognizes other educated men, which is to say men of the city—of every city, as Vitruvius tells it. The Stoic view, as reported by Arius Didymus, Augustus's second philosophical advisor, was that the rusticity of wild men who are *agresti* (literally "of the fields") was a sign not only of brutishness but of wickedness as well.[255] The citification of such brutes, both in Cicero and in Vitruvius, is reciprocally concomitant with their education: with *humanitas,* a term Cicero more than once equates with *urbanitas.*[256] That "a city teaches a man" was already recognized by the time of Simonides in late archaic Greece.[257] The great Hellenistic cities—Rhodes, Antioch, Pergamon, and above all Alexandria—were all centers of learning. The heroes of the Hellenistic literature of the third and second centuries B.C.—at once men of action, "philanthropic," educated, and, unlike countrymen, able to appreciate what is beautiful—are all city dwellers.[258] It has been pointed out that in this context even love, a special form of such appreciation, was an urban phenomenon.[259] Before they are citified, the men at the beginning of Vitruvius's primitive hut chapter mate like animals.[260]

Cities are the common thread that runs through the various, notoriously difficult to pin down aspects of *humanitas,* whether the term is taken as a translation of *philanthropia* and *paideia* or as the softness that stands in contrast to barbarian harshness.²⁶¹ Near the end of his second book, Vitruvius writes of a spring near a temple of Venus and Mercury in the Greek city of Halicarnassus, whose water was said to afflict men with lasciviousness (*veneris morbo*), making them effeminate and shameless (*molles et inpudicos*). Not so, says Vitruvius, revealing an awareness of how easily the "softness" of *humanitas* can be confused with degeneracy and carefully underscoring the difference.²⁶² He explains that the reason for the spring's false reputation was that the barbarians who, a little like the brutes at the beginning of book 2, lived in the hills surrounding the city were drawn into civilized society by the clear, pure water, next to which an astute innkeeper had built an inn. "So down they came one by one to meet together in assembly and, returning readily by choice, gave up their rough and savage ways for the delights of Greek customs. That is how the water acquired its reputation. Not from a corrupt and shameless disease, but from the souls of the barbarians being softened by the sweetness of *humanitas*."²⁶³

In *humanitas* lay not only the power to soften the souls of barbarians but also the means, as Strabo pointed out, for dealing with Greeks.²⁶⁴ The essence of its power, whether as *paideia, philanthropia,* or mollification, lay in the ability to gather people into one place and keep them there ("returning readily *by choice* . . . ").²⁶⁵ Cicero understood that power as residing in the speech of the cultivated Roman. Vitruvius's insight—and it was brilliant—was to see its demonstration, its "proof," in *architectura,* the judiciously exercised knowledge of the architect. That, ultimately, is what makes the art of the orator his model, and that is why he makes architecture a liberal art. Not just one of several: all of them together.

And the *artes* specific to Rome, Virgil proclaimed in the very best-known lines of the *Aeneid*, were conquest and world dominion, "to rule peoples with supreme command . . . to spare the vanquished and war down the proud."[266] Of these arts *architectura*, being Herculean, is also proof.

Tacitus's acerbic remarks on Rome's civilizing mission show that architecture indeed came to play (or at least was assumed by Roman conquerors to play) the very role for which Vitruvius's theoretical demonstration, written over a century earlier, appears to be, if not demonstrably prescriptive, at least uncannily clairvoyant. In the mid first century A.D., the Roman *orbis* expanded to include Britain. Agricola, Tacitus's father-in-law, governed there from 77 to 84. During his first winter, writes Tacitus, Agricola undertook "most salutary measures."

By private encouragement he set about persuading men who were scattered, ignorant and easily aroused to warfare, to become peaceable and accustomed to the pleasures offered by leisure. In public he assisted them to build temples, fora *and homes, praising those who were quick to follow his advice and criticizing those who were slow. . . . He went on to give the sons of the nobility a proper education . . . so that the natives who used to reject the Latin tongue, now aspired to rhetoric; even the wearing of our dress came into fashion and little by little, the Britons were seduced into alluring vices: the portico, the baths, the well-appointed dinner table. The simple natives called all this* humanitas, *when it was really a facet of their enslavement.*[267]

In another context, Tacitus reports that when Clodius Thrasea, a dissident of Nero's day, was sentenced to death in 66 A.D., his accusers, who viewed him as fundamentally and irredeemably un-Roman, condemned him as a man who "shunned the fora, the theaters and the temples."[268] *Fora, theatra,* and *templa:* the topics that form the bulk of Vitruvius's three books (3, 4, and 5) on public building; the essentials of the Roman city—the essentials, as Paul Veyne would have it, of *humanitas* and the Roman way of life.[269]

Humanitas begins when people come together in one place. The place is the city. *The* City, Rome, the *Urbs* that was rhetorically identical with the *orbis.* "Romanae spatium est Urbis et orbis idem," wrote Ovid, famously reiterating an alliterative commonplace that had been current since the late republic.[270] "The world and the city of Rome occupy the same space."[271] Varro, ever eager to find evidence in the forms of the words themselves, derives *urbs* from *orbis* (circle) because, he says, the boundary of the city was first plowed in a circle.[272]

The sum of learning is also a circle. *Orbis doctrinae* was the Latin for what the Greeks called the *encyclios paideia.* Vitruvius mixes Greek and Latin terms (as he sometimes does) when he writes in book 1 that the *encyclios disciplina,* the whole of learning, "is put together just like a single body from its members."[273] Similarly, in his sixth preface, he thanks his parents for having educated him in an art that cannot be "proven" (*probata*) without knowledge of letters and the *encyclios disciplina* that includes all branches of learning.[274] An art that cannot be proven without *humanitas,* in other words. Its power, Vitruvius claims in his second preface, lies in the Herculean body not of a Dinocrates, but of his own "knowledge and writings"—*architectura* and *De archi-*

Gilded bronze statue of Hercules, from the Forum Boarium, Rome, first century B.C., detail. Musei Capitolini, Rome (inv. 1265).

tectura; in the scrolls (a whole, complete, and perfect ten of them) which he earlier said he hoped would vouch for "the power of the art and the *rationes* in it, beyond question and with the greatest authority—not only to builders but to all learned men."[275] The demonstration lies in showing how *architectura* can make the circle of learning and the circle of the world coincide in the single geometrical footprint whose center and circumference are Rome. Beyond question and with the greatest authority.

3

THE BODY BEAUTIFUL

Vitruvian Man.

Religio.

Venus, *venustas*.

Corinthia.

Likewise in sacred dwellings, the symmetry of the members ought to correspond completely, in every detail and with perfect fitness, to the entire magnitude of the whole. By the same token, the natural center of the body is the navel, for if a man were placed on his back with his hands and feet outspread and the point of a compass put on his navel, both his fingers and his toes would be touched by the line of the circle going around him. You could also find a squared layout in the body in the same way as you made it produce the circular shape. For if you measured from the bottom of his feet to the top of his head and compared that measurement to his outspread hands, you would find the breadth the same as the height, just as in areas that have been squared with a set square.[1]

VITRUVIAN MAN

If Vitruvius can indeed be said to have written the body of architecture, this is its epitome, its geometrical proof. But the picture these words inevitably bring to mind—the arresting image of a naked male body circumscribed by a circle and a square—was not drawn by Vitruvius. Leonardo da Vinci drew it a millennium and a half later, near the end of the fifteenth century.[2] And Leonardo's figure, like the images that appeared after it in architectural treatises and illustrated editions of Vitruvius, says more about Renaissance humanism than about the geometrical footprints of Roman *humanitas*. The drawings, Leonardo's especially, are familiar to the point of utter banality—more so by far than Vitruvius's text—which oddly encourages an absurd, anachronistic tendency to read the words as a transcription of the images. The words, for this study, are the primary source, and the person who wrote them ca. 25 B.C. was obviously not describing the pictures Leonardo and the others drew. Although Vitruvius's intentions could and did resonate richly well beyond their initial textual formulation, it is well to insist that the context of that formulation was early imperial Rome.

There is no evidence that Vitruvius himself ever made a drawing to accompany this passage. He makes no reference to any appended *schema* or *forma,* as he does elsewhere in the few instances where it is generally agreed that drawings were originally included.[3] That he favored writing over drawing, in any event, and his reasons for doing so were discussed earlier.[4] Most of the ten no longer extant figures he does refer to are of a technical, how-to nature: the schematic for the entasis of columns, for example, or that for Ionic volutes.[5] Vitruvian man can hardly be called a how-to description: the text at the beginning of Vitruvius's third book is not meant to supply directives for putting together a male body. Moreover, Vitruvian man is not *produced* by geometry like the entasis of a column or an Ionic volute. As Vitruvius describes him, the man is geometry's *source.*

The man is *given* passively, *conlocatus,* placed on his back. A compass point, passively again, is *conlocatum* on his navel. His fingers and toes are touched (passively once more: *tangentur*) by the line the compass makes as it goes around him. Who, if anyone, is to hold the compass in this hypothetical situation ("*if* a man were placed on his back . . ."), Vitruvius does not say. The Vitruvian men of Renaissance images are invariably standing.[6] Vitruvius lays his flat on the ground—a man without thickness

Náqʒ nõ põt ædes ulla fine fymmetria atqʒ pportióe rónem habere cõpofi/
tionis,nifi uti ad hoís bene figurati mébroꝛ habuerit exactã rónem. Cor/
pus.n.hoís ita natura cõpofuit, vti os capitis a mento ad fronté fummã &
radices imas capilli effet decimæ partis,Ité manus palma ab articulo ad ex/
tremũ mediũ digitũ tãtũdé,Caput a mento ad fũmũ verticé octauæ,Tãtun/
dem ab ceruicibᵒ imis, Ab fũmo pectore ad imas radices capilloꝛ fextæ, ad
fũmũ uerticé quartæ,Ipfius aũt oris altitudinis tertia pars eft ab imo mento
ad imas nares,nafus ab imis naribus ad finé mediũ fupercilioꝛ tantũdé , ab
ea fine ad imas radices capilli,vbi frons efficit ,item tertiæ partis,Pes uero al
titudinis corporis fextæ, Cubitus quartæ, Pectus item q̃rtæ,Reliqua quoqʒ
membra fuos habent cõmenfus proportionis,quibus etiam antiqui picto/
res & ftatuarii nobiles ufi magnas & infinitas laudes funt affecuti, Similiter
uero facrarũ ædiũ mébra ad uniuerfam totius magnitudinis fũmã ex parti/
bus fingulis cõueniétiffimũ debét hére cõméfuũ refpófum,Ité corpis cétrũ
mediũ naturaliter eft umbilicus,Náqʒ fi hõ col'ocatus fuerit fupinus mani
bus & pedibus panfis circiniqʒ collocatũ cétrũ,in vmbilico eius, circũagen
do rotundationem utrarunqʒ manuum & pedum digiti linea tangentur.

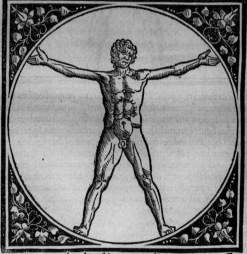

Non minus quemadmodum fchema rotundationis in corpore efficitur,
item quadrata defignatio in eo inuenit̃,Nã fi a pedibus imis ad fummũ ca/

put menfum erit,eaq₃ menfura relata fuerit ad manus pãfas,inuenietur ea
dem latitudo,vti altitudo,quéadmodũ areæ,quæ ad normã fũt quadratæ,

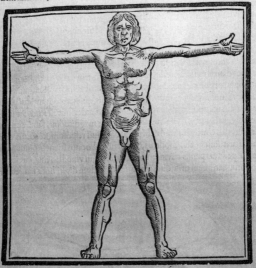

Ergo fi ita natura compofuit corpus hominis ,vti proportionibus mem
bra ad fummam figurationem eius refpondeant,cum caufa conftituiffe ui
dentur antiqui,ut etiã in operũ perfectionibus fingulorũ membrorum ad
vniuerfam figuræ fpetiem habeant commenfus exactionem,Igitur cum in
omnibus operibus ordines traderent,id maxime in ædibus deorum,in qui
bus operum laudes & culpæ æternæ folent permanere,Nec minus mẽfura
rum rationes quæ in omnibus operibus uidentur neceffariæ effe,ex corpo
ris membris collegerunt,vti digitum,palmum,pedem,cubitũm,& eas di
ftribuerunt in perfectum numerum,quem græci τέλειον dicunt,Perfectũ
autem antiqui inftituerunt numerum,qui decem dicitur,namq₃ ex mani
bus denarius digitorum numerus,ex digitis vero palmus:& ab palmo pes
eft inuentus,Sicut autem in vtrifq₃ palmis ex articulis ab natura decem fũt
perfecti,ita etiam Platoni placuit effe eum numerum ea re perfectum,q₃ ex
fingularibus rebus,quæ μόιαλες apud græcos dicuntur,perficitur decuf
fis,quæ fimulac vndecim aut duodecim funt factæ,q₃ fuperauerint,nõ pñt
effe pefectæ,donec ad alterum decuffim peruenerint,Singulares enim res

who is at once a metaphysical proposition, a ritual formula, and a template.[7]

To begin with the metaphysical proposition. The Stoics followed a long tradition in upholding the view that the universe was spherical because the circle and the sphere alone possess, as Cicero put it, "the property of absolute uniformity in all their parts, of having every extremity equidistant from the center. There can be nothing more tightly bound together."[8] As already established, the ultimate criterion for qualifying bodies *as* bodies and, concomitantly, for determining how long they might be expected to last was coherence. That Vitruvian man can be made to produce a circle thus clearly allies him with the highest degree of coherence and indestructibility. No other shape, Cicero continues, could maintain the uniform motion and regular disposition of the heavenly bodies.[9]

Like all the bodies in it, the spherical body of the Stoic universe is constituted by the four elements, whose up-down, side-to-side motion maintains its continuous nature, gives it unity, and guarantees enduring stability.[10] It would seem that the coherence endemic to perfect circularity is, alone, not necessarily self-maintaining. It needs in addition the ordering vertical-horizontal action of the four elements. Cicero notes that when philosophers had observed the perfect regularity of the universe, they rightly inferred "not only the presence of an inhabitant of this celestial and divine abode, but also of a ruler and governor, the architect as it were of this mighty and monumental structure."[11]

The late Augustan poet Manilius devotes over 500 lines of the first book of his *Astronomica* to various aspects of the universe's perfect roundness.[12] This, he says, is the shape of nature, which "continues forever and most resembles that of the gods: nowhere in it is there beginning or end."[13] Like other Stoics, Manilius understood the universe as a great body.[14] For him, as for Cicero, its order is fixed by the movements of the four elements.[15]

Also circular is the horizon that "girdles the sky with a level boundary line"—the *orbis* that embraces the earth to limit (*horizein,* in Greek) human sight.[16] *Quattuor in partes caeli discribitur orbis,* Manilius writes later on, "the circle of the sky is divided into four parts," by the rising and falling of the day, the noonday heat, and the Great Bear, as he puts it: the four cardinal points.[17]

Both the universe and the earth (the latter as limited by the vision of the indwelling human subject) are circular, unlimited insofar as circles have no beginning or end, yet perfectly coherent. But the horizon, as Cicero notes, varies "without limit for different people in different places."[18] Constant within this infinite multiplicity of circles are the cardinal points whereby the earth, whatever the location of its occupant, is divided in four: *quadrata,* in Latin. Four is the number of cosmic order. As demonstrated earlier, with pebbles used instead of numbers and expanded into its constituents, four is also ten.[19] Drawing on Pythagorean sources, John Lydus called ten "the circle and limit of all the numbers," following a tradition which, significantly, made ten circular as well as fourfold.[20]

Like the circle that bounds Vitruvian man, whose ten extended fingers and toes are touched by the line the compass makes as it goes around him, ten is both the coherent circular totality of things and the fourfold "squaring" that makes that totality a constant for all peoples in all places. Read against this background, the circle and square that are Vitruvian man's key geometrical attributes are also the attributes of the perfect ten Vitruvius discusses in the paragraph almost immediately following, where its appearance in precisely this context tends to confirm the tenness implicit in the body of Vitruvian man.[21] Thus, the ten-scroll body of *De architectura* can also be read both as a coherent totality and as the "squaring" limit of that totality which, in its tenness, acquires metaphysical (or at least metaphorical) congruence with the geometry of Vitruvius's outstretched man.

Vitruvian man is a metaphysical proposition. He is also a ritual formula. It was initially in the late republic but especially during the reign of Augustus that the geometry of circle and square became a topic of particular interest in connection with the city of Rome and its origins.[22] Varro, as often, is the earliest source, writing in *De lingua latina* that Rome was first plowed in a circle, and so deriving *urbs* from *orbis*.[23] But Varro also said that Rome was first *quadrata* "so that it might be placed in equilibrium": stable, certainly; immovable by implication; and here, with *quadrata* used as a participle, not "square" but "squared."[24] Solinus, the third-century A.D. grammarian who cites Varro on this, further locates *Roma quadrata* on the Palatine, in front of the Augustan Temple of Apollo, near the hut of Romulus.[25]

Another explanation for Rome's being initially *quadrata* is given in the lacunary text, supposed to be Augustan or earlier, preserved in a papyrus fragment from Oxyrhincus. "In the first district was the place where Rome was founded and where Rome was fortified with squared masonry so that no one could penetrate into *Roma quadrata*. For they considered *Roma quadrata* to be the head of empire."[26]

That the Palatine foundation was called *Roma quadrata* "because in the beginning it was fortified with squared masonry [*in speciem quadratam*]" is also reported by the second-century A.D. lexicographer Festus, who, like Solinus, locates his *Roma quadrata* in front of the Augustan Temple of Apollo on the Palatine where Festus says the "things of good omen usually used for city-founding were kept."[27]

What "things"? A *lituus,* or crooked augural staff, almost certainly. Probably *the* original *lituus* from which, Cicero says, all augural *lituí* are derived—the one with which Romulus had founded the city, that had been stored in the *curia* of the Salii on the Palatine and, miraculously, alone survived when the Gauls set fire to the Palatine in 390 B.C.[28] Also, perhaps, among other "things," the plowshare that was used for plowing the furrow that was a new colonial foundation's first, sacred boundary, set out in keeping with the ritual prescriptions of the *etrusca disciplina,* wherein lay the foundations of much Roman civil theology. Such "things of good omen" are reported to have been enshrined in the precinct of the temple that Augustus dedicated in 28 B.C. to the Greek god Apollo, who had championed his victory over Antony and Cleopatra at Actium three years earlier.[29] The temple, exceptionally, was itself built of solid marble, with "squared stones."[30] Building *a quadrato* makes for tight joints and continuous, solid walls that last forever, Vitruvius says, voicing a clear preference for such walling methods.[31]

On the Palatine, near the Augustan Temple of Apollo, stood the hut of Romulus that was duplicated by the one on the Capitol, as discussed in the previous chapter.[32] The gleaming white Luna marble temple that overlooked the Circus Maximus stood within a complex of buildings that included Augustus's

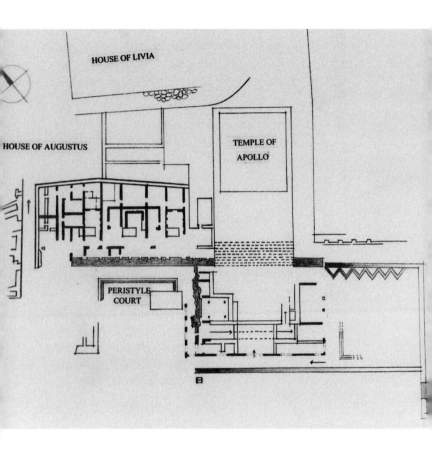

Plan of the House of Augustus and the Temple of Apollo Palatinus,
Rome, dedicated in 28 B.C.

own residence. Suetonius calls the temple an actual *part* of the Augustan *domus,* which means that Augustus kept the "things . . . usually used for city-founding" at home.[33] Ovid called the Palatine *domus* the "single . . . abode of three immortal gods," Apollo, Vesta, and Augustus.[34]

Patrizio Pensabene has recently located these "things" in a pit under the altar of a rectangular *tempietto* on the eastern edge of the square peristyle court directly in front of the lower terrace of Augustus's house, just southwest of the podium of the Temple of Apollo.[35] Not in front of the temple, as Festus and Solinus report, but in front of Augustus's house, from which, if Pensabene is correct, Festus and Solinus obviously did not differentiate the temple itself. As already noted, Augustus's name was attached to the countless Roman colonies that were founded during his reign, and later: Augusta Emerita (now Mérida), Augusta Praetoria (Aosta), Augusta Raurica (Augst), Augusta Taurinorum (Turin), Augusta Treverorum (Trier), to name but a few.[36] Suetonius says that Augustus received his new name from the Roman Senate in January of 27 B.C.,

on the ground that [Augustus] was not merely a new title but a more honorable one [than Romulus], inasmuch as both sacred places and those in which anything is consecrated by augural rites are called augusta *from increase* [ab auctu] *in dignity, or from the movements or feeding of the birds* [ab avium gestu gustuve], *as Ennius also shows when he writes, "After by augury august* [augusto augurio] *illustrious Rome had been founded."*[37]

Squaring is fundamental in augury.[38] Not the drawing of squares, but the division into four with two lines crossing at right angles, as Arpad Szabo pointed out when he argued some years ago that *Roma quadrata* referred therefore not to a "square" Rome but to one that was at least notionally circular and then *quadrata,* "squared"; a circle quartered and ritually set in proper order by its squar*ing*.[39]

An augur who set out to take the auspices needed, first of all, an unobstructed view of the area surrounding him, limited only by the horizon.[40] At Rome, he would normally position himself at the *auguraculum* on the *Arx,* which was the highest, easternmost of the two peaks of the Capitoline hill.[41] Only after "quartering" or "squaring" a given area within this encompassing circle, using, usually, his *lituus,* could the auspices properly be taken and the decision reached as to whether or not the gods favored whatever was at issue. This would be revealed by the "quarter" in which, for instance, birds of good omen appeared, by whether or not they alighted to feed, and by how many of them there were.[42] So, it was said, did Romulus "mark out the quarter for taking observations when he founded the city."[43] Squaring or quartering, originally performed when Rome itself was *quadrata,* was something of an essential prerequisite for determining the approval of the gods, and therefore also the condition for Roman success. Augury, it has been pointed out, provided the major axis of communication between gods and men.[44]

Any ritually inaugurated or oriented place—technically a *templum minus* (town, military camp, public building, or *aedes sacra,* which is to say temple proper)—was square or quadrangular and evidence that such "squaring" had indeed been properly performed. Thus, any official action undertaken in such a location came, at least ideally or in theory, with divine approval.[45] Although repeated auspices were taken as the prelude to, for example, Senate sittings and battles, the squared *place,* of which by Augustan times Rome itself had become the paradigm, remained the first requirement for any correctly initiated political, religious, or military activity—activities that in the Roman world were of a piece. "The highest and most important authority in the commonwealth is that of the augurs," wrote Cicero in his *Laws;* "no act of any magistrate at home or in the field can have any validity without their authority."[46]

Because, as Suetonius explains, "both sacred places and those in which anything is consecrated by augural rites are called *augusta,*" Augustus, upon acquiring his new name, became personally allied with all places so squared, as indeed the "Augusta" attached to the names of so many new imperial foundations attests. Augur since the 40s B.C. and custodian of the (perhaps original) Romulean *lituus* that, among the other "things of good omen," was enshrined within the precinct of his Palatine *domus,* Augustus, by virtue of his name, was not only the paradigm—like Rome—of all squared places. He was the agent of such squaring as well, and as such principal guarantor (*auctor*) of Rome's correct relation with the gods. The countless portraits that showed him holding the augural *lituus* and the many Augustan coins on which it was featured insisted on this.[47]

A military man during the period of his attachment to Julius Caesar, Vitruvius would often have participated in, or at least witnessed, the setting up of military camps. These were invariably square installations and were crossed by two main thoroughfares, as were most Roman towns. At their crossing in a camp, on the spot chosen for its best overall view, was pitched the general's tent, the *praetorium* that also served as an *augurale,* or *auguratorium,* from which, as from the *auguraculum* on the citadel at Rome, the auspices were taken.[48] It was to his augural power that Augustus overtly attributed his own military success.[49] After his victory at Actium, he founded the city of Nikopolis ("city of victory") on the site of his camp. "On the spot where he had had his tent, he laid a foundation of square stones . . . and erected upon it, open to the sky, a shrine of Apollo."[50] Horace more than once qualifies this Augustan Apollo as *augur* in a poetic "theology" whereby the god, while remaining the Greek god of healing on whose oracular authority the Greeks had founded their colonies, became, simultaneously and conspicuously, a god of victory and the new *Roman* founder's personal authority.[51]

It is essential to recall traditional practices when founding a new city, Vitruvius says, referring in book 1 to that branch of the Etruscan science of divination that involved examining the livers of sacrificed animals in order to determine whether or not the proposed site of a town or a camp was a healthy one.[52] Reference to such practices is buttressed by far lengthier explanations of what to look for in terms of Greek science: the theory of the four elements, the necessity of maintaining their proper balance, and so on. Greek science (or "natural theology," as Varro would have called it) was respected and understood by all learned men everywhere. The arcane practices of divination, virtually impossible to explain, were only properly understood by their Roman practitioners.[53] Thus it is not surprising that, when Vitruvius invokes the universal benefits of squaring in the preface to book 9, he should do so with reference to Plato and Pythagoras, and not to augural practice.[54] But in book 1, when he gives instructions for drawing the wind rose that determines the directions of the prevailing winds to be avoided in laying out the streets of new cities and divides his diagram into sixteen parts, the Etruscan discipline of augury is implicit, for the Etruscans divided the sky into sixteen parts for the purposes of divination.[55] In the pebble diagrams of Pythagorean mathematicians, sixteen was a square number.

The *disciplina etrusca* also appears to be assumed in book 9, two-thirds of which is an exegesis of Greek astronomy. Writing about the constellations and the yearly course of the sun, Vitruvius twice refers to the world as having a left and a right.[56] In Greek texts, from Homer on, the east is the world's right and the west its left.[57] Roman writers, on the other hand (all of them Augustan, like Vitruvius), have north as the right and south as the left.[58] "Varro has ascribed the original source of limits to the Etruscan discipline," writes Frontinus in his *De limitibus,* a work on surveying,

because the haruspices divide the world into two parts, from east to west. They called the one that falls in the north the right and the one in the south the left, because the sun and the moon look to the west, even as certain architects have written that shrines, properly, should face west. The haruspices divide the earth with another line from north to south, and have named the part from the midday line forward antica *[front], the other* postica *[back]. From this foundation our ancestors established the principles of land measurement.*[59]

nonte nascatur siue decim   quomodo potest cur
us recte comprehendi · cum ferramento sol occider
'trans montem adhuc luceat · & eisdem ipsis adhuc
is inulteriori parte resplendeat,

Quaerenda est primum quae sit mundi magnitud
quae solis · quae ratio oriundi aut occidendi · quant.
'it mundo terra aduocandum est nobis gnomonic
'ummae ac diuinae aras elementum · explicari enim

Solis cursus ("the course of the sun"), from the ninth-century Codex
Palatinus of Hyginus Gromaticus's *Constitutio limitum*. Bibliotheca
Apostolica Vaticana (Vatic. lat. 1564, fol. 92r).

Why temples are to face west. Folio 44r of the sixth-century A.D. Codex Acerianus of Hyginus Gromaticus's *Constitutio limitum*. Herzog August Bibliothek, Wolfenbüttel (Cod. Guelf. 36.23 Aug. 2, fol. 44r).

The Roman land surveyors squared a flat earth, as did the augurs Frontinus calls haruspices in whose methods, he says, the first principles of surveying are grounded.[60] The world of itself is without left, right, front, or back; to say that north is on the right assumes an indwelling human subject who must be facing west. The augur takes this position, says Frontinus, because that is the way the sun faces, "east" being its *oriens* (rising) and "west" its *occasus* (going down)—the direction of the sun's forward movement and hence, anthropomorphically, the direction in which it "looks." Land surveyors are also to adopt this practice for, by aligning themselves with the forward movement of the sun at midday, they make "the constitution of limits identical throughout the whole world."[61]

Varro, in a *locus classicus* on the augural quartering of *templa,* has his augur face south, not west, with east on the left, west on the right, south in front, and north in back, a stance that cannot, obviously, have been taken in direct imitation of the sun or the moon.[62] Varro elsewhere has temples face south, giving them an orientation in keeping with the south-facing augural stance he stipulates.[63] Although he cites Varro at the opening of his account, Frontinus departs from him when he faces augurs and temples to the west. Likewise the Augustan authors who made north and south right and left respectively.

Correctly oriented shrines are to face west for the same reason that augurs do: to be in tune with the sun's course, in deliberate mimetic recognition of the sun as the origin of all "squaring" and of the "limits" so established. Or so certain architects have written, says Frontinus.[64] So, certainly, wrote Vitruvius.[65]

This is how to determine which regions of the sky the temples of the immortal gods should face. If no reason stands in the way, and given the unrestricted power to do so, both the temple and the statue placed in the cella are to look toward the evening region of the sky, so that a person approaching the altar to make offerings or sacrifices looks to the part of the sky where the sun rises and also at the statue in the temple. In this way, when people undertake vows they will gaze at once upon the temple, on the sun rising in the eastern sky, and on the images themselves that seem to rise in the east along with the sun and gaze back upon those praying and making sacrifices—which obviously demands that all the altars of the gods face east.[66]

Unless it is *quadrata*, the sky has no "regions" or "parts," and neither a temple nor its cult statue has a "region" to look upon—regions which here, as in Frontinus, refer with considerable emphasis directly to the sun's course, whose westward direction the temple, like Frontinus's augur, is to imitate. A supplicant stands at the altar in front of the temple and gazes at once upon the shrine, the cult statue in the cella, and the sun with whose rising at daybreak the statue is confounded. The statue and the sun return his gaze. Not that this could have worked in practical terms. Even if, as Vitruvius implies, the temple doors were open, the sun rising behind a west-facing temple would reduce it to a silhouette and prevent anyone from seeing into the cella, plunged as it would be into total darkness by the contrast.[67]

Implicit in the exchange of gazes that Vitruvius gives as the reason for west-facing temples is the partnership of gods and men, a pact sealed when the pious gaze of the supplicant is acknowledged in the benevolent, joint return gaze of the gods (statue) and nature itself (sun): an exchange that—ideally, if unrealistically—can only take place at daybreak if the temple is made to face west to give the supplicant his proper orientation. The same pact was endorsed every time the auspices were taken in order to determine the gods' approval of a proposed undertaking.

Hellenistic temples, particularly those in Asia Minor, sometimes faced west, notably the great Temple of Artemis at Ephesus which Vitruvius lists, without mentioning its orientation, when he enumerates the works he considers architectural masterpieces in the preface to book 7.[68] But in the Greek world an eastward orientation, whereby the cult statue would indeed be illuminated at sunrise, was far more common.[69] Unlike Roman ones, Greek altars—whichever way the temple faced—were usually not strictly on axis with the temple. This meant that even a west-facing Greek temple did not necessarily have an east-facing altar directly in front of it: an altar whose orientation Vitruvius seems to consider just as important as that of the temple, if not more so, since he repeats the east-facing requirement for altars at the end of book 4, stipulating further that these should always be lower than the statues so as to oblige the supplicant to raise his eyes to the divinity.[70]

Roman temples seem to have had no fixed, or even preponderant, orientation. Only later in Christian architecture did west-facing churches and east-facing altars become canonic. Pierre Gros's survey of Augustan temples at Rome has shown that their orientations fanned out over virtually all the points of the compass, with the exclusion of an 83-degree quarter to the north.[71] Was Vitruvius here, once again, demonstrating the disconnectedness from reality for which his critics have so often taken him to task?

Augustus Caesar's triple triumph of 29 B.C. marked the end of the civil wars and, so the poets agreed, ushered in the dawn of a new era. Virgil says that the celebrations were accompanied by the dedication of "three hundred mighty shrines throughout the city."[72] In fact, although he would indeed go on to dedicate a great many more, on that particular occasion Augustus consecrated only one temple, the Temple of Divus Julius dedicated to Julius Caesar, his deified father and the first Roman since Romulus to be so honored.[73]

The temple was built at the eastern end of the Forum Romanum, which it dominated from a three-and-a-half-meter-high podium that was not accessible from the front, but only indirectly by a circuitous route from the back.[74] The almost square Corinthian temple building, which Vitruvius knew and identifies as having a dense, pycnostyle intercolumniation, appears to have had an exceptionally shallow cella in which stood a colossal statue of Caesar himself.[75] The statue's visibility from below was enhanced by the wide cella door and also, possibly, by an enlarged intercolumniation in front of it.[76] The configuration, stressed in coinage even before the temple was dedicated, made the temple almost secondary to the statue, for which it seems to have served as a showcase.[77]

Uniquely among Augustan foundations at Rome, the Temple of Divus Julius faced west. Looking toward the Capitol, it faced the sunset of the summer solstice in the west-northwest, to be precise.[78] The complementary point on the horizon, directly

Aureus of 36 B.C., African mint, with the head
of a bearded Octavian (not yet "Augustus"),
and on the reverse the Temple of Divus Julius.
British Museum, London (Crawford 1974, 540.1,
BMC Africa 32).

opposite in the east-southeast, was the point at which the sun rose in December, at the winter solstice. Thus the temple, sitting squarely on the line from midwinter sunrise to midsummer sunset, sat squarely on a line that divided both the world and the year into two equal parts. It faced west in mimetic sympathy both with the direction of the sun at the dawning of a new day and with the precise direction of its ascent during the first half of the solar year. At the winter solstice, the sun rose under Capricorn, which was why Capricorn was considered the sun's birth sign. Although Augustus was born in September, under Libra, Capricorn was the sign predominantly disseminated in the literature and imagery of the period as Augustus's own.[79]

Also perforce facing west along with the new temple in the Forum was Caesar's statue in the cella, which appeared *capite velato,* with its head veiled in keeping with the Roman requirement for proper ritual performance, and holding—it seems almost unnecessary to add—the augural *lituus* in its right hand.[80]

From the beginning of the Augustan principate, when the sun was "born" at the winter solstice it rose, in the Forum Romanum, directly behind the Temple of Divus Julius. When, as Vitruvius writes explaining the westward orientation of temples, a person approached the altar of this particular temple at sunrise, he would have faced the dawning of the year.[81] Looking into that rising sun, the supplicant would, simultaneously, have lifted his eyes to Divus Julius and to the temple that Augustus dedicated to mark his own triumph and the return of peace. In this specific location, the supplicant's pact with the gods and nature became, concurrently, a pact with Caesar and the temple builder who was Caesar's legitimate heir. In the practical terms outlined earlier, it seems unlikely that even this especially prominent cult statue could have literally appeared to surge up out of the east along with the sun to return the supplicant's pious gaze. But read through the paradigm of the Temple of Divus Julius, Vitruvius's description makes flawless rhetorical sense. From the early empire on, the right, left, back, and front of the world (its north, south, east, and west) were the left, right, front, and back of the augur in the temple that here, at the world's center, faced west. And so, writes Vitruvius, "if no reason stands in the way," should all temples.[82] The temples that did end up facing west were not, principally, at Rome but elsewhere: those dedicated to the imperial cult which replicated the rhetoric of the Temple of Divus Julius in other parts of the Roman world.[83]

As it turned out, the Temple of Divus Julius was the initial move in Augustus's subsequent "squaring" of the geometrically rather amorphous republican Forum and his concomitant transformation of it into a dynastic monument.[84] The augural squaring function on which, from the time of Romulus, Rome's unique collusion with the gods was claimed to have depended, depended now on Rome's collusion with the imperial dynasty that now controlled it.[85] In the signifying power of the architecture of the Forum Romanum lay its incontestable "proof."[86]

So too in the signifying power of Vitruvian man, whose progeny (Man) may be legion, but who materializes out of nowhere in a text that appears to have no identifiable source other than the historical circumstances of its composition.[87] For if, as argued earlier, the Augustan Vitruvius who is the focus of this study cannot be severed from the emperor for whom he wrote his treatise, no more can the man who produces the circle and the square at the beginning of the first of Vitruvius's two books on temples. But, strictly speaking, the man does not *pro-*

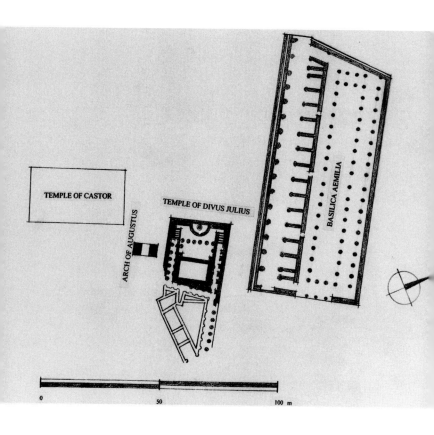

TEMPLE OF CASTOR

ARCH OF AUGUSTUS

TEMPLE OF DIVUS JULIUS

BASILICA AEMILIA

0   50   100 m

Plan of the eastern end of the Forum Romanum in 29 B.C.,
with the west-facing Temple of Divus Julius.

Denarius of Augustus with head of Augustus
and, on the reverse, Capricorn, the sun's birth
sign. Spanish mint, ca. 29 B.C. British Museum,
London (BMC 345).

duce the geometry in question. Flat on his back and passive, he is *made* to produce it. The active agents, as Vitruvius tells it, are the compass and the set square. At once a metaphysical proposition and a ritual formula, Vitruvian man is also and above all the architect's template.

Vitruvius introduced his man with, "in sacred dwellings the symmetry of the members ought to correspond completely, in every detail and with perfect fitness, to the entire magnitude of the whole."[88] The description that follows is presented as a demonstration of the pertinence of this insistent directive, repeated with almost equal force at the opening of the paragraph immediately following. Given the metaphysical subtext reviewed earlier, the "magnitude of the whole" invokes the whole body of the world; a magnitude which, allowing the ritual background just discussed, is also (interchangeably) the Roman *orbis* "limited" by the imperial augur at its center. The compass and the set square—the tools of the architect—make Vitruvius's outstretched man commensurate with these two mutually entailing totalities.

The compass, centered on the man's navel, produces a circular shape by "going around" him. Similarly, a squared layout (*quadrata designatio*) can be found in his body by measuring his arm span and comparing it to his height, with which it will be found to be equal, "just as in areas that have been squared with a set square."[89] As in a squared "area," whose length is equal to its width, the commensurability of the man's height and arm span is evidence of squar*ing:* metaphysical, ritual, and here explicitly architectural. What exactly does Vitruvius mean by an "area"?

A ground plan (*ichnographia*), he writes in book I, is "the properly related use of compass and ruler that renders how figures are marked out on the grounds of areas."[90] Geometry, without which there are no plans, "teaches the use of straight lines and the compass (especially important for readily delineating the way buildings are marked out in areas) as well as the use of set squares, levels, and lines."[91] "An area, strictly speaking, is an empty place," wrote the lexicographer Festus.[92] In cities, corroborates his contemporary Florus in the second century A.D., an area is a place without buildings, in the country, a field.[93] Varro links urban "areas" to those places, also known as *areae*, "where the cut grain-sheaves *arescunt* [dry out] for threshing," which is why, so he says, "clean places [*loca pura*] in the city are called *areae*."[94] Perhaps, Varro continues, altars (*arae*) are so called because they too are clean; or maybe because of the fire (*ardor*) that burns on an altar. An area—the site of some future urban development—is (following Varro) more than just empty. It is *clean*, the way an altar is clean: ritually pure, a "squared" place.

Geometrically, threshing floors—*areae* where grain is separated from chaff—are circular. "Clean" or empty places in cities are squared. Once the walls of a new foundation are laid out, the future city must, writes Vitruvius, be divided up into areas by laying out the streets and lanes.[95] Determining the orientation of these thoroughfares requires the use of a compass and set square to draw the wind rose that is, essentially, a squared circle.[96] Roman foundations were almost invariably rectangular or square. But their division into areas depended upon the initial compass rendering of the horizon's circularity so as to locate the cardinal points. It is into such always operationally *flat* areas that Vitruvius insinuates his paper-thin imperial man whose replication in the empty places of new Roman cities worldwide is the source of the squaredness that makes them well and truly *augus-*

tae. Which—and this is the crux of Vitruvius's argument—only the agency of compass and set square, only architecture, can bring about.

RELIGIO

Crucial though he may be as an index of his author's intentions, Vitruvian man does not introduce *De architectura* as a whole. As it happens, his *locus* is even more significant: at the beginning of book 3, the first of the two books Vitruvius devotes to the "sacred dwellings of the immortal gods."[97] These two books, in turn, are the first of the three that deal with public building.

Public building has three parts, Vitruvius explains in book 1. The first concerns defense, the second *religio,* and the third convenience.[98] To defense belongs the arrangement of city walls, towers, and gates; to convenience, the laying out of harbors, fora, porticos, baths, and theaters. To *religio* belongs the "putting together of the sanctuaries and sacred dwellings of the immortal gods."[99]

Strategically located at the beginning of Vitruvius's account of these sacred dwellings, Vitruvian man also perforce belongs to *religio.* If he had not been meant to, Vitruvius would almost certainly have put him somewhere else. *Religio* is best left untranslated. "Religion," its usual English equivalent, is colored with too many misleading assumptions, among them the assumption that separating church (religion) and state (politics) is both necessary and desirable and that, since real religion is untainted by politics, Roman *religio,* which was political through and through, was not really religion at all. This conventional modern western view, shaped principally by the Christian tradition, has religion dependent upon belief, otherworldly in focus, and directed toward personal salvation.[100] A person's "religion," if he or she has one, tends to be measured in terms of sincerity and spiritual commitment. The incommensurability of such impalpable yardsticks with Roman *religio* points less, perhaps, to a failure of *religio* to qualify as religion than to an inappropriate choice of criteria.

Like many ancient religions, *religio* was entirely worldly.[101] This worldliness was, to an overwhelming degree, what unleashed the indignant Christian polemic of St. Augustine's *City of God* in the fifth century A.D. and fueled his imagining of that other, otherworldly city.[102] St. Augustine's unrelenting condemnation was unabashedly partisan of course. But, abstracted from the censure that invariably accompanies it, his recognition of the older *religio*'s worldliness remains perfectly accurate. What St. Augustine clearly recognized, and found unacceptable, was that worldliness—glory, success, wealth, power—was virtually the entire point of Roman *religio,* aimed as it was at ensuring that no enterprise was initiated without the gods' approval. What a Roman truly believed, or the state of his soul, had very little to do with it. It was what he *did* and, even more importantly, what he was *seen* to do that counted.[103]

Religio was emphatically public. "*Religio* regularly refers to the traditional honours paid to the gods by the state . . . the focus of the term was on public, communal behaviour toward the gods of the state," is the assessment of a recent major study.[104] That which is sacred, writes the second-century A.D. lexicographer Festus, "is anything that has been dedicated and consecrated to the gods by the city according to law and custom: a dwelling [*aedes*], an altar, a statue, a place, or money. The Roman pontiffs do not consider any of these things sacred if they are dedicated to a god on account of private *religio*."[105]

"Private *religio*" belonged to what the Romans called *superstitio*, an unregulated and therefore suspect perversion of proper, public *religio*, for which *superstitio* supplied something of a defining, if shifting, limit.[106] Often excessive and following no officially sanctioned rules, *superstitio* did not contribute (as *religio* did) to the well-being of the city. It was, rather, a threat to its stability. Cicero, tellingly, regularly couples *superstitio* with the practices of old women.[107] Old women were among those least likely to take part in Roman public life, and would therefore have been incapable of *religio* by definition. By the second century A.D., Christianity, condemned among other transgressions by its brazen novelty, came to be considered the nadir of *superstitiones*.[108]

"*Religio* honors the gods, *superstitio* wrongs them," wrote Seneca in the late first century A.D.[109] *Superstitio* undercut the community of interest underwritten by Rome's exclusive pact with the gods that sanctioned what Vitruvius and his contemporaries took as her divinely ordained mission of world conquest.[110] The divine mind placed Rome at the center so that she might rule the world, Vitruvius writes.[111] Vitruvian man, the man at the center who, as the architect's template, is to square that world and make it whole, is diagrammatic shorthand both for *religio* itself and for the imperial mission it underwrites. The temples that are the context and the reason for his appearance in *De architectura* signified *religio* as the measurable index and proof of the inseparability of these two sides of the same Roman coin.[112] Separating the spheres of God and Caesar was a Christian innovation.[113]

"You will continue to atone for the sins of your ancestors undeservedly, Roman," wrote Horace around 25 B.C., "until you have rebuilt the temples and crumbling houses of the gods and the images fouled with black smoke. You rule because you keep yourself lesser than the gods; with them all things begin, to them refers each outcome."[114] Horace's was a common lament. Roman piety was, or had been, in a state of appalling decline.[115] It must have been. The political havoc of the civil wars and the near destruction of Rome itself were clear evidence that the gods had not been properly honored.[116] The clearest evidence of all was the sorry state of Roman temples.[117] That less attention was in fact paid to the building and repair of temples during the late republic than in earlier times is perhaps questionable, but the "crumbling houses of the gods" were not just the impious foreground poets and orators projected against the ostensible piety of bygone days.[118] Decaying temples, real or imagined, in turn and even more importantly supplied essential rhetorical background for the shining new ones built during the Augustan principate.

As long as temples were left to moulder, there would be no renewal of Rome's ruptured pact with the gods, Horace infers, nor any ratification of Roman power. "You rule because you keep yourself lesser than the gods." Of all the many signs through which Romans communicated with their gods and the gods with them, the visibility, permanence, and incontestable *factuality* of temples made them preeminent.[119] In the ode just cited, Horace does not point to sloppily performed rituals as evidence that normal channels of communication with the gods have broken down. He points to decaying temples.

When Augustus celebrates his triple triumph in book 8 of the *Aeneid*, Virgil makes the event concurrent with the consecration of "three hundred mighty shrines throughout the city."[120] Utterly faithful to the economy of *religio*, the poet projects Augustus's "immortal gift" of three hundred temples and the divine approval signaled by the triumph itself as mutually entailing. The exaggerated number of temples at once compels appreciation of the magnitude of the triumph (losers built no temples) and dispels any doubt as to who, thus exceptionally favored by the gods, now controls access to them: the man who, as Horace wrote in another ode, in the guise of Mercury, winged messenger-god of right relations, would repair the ruptured channels of communication between gods and men to which recent civil discord had testified.[121] The custodian of the augural *lituus* on the Palatine and chief holder of the augural function that kept those channels open. The builder of the Temple of Divus Julius in the Forum Romanum—west-facing showcase for Caesar's statue, clad in priestly robes, holding up a *lituus*—that located that augural function in the most public of all Rome's public places, allied it with the order of nature, and made it Augustus's, the temple builder's, legitimate inheritance. The person rendered diagrammatically memorable in Vitruvian man.

Livy, writing at about the same time as Vitruvius, names Augustus as "the restorer and founder of all our temples."[122] All temples, writes Ovid of Augustus a decade or so later, "would have fallen into complete ruins, without the far seeing care of our sacred leader, under whom the shrines feel not the touch of age; and not content with doing favours to humankind he does them to the gods. O holy one, builder and rebuilder of temples, I pray the powers above may take such care of you as you of them."[123]

The hyperbole of the "three hundred mighty shrines" Virgil prophesies in the *Aeneid,* and the fulsomeness of Ovid's address to their "builder and rebuilder" in the *Fasti,* are poetic enhancement of what was indeed an intensive period of temple building of which Augustus, from 33 B.C., assumed sole charge, at least in the city of Rome.[124] Augustus himself lays particular stress on this in the central, architectural paragraphs of his autobiography, listing thirteen new temples, and claiming eighty-two restorations in his sixth consulship of 28 B.C. alone.[125] His monopoly of temple building was complemented by his exclusive right to triumph and his gradual appropriation of all the major Roman priesthoods, culminating with that of *pontifex maximus* to which he was finally elected in 12 B.C.[126]

The person of the first emperor was central to all aspects of Roman religious life. This undisputed fact is less usefully interpreted as a shameful case of a master politician manipulating popular piety to his own ruthless ends than taken on its own terms and in its own Roman context—one where political manipulation of religion was, strictly speaking, a logical impossibility. The notion of manipulation assumes, on the one hand, an unbelieving political manipulator and, on the other, a credulous populace innocently available for manipulation. It assumes two distinct and separate things, politics and religion. But the two were not separate. The one, political hand and the other, religious one were, so to speak, the same ruling hand, and it is not only logically but also anatomically impossible for a hand to manipulate itself. And belief, as pointed out earlier, was not an issue. Those who held political power controlled access to the gods; those who controlled access to the gods held political power. It was ever thus. And rightly so, wrote Cicero.

Among the many things . . . that our ancestors created and established under divine inspiration, nothing is more renowned than their decision to entrust the worship of the gods and the highest interests of the state to the same men—so that the most eminent and illustrious citizens might ensure the maintenance of religion by the proper administration of the state and the maintenance of the state by the prudent interpretation of religion.[127]

In the thirty or so years that elapsed between 57 B.C., when Cicero delivered the speech that opens with the solemn words just cited, and the early Augustan principate when Vitruvius (and Horace and Virgil) were writing, the situation had changed. Not the fundamental principle that made Roman *religio* political and its politics religious: that power depended on knowing how to access the gods and vice versa. This remained the same. What changed with the fall of the republic and the rise of Augustus was the *localization* of that power.

In the republic, both magistracies and priesthoods were loosely distributed, usually for limited periods, among various, changing members of the ruling aristocracy.[128] Different people at different times celebrated triumphs and dedicated the temples that left permanent traces of those celebrations in the urban landscape.[129] The mediating power Mary Beard has called the defining function of priesthood belonged, paradoxically, not to priests but to the 300 men who made up the Roman Senate.[130] Augustus did not abolish the Senate nor does he appear to have substantially altered other traditional republican political structures, claiming with some degree of justification in his autobiography that he *restored* the republic and that after that time (27 B.C., when he was given his symbol-laden new name) he "excelled all in *auctoritas,* although [he] possessed no more power than others who were [his] colleagues in the several magistracies."[131] What did change, and changed irrevocably, was the localization of the mediating power that secured *religio* by channeling access to the gods through Augustus and through no one else.[132] Given the economy of *religio,* the exclusiveness of his mediating position was what empowered Augustus, excelling all in *auctoritas,* to reign as de facto monarch in an ostensibly restored republic.

The signs were evident in the city of Rome right from the beginning: in the Temple of Divus Julius in the Forum Romanum dedicated in 29 B.C., for instance, and in the Temple of Apollo on the Palatine, dedicated a year later. And not just in the new temples. When Augustus restored the monuments of his predecessors, he often had the temples' dedication days (*dies natales*—"birthdays" subsequently celebrated as anniversaries) altered from their original ones to ones that referred to himself. The birthdays of no fewer than six restored temples in and around the Circus Flaminius, a site traditionally linked to the celebration of triumphs, are known to have been changed to September 23, Augustus's own birthday.[133] In the years that followed, every year on the same day in September, the concurrent celebration of these six temples' birth would have simultaneously celebrated the birth of their restorer, fusing their identities and obviating any connection with the temples' original dedicators.

Augustus also devoted considerable attention to the Capitol. In the late thirties B.C., allying himself with Rome's founder from the outset, he first restored the tiny, ancient Temple of Jupiter Feretrius, allegedly the first of all Roman temples, which

Romulus, it was said, dedicated to receive the *spolia opima*, the armor he had stripped from the enemy king he had killed in single combat.[134] Augustus also restored the Temple of Jupiter Capitolinus, Tacitus's "guarantee of empire," greatest and most visible of all the signs of Rome's alliance with the gods.[135] Although this restoration was carried out "at great expense," Augustus did not, as he himself points out, inscribe his name on it.[136] Rome's collective pact with the gods was not Augustus's personal one. He was its mediator; he guaranteed the guarantee. Jupiter himself had given him a sign.

"On his Cantabrian expedition [26–25 B.C.] during a march by night," writes Suetonius, "a flash of lightning grazed his litter and struck the slave dead who was carrying a torch before him."[137] There was more to this than a terrifying close call for a man who was inordinately fearful of lightning.[138] Lightning was among the most portentous—certainly the most visible and dramatically direct—of the many celestial signs on whose proper interpretation good government depended. An entire department of the Etruscan science of divination was devoted to its exegesis, with instructions recorded in the *libri fulgurales* ("lightning books") that served as a guide for the interpreters.[139] Lightning of course came from Jupiter, and was usually a sign of divine favor. If it struck a prince or a king without killing him, he would have illustrious descendants.[140] It promised unhoped-for honors to the powerful.[141] When, at the time of Rome's foundation, Romulus took the auspices to determine whether Jupiter approved of his being king of the new city, the affirmative reply was conveyed in a flash of lightning.[142]

Some years before Augustus's Cantabrian campaign and his near death by lightning, lightning had struck a part of his house on the Palatine, indicating, according to the soothsayers, Apollo's desire for a temple there.[143] Much earlier, before he was born, Augustus's world rule had been foretold, so it was said, when a lightning bolt struck the walls of Velitrae, his birthplace.[144] In Cantabria lightning all but struck the world ruler himself.

The sign received due acknowledgment. A temple was vowed, built (exceptionally, like the Temple of Apollo, another temple born as it were of a thunderbolt and intimately connected with the *princeps*'s own person) of solid marble in *opus quadratum*, and dedicated four years later in 22 B.C.[145] This hexastyle Corinthian Temple of Jupiter Tonans (the Thunderer) was situated on the southeastern brow of the Capitoline at the entrance to the *area Capitolina*.[146] When people climbed to the Capitol, it was the first temple they encountered, before reaching the Temple of Jupiter Capitolinus. It was much frequented, especially by Augustus himself but also by the general populace.[147] Suetonius writes that Jupiter Capitolinus, thus relegated to second place, visited Augustus in a dream to complain about the loss of popularity. To this Augustus is said to have replied that he had placed the Thunderer there to act as Jupiter Capitolinus's doorkeeper and afterward hung bells, like those hung in doorways, on the temple pediment in confirmation.[148]

Augustus's dream is eloquent on the new politico-religious order. But far more eloquent in its day was the primary architectural *fact* that the dream elucidates. The temple itself—solid marble sign of a life spared, divinely favored, and permanently anchored with squared stones at the point of access to the *area Capitolina*—was incontrovertibly *there*, and it altered the temple's signified matter not one iota whether or not Augustus

Aureus (above) and denarius (below) of Augustus, with heads of
Augustus. On the reverses, the Temple of Jupiter Tonans. Spanish mint,
ca. 17 B.C. British Museum, London (BMC 362 and 363).

really dreamed the dream in question or, for that matter, was really almost struck dead in Cantabria. Indeed the temple, in a sense, *made* the story true, for if it were not true, why would the temple have been built? In the experience of any Roman who climbed to the Capitol after 22 B.C., the Temple of Jupiter Tonans was, literally, the gateway to the precinct of Rome's chief deity where it occupied the mediating position between Romans and their "guarantee of empire." This, with the advent of the principate, was Augustus's own mediating position. But in the absence of architectural signifiers such as this and other temples, his gateway position had no spatial reality, no palpable truth. Without temples (paradigmatically, the Temple of Jupiter Tonans), Augustus *had,* in the strictest spatial sense of the term, no mediating position.

The primacy of temples in the climate of the early principate is mirrored in the weight (two of the total of ten books; two of the three on public building) and central importance Vitruvius gives them in *De architectura.*[149] Vitruvius, Horace, and Virgil—and of course the man for whom they all wrote—fully realized the degree to which temples were crucial in the new world order. Unlike Virgil, Horace, and Augustus, however, Vitruvius was an architect. More than to stress their importance and to praise their builder, his task was to set forth the principles governing how temples were to be put together.

It has become clear that Vitruvius argued with rather greater subtlety than modern critics usually credit him with, and that both the manner and the matter of his argument were deeply colored by the time and place of their formulation. The alliance of architecture with *humanitas* in the "Herculean" body of *De architectura* made architecture concurrently the benchmark of civilization, the means of conquest, and the measurable index of Roman world dominion. Similarly, allowing the importance of the cultural matrix and the central role of *religio* in it, it is unlikely that Vitruvius's presentation of the principles governing temple construction should themselves bear no relation to how temples performed in the space and climate of early imperial Rome. It is unlikely, in other words, that Vitruvius, a Roman writing at Rome for Rome's new ruler in ca. 25 B.C., should simply have acted as a not very sophisticated, neutral channel for outdated principles of Greek temple building, which appear in any case to have been neither correctly transmitted nor, as scholars have often pointed out, in fact applied.[150]

One of the most important of these is unquestionably the principle of *symmetria*, a notion apparently so Greek that, as Pliny pointed out, the Romans did not even have a word for it.[151] "The putting together of temples depends on symmetry," Vitruvius begins the first chapter of book 3.

Architects must grasp this principle thoroughly. It is produced from proportion, which is called analogia *in Greek. Proportion is the correspondence of members to one another and to the whole, within each work, measured by means of a fixed part. That is how symmetries are calculated. No temple can be put together coherently without symmetry and proportion; unless it conforms exactly to the principle relating the members of a well-shaped man.*[152]

Symmetry is the condition of coherence. It is the result of calculated relationships or proportions which, through measured correspondence (*commodulatio*) based on a fixed part, bind each member of a work at once to every other member and to its overall configuration.[153] This general principle, initially introduced in book 1, is of particular—apparently critical—importance in the case of temples, judging from Vitruvius's obsession with it in the first chapter of book 3, where he drives the point home in no fewer than four of its nine constitutive paragraphs.[154]

Coherence, as discussed earlier, is the key requirement and defining characteristic of all bodies, from that of the cosmos and the Roman world to that of building materials and the "perfect body" of *De architectura,* but especially of the man's body that is their common ground and universal, if not always entirely explicit, chief referent. The binding agent of coherence, the glue of bodies as it were, is their *ratio,* the principle or calculation that governs how they are put together. The man who is Vitruvius's referent for the symmetry on which he says the putting together of temples depends is particularly coherent—more of a body than most—thanks to the especially concentrated degree of *ratio* present in the "canonic" proportions, which Vitruvius details in the second paragraph of book 3, chapter 1, and which are usually taken to be based on the lost canon of the fifth-century B.C. Greek sculptor Polykleitos.[155] It is by imitating these proportions that painters and sculptors of ancient times won everlasting fame, Vitruvius says.

The canon of Polykleitos had two complementary iterations, a written work and a statue that confirmed the *logos* of the text. According to Galen, the statue was also called Canon.[156] But Vitruvius is not referring to a statue; he is referring to a man— one who is well-shaped (*bene figuratus*). "Likewise," he continues, "in sacred dwellings the symmetry of the members ought to correspond completely, in every detail and with perfect fitness, to the entire magnitude of the whole."[157] There follows the paragraph on Vitruvian man, presented as geometrical proof of the perfect coherence conferred by symmetry. It goes without saying that Vitruvian man and the well-shaped man of canonic proportions are one and the same. Only a man well shaped by symmetry can be made to produce the circle and the square. And only such an ideally circumscribable man can, as the architect's template, carry coherence with him wherever he goes, so to speak: at Rome, sole mediator of divine will, and beyond it, universal model for the order on which the Roman world's own unity depended.

Historically, Vitruvius's insistence on the identity of temple and man, whose defining condition is their mutual dependence on being put together symmetrically, is to be understood in this light. To what degree Vitruvius's lost sources made the precise identification of man and temple that has been defended as an anthropological constant is at least debatable.[158] In fact, Vitruvius does not report that the "ancients" made the identification at all. The way he puts it (twice), it is *because* a man's body is symmetrical that architects should follow ancient precepts about symmetrical building. In other words, Vitruvius introduces the man as the reason for following those precepts, not as part of the inherited tradition itself.[159] Be that as it may, even if Vitruvius was following precedent on the matter, the precedent, like so many Greek precedents, took on specifically Roman meaning through its incorporation into the Roman context.[160]

When Vitruvius completed his treatise, every single new temple in Rome was being built by the same man, who, in the absence of such temples, would have had no *real* position in the public places that were the spatial condition of *religio*, and who, consequently, would have had no *real* position in the new politico-religious order. The countless portraits of this man, Augustus, invariably presented him as particularly "well shaped," which Suetonius reports he was.[161] Birthdays identical with that of their rebuilder were, in many cases, assigned to the temples Augustus restored. When new temples appeared on the reverses of coins, his exquisite profile was, inseparably, their obverse type.[162] "Quis locus est templis augustior?" asks Ovid rhetorically, punning on Augustus's name. "What place is more august [or 'more Augustus'] than temples?"[163] The identity of well-shaped man and temple—the identity of Augustus and temple—was a given in Augustan Rome. Book 3, chapter 1 of *De architectura* is its theoretical ground. No Augustan reader of Vitruvius, certainly not his dedicatee, could have failed to be struck by the inescapable convergence of this given with the theory that showed it to be natural, universal, and necessary.

VENUS, *VENUSTAS*

It is not enough for Vitruvius that the bodies of temples be symmetrical and therefore coherent, like the body of the man who is their model. They must also *appear* to be so. The built analogue for a man's well-shapedness, the *appearance* of symmetry, is what Vitruvius calls eurythmy, "the beautiful appearance [*venusta species*] and fitting aspect of the parts once they have been put together";[164] the utterly convincing, *visible* coherence of form that an architect must strive for by adjusting or "tempering" proportions so as to flatter the eye of the beholder.[165]

The emphasis here is on the relation between the built work and its public. In this, eurythmy again allies Vitruvius's discipline to the art of the orator, whose reasoned speech is the bond of civil society.[166] But *ratio* alone has no power of persuasion. In order to bring people together "into one place," the *ratio* of a speech must be heard, that of a built work—its *symmetria*—seen.[167] "It is in calming or kindling the minds of those who hear that the full power and *ratio* of speaking are disclosed," wrote Cicero.[168] The ultimate proof of an orator's worth, Cicero says elsewhere, is his *effect* on his audience: the degree to which his listeners are instructed or given pleasure or their emotions stirred.[169] Plutarch explicitly names *eurhythmia* as the accord between the speaker and the hearer of a discourse, reminding one of the gold and amber chains that, in Lucian's story, tie the tongue of the Gallic Hercules to the ears of his willing followers.[170] Recognition of "well-shapedness" (literally, *eurhythmia* in Greek) is what conveys the *ratio* of a speech, making it persuasive and binding speaker to listener in the public domain—where built works, through analogous means, are to carry the same force of conviction.[171]

Eurythmy, *venusta species*, is the ultimate aim of symmetry in building. It is a quality, not a quantity.[172] In the end immeasurable, it outweighs quantitative, calculated symmetries as a guiding principle. As explained earlier, qualities were the condition for the appearance of bodies in the world.[173] Without qualitative visibility in *venustas* (beauty), symmetries had no earthly use in the public sphere where built works—the temples that belonged to *religio*, above all—operated.

When executing the works of architecture, writes Vitruvius in the most frequently cited phrase of his entire treatise, you must take three things into account: *firmitas* (strength), *utilitas* (use), and *venustas*.[174] "When *venustas* is taken into account, the appearance of a work is select and pleasing, and its members correspond with rightly calculated symmetries."[175] *Venustas*, visible coherence achieved through the judicious choice of correct proportions, is the special province of the architect. Magnificence in a work credits the builder; fine workmanship, the master craftsman, writes Vitruvius near the end of book 6. "But when, through its proportions and symmetries, beauty gives a work authority, the glory is the architect's."[176] Laymen can appreciate beauty once it is already present. Only the architect knows in advance how to bring it about.[177]

Pulchritudo was another word for beauty in Latin, but Vitruvius never uses it, nor the related adjective *pulcher* (beautiful).[178] J. J. Pollitt has argued that in the aesthetic vocabulary of classical antiquity the Latin *pulchritudo* was equivalent to the Greek *to kallos* (invisible, ideal Platonic Beauty), whereas *venustas*, "more mundane in its associations . . . [an] immediate sort of beauty which is known through simple sense perception," translated the Greek *charis* (grace, charm), as Pliny the Elder attests.[179] For Vitruvius, the proof of *venustas* is the pleasure (*voluptas*) it gives, which indeed anchors architectural beauty in the world of the senses.[180] Such beauty is not necessarily "mundane" or trivial but, operating in the world like rhetoric and *religio*, it *is* clearly worldly—a beauty whose worldliness the total exclusion of otherworldly *pulchritudo* from the vocabulary of *De architectura* appears to corroborate. But there is more to *venustas* than an aesthetic category and a translation of *charis*.

To begin with, one might recall with Cicero that *venustas* comes from *Venus*.[181] According to Varro, Venus (love)—like proportion and symmetry, as Vitruvius repeatedly defines them—is a force that binds.[182] Varro presents the birth of Venus herself from the sea foam in a fusion of fire and water as the mythical paradigm for the binding force at the origin of all life.[183] This force is the origin of coherence, universal concord, and community, wrote Plutarch, citing Greek sources, later in the second century A.D.;[184] of all appearing in the world, according to Lucretius, whose *De rerum natura* Vitruvius knew, and who invokes Venus as "the pleasure [*voluptas*] of gods and men" at the opening of that great poem of cosmic order.

Mother of Aeneas and his race [Aeneadum genetrix] . . . *nurturing Venus, who beneath the smooth-moving heavenly signs fill with yourself the sea full-laden with ships, the earth that bears the crops, since through you every kind of living thing is conceived and rising up looks on the light of the sun . . . since . . . you alone govern the nature of things, since without you nothing comes forth into the shining borders of light, nothing joyous or lovely is made, you I crave as partner in writing [these] verses.*[185]

Despite the absence of any etymological link between the aesthetic quality of *charis* and Aphrodite, the seductive power of *charis*—grace, charm—belonged as much to the Greek goddess of love as *venustas* did to the Roman Venus. The earliest versions of the myth of the birth of Venus that Varro evokes are of course Greek.[186] Lucretius's cosmic Venus can also be traced to Greek sources.[187]

But the Venus Lucretius invokes at the opening of his poem is *Aeneadum genetrix,* mother of Aeneas's race, ancestress of all Romans. She, Aeneas's mother, had protected her son on his treacherous sea voyage to Italy, where he came from Troy after its fall to father a new race of heroes. That this was so had been common knowledge since the third century B.C. in the foundation legend that Virgil later made epic and Augustan in the *Aeneid*.[188] The Romans called the goddess they claimed as their *genetrix* Venus, however, not Aphrodite. And this Venus, arguably, named the very essence of the correct relations with the gods that, if properly maintained, guaranteed Roman might.[189] It is in this that Venus might rightly be understood as the "mother" and origin of Rome, for the foundation legend naming her as the ancestress and divine source of Roman power became current in the century that saw the beginning of Rome's conquest of the Mediterranean world.[190]

Venus is also a common noun, *venus,* which means "charm": a thing, fact, or function that became personal in Venus between the sixth and fifth centuries B.C.[191] Robert Schilling has argued that, in the religious sphere, the Latin *venus* is less charm as an aesthetic quality than charm in the sense of a magic formula or spell. The verb *venerari* ("venerate") is to exercise that charm: to "exercise *venus.*" One did not "exercise *venus*" indiscriminately. Only gods were to be so venerated.[192] *In primis venerare deos,* "above all venerate the gods," Virgil writes in his *Georgics.*[193] Not worship the gods in any vague spiritual sense, but perform the correct rites, for indeed Virgil continues: "and pay great Ceres her yearly rites." Ceres's rites were not the same as those of Juno, say, or Minerva. In order to venerate or exercise *venus* on a god or a goddess, one had first of all to select or pick out the right ritual, a procedure which Cicero, adducing etymological evidence, gives as a defining condition of true *religio.* "Those . . . who carefully reviewed and so to speak retraced all the lore of ritual were called *religiosi,* from *relegere* (to retrace or re-read), like *elegans* from *eligere* (to select), *diligens* from *diligere* (to care for), *intellegens* from *intellegere* (to understand); for all these words contain the same sense of 'picking out' (*legere*) that is present in 'religious.'"[194]

Proper selection is also a condition of *venustas* in architecture, where correct choice of the right proportional relationships yields the reward of pleasurable effect. "When *venustas* is taken into account, the appearance of a work is select [*elegans*] and pleasing [*grata*], and its members correspond with rightly calculated symmetries," Vitruvius writes.[195]

If, in the religious sphere, a supplicant made the correct selection and properly performed the prescribed rite, he was rewarded with *venia,* another cognate of *venus,* which meant divine grace or favor.[196] Seen in this light, Venus becomes less a personalized thing than a personalized *relationship* forged at the intersection of *venerari,* "to venerate," and the *venia* obtained thereby—the interchange that, precisely, defined the mediating position that underwrote Rome's special covenant with the gods and, reciprocally, her power.[197]

Thus it is not surprising that, in the dying years of the republic, the individual Romans who craved a monopoly of Rome's power all sought to harness Venus to personal ambition. The dictator Sulla claimed Venus *felix* (bringer of success or good fortune) as his special patroness in the early part of the first century B.C.[198] Pompey later made the same claim for Venus *victrix* (bringer of victory), and crowned the vast theater complex he built as a victory monument in the Campus Martius with a temple dedicated to her in 55 B.C.[199] Both Sulla and Pompey linked the patronage of Venus to their possession of the augural function that, as already noted, was the major axis of communication between gods and men.²⁰⁰ So, to an even greater degree, did Julius Caesar.²⁰¹

The contest over who would monopolize Venus was endemic in the power struggles of the mid first century B.C. To Pompey's Venus *victrix,* his rival Julius Caesar replied with his champion, Venus *genetrix,* the mother of all Romans whom he claimed as his personal ancestress and genealogical protectress and who became perforce the ancestress of Augustus, his adopted son. This direct line of descent, which underpins the whole of Virgil's *Aeneid,* distilled as it were in the blood of the Julians the essence of the power that Venus (or *venus*) gave to Romans in general, making Caesar and Augustus, in whom it was thus concentrated, naturally more Roman, religious, and powerful than others. And so they were. Architectural proof lay in the Temple of Venus Genetrix which dominated the splendid new forum Caesar built adjacent to the old Forum Romanum in the early 40s B.C. to outbid Pompey's Temple of Venus Victrix on the other side of the city.²⁰²

Further, if somewhat more equivocal, evidence of Caesar's intimate connection to Venus lay in his own person: in his good looks, especially the "bloom of youth" he said he had received from his divine ancestress, whose image was carved on his seal ring.²⁰³ This "bloom" or "flower" of youth (*flos aetatis* in Latin) could also be virginity, a "bloom" that Cicero, in malicious reference to Caesar's claim, said Caesar lost early in the company of King Nicomedes of Bithynia.²⁰⁴ No literary record survives to affirm whether a similar claim was ever made for Augustus, either by himself or by others. But that Augustus, or at least his public persona, was meant to be understood as possessing such a "bloom" is inherent in the relentlessly youthful beauty that radiates from the countless portraits made of him, even those made when he was an old man.

Beauty is important in the best kind of ruler according to Philodemus, who wrote his *The Good King According to Homer* in about 45 B.C. and dedicated it Lucius Calpurnius Piso, Caesar's father-in-law.[205] Beauty in Homeric kings inspired awe and allied them with the gods.[206] At the dawn of civilization, writes Lucretius, Philodemus's near contemporary, when kings first founded cities, beauty had great power; strength had esteem.[207] In a kingship treatise of uncertain date, one Diotogenes advises that a king "wrap himself about with such decorum and pomp in his appearance . . . that he will put in order those who look upon him. . . . For to look upon the good king ought to affect the souls of those who see him no less than a flute or harmony."[208]

In 29 B.C. Augustus dedicated the Temple of Divus Julius in the Forum Romanum, where its position, orientation, and cult statue of Divus Julius as augur made the world-ordering role of Rome and its new ruler measurable, spatial, and real. The statue of Divus Julius was not the only artifact Augustus placed in the west-facing temple cella, however. In it he also placed a painting, dedicated to the new god, his father: Venus Anadyomene, Venus emerging from the sea, wringing the water from her hair, seized at the mythical moment Varro evokes as the paradigm for the binding force he names "Venus."[209]

The painting had been painted in the late fourth century B.C. by Apelles, Alexander the Great's favorite portraitist, whom Pliny judged to have surpassed all the painters who came before or after.[210] Apelles' works were known for their ineffable quality of *charis,* for which Pliny, as already noted, gives *venustas* as a

Entablature fragment from the Temple of Venus Genetrix in the Forum
Julium, Rome, dedicated 46 B.C.

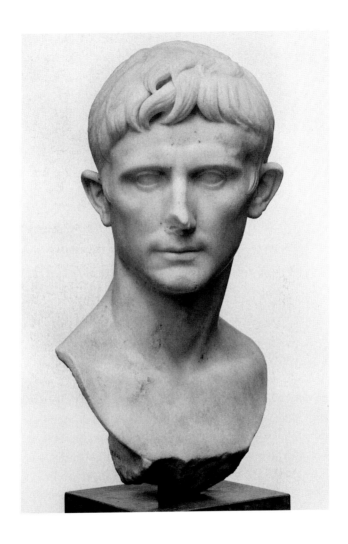

Marble bust of Augustus from Fayum, sculpted between 4 and 14 A.D. when Augustus was in his late sixties or early seventies. Ny Carlsberg Glyptotek, Copenhagen (cat. 610, I.N. 1443).

Latin equivalent. His Venus Anadyomene, the most charismatic of his works, had hung in the Asclepion at Cos, famous for its medical school, until its transfer to Rome, for which Augustus compensated the Coans with a remission of 100 talents in tribute.[211]

This Venus was by all accounts—and the accounts are many—one of the most beautiful paintings in the world.[212] The earliest surviving description dates from the third century B.C. and sets the tone for the rest.

Apelles having seen Cypris [Aphrodite], *the giver of marriage blessing, just escaped from her mother's bosom and still wet with bubbling foam, figured her in most delightful loveliness, not painted but alive. With beautiful grace she wrings out her hair with her fingertips, beautifully calm love flashes from her eyes, and her breasts, the heralds of her prime, are firm as quinces.*[213]

Obviously a work of considerable seductive power, this Venus: the "bloom of youth" personified, meltingly lovely in her newborn grace. If Apelles had never painted her, Ovid reflects, she would still be lying at the bottom of the sea, invisible, unknown, and undesired.[214] And if Augustus had not brought her to Rome, she would have remained in the Asclepion at Cos with no visible connection to the Roman dynasts who were now the mediators of *religio.*

That her relocation was meant to reaffirm Caesar's divine descent is obvious.[215] But why this particular painting? The cult statue Caesar commissioned for the apse in the cella of the Temple of Venus Genetrix made the same point, but was modestly draped in a long belted tunic and mantle. It had a Cupid (Venus's child, Eros or Amor) on its shoulder and set the matronly precedent for future official Roman representations.[216] There was nothing matronly about the Anadyomene.

As already noted, the west-facing Temple of Divus Julius sat squarely on the line that divided the world and the solar year into two equal parts, in mimetic sympathy with the yearly course of the sun. Its orientation made the dawn of the new era heralded by Augustus's triple triumph of 29 B.C. a cosmic dawn. If, following Vitruvius's exegesis of west-facing temples, Caesar's statue holding its augural *lituus* is to be imagined as surging up out of the east along with the rising sun, its appearing collapses in the mind with the emergence in the temple cella of the incomparably beautiful newborn Venus rising from the sea at the world's daybreak.

In 44 B.C., not long after Caesar's assassination, during the games Augustus held in honor of Venus Genetrix, a comet, the *sidus iulium*, had appeared to announce Caesar's apotheosis.[217] This star was figured on the head of his posthumous portraits, on coins, and also in the pediment of the new temple building.[218] Validated by the painting, the star's significance expanded to include the planet Venus: "Lucifer," as she was called when she appeared in the morning, "bringer of light," the star that announces the dawn.[219] In the Temple of Divus Julius, the binding force of augury that ordered the world—the *ratio* of the "squaring" function that guaranteed Rome's pact with the gods—became, thanks to Apelles' Venus, plainly evident in the irresistible beauty of the cosmic, Roman, and, here above all, Julian *genetrix*.

In architecture, especially temples, carefully selected proportions and symmetries bind each part to every other and to the whole, just as they do in the bodies of well-shaped men.[220] Proportions and symmetries are the indispensable condition of coherence, as coherence is of bodies. *Venustas,* through the pleasure it gives, is evidence of this coherence, and great care must be taken to ensure its visibility, even to the point of bending canonical rules, for beauty, the *appearance* of proper proportional relationships (whether or not these are in fact measurably present), is paramount.[221]

Does Vitruvius mean to say that the architect's ultimate aim is to give pleasure? That would make him an Epicurean, and he is far too earnest, too politically engaged, too Stoic in his way of thinking for that. But what earthly use *is* beauty, then, beyond pleasure? How is the role of *venustas* to be understood in this early Augustan context?

For the Stoics, beauty's part in the order of things was to inspire love. By love they meant good will, friendship, and fellow feeling more than erotic love, although they did allow that erotic love might be the initial impetus for friendship. Love, thus understood, was the basis for civic concord and the root cause of cities.[222] So, for Romans, was augury and the correct performance of ritual that seems to have been metonymic in the Roman Venus. So was architecture. Against this background, the architectural beauty Vitruvius names *venustas* becomes crucially determinant.

The Stoic theory never refers to rarefied ideal Beauty but always, explicitly, to *apparent* beauty, and, as often as not, to a visible or "appearing" beauty of a specific kind: that of adolescents, of beautiful young men, of "young men in bloom." Arius Didymus, the Alexandrian Stoic who was Augustus's philosophical intimate for twenty years after the conquest of Egypt, transmits the following definition. "Love is an attempt to make friends on account of visible beauty appearing [*dia kallos emphainomenon*] with young men in bloom [*neôn hôraiôn*]."[223] Later in the same work Arius writes, "it is clear that beauty when it appears [*to kallos, emphanes*] has by itself some attraction, and everybody feels naturally drawn towards beautiful people, even without any consideration of usefulness, and so beauty is seen to produce good will."[224]

Similarly, in Diogenes Laertius's doxography, we have, "Their [the Stoics'] definition of love is an effort toward friendliness due to visible beauty appearing [*dia kallos emphainomenon*], its sole end being friendship, not bodily enjoyment . . . and beauty they describe as the bloom or flower of virtue [*hôran anthos aretês*]."[225] Cicero, in a Latin version, says that "the Stoics . . . define love as the endeavor to form a friendship inspired by the appearance of beauty [*ex pulchritudinis specie*]," rendering the Greek *kallos* as *pulchritudo,* and corroborating what J. J. Pollitt has said about the equivalence of the two terms.[226]

For Vitruvius eurythmy, the appearance of beauty in architecture, is not *pulchritudinis species* but *venustatis species.*[227] It occurs when the temples and other buildings without which there are no cities are put together in the same way as nature puts together the bodies of well-shaped men.[228] At the time Vitruvius wrote, and increasingly in the years that followed, the general principle had, or was made to have, a concrete exemplar in the beauty of Augustus Caesar, direct descendant of Venus, whose appearance, Suetonius writes in confirmation of the patent contention of innumerable images, was superlatively beautiful—

venustissima—at all periods of his life, with finely proportioned, symmetrical limbs.[229]

He was also short, sickly, weak, had bad teeth, limped, and, of course, grew old.[230] This does not appear in the portraits.[231] Because, as Vitruvius writes about architecture, the eye is greedy for beauties (*venustates*), the pleasure it seeks must be flattered with suitable curative measures so that a building does not present viewers with an ungainly and graceless appearance (*vastus et invenustus aspectus*).[232] In architecture as in Augustan portraiture the *appearance* of beauty was paramount. It was a sign of virtue and without it, the Stoics claimed, there was no love or friendship—nor any city.

The person who says that love is "an attempt to make friends" simultaneously implies "with young men in bloom," even if he does not say so overtly, for no one loves old men and those who do not have the bloom of the prime of love.[233]

CORINTHIA

Youth became permanent and perennially new in the representations of Augustus, who "bloomed" not only in sculpture and on coins, but also—less personally, at a larger scale (more symbolically, more powerfully)—in the beauty of Roman architecture. Particularly so in the phenomenon scholars have called "corinthianization," which includes not only the increasing and eventually exclusive use of the Corinthian columnar order at Rome and throughout most of the Roman empire, but also the invasion of flat surfaces by flourishing scrolls of acanthus, the vegetation that is the hallmark of the Corinthian capital.[234] The highest concentration of "corinthianized" buildings appears among those linked, specifically, to the power and *religio* of the imperial dynasty. Of these, the Ara Pacis Augustae, the altar of Augustan peace in the Campus Martius, with the lush acanthus frieze of its encompassing screen wall is among the best known.[235]

Vitruvius accounts for the origin of the Corinthian capital as follows.

This, so it is recorded, is how the capital was first invented. A virgin citizen of Corinth was just ripe for marriage when she was overcome by disease and died. After she was buried, her nurse filled a basket with things [pocula: literally, small cups or vessels] that had delighted the virgin when she was alive, brought it to the tomb, and placed it on top. Then, so that the things in the basket would last longer in the open air, she covered it with a tile. As it happened, the basket was placed on the root of an acanthus plant. After a time, in the spring, because of the weight pressing down on the middle of it, the root put forth leaves and small stalks which grew up around the sides of the basket. Because of the weight of the tile, the ends of the stalks were forced by necessity to curl back into volutes at the corners.

Then Callimachus, called Catatexitechnos by the Athenians because of the refinement and skill of his marble carving, passed by the tomb and noticed the basket and how tender the leaves growing

Frieze fragments from the Temple of Divus Julius, Rome, dedicated in 29 B.C.

up around it were. Delighted by the freshness of this new form, he used it as a model to make columns for the Corinthians, established their symmetries, and assigned the rules for completing works of the Corinthian order.[236]

Although he presents his story as matter of record ("sic memoratur")—from Greek sources, it is usually assumed—Vitruvius's story is in fact unique in surviving literature. He is also the earliest known writer to give the name "Corinthian" to the foliate acanthus capital that in time became ubiquitous as an emblem of Roman power.[237]

Scholarly attempts to account for Vitruvius's story have been complicated by the difficulty of reconciling its details with the historical and archaeological evidence.[238] To begin with, it is fairly certain that the *genus* Vitruvius calls Corinthian did not, as he claims, originate at Corinth. Even the acanthus that figures so crucially in the narrative is unlikely to have grown in the area.[239] The plant's funerary symbolism has been demonstrated by a number of scholars, but the evidence for this comes from Attica (mainly Athens) and southern Italy, not Corinth, which is not surprising if acanthus did not grow there.[240] According to recent scholarship, the earliest prototypes of the "Corinthian" column capital were developed at Athens, not Corinth, in the second half of the fifth century B.C., close to the time of the Athenian sculptor Callimachus, named by Vitruvius as its inventor.[241]

Subsequent developments are in no known instance linked to Corinth either.[242] The prototype long thought to be originary is the single Corinthian column in the cella of the late fifth- or early fourth-century B.C. Temple of Apollo Epikourios at

Bassae, in the mountains of Arcadia.[243] A later example, somewhat more familiar in appearance, is the interior order of the third-century B.C. tholos in the sanctuary of Asclepius at Epidaurus in the Argolid.[244] The so-called "normal" Corinthian capital that first appeared on the propylon built by Ptolemy II Philadelphus on the Aegean island of Samothrace in the early third century B.C. was also its first use on the exterior of a building.[245] Closer to Vitruvius's own time are the Corinthian columns of the dipteral peristyle of Antiochus IV Epiphanes' colossal, second-century B.C. Temple of Zeus Olympios at Athens, designed by the Roman architect Cossutius, according to Vitruvius, who singles the temple out as the acme of architectural excellence.[246]

In sum, there is little, if anything, in known evidence from the Greek past to connect the appearance of the new kind of column capital with the city Vitruvius names as its place of origin, either symbolically, historically, or archaeologically. What of the Roman present?

Corinth, a seaport on the isthmus that separates Attica from the Peloponnese, was one of the largest, wealthiest, and most notoriously extravagant of Greek cities.[247] Its patroness was Aphrodite Ourania *poliouchos,* heavenly "defender of the city," to whom young Corinthian women were dedicated as sacred prostitutes.[248] In the fifth century B.C., Aristophanes tellingly used the verb *korinthiazomai,* "to corinthiate," as an alternative for "fornicate."[249] Over a thousand prostitutes had been attached to Aphrodite's temple on Acrocorinth, a great attraction to visiting ship captains, apparently, and another source of the city's wealth.[250]

Wallowing in the cognate vices of lust and luxury Romans

professed to abhor, Greek Corinth must have typified what the Romans had in mind when they claimed that the Greeks had invented civilization, but had lost it; an exemplar of the kind of decadence for which Roman conquest in the Greek world—so went the argument in late republican Rome—was to be justified as a moral corrective.[251]

In 146 B.C. Corinth was destroyed by the Roman general Lucius Mummius who razed the city, sold the Corinthian women and children into slavery, and killed its entire male population.[252] His war booty—works of art mainly—was fabulous, and paid for the temple he dedicated to Hercules Victor as his victory monument.[253] A century later, profit continued to be gained from the city's destruction through the sale to eager Roman buyers of grave goods known as *nekrocorinthia,* chiefly pottery and bronze ware, looted from Corinthian tombs.[254]

For over a hundred years the site of Corinth lay waste, an *ager publicus* (public land) of Rome, under Roman administrative tutelage.[255] In 44 B.C., shortly before his assassination, Julius Caesar refounded the city as a Roman colony, renaming it Colonia Laus Julia Corinthiensis (the Corinthian glory of Julius).[256] Duly squared and divided into "areas," the new city subsequently rebuilt under Augustus with a typical Roman monumental center became a model of *romanitas* in the Greek east.[257] Pierre Gros has noted a close correspondence between the basilica at the eastern end of the forum at Corinth and the description of the basilica Vitruvius claims he built at Fano in northern Italy with an *aedes augusti* (shrine of Augustus) in it.[258] The new west-facing Julian basilica in Corinth also appears to have included just such an *aedes,* which must have contained the famous statuary group of Augustus flanked by his grandsons

Gaius and Lucius Caesar that was found there.[259] North of the forum, the east-facing archaic Greek Temple of Apollo was rededicated to the cult of the Julian dynasty and reoriented to the west in a rather forcible instantiation of Vitruvius's prescription on the matter.[260]

Vitruvius's early attachment to Caesar makes his knowledge of, and almost certain interest in, the rebirth of Aphrodite's city as Caesar's "Corinthian glory" a given. Allowing this, and against the background of Rome's relations with Corinth, the etiology of the order Vitruvius names Corinthian fairly begs for an allegorical reading. The Corinthian virgin, *virgo civis corinthia,* is Corinth itself.[261] The disease (*morbus,* also "vice") that overcomes her figures the city's decadence and is the reason for her death, which is Corinth's destruction. Being "just ripe for marriage" put her at the peak of the sexual attraction that would have made her a choice victim of the rape that invariably accompanied a city's *direptio,* the procedure whereby a city was literally "torn to pieces" by Roman soldiers when they sacked it.[262] Rome is the dead city's nurse for a hundred years until her rebirth under Caesar, whose "bloom" (his "Corinthian glory") flourishes in the acanthus plant and testifies to his descent from the tutelary goddess of the city he brings back to life. Even the *pocula,* cups or vessels, source of the virgin's former delight, which the nurse piles into the basket she puts on the girl's tomb resonate singularly with the pottery and bronze *nekrocorinthia* dug out of Corinthian graves for sale at Rome, for Corinth's "delight" in its lifetime had indeed been the pottery and bronze for which it had been famous. It is, admittedly, almost too neat to be true.

But then so is the exact correspondence between the story of the Corinthian virgin and the late form of the Corinthian cap-

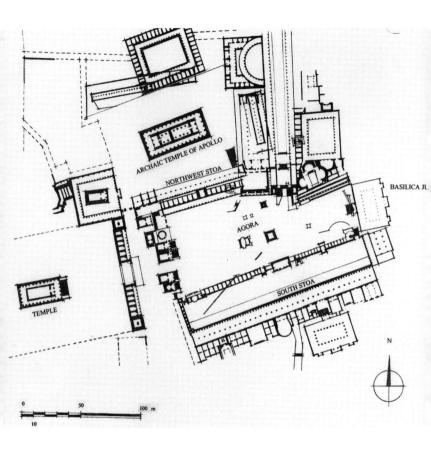

The monumental center of Roman Corinth.

ital that Vitruvius's etiology matches with all too uncanny perfection. The etiology has clearly been fashioned so as to account for every detail of the capital's current, approved form—in, for example, the Temple of Zeus Olympios that Vitruvius admires so much and that Suetonius says was to have been completed as a temple dedicated to Augustus's *genius*.[263] By the same token, and in parallel, the recent history of Corinth supplies Vitruvius with an identifiable historical form, a place and Roman meaning to which to assimilate, and by which to retrospectively explain, the resonant symbolism of death and rebirth already inherent in the arguably as yet unnamed acanthus leaf capital. Once named and located, the Corinthian order was no longer just about Corinth, of course, but about Rome and her civilizing mission. The specific architectural form into which Vitruvius encapsulates the city's rebirth could then go on to herald the rebirth of the entire world. Generated by natural forces, the Corinthian order was the order of future renewal, not, like the venerable Doric and Ionic, an order of the past.

Vitruvius is brief on the proportions of the Corinthian order, allowing it only two paragraphs which deal exclusively with the design of the capital.[264] His accounts of the Doric and Ionic are much more detailed and extensive and cover base, shaft, capital, and entablature.[265] There were probably more written sources on these two orders, both of which were of greater antiquity and, at the time, more widely used than the Corinthian, which may partially account for the imbalance.[266] But, if one reads Vitruvius carefully, this ostensible imbalance does not really diminish the Corinthian order's relative importance or contradict the implications of the powerful, prophetic etiology he endows it with.

Restored southeast corner of the Maison Carrée at Nîmes, a dynastic temple dedicated between 1 and 10 A.D. to the cult of Augustus's grandsons, Gaius and Lucius Caesar. After R. Amy.

Corinthian columns have pride of place in the opening words of book 4, where Vitruvius writes, "except for their capitals, Corinthian columns have all the same symmetries as Ionic ones."[267] This means that everything he said about Ionic columns in book 3 applies to Corinthian ones, leaving the reader beginning book 4 with the distinct impression that Vitruvius has been leading up to the Corinthian order all along. It is because of the loftiness of their capitals, higher proportionally than those of the Ionic order, that Corinthian columns present a more slender appearance.[268]

The base and shaft of the Corinthian column have Ionic proportions and are therefore strictly speaking Ionic. Vitruvius says that the Corinthian column does not have an entablature proper to it either, but can be placed under either a Doric or an Ionic one.[269] He is mistaken here, for the Corinthian order did, in fact, end up having its own distinctive entablature, but he does not anticipate this, or does not want to.[270] What he seems to be saying is that Corinthian columns, whose only distinctive feature is their capitals, are infinitely adaptable—they can fit in anywhere.[271] So it was, he concludes, that "when the [Corinthian] capital had been put between them in built works, the two orders [Doric and Ionic] engendered a third one."[272]

As Vitruvius tells it, the Doric order is male, the Ionic female.[273] The Corinthian capital that he says was inserted (*interposito*) between them is what joins them together.[274] Thus the Corinthian capital, emblem of the world's regeneration through Rome, is not only potentially ubiquitous. It is also, simultaneously, both the evidence and the agent of coherence. The built works in which the new order has thus been "engendered" (*procreatum*) can make such coherence ceaselessly fruitful every-

Corinthian capital of the Temple of Zeus Olympios at Athens, after
W. Dinsmoor.

where because, taking Vitruvius at his word, each time a Corinthian capital is placed in a work, the Corinthian *genus* is born anew.[275]

Venus, as noted earlier, was the name Varro gave to the procreative force that joins fire to water, male to female. This force, he says, is inherent in Victory as well, because when Victory overpowers, she also binds.[276] Like the newborn Venus rising from the sea, *venustas,* apparent beauty, is the visibility of the binding force that beauty generates through its power to inspire love. The Corinthian order, being young and slender, is capable of more beauty and can therefore inspire more love than the others. This is its chief attraction. "The third kind, which is called Corinthian, imitates virginal slenderness, because virgins have more slender limbs due to their tender age, and thus can carry off more beautiful effects [*effectus venustiores*] in ornament."[277]

The acanthus leaves that grow up in the spring around the basket on the dead virgin's tomb are, like the girl, also "tender" and "new."[278] Their tenderness and newness are what inspire Callimachus to invent his new column capital, writes Vitruvius. Transfigured by his story, the flower of the Corinthian virgin's youth could go on to bloom in the built works whose imperious beauty made them the irresistible source of kingly power endlessly renewed.

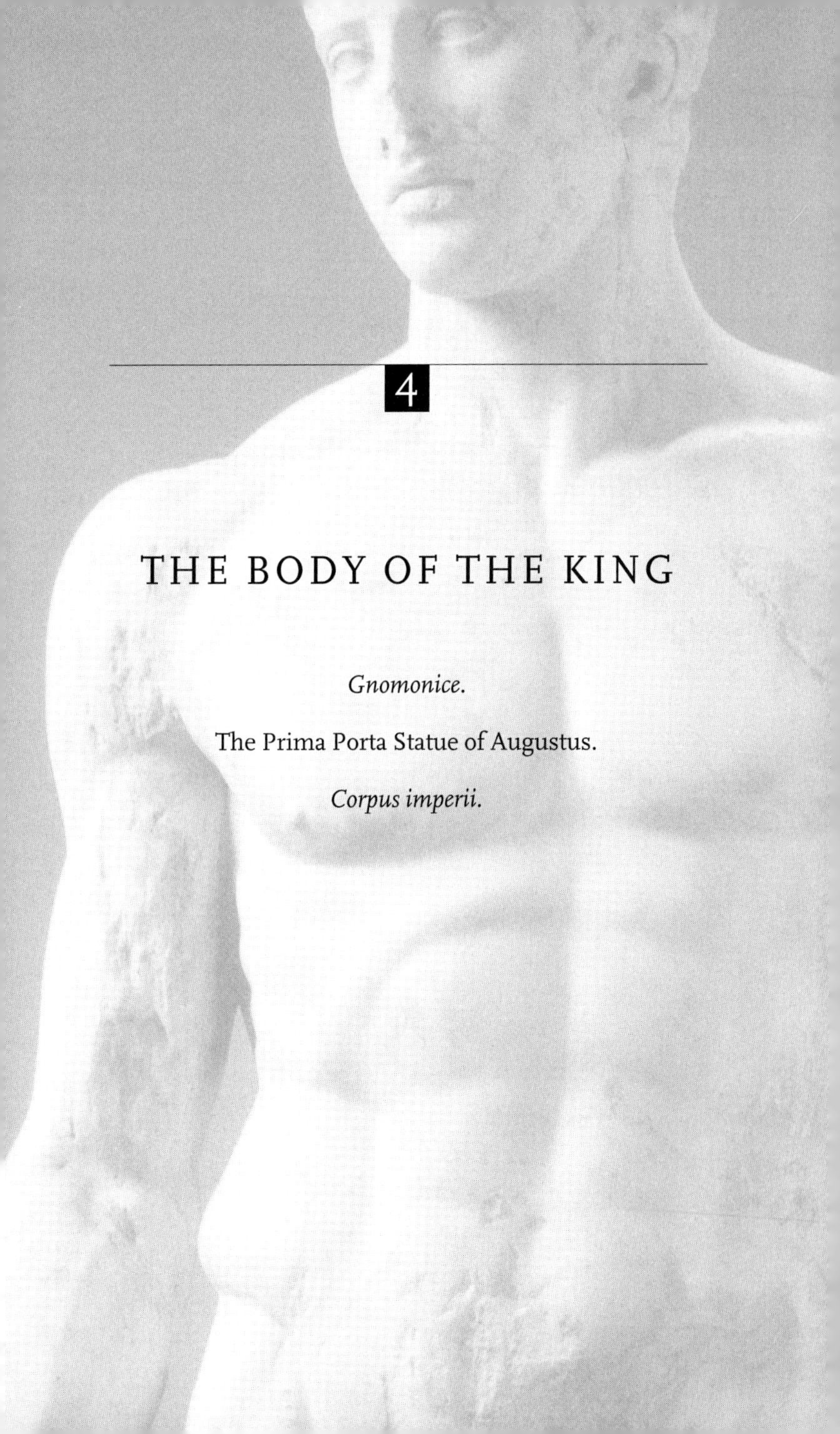

4

THE BODY OF THE KING

Gnomonice.

The Prima Porta Statue of Augustus.

Corpus imperii.

Vitruvius was active during the hectic years that marked the transition from republic to empire—the transition from oligarchy to de facto monarchy.[1] The argument of this study has been that *De architectura* was shaped in most major respects by that specific Roman context, particularly the circumstances attending the Augustan renewal that followed the civil wars.

Renewal (*renovatio*) for Stoics was the world's cyclical rebirth through fire, the "seed" of all things—"a living being and a god," according to Augustus's friend the philosopher Arius Didymus.[2] Varro derived fire, *ignis,* from *gnasci,* to be born, "because from it there is birth, and everything which is born the fire enkindles."[3]

In Vitruvius's chapter on the origin of building, fire draws the savage multitude together into one place and makes them builders. Unlike other animals, men walk upright, can contemplate "the magnificence of the world and of the stars," and are uniquely endowed with hands and fingers.[4] For Vitruvius, the power of fire to renew the world works through the hands and fingers of builders. Architecture is the proof of its power.

Augustan renewal did indeed mean rebuilding, and rebuilding referred, almost unwaveringly, to the person of the *princeps.* His care for the fitness of the public buildings that provide "eminent guarantees of the majesty of empire" was what prompted Vitruvius "to set out . . . [his] writings on these matters" for the new ruler.[5] *Architectura,* the art of the geometrical footprint, the art that "demonstrates everything the other arts achieve," was the passport to Roman ubiquity and, reciprocally, to that of the new ruler.[6]

A passage in Dio Cassius's third-century A.D. *Roman History* makes ubiquity concomitant with kingship. The context is an imagined debate, set in 29 B.C., about how Augustus, having seized command of the world, is now to govern it.⁷ Agrippa, his general, argues for a republican form of government. Maecenas, another close friend and advisor, pleads for monarchy but counsels against making images of the king or building temples to him, because, he says, "if you are upright as a man and honorable as a ruler, the whole earth will be your sacred precinct [*temenos*], all cities your temples, and all men your statues, since within their thoughts you will ever be enshrined and glorified."⁸

Written some 250 years after the time of Vitruvius, this is obviously a post-factum prophecy. When Dio wrote, Augustus and his successors had already been enshrined everywhere for over two centuries, and the Roman world had indeed become the emperor's *temenos*. But if his virtue had, or seemed to have had, made this so as Maecenas predicted it would, it was *because* of the cities that were built as his temples, and *because* of the images that were made to populate them: because of the signifying power of architecture that gave the king's image, and so his virtue, real coordinates in space and time.⁹

During the Augustan principate, the Roman world became for the first time an imagined body permeated by the ubiquitous ruler, the "divine mind" (the *ratio*) that made it cohere.¹⁰ The argument of this final chapter is that in writing the body of architecture, Vitruvius was writing the body of the king.

Ernst Kantorowicz's *The King's Two Bodies* is the indispensable referent here.¹¹ Kantorowicz showed that in the culture of the Christian west the king had two bodies: a visible one, subject to imperfection, infirmity, old age, and death, and an invisible body politic that was eternal, ubiquitous, and perfect.¹² The first was "natural" or real, the second a legal fiction. The first, worldly one was sustained and made continuous from generation to generation by the infusion of the second which was spiritual—a soul beyond time.

Given this interpretive framework, it is tempting to infer that the body Vitruvius claims he was writing is to be understood as the second, eternal one of the king's two bodies. His written or "angelic" body is, after all, a *book*.[13] Constituted by ten scrolls, and containing, its author claims, "all the *rationes* of the discipline," it is perfect.[14] Unlike Vitruvius himself, his book is neither old nor infirm.[15] Nor will it ever be. The bodies of Olympic athletes grow old and die as quickly as their short-lived glory, he writes in his ninth preface, but the opinions of writers like Cicero, Lucretius, and Varro, "their bodies absent, will flower in old age ... and have greater authority than all those who are present."[16] Into this ever-youthful company Vitruvius means to insert both himself and *architectura,* the knowledge of the architect that, judiciously exercised, makes Rome, its civilization, and its king at once ubiquitous and ageless.

A Roman emperor's agelessness was not out of time, however. Timelessness would have been unimaginable in Vitruvius's day, when nature, with its inherent *ratio,* was the ally, not the enemy, of all perfection. Nature's perfection lay in the pattern (also *ratio*) of the changes that, being cyclical, were the source of time itself. The body of architecture perfects and renders visible the body of a king whose unending renewal *in* time makes him ageless. This body, presented as fundamentally and essentially *natural,* could only give the kingly one its visible worldly identity by operating *within* time, which was the generative agent of the world's perpetual rebirth.

Granting the integrity of the early imperial context that

produced *De architectura,* the body that Vitruvius deploys in his treatise cannot be deconstructed as a pretense, deliberately fabricated to mask a suspect and corrupt reality—or any kind of alternative reality, corrupt or not. If it is perfectly coherent with nature, a mask *becomes* reality. Paradoxically transparent because it is impenetrable (revealing all and hiding nothing), a perfect mask can never be construed as a misrepresentation. Being perfect, it *is* what it represents. Perfection—completeness, wholeness—is crucial because, if perfect, the representation is by definition unique and makes all alternative realities unimaginable. Imagined realities *un*founded in nature threaten the perfect coherence of such representations.

This, and not a crusty conservative's inability to appreciate the currents of contemporary art, is, for instance, what underlies Vitruvius's celebrated invective in book 7 against the depravities of what is now identified as late second style mural painting.[17] Images of things that "are not, were not, nor can be" are unnatural and therefore subversive.[18] They are irrational. They endanger coherence.

That is why the body of architecture had to be written, as Vitruvius puts it, *emendatum,* "without a flaw": to present the king for whom he wrote it in a body as self-contained and single, as flawless and entirely natural, as the world it would occupy and make perfectly Roman.

GNOMONICE

"Architecture itself has three parts: building, the construction of clocks [*gnomonice*], and mechanics," Vitruvius writes in book 1.[19] This tripartite structure makes architecture complete and whole, as do the ten scrolls that constitute his treatise. The inclusion of building as a "part" of architecture needs no comment. Making mechanics, particularly the machinery of war, another of its constituents is concomitant with presenting *architectura* as a Herculean body which benefits the world through conquest, as discussed earlier. Furthermore, by the time Vitruvius wrote, mechanics had already long been entrenched as an integral part of an architect's expertise.[20]

This is not true of *gnomonice*.[21] Vitruvius is the first known author to make it a part of architecture, and his account of it is unique in surviving literature.[22] Even after Vitruvius, at the end of the first century A.D., when Pliny the Elder writes of Augustus's great sun clock in the Campus Martius, he calls Facundus Novius, the man he says devised it, a *mathematicus* not an *architectus*.[23] Why, apart from inserting it as the structurally indispensable middle term for completing the threefold rubric of architecture, does Vitruvius make clock construction one of its "parts"?

Generalities can readily be marshaled in his defense.[24] The *gnomon*, sundial pointer, is essentially the same tool as the architect's *norma*, set square. Both pointer and set square are referred to by the Greek word *gnomon* (generically, any upright), from which the Latin *norma* derives.[25] Both, interchangeably, are agents of the "squaring" that establishes the 90-degree relation between verticals and horizontals without which there can be neither sundials nor cities nor buildings, nor yet the exclusively human upright posture that makes a man in his prime architecture's fundamental human referent.[26] Before the use of gnomons and sundials became widespread in the third century B.C., a man's shadow, along with the tables that recorded its varying

Conical sundial from Pompeii.

length, provided a rough guide for chronometry in the Greek world.[27] "What," famously asked the Sphinx, "is that which has one voice and yet becomes four-footed and two-footed and three-footed? . . . Oedipus found the solution, declaring that the riddle of the Sphinx referred to man."[28] Upright and two-footed at midday, architecture's ultimate referent is also the measure of time.

One can be less general than this. In the ninth preface that introduces his book on gnomonics, Vitruvius presents examples of the kind of learning he sees as paving the way for the spread of *humanitas*.[29] As already noted, pride of place is given to geometrical operations that involve precisely the kind of "squaring" that was fundamental in centuriation, the process whereby Romans inscribed the order of the cosmos and of Rome onto its conquered territories.[30] Whether the operations of Roman land surveyors were founded in augural practice, as Varro attests, or in the Greek learning that Vitruvius claims is a source of universal benefit, these practices depended on proper deployment of the *groma*—another cognate of *gnomon*—that was the chief tool of the Roman land surveyor who was called a *gromaticus*.[31]

Evidence points to a convergence of augury and Greek science, dating from the late republic and early empire, which made them subsequent partners, not mutually exclusive alternatives, in underwriting the "squaring" of the world. In earlier days, the practice and orientation of augurs appears to have been largely dependent on the place from which the auspices were taken. On the Capitol at Rome, says Varro, augurs faced south, and pronounced a ritual formula that was not the same as that pronounced elsewhere.[32] Livy has the augur who took the auspices for the inauguration of Numa, Rome's second king after Romulus, position himself on the citadel next to the Capitol, and face not south but east when he performs his ritual quartering of the sky.³³ The way an augur faced seems to have been determined more by the direction of the best possible overall view, which would account for many possible variations in position, than by any strict alignment with the cardinal points.³⁴

Variations tied to locality appear to have disappeared in the imperial period, at least in theory. Land surveyors, writes Frontinus in the late first century A.D., are to follow the practice of augurs and face west because, he says, that is the way the sun faces.³⁵ So, according to Vitruvius and to Frontinus who follows him, are temples, as already discussed.³⁶ Mimetic sympathy with the forward movement of the sun was not dictated by tradition or locality but by nature. It made the practice of augurs and surveyors everywhere uniform and, Frontinus writes, rendered "the constitution of limits identical throughout the whole world."³⁷ He means the *Roman* world, of course, whose order, now explicitly tied to the movement of the sun, became not only ritually correct (because divinely sanctioned through its grounding in augury) but necessarily, universally, and invariably so in graphic projection of the sun's rule over the cosmos.

That the sun was *hêgemonikon* of the universe—its ruling principle—was the view of the Stoic Cleanthes whom Cicero calls "the Stoic of the older families."³⁸ In *De republica,* Cicero has Scipio Africanus, a famous member of one such older family, describe a universe ruled by the sun which he calls the "lord, chief and ruler of the other lights, the mind and guiding principle of the cosmos."³⁹ The fullest surviving transmission of Cleanthes' view of the sun as *hêgemonikon* appears in a passage from Arius Didymus, Augustus's philosophical advisor from 30 to 10 B.C., who also, in the same work, transmits the key ideas about beauty, love, and the Stoic city discussed in the last chapter.[40] "Cleanthes invoked the sun as the ruling principle of the universe [*hêge-monikon de tou kosmou*] because it is the largest of the stars, and because it makes provision for the most things to unite together into the whole, creating as it does the succession of hours in the day and of the seasons in the year."[41]

When Cicero cites the same view in his *Academica*, his phrasing in Latin has Cleanthes hold that "the sun is lord and master of the world": "solem dominari et rerum potiri putat."[42] *Rerum potior* means to have complete or supreme mastery of things.[43] The same verb, *potior*, appears in Vitruvius's address to Augustus in his first preface: "When your divine mind and power, Imperator Caesar, were seizing command of the world . . .".[44] It reappears in the opening of his second preface with reference to Alexander the Great: "When Alexander was taking mastery of the world . . .".[45] In the first chapter of book 6, Vitruvius says that the divine mind has given the Roman people their ideal position at the center so that they might "seize command of the world."[46] In Latin, the terms that express the sun's rule over the universe are the same as those that Vitruvius uses to describe the rule of Rome and of Augustus.[47]

Cleanthes said the sun was *hêgemonikon* of the universe because, Arius Didymus explains, it creates the succession of days and seasons, and "makes provision for the most things to unite together into the whole." None of the other four sources that report Cleanthes' view of the matter say anything about the sun's unifying power being the source of its hegemony, which rather suggests that Arius was interpolating here.[48] As Augustus's philo-sophical advisor reports it, the condition of coherence in the body of the world is the sun that created the pattern of time.[49]

"This book is on the principles of gnomonics," Vitruvius writes at the end of the preface to book 9. "In it I will explain how they were discovered from the sun's rays in the universe, by means of the shadows of gnomons, and how it is that these grow longer or shorter."[50] The shadow of the gnomon at the equinox, which, Vitruvius notes, varies in relative length from place to place, determines the configuration of the analemma, or "face" of a sundial.[51] An ancient sundial was not only a clock in the conventional modern sense; it was also a calendar. "The shadow of the gnomon appearing on the lines [of the analemma] indicates the hours of the day and the seasons of the year," explains the inscription on a Greek sundial from Samothrace.[52] This is the same temporal order that Arius Didymus, in almost identical terms, credits to the sun as the source of its cosmic hegemony. The sun *creates, makes* (*poieiô* is the Greek verb Arius Didymus uses) the succession of days and seasons, which the sun clock *indicates* or *signifies* (*semainei,* in the inscription from the sun clock at Samothrace).

The sun's rays strike the mediating gnomon whose projected shadow transforms the temporal order into the spatial one of the analemma, giving heavenly order and the sun's hegemony over it the reality of measurable extent. In this, the proportional relationship between the shadow's and the gnomon's length at noon on the equinox (at Rome 8:9, at Athens 3:4, and so on) is the key to the transfiguration of cosmic order into worldly reality, a process Vitruvius claims is *architectural*.[53] "The analemma is the pattern obtained from the course of the sun and discovered by observing the shadow of the gnomon as it lengthens to the winter solstice. It is by means of architectural principles and the tracings of the compass that the analemma discloses how the universe operates."⁵⁴

The universe, "the all-encompassing vessel of the whole natural order," revolves on its axis thanks to the power of nature that, according to Vitruvius, itself operates architecturally.⁵⁵ Crediting the operation of the cosmic mechanism (whose revolution Vitruvius also says generates the principles of machinery) to an architectural power which the earthly architect imitates is unlikely to have originated with Vitruvius.⁵⁶ In Plato's *Timaeus,* a work that held particular fascination for late republican intellectuals, a universe very much like the one Vitruvius describes in the first seven chapters of book 9 is constructed by a *dêmiourgos,* a divine craftsman.⁵⁷ Similarly, when Cicero presents the Stoic view of the universe in book 2 of *De natura deorum,* its spokesman Balbus infers "the presence not merely of an inhabitant of this celestial and divine abode, but also of a ruler and governor [*rector et moderator*], the architect as it were of this mighty and monumental structure."⁵⁸

But even if Plato's *dêmiourgos* can be taken as the precursor or model for Vitruvius's cosmic architect, and even if the translation of cosmic into earthly order through the projections of *gnomonice* was considered an architectural process before Vitruvius declared it to be one, no one before Vitruvius had made *gnomonice* part of a written "body of architecture," because no one before him had ever attempted to write such a body.⁵⁹ And for all its reliance on Greek components, this newly assembled body was quintessentially imperial and Roman.

Vitruvius supports the view of the sun as *hêgemonikon*— "lord, chief, and ruler" of the universe.⁶⁰ The sun not only determines the lengths of the hours and the days as it travels through the twelve signs of the Zodiac;[61] its light penetrates the entire universe, so that, contrary to the view of some people, none of the planets is ever invisible.[62] The progressions and retrogressions of the stars are also accounted for by the "mighty force of the sun," for just as plants and moisture rise toward its heat, so the sun attracts the stars that follow it and, "curbing and restraining those that run ahead, does not allow them to move forward, but makes them turn back toward itself."[63] The description projects the image of an expert charioteer in perfect control of his team—of a sun whose power, if it is to be a unifying force, *must* be uniformly attractive.

The conventional ancient view, transmitted by the elder Pliny, is more complex.[64] It accounts for erratic planetary motion by having the sun sometimes attract and sometimes repel the other stars, depending on the direction from which they are struck by its rays. A sun that sometimes attracts and sometimes repels is neither a true *hêgemonikon* nor a good charioteer. Such a sun would make no proper provision "for the most things to unite together into the whole."[65]

Vitruvius's unconventional account is clearly generated by the assumption that the sun is a source of cosmic coherence. Only if the sun is, first and unequivocally, a unifying force in the celestial order can it become, as a consequence, a unifying force in the terrestrial one through the proportional mediation of *gnomonice,* which Vitruvius claims for his architectural body as the middle one of its three parts.

With the advent of the principate, access to the gods was channeled through Augustus Caesar who became its exclusive mediator. A single channel of access to the gods meant that the power so conferred was now concentrated in a single person, who thus became sole ruler.

In the late republic, *religio* was projected beyond the ineffability of ritual performance and into the realm of rational discourse, in a move that was part of the more general effort to reconcile Greek learning (*ratio*) with Roman tradition (the *mos maiorum*). Cicero's *De divinatione* has been taken as an early case in point.[66] The tripartite theology of Varro's *Antiquitates rerum divinarum* can be taken as another, with his "natural theology"— the second of its three parts—complementing the "civil theology" that was an account of the Roman gods and their traditional rites.[67] Natural theology was the special domain of philosophers and concerned the universe (*mundus*), "the most important of all existing things."[68] Perhaps the most telling index of what one might, with Varro in mind, call the naturalization of *religio* was the naturalization of augury, principal guarantee of Roman power. Through its naturalization, augural practice and the surveying procedures that were claimed to be grounded in it became an unvarying reflection of the sun's course in the heavens. The power that had been guaranteed by the traditional Roman covenant with the gods was now jointly underwritten by the natural order, with the latter—being rational and, as Varro would have it, concerned with the universe—naturally carrying more weight worldwide than the first. Utterly characteristic is Vitruvius's enthusiastic, rather elaborate account of how and why Rome's world dominion was the necessary concomitant of her naturally determined central position under the sun.[69]

It was inevitable, in this context, that when Augustus became sole mediator of *religio* he should also have become sole mediator of the natural order and its solar *hêgemonikon,* duplicating in this precisely the role Vitruvius assigns to the mediating gnomon through whose shadow the sun's rule over the cosmos is projected onto the world.

Early in Augustus's reign, the west-facing Temple of Divus Julius in the Forum Romanum was an architectural demonstration of how Roman rule was now grounded both in augury and in nature. The temple's mimetic sympathy with the rising sun, on which Vitruvius's exegesis of west-facing temples has proven to be so enlightening, coupled the advent of the Augustan principate with the "birth" of the sun at the sunrise of the winter solstice under Capricorn, the zodiacal sign that—possibly because it presided over his conception—was disseminated in literature and in imagery as Augustus's own.[70] The precisely calculated orientation of the Temple of Divus Julius that thus confounded Roman civil *religio* at once with the order of the solar year and with the rule of the Julian dynasty could not have occurred without thorough understanding of that order and acknowledgment of solar hegemony over it.

Precise knowledge of the temporal order ruled by the sun had been essential in Julius Caesar's reform in 46 B.C. of the Roman calendar, which until then had been lunar, not solar.[71] According to Macrobius's *Saturnalia* of the fifth century A.D., Caesar acquired this knowledge from the Egyptians.[72] "Copying the Egyptians, the only people who fully understood the principles of astronomy," writes Macrobius, Caesar "endeavored to arrange the year to conform to the duration of the course of the sun, which takes three hundred and sixty-five days and a quarter to complete."[73]

In the Julian calendar, as in the modern one that is based on it, months are entirely arbitrary units of time and bear no relation to the lunar cycles that had governed Roman calendars before Caesar's reform, and made the reckoning of years and seasons notoriously complex.[74] The solar calendar, which obviated such complexities by the simple expedient of eliminating lunar months from its calculations, was much more coherent. The calendar reform also entailed the reordering of civic time (the sequence of feast days, market days, etc.) in which lunar time had been imbricated along with the traditions (*mores maiorum*) that had hitherto shaped their observance.[75] The Egyptians, who since early pharaonic times had used a solar calendar of 365 days which indeed was the source for the new Roman one, maintained a lunar religious calendar in parallel with the solar civic one.[76] There was no parallel lunar calendar in the new Roman system, only a single order of time ruled by the sun.

Stefan Weinstock has shown that the solar symbolism that had become integral to the imperial cult by the end of the first century A.D. "began under Caesar and for Caesar."[77] Far more fundamental in this than the adoption of solar attributes, such as the radiate crowns formerly worn by the Hellenistic kings whose kingdoms were now part of the Roman *orbis*, was the new calendar in which Caesar decreed that his victories be recorded along with his birthday and that, with the month of Quintilis renamed Julius (July), bound solar hegemony to that of Caesar.[78] Augustus carried on the good work, fine-tuning the calendar to make it even more consistent, and commanding that "its entire arrangement be consigned by inscription to the eternal custody of a bronze tablet."[79] In 8 B.C. the month of Sextilis was renamed Augustus.[80] That was by no means all.

When Augustus conquered Egypt in 30 B.C., the last and richest of the Hellenistic kingdoms fell to Roman rule. In Egypt, the king, the sun, and time itself had been bound together in a particularly intimate relationship from the time of the Old Kingdom pharaohs down to the Ptolemies, whose rule ended with Augustus's conquest and Cleopatra's, the last Ptolemy's, suicide.[81] The king's titles—formulaic epithets attached to his name which stressed the privileged relationship to the gods that was the source of his legitimacy and of his cosmocratic power to uphold the order of the world—were, with certain adjustments, almost immediately transferred to Augustus, whose name appeared enshrined in the pharaonic cartouche less than eight months after the conquest.[82] A colossal red granite statue of a pharaoh from the Temple of Amon at Karnak has been identified as a portrait of Augustus and assigned to the same early date.[83]

Heliopolis, the "city of the sun" north of the ancient Egyptian capital of Memphis, was the center of the Egyptian solar cult where pharaohs had been dedicating obelisks to the sun's power, chief source of their own, since the third millennium B.C.[84] It was no doubt during this visit to Egypt in 30 B.C. that Augustus decided to have two Heliopolitan obelisks sent to Rome, and two others to Alexandria.[85] One tends to forget, in view of the long subsequent history of their removal, that the displacement of obelisks was, at the time, a wholly novel undertaking; that their transportation began when the first Roman emperor "seized command of the world."[86]

The two obelisks Augustus had sent to Alexandria had been a pair, dedicated by the fifteenth-century B.C. pharaoh Thutmosis III to "his father the Rê-Harachte," and set up at the entrance to the sun god's temple.[87] At their new location near the port of Alexandria, they were again set up as a pair, this time in front of the Temple of Caesar, and rededicated by Augustus to

Lower half of the gnomon-obelisk of the Horologium Augusti, Rome, after James Stuart. Plate II from Bandini 1750. Collection Centre Canadien d'Architecture / Canadian Centre for Architecture, Montréal.

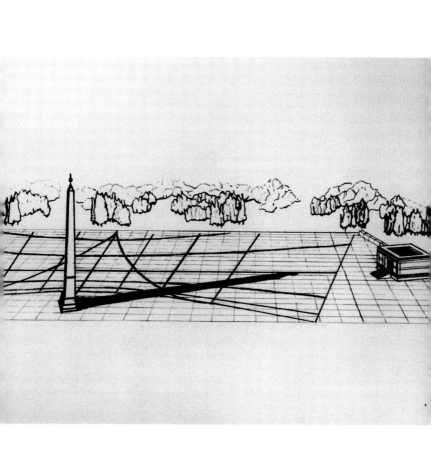

The Horologium Augusti and the Ara Pacis, Rome, after E. Buchner.

his deified father in 13 or 12 B.C.[88] Each of the two obelisks stood on the backs of four bronze crabs, no doubt because Julius Caesar, whose birthday was July 13, was born when the sun was in Cancer, the crab.[89]

Of the two obelisks sent to Rome, one, originally dedicated at Heliopolis by Ramses II in the thirteenth century B.C., was raised on the *spina* of the Circus Maximus in 9 B.C., where it faced the ancient Roman Temple of Sol that was integrated into the seats on the southwest side of the *cavea*.[90] Overlooking the Circus from the north, on the gable of the pediment of Apollo's gleaming new temple on the Palatine, Sol surged forward in his sun chariot, a victor's *quadriga*.[91] According to Tertullian's *De spectaculis* of about 200 A.D., the Circus itself was dedicated to Sol.[92] Each team, says Tertullian, raced around the *spina* as the representative of a different season over whose revolutions the obelisk presided, just as the sun presided over the courses of the stars in the charioteering vocabulary Vitruvius used to describe the sun's cosmic hegemony.[93] On either side of the base of the Circus obelisk, duplicate inscriptions read, "Imperator Caesar, son of the god, Augustus, Pontifex Maximus . . . Egypt having yielded to the power of the Roman people, gave this gift to the sun."[94]

A pair of identical inscriptions was chiseled onto the base of the second obelisk Augustus had shipped to Rome.[95] This last and, for present purposes, most important of Augustus's Egyptian trophies had been dedicated at Heliopolis by the sixth-century B.C. pharaoh Psammetikos II. In 9 B.C., it was raised as the gnomon of Augustus's huge sun clock in the newly developed Campus Martius. This clock was both a calendar and an hour indicator, and was part of a far vaster complex which included the

Ara Pacis Augustae (the altar of Augustan peace, dedicated the same year) to the east and Augustus's mausoleum to the north.[96]

Edmund Buchner has argued that all three of these monuments were geometrically bound in an ideological narrative whose hero was Augustus and whose plot line was traced out by the movements the gnomon-obelisk's shadow over the pavement of the analemma.[97] The geometrical relationships Buchner saw within this complex—that the obelisk-gnomon's shadow pointed directly at the Ara Pacis on Augustus's birthday, for instance—may not be as precise as he claims, depending as they do, among other things, on what has subsequently been pointed to as a somewhat arbitrary choice of site for the obelisk's original location.[98]

Whatever the differences of scholarly opinion on the matter, however, it is beyond dispute that the sun clock's meridian line began at the northern edge of the analemma, whose northern, exterior limit was established by the length of the gnomon's midday shadow at the winter solstice, when, as already noted, the sun was "born" under Capricorn, the sign Augustus repeatedly claimed as his own.[99] The interior endpoint of the meridian line closest to the gnomon was determined by the length of its short noonday shadow at midsummer, when the sun was in Cancer, Julius Caesar's birth sign. This meridian was crossed at right angles by a parallel—the equinoctial line. The point of intersection would have been determined at noon on the equinox when, as Vitruvius points out, the shadow of the gnomon at Rome measured eight-ninths of its height. The same key proportional relationship determined the point of departure for setting up the whole configuration.[100] This occurred in March, of course, and also (more pertinently) on September 23, Augustus's birthday. Rome, the center of the world, whose position Vitruvius claims as the natural source of its power, was precisely located by the crossing of this meridian and this parallel at a center made congruent with the intersection in real lived space of the two astral plot lines of its ruler's solar being: a center from which the world was "squared" by nature herself, and all, Vitruvius would claim, thanks to *architectura*.

Virtually concurrent with the inauguration of the sun clock and the dedication of the Ara Pacis nearby was the adoption of Augustus's birthday as the beginning of the new year in the Roman province of Asia, a change that dovetailed perfectly with the time-reckoning practice adopted earlier in some Asian cities where, since Augustus's victory at Actium, the years were numbered from the new "era" that began in September 31 B.C., which was the date of that victory.[101] Paulus Fabius Maximus, proconsul for that province who proposed that new year's day be celebrated on Augustus's birthday, called it a day "equal to the beginning of the world," to which he said Augustus had given "a whole new appearance."[102] Both the proposal, greeted as the bearer of "good news" (*euangelia*), and its acceptance were inscribed in the public places of cities throughout the province.[103] At Rome, the new year began at the winter solstice, on the anniversary of Augustus's conception, when the sun was born in Capricorn. In Asia it began at the fall equinox with the birth of Augustus himself.

Egyptian kings, writes Pliny, dedicated obelisks to the power of the sun, "of whose rays the obelisk is a sign in effigy."[104] What, one might ask, could be less like a sunbeam than a solid granite monolith weighing several hundred tons? But Pliny does not say that the obelisk *represents* the sun's rays. He says the

The gnomon-obelisk from the Horologium Augusti, now in front of the
Palazzo Montecitorio, Rome.

obelisk is their *argumentum*, their sign or "argument," in effigy, "for so its Egyptian name signifies."[105]

Every obelisk is topped by a four-sided pyramidal cusp usually referred to as a pyramidion. Their large-scale counterparts, the pyramids themselves, were sometimes said to "devour their own shadows," for when the sun was at a certain altitude, the shadow of a pyramid's apex fell within the area of its base, making it uniquely shadowless among worldly phenomena.[106] With their shadows *inside* of them, pyramids contained time. Casting no shadow, they were timeless. A late source which credits Varro for the information says that "Dinochares" once designed such a four-square, shadow-devouring pyramid.[107] The pyramidions of obelisks also ate their shadows, which made them traps for the sunbeams that disappeared into their pinnacles leaving no trace. Pliny refers to precisely this phenomenon when he says that the pinnacle of the obelisk Augustus brought to the Campus Martius for his sun clock "gathered its shadow into itself."[108]

Now this presented a problem, for the whole point of gnomons is that they *do* leave traces—that they *tell* time, not entomb it. Obelisks were not meant to translate solar power as gnomons were, but to contain it. Pliny points out that, because of its shadow-eating cusp, the Campus Martius obelisk would have cast what he calls an "irregular" shadow—one that bore a false proportional relationship to the monolith's height, and that would therefore have been useless for telling time.[109] Facundus Novius, the *mathematicus* who devised the sun clock, recognized the difficulty and fixed a golden globe to the top of it, taking his cue, Pliny reports, from how a man's head defines the shadow he casts.[110] Attaching a "head" to the pyramidal cusp, which thus be-

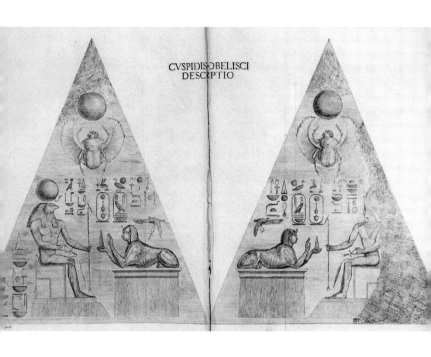

CVSPIDISOBELISCI
DESCRPTIO

Cusp of the gnomon-obelisk of the Horologium Augusti, after James Stuart. Plate III from Bandini 1750. Collection Centre Canadien d'Architecture / Canadian Centre for Architecture, Montréal.

came shoulders, restored the correct proportional relation between the monolith and its shadow by making it anthropomorphic, and transformed the obelisk from an effigy whose "argument" was the sun's rays into a gnomon whose significance was the unifying power of the man who was their mediator.

THE PRIMA PORTA STATUE OF AUGUSTUS

Vitruvius himself may not have anticipated the construction of the sun clock which was inaugurated some fifteen years after the appearance of *De architectura,* although the obelisk would already have been claimed as a trophy by then, and its intended avocation as a sundial pointer probably decided as well. But the difficulty of establishing demonstrable causal connections between Vitruvius and the sun clock in no way obviates their interconnectedness as constituents of the same cultural matrix. For if Vitruvius's ninth book, the only surviving work on *gnomonice,* has been indispensable in scholarly attempts to reconstruct the clock's physical appearance, it is just as indispensable in any attempt to understand the clock's significance.[111] And, perhaps more importantly, vice versa: the clock is key for grasping why Vitruvius made *gnomonice* the middle "part" of a written body of architecture that was meant to double the king's.

One of the best-preserved and best-known images of the latter survives in the Parian marble statue of Augustus, just over two meters high, found in 1863 in his wife Livia's villa at Prima Porta on the northern outskirts of Rome.[112] Like the sun clock, it also postdates Vitruvius, but by fewer years, if one accepts the current consensus that the statue (or, as many scholars believe, the bronze original of which it is a copy) was made shortly after

20 B.C.[113] Unlike the sun clock, the statue cannot, obviously, be assigned directly to any one of Vitruvius's three parts of *architectura*. What the statue does provide—for the historian, not for Vitruvius who probably never saw it—is something of a summation of all three parts together, a microcosm in patently human form of the written body Vitruvius presented to the king in order to show him, as in a mirror, the power of *architectura* to furnish his ubiquitous corporeal presence in a world to be renewed and rendered perfectly coherent thereby.

In the statue as in *De architectura,* Augustus appears as *imperator,* an armed conqueror, with (in the statue) his general's *paludamentum* (military cloak) draped around his hips and over his left forearm.[114] The date of 20 B.C. scholars take as a *terminus post quem* for the statue is based on the central image on the breastplate of the statue's figured cuirass. This image, all agree, refers to the return in that year of the Roman standards captured by the Parthians in three humiliating defeats earlier in the century.[115] Augustus, who considered recovery of the standards a great diplomatic victory, "received them as if he had conquered the Parthian in war, for he took great pride in the achievement, declaring that he had recovered without a struggle what had formerly been lost in battle."[116]

The famous cuirass on which the image appears figures an exceptionally well-muscled male torso, projected as the double of its wearer whom, one assumes, it fits perfectly. Imbricated into the "flesh" of this cuirass, along with the image just mentioned, is the entire natural order deployed in a highly charged cosmic-imperial narrative which—and this is the overriding point of the representation—owes its perfect coherence to the wearer's body into which it has been written.[117]

ABOVE The statue of Augustus from Prima Porta, ca. 19 B.C. Vatican
Museums, Braccio Nuovo (inv. 2290).

RIGHT Parthian returning a Roman standard at the center of the cuirass
of the statue of Augustus from Prima Porta.

The Parthian, who holds aloft the eagle-topped standard he is ostensibly returning to the Roman, in fact pays no attention at all to the armed figure opposite him, whom some identify as Tiberius, Augustus's stepson who was delegated to receive the standards.[118] Instead, the Parthian's eyes are raised to the eagle that leads his, and the viewer's, gaze further upward, to the face of Sol who appears over Augustus's right breast, whom the Parthian thus salutes as the true and rightful owner of the standard, whose return entails a diagonal transfer from the lower left of Augustus's stomach to the upper right of his chest. The sun looks down on the Parthian and returns his reverent gaze, recalling in this precisely how Vitruvius says the rising sun is supposed to gaze back benevolently at supplicants who pray in front of west-facing temples at dawn.[119]

Sol has his right arm raised above his head to grasp the edge of the sky-canopy above—of which the gesture clearly makes him *hêgemon*—and rides in a sun chariot, the hub of whose wheel might almost be mistaken for Augustus's right nipple. With his left hand, he guides his fiery team across the conqueror's bosom bringing perennial sunrise. It must be daybreak because on Augustus's left breast Venus, the morning star the Romans called Lucifer (bringer of light), runs ahead of Sol's four onrushing horses carrying a torch.[120] She is borne aloft by Aurora, the dawn, who, winged like a Victory, sprinkles morning dew from a pitcher. The conditions of procreation, wrote Varro, are two,

fire and water. Thus these are used at the threshold in weddings, because there is union here, and fire is male . . . and the water is the

The Prima Porta cuirass, upper torso.

female . . . and the force that brings their vinctio *"binding" is* Venus. *Hence the comic poet says, "Venus is his victress, do you see it?" not because Venus wishes* vincere, *to conquer, but* vincire, *to bind. Victory herself is named from the fact that the overpowered* vinciuntur, *are bound.*[121]

Bound indeed is the overpowered nation figured in the dejected person seated near Augustus's armpit under the curve of his left breast, just below the procreative fire and water carried in tandem by torch-bearing Venus and the dew-dispensing dawn. The sun will rise there first in its circular trajectory around the *imperator*'s torso, so the nation represented by this figure must be an eastern one—like Parthia, whose barbarian representative is located on the same left side of his body.[122] Always moving forward, Sol will eventually circle around to rise over the west on Augustus's right side, where another overpowered nation is bound to his rib cage in symmetrical dejection behind the armed western Roman. "East and west together" was a fairly common way of referring to the whole world.[123] The *princeps*'s body is the condition of its totality.

Below Augustus's navel, emerging from the twisted folds of the *paludamentum* that bulge out thickly over his genitals, is the female figure of Earth with two small babies, a cornucopia, and other attributes of fecundity.[124] On his right hip Apollo, Augustus's champion at Actium, rides a griffin—half lion, half eagle, another solar emblem—and carries his lyre, source of civilizing harmony.[125] Riding a stag on Augustus's left hip is Apollo's twin Diana, goddess of the moon and of the wild lands that her brother and his lyre will tame and bring to solar order.[126]

A strict geometry, generated by the wearer's body, governs the images on the cuirass. In the "heaven" of Augustus's upper chest, under the sheltering canopy held by the sky god Caelus, Sol as noted is in motion, rushing forward with his celestial precursors around the stationary world below (Augustus's stomach) in the circular orbit described by the images carved in relief around the edge of the cuirass. "Squaring" this circle, joining heaven to earth and east to west in the flesh that generates their geometrical footprint, a vertical and a horizontal intersect at right angles.

Anatomically, there is usually an interruption between the *linea alba* or median line of a well-muscled man's stomach and the line between his breasts. Here, where the first (the *linea alba*) appears to extend upward to join the second (the line between the breasts) in an unbroken vertical, the usual interruption disappears. Also usually discontinuous is the horizontal line under the breasts that here joins east to west in unbroken flesh, a bodily contour which east and west in turn render at once geographical and cosmic. The pectoral triangle that, even here, would if one could see it interrupt both these contour lines has been filled with the eagle at the tip of the surrendered Roman standard: precisely located agent of their (the lines') and the world's continuity at the still point of the revolving cosmos in the middle of Augustus's chest.

Augustus, writes Suetonius, received his new name from the Roman Senate in January of 27 B.C. "on the ground that [Augustus] was not merely a new title but a more honorable one [than Romulus], inasmuch as both sacred places and those in which anything is consecrated by augural rites are called

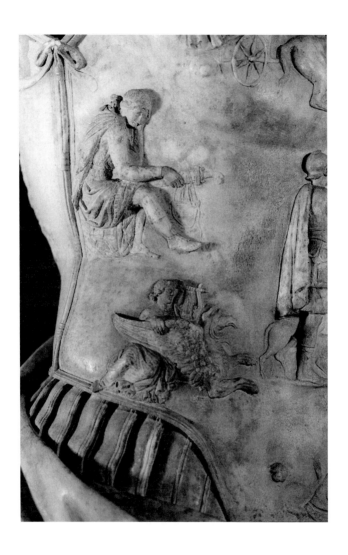

Right side of the Prima Porta cuirass, with subjected Spaniard
and Apollo on a griffin.

Left side of the Prima Porta cuirass, with subjected Galatian and
Diana on a stag.

Breastplate of the Prima Porta cuirass.

augusta."[127] The "squared" torso of the Prima Porta Augustus is just such a place—the same that generated Vitruvian man.[128]

As a bloodless, ostensibly negotiated victory, the diplomatic victory celebrated by the image at the center of the cuirass is a victory of the *logos* or *ratio* that, according to Stoic theory, was the condition of coherence in bodies and the world. One rather suspects that that is why so much was made of the event.[129] It was a victory not only of speech over brute force but of speech (*logos*) made one, as in the statue, with the binding force of the cosmic *logos* whose agent here is the Roman eagle lodged above Augustus's sternum. The eagle belonged to Jupiter who, as king of the gods to whom the "squaring" augural power referred, was the emblem of Roman might above all others. It was in the chest, where the statue locates this eagle, that Stoics situated a man's *hêgemonikon,* identified in Latin as the *mens* or intelligence that ruled his soul, which soul this intelligence dispersed as unifying currents of warm breath throughout his body.[130] Varro, citing Ennius, said that human intelligence was fire taken from the sun.[131] In about 50 A.D. the Stoic Seneca hopefully admonished Nero: "the gentleness that comes from your spirit will spread little by little through the whole great body of empire, joining all things in the shape of your likeness."[132] Before Seneca, there was the Prima Porta statue.[133]

At Rome, monarchy was inevitably concomitant with channeling access to the gods through a single person, which was how Augustus could be in effect a king.[134] Late republican intellectuals, particularly Cicero, had already been entertaining the notion that it was also the most natural form of government.[135] In the first chapter of Cicero's *De republica,* the younger Scipio argues for monarchy as a reflection at once of the divine order where Jupiter reigns "with a nod," of a natural order ruled by a divine mind, and of wise men ruled by the "kingly power" (*regale imperium*) of reason within themselves.[136]

All of this is deployed not only in the cuirass of the Prima Porta statue but also by Vitruvius. "When your divine mind and power, Imperator Caesar, were seizing command of the world . . . and all subjected peoples awaited your nod . . .".[137] This, the opening address of his first preface, is not affixed as an extraneous appendage to the rest of the treatise any more than the Prima Porta cuirass is affixed as an extraneous appendage to the body wearing it. The cuirass is the *appearance* of the king's body in the world as a mask which (while remaining, overtly, a mask) is made so entirely continuous both with its wearer and with the natural order it represents as to render unaskable any questions about realities behind it. With no chinks in his armor, the king had only one body.

The wearer of the cuirass extends his right arm, his hand raised almost to the level of his head. The hand, of whose fingers all but the ring finger are restored, may originally have held some object such as a spear or a branch of laurel.[138] Alternatively, it may have held nothing and have been raised in the gesture of *adlocutio,* or public address.[139] This last is by far the likeliest option, and not just because, as John Pollini has recently established, the tendons on the back of the hand are represented in a way that precludes its ever having grasped anything.[140]

The cuirass celebrates the Parthians' return of the standards as a negotiated settlement, and presents the alleged diplomatic victory as the operation of the cosmic *logos* in historical time. The body of Augustus is entirely continuous with the cuirass. So, with this narrative, is the authoritative gesture of his

Two Augustan aurei with heads of Augustus. On the reverses,
Capricorns with the legend *signis receptis* ("standards recovered").
Asian mint, ca. 19 B.C. British Museum, London (BMC 679 and 680).

raised right hand. The power of speech was man's privileged channel of communication with the *logos* of the Stoic universe.[141] It was, according to Cicero, speech-as-*ratio* that gave great orators the power to lead people from their savage ways and gather them together "into one place."[142] Therein, argues Vitruvius, lies the power of architecture.[143] The place, here, is the body of the king to whose flanks the chastened peoples of east and west cling abjectly—the *gentes omnes subactae* of Vitruvius's first preface, drawn to the circumference of the Roman *orbis* by the power of the cosmic-imperial Word.[144]

The model for the Prima Porta statue is generally thought to have been the so-called Doryphoros—the spear carrier that was the fifth-century B.C. Greek sculptor Polykleitos's most famous work, and of which a number of Roman copies survive.[145] Both the Prima Porta statue and the two best surviving copies of the Doryphoros measure almost exactly the same height of two meters; both have the same, typically contrappostal or "chiastic" Polykleitan stance, with the subject, whose weight is carried on his forward right leg, perfectly balanced between motion and stasis.[146] Similarities have also been noted in the heads, in the impassive "classical" beauty of the features, in the arrangement of the hair. Both statues, as well as can be judged, have the same proportions, to the degree at least that they both *look* very similarly proportioned.[147]

There are also a number of significant variations, notably in the position of the arms.[148] The most obvious difference of all is that whereas the Doryphoros is nude, the Augustus from Prima Porta is clothed, dressed as a military commander. The musculature of his cuirass, presented as the mask and double of the *imperator*'s own, reproduces (nearly) that of the torso of the

Doryphoros, marble copy of the fifth-century B.C. statue by
Polykleitos. Minneapolis Institute of Arts (86.6).

Polykleitan statue, whose contours, principally those of the stomach muscles, have been attenuated just enough to enhance the legibility of the intersection in the Roman eagle of the vertical and the horizontal discussed earlier.

Andrew Stewart has called the "highly-contrived articulation" of the Doryphoros's torso "one of the most characteristic hallmarks of the Polykleitan style," following precedent in labeling it (fortuitously, but with no reference to the Prima Porta statue) its *cuirasse esthétique*.[149] The sculptor of the Prima Porta statue was by no means the first artist to take Polykleitos as his model. Other sculptors had made the torsos of their statues display the same monumental aesthetic *cuirasse*.[150] But like the Doryphoros, such statues are nude. They were made to imitate the ideal *in the flesh*, not to *wear* it as a piece of clothing. Augustus's cuirass fits him perfectly, but he can still in principle take it off. As a piece of clothing, it defines his appearance, his role: Roman *imperator* as mediating "wearer" of the Greek ideal. It is almost as if to stress the self-conscious deliberation with which the Polykleitan armor has been *put on*—almost, indeed, as if to confirm the very nature of that armor—that, on the back of the cuirass where few if any would have seen it, the statue's sculptor has carved a trophy—another, much smaller cuirass, emptied of its vanquished owner, and mounted like a scarecrow, as Romans did their trophies, on a cross-shaped tree trunk. The flesh of the Doryphoros has been made part of the king's mask. Why?

Rightly or wrongly, Romans thought that the Doryphoros was the statue Polykleitos made "to confirm in action," as Galen put it in the second century A.D., the *logos* of a written work that for the first time "gave all the explanations of the symmetries of the body," calling the statue Canon just like his book.[151] Pliny,

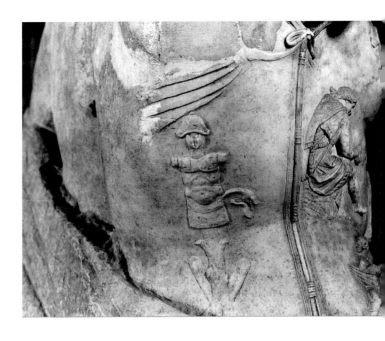

Rear of the Prima Porta cuirass with trophy.

who explicitly identifies the Doryphoros with the famous Canon statue, asserts that Polykleitos alone among men was "judged to have fashioned the art itself in a single work."[152] The essence of the *ars* so fashioned in the work whose lineaments, according to Pliny, artists followed as one might a law (*veluti a lege*) is the precise commensurability (*symmetria*) of all the parts with one another; of "finger, obviously, to finger, of all the fingers to palm and wrist, of these to forearm, of forearm to upper arm, and of all to all."[153] In donning the flesh of the Doryphoros, Augustus put on the canon, and with it the symmetrical correspondences that simultaneously endowed his body and the world with perfect coherence in measurable confirmation both of the binding force of the cosmic *logos* deployed on his chest and that of the *ratio*-as-speech latent in the rhetorical gesture of his raised right hand.[154]

Symmetrical correspondences, carefully selected from "many numbers," are the source, interchangeably, of excellence (*to eu*) and beauty (*to kalos*).[155] "Quite perfect" is how Cicero judged the beauty of Polykleitos's statues.[156] Varro, who attributed to Polykleitos the discovery of making statues throw their weight on one leg in the famous "chiastic" pose, called them *quadrata* and "almost all made on one model."[157] This *quadrata* is usually taken as pejorative: "squarish" or "blocklike"—with heavy, tedious, and repetitive read as the implicit subtext.[158] But Varro also said elsewhere that Rome was first *quadrata* "so that it might be placed in equilibrium."[159] With this in mind, one is led to suspect that the squareness Varro attributes to Polykleitos's works, while referring to their blocklike appearance, referred equally to the equilibrium of the contrappostal stance which, weighted by the solidity of blocklike appearance, rendered visible the harmonious balance of carefully selected "canonic" symmetries to give them the beauty Cicero considered entirely perfect.

This "squared" perfection also had, traditionally, a moral dimension—*tetragônos* was how the Greek poet Simonides described the good man in the fifth century B.C., "foursquare in hands and feet and mind, fashioned without a flaw."[160] To attempt to disentangle Simonides' moral squaredness from the squared or blocklike appearance Varro assigns to the works of Polykleitos by assuming the first to be metaphorical and the second purely descriptive, as scholars sometimes do, is an anachronistic not to mention futile endeavor.[161] Simonides' good man is squared not only in mind but also in hands and in feet. In the ancient world, the one was unimaginable without the other. And Simonides and Polykleitos belonged to the same Greek century of whose civilizing ideal Augustus appointed himself the self-conscious mediator when he put on his Polykleitan armor. "They say," wrote Diogenes Laertius of the Stoics, "that the perfect good is beautiful from its having all the numbers according to nature, or because of perfect *symmetria*."[162]

The squaredness of Rome and of the Doryphoros are, in equal measure, the squaredness of the Augustus from Prima Porta, in whose body the imperial world city is "placed in equilibrium." Indeed, it has been noted that the Roman statue is somewhat more solidly planted than the Greek one.[163] Just as rightly calculated symmetries generate beauty in the squared, perfectly balanced body of the statue, so beauty in turn generates the binding power of love, even as the Stoics said it should.[164] Riding on a dolphin, behind the calf of Augustus's right leg, a small winged Amor reaches up to the hem of the general's *paludamentum*. The Amor (son of Venus, the Julian dynasty's divine ancestress) represented here is also, almost certainly, Gaius, Augustus's first grandson and future heir whose birth was celebrated the same year as the Parthians' return of the captured standards.[165] In this Stoic world city, where every referent is at once universal and historically specific, the Venus-born power of love is dynastic. It belongs to the king whose perfect body generates it.

Vitruvius was *writing* the body of architecture, not sculpting it—a perfect *corpus* he describes as *emendatum* at the end of book 9, "flawless." But then Polykleitos himself, at least according to Galen, *wrote* his *Canon* before he fashioned it in the statue he also called Canon.[166] The passages from book 3, chapter 1 on proportion and symmetry discussed earlier do not refer explicitly to any canon, written or sculpted, although in book 1 Vitruvius notes that an architect, even if he neither is nor can be a sculptor like Myron or Polykleitos, should not be ignorant of the *rationes* of modeling.[167] He again lists Polykleitos along with Myron, Phidias, and Lysippus as examples of artists who benefited from recognition during their lifetime and undying fame after their death.[168] But even with no explicit reference to a canon, it is beyond question that there *is* a canon (and very probably that of Polykleitos) behind the well-shaped man whose commensurate proportions, Vitruvius says, "famous ancient painters and sculptors adopted, and so attained great, unlimited praise"—the same man whom Vitruvius encircles and then "squares" as geometrical proof of his overall commensurability.[169] This man, like the Prima Porta statue and indeed like "Vitruvian" architecture, is informed by Greek precedents, but his proper subject is itself no more Greek than the Augustus wearing the Polykleitan armor is.

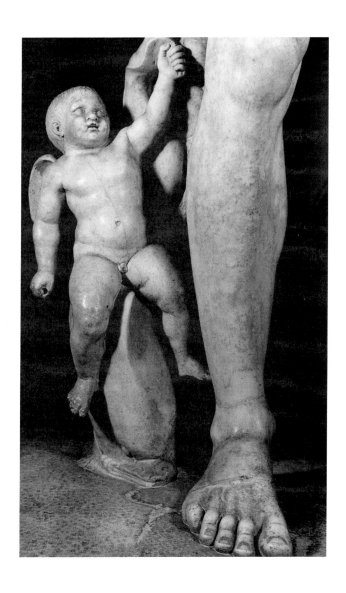

Amor behind the right calf of the statue of Augustus from Prima Porta.

Like the subject of the Prima Porta statue, the "squared" man at the center of *De architectura* is Roman.

It is this man whom Vitruvius cites as the reason for following ancient precepts about commensurability in building, where carefully chosen symmetries in turn generate *venustas.* There is no evidence, in Vitruvius or elsewhere, that the authorities Vitruvius refers to as "ancients" themselves ever invoked well-shaped men as the reason architects should adhere to symmetrical principles.[170] There *is* evidence, however, that the ancients evoked the well-shaped man to urge what one might call "symmetrical" principles in public speaking. That a good speech should be put together like a well-shaped man, with all its parts "adapted to one another and to the whole," as Plato put it in the *Phaedrus,* was a notion Vitruvius's readers, Roman aristocrats trained in rhetoric, would have been entirely familiar with.[171] They may not have understood that (or how) the "the putting together of temples depends on symmetry," but once Vitruvius presented his well-shaped man as its exemplar, the importance of architectural symmetry would have acquired the force of obvious truth.[172] Allied to rhetoric through the man of commensurate parts, so too would the importance of architecture itself.

As familiar to Vitruvius's readers as the imagined body of a symmetrical speech, just as much of an acknowledged ideal, and not unrelated to it, was commensurability in the *corpus rei publicae,* the body of the Roman commonwealth, which Cicero made a favorite trope and Caesar loftily dismissed as a fiction.[173] Unity in the body politic depended on cooperation between its members. In a fable related independently by Livy and Dionysius of Halicarnassus, two of Vitruvius's contemporaries, the senator Menenius Agrippa allegorizes the members of the Roman commonwealth as different body parts, all mutually dependent in their common project of keeping the body alive and well, a fable with particular point at this historical juncture in the wake of the civil wars.[174] In the unfamiliar trope of well-shaped man as the ground for architectural symmetry, Vitruvius's readers would have recognized this other, already familiar one, and with it another powerful argument for architecture's importance. Except of course that Vitruvius's well-shaped man now had a referent that was at once more personal and more universal than Cicero ever entailed in his "corpus rei publicae."

The measurements that the Greeks, and until relatively recently most peoples, used for building were of course based on the members of the human body, and indeed usually related proportionally, as they are more or less in the human body itself.[175] But this does not necessarily lead to the conclusion that *because* men's bodies are commensurable buildings should be so. The causal connection itself may just conceivably be Vitruvius's own; the stress laid on it, as *the* justifying principle for having all the parts of buildings (particularly temples) relate to one another proportionally, almost certainly is. And, allowing that the context in which *De architectura* was written ("When your divine mind and power, Imperator Caesar, were seizing command of the world") is the same as the one that produced the Prima Porta Augustus, one is led to conclude that Vitruvius's insistence has to do not only with the precedents already mentioned, but even more precisely with the conqueror who, as civilizer, "wears" the canon, and whose speech mediates its cohesive *logos*. To relate the symmetrical principles that the ancients handed down for building to the symmetrical principles governing how nature puts together a man, and to cite the latter as the reason for adhering to the former, is to ally architecture with the same imperial project.

The numbers of human measurement—finger, palm, foot, cubit—were "arranged," as Vitruvius puts it, "into the perfect number which the Greeks call *teleon*": the number ten that is at once the "number" of the human body and the number of scrolls in which Vitruvius, very deliberately, deploys his "perfect body of architecture."[176] This number—four expanded to ten through pebbles or points laid out in the Pythagorean *tetractys*—was the "organizing idea of cosmic events," "the circle and limit of all the numbers," the container and content of time itself.[177] In the Pythagorean way of thinking, four, the number of cosmic order, *was* ten.[178] Squared, it produces sixteen, the number Vitruvius says is Roman and "supremely perfect."[179]

J. E. Raven pointed out over 50 years ago that Pythagoreans appear to have coupled the perfect nature of the decad with the Polykleitan canon itself.[180] Vitruvius, whose argument moves sequentially from well-shaped man to Vitruvian man to the arrangement of human "numbers" into the *teleon*, makes the same connection, as Raven noted. Following this line of reasoning, a statue like the Prima Porta Augustus whose perfect beauty would have led to the assumption that it was canonic (even if, measurably, it may not have been) would, concomitantly, have represented the *teleon* in action: organizer of cosmic events, container and content of time, and so on—just as illustrated on his cuirass.[181]

The *teleon* contained in the Prima Porta Augustus has the world cohere in a single body, one that, unlike its model the Doryphoros, has a specific historical identity.[182] The *teleon* Vitruvius contains in *De architectura*, which he allies to the same historical person, also makes the book a body. This body, like all bodies, coheres through *rationes*—the same that Cicero claimed were the prerequisite for the formation of any *ars* (geometry, oratory, grammar, etc.) in order to cement fragmentary knowledge, formerly "diffuse and all in pieces," and bind it together.[183] Unlike the *rationes* that bind the other arts, however, or those that bind other bodies, the *rationes* that bind architecture at once into an art and into the historically specific body of *De architectura* have, as Vitruvius presents them, the unique potential to lay the king—or rather his mask—out over the contours of the imperial landscape, and by so doing to palpably bind "all to all" in the lived world of spatial extent. In *De architectura* the world-body the Prima Porta statue presents as an image becomes a real possibility.

CORPUS IMPERII

The year the Parthians returned the captured standards in the event that was made the focus of the Prima Porta cuirass was also marked by the birth of Gaius, Augustus's first grandson and successor, whom the winged Amor at the feet of the statue probably represents, as already noted.[184] The same year Augustus was named *curator viarum* and put in charge of all the highways in the vicinity of Rome.[185] In this capacity he set up the so-called *miliarium aureum,* the golden milestone at the northwest end of the Forum Romanum near the Temple of Saturn, where it marked the convergence of the main roads that led to the city, and commemorated the curatorship of the *princeps* who was, ideally, the point where they all converged.[186]

The notion of what we call the Roman empire—a spatial

unit with a center, Rome, and a clearly marked limit or periphery—first took shape under Augustus Caesar, through whom, as through the golden milestone and the Prima Porta statue, all expressions of unity were initially formulated. There had been, Dietmar Kienast has pointed out, no preconceived idea of a fixed, geographical empire.[187] It did not exist prior to or independently of Augustus; there are virtually no expressions concerning "the" empire during the Augustan period that do not refer to the emperor himself.[188]

Ovid is the first to use the phrase *corpus imperii,* the body of empire, in his *Tristia,* the series of poems he wrote from exile on the Black Sea around 10 A.D. near the end of Augustus's reign. This phrase concludes a panegyric Ovid opens with an address to Augustus, now over 70, as "imperii princeps" (prince or originator of empire) on whom, he says, the world depends, to whom Parthians return standards (an event now thirty years in the past), and whose youthful vigor is renewed in the German conquests of his son and current heir, Tiberius.[189] Although vaster now than ever, Ovid writes, there are no shaky (no loosely connected) members in the *corpus imperii,* the body of empire.[190]

By the time Florus wrote his epitome of Roman history in the second century A.D., the phrase *corpus imperii* had become something of a cliché.[191] Florus writes that at the end of the civil wars,

the chief power passed to Octavius Caesar Augustus, who by his wisdom and skill set in order the body of empire, which was all overturned and thrown into confusion and would certainly never have been able to attain coherence and harmony unless it were ruled by the nod of a single protector: its soul, as it were, and its mind.[192]

So what was *imperium* before it acquired spatial extent and (as Florus phrases it in terms that are so uncannily close to those of Vitruvius's first preface) perfect coherence in the *corpus* ruled by the nod, the soul, and the mind of Augustus?

Until the time of Augustus the Latin word *imperium* meant the legally vested power of command, confirmed by Jupiter through the taking of auspices. The power—in equal and interdependent parts religious and political—was conferred on magistrates when they entered office.[193] Magistrates were elected by the people, but they received *imperium* from Jupiter.[194] Since they were elected for periods usually limited to a year, no one person ever held *imperium* for very long. This was true both of city magistrates and of proconsuls and others who governed in their provinces, with *provincia* understood more as the "official duty, office, business or charge" of those who exercised *imperium* there than territorially, as geographical "provinces" independent of that command.[195] It was also true of military commanders in the field. *Imperium,* the right of command, did not exist independently of the person who temporarily held it, and it could belong to as many or as few people as circumstances dictated. A proconsul might for instance have *imperium* in Asia, but Asia was the *provincia* of his *imperium,* not an *imperium* itself. Romans in the late republic told themselves that they ruled the world, but the Roman *orbis* they claimed to rule was itself not called an *imperium.*[196] Even in Virgil, the "imperium sine fine" that Jupiter promises the Roman people is *temporally* "without limit"—a power endlessly renewed—not a spatial entity.[197] Because *imperium* had no body, before Augustus took the name Imperator there was, as conventional usage now designates it, no Roman "empire."

Indeed, before Augustus adopted it as a *praenomen* in 29 B.C., Imperator had not been a name at all, attached permanently to any single person.[198] The man designated by the common noun *imperator* was a military commander, who exercised *imperium* in the field.[199] If, after a major victory, his troops acclaimed him "Imperator," he could carry the title only until after the celebration of his triumph, after which he had to relinquish it.[200] The role of a military commander (an *imperator*) was not exclusive, nor the acclamation permanent. In the name Imperator Caesar Augustus, it became both. "Regarded as a personal name," wrote Sir Ronald Syme, "'Imp.' is exorbitant, far outdistancing any predecessor or competitor . . . 'Imp.' is a name of power, precise yet mystical, a monopolisation of the glory of the *triumphator.*"[201] This is the name by which Vitruvius addresses the man for whom he wrote *De architectura.*

Renewed yearly in different elected officials, *imperium* was, like the title *imperator,* entirely time-dependent until Augustus became the single and permanent Imperator in whom *imperium* was perpetually renewed. When the locus of *imperium* became the body of the Imperator who ruled the world, its localization transformed a hitherto temporal phenomenon into a body of power whose objective reality was at once spatial and— as in the Prima Porta statue—"canonically" measurable.

These are the terms governing Vitruvius's presentation of architecture as the privileged means for spatializing *imperium,* which, given its *locus* in the man he acclaims as Imperator, is identical with the project of shaping the world in the king's own image. "When I realized," he writes to Augustus in his first preface,

> that you had care not only for the common life of all men and for the regulation of the commonwealth but also for the fitness of public buildings—that even as, through you, the city [civitas] was increased with provinces, so public buildings were to provide eminent guarantees for the majesty of empire [maiestas imperii]—I decided not to hesitate and took the first opportunity to set out for you my writings on these matters, for it was concerning this that I was known to your father [Caesar] and this is what first attached me to his might. And when . . . your father's imperium was conveyed into your power, my enduring attachment to his memory likewise brought your favor with it.[202]

Vitruvius presents Augustus's conquests not as a territorial expansion but as an increase in the *provinciae* of the Roman *civitas,* a phrasing that puts less emphasis on increase in the size of an "empire" in the conventional sense than on collective power accrued—a power now located in the person explicitly addressed as the agent of that increase. Buildings are the "eminent guarantees," the evidence and proof, of the majesty of *imperium* so augmented.[203] They localize *imperium* and make it spatial. They also, as Vitruvius tells it, localize the achievements of Imperator Caesar.[204] *De architectura*—the ten scrolls that delineate the complete body of architecture—is Vitruvius's single schema or diagram for situating both.[205] It is a body less usefully understood as an exhaustive set of specific instructions (it is not) than as an overall mnemonic figure meant to supply the diagrammatic frame for giving *imperium* the world-scale locus Ovid and others called *corpus imperii*—what is now called the Roman "empire."[206]

The phenomenon of worldwide Roman colonization that began as a trickle under Caesar swelled to an unprecedented and never-to-be repeated tidal wave under Augustus. By his own account, he founded twenty-eight new cities in Italy itself; others in Gaul (both Gallia Narbonensis and the "three Gauls" recently conquered by Caesar), Spain, Africa, Mauritania, Sicily, Corsica, Sardinia, Macedonia, Achaea, Asia.[207] There was more to this than the provision of land for the more than 100,000 veterans he demobilized after his victory at Actium.[208] "Colonies," explains the miscellanist Aulus Gellius in the second century A.D.,

do not come into citizenship from without, nor grow from roots of their own but are as if transplanted from the [Roman] civitas and have all the laws and institutions of the Roman people, not those of their own choice. This condition, although more subject to control and less free, is nevertheless thought to be preferable and superior because of the greatness and majesty of the Roman people of which those colonies appear rather as small effigies and, as it were, images.[209]

Colonies are images not of Rome, but of Roman majesty and greatness: precisely the terms Vitruvius uses with respect to Augustan building activity in the preface to book 1. Founded by

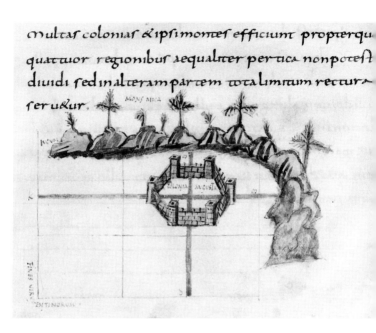

"Colonia augusta," image from the ninth-century Codex
Palatinus of Hyginus Gromaticus's *Constitutio limitum*.
Bibliotheca Apostolica Vaticana (Vatic. lat. 1564, fol. 90r).

illustrious men like Caesar and Augustus, for the sake of "increasing" the Roman commonwealth (*augendae rei publicae causa,* as Hyginus Gromaticus writes), their creation everywhere followed an identifiable pattern.[210]

Greg Woolf has recently documented the case of Gaul, whose urbanization under Augustus followed Caesar's conquest of it in the 50s B.C.—the latter, almost certainly, with Vitruvius's active participation.[211] Cities, the measurable index of *humanitas,* were also the measurable evidence of the conquest in whose wake their foundation followed, which founding, as a systematic enterprise, dated from the early Augustan period.[212] Their creation in Gaul began with the choice of site, which changed from the hills, where Gauls had built the forts that had characterized traditional settlement patterns for more than five centuries, down to the neighboring plains.[213] Next came the organization of urban space: the limitation of its perimeter, and the "squaring" of the territory so limited in an operation whose laborious execution through the large-scale earth removal entailed by leveling and terracing appears to have been more than compensated by the evidence of coherence so established.[214]

The building of the monumental center followed. Significantly, although there is evidence for the foundation of a very few colonies in Gaul before the Augustan period, none exists for the construction of any urban monument before 30 B.C.[215] The exact sequence and details of their building varied, but the general pattern did not: a forum complex (enclosed, continuous, coherent) that included temples, a basilica, a *macellum* or monumental market, bath buildings, and theaters. Rarely amphitheaters, whose initial appearance in Gaul at the end of the first century

A.D. considerably postdates the Augustan period—an interesting delay, in view of Vitruvius's failure to discuss them.[216]

After the city had been gridded out and its monumental center at least located, Gallic city builders turned to the construction of their own residences. At first, those who settled around the recently cleared *fora* of these sparsely populated new cities lived in houses built of wattle and daub—a quick and easy but highly impermanent building technique that Vitruvius condemns as a public calamity and wishes had never been invented—one he includes in the discussion of primitive huts that opens book 2.[217] Within a generation, and only after the monumental center had been built, the Gauls, or at least those who could afford to, mended their ways and built aristocratic *domus* with tiled roofs, mosaic floors, and walls of *opus caementicum,* whose smooth-plastered interior surfaces were painted with murals.[218] The progress of civilization Vitruvius describes in his primitive hut chapter concludes with his now sedentary hut builders constructing, no longer huts, but houses (*domus*) with foundations, stone walls, and tiled roofs, and learning to grace their lives with the pleasures of refinement.[219]

The order of operations in the urbanization of Gaul (choice of site, organization, public buildings, private buildings, finishes) is precisely the order of the first seven books of *De architectura.* Available evidence leaves little room to doubt that the same general order obtained in the urbanization of the Iberian peninsula, for instance, or in other areas of Augustan colonization, at least in the western provinces.[220] In spite of many variations in their size and shape, archaeologists have little difficulty in identifying the vestiges of any Roman town, temple, or house as indeed Roman.

Some towns were built in previously uninhabited locations; others, like Conimbriga in Lusitania for example, over existing towns.[221] All, in recognizable conformity with the civilizers' schema, left little or no trace of the many heterogeneous cultures so effaced; all, through their newly acquired coherence (each with each, and all to all), "increased" the *corpus* of Roman *imperium* and testified to its greatness and majesty. And if adherence to the schema was eager and willing, the persuasive force of the testimony and the majesty of the *imperium* to which it testified increased proportionally.[222]

These cities also, invariably, testified to the greatness of the Imperator who was their center and origin: in the temples dedicated to his cult which were sometimes the first monumental building to be erected in a new city, in his statues, in the coins that bore his image, in the Latin inscriptions that recorded his deeds, and of course in their names: Augustodunum (Autun), Augusta Emerita (Mérida), Augusta Raurica (Augst), Augusta Suessionum (Soissons), and so on.[223]

Systematic urbanization like that carried out in the western provinces was not undertaken in the Greek east, where, Romans acknowledged, civilization had been invented, but where, they also claimed, civilization was now in a sorry state of decline.[224] Roman architectural activity in the east—again there is little or none that dates from before the time of Augustus—while it included the foundation of colonies, was less a question of creation *ex* (barbarian) *nihilo* than one of renewal and reform. In the preface to book 9, Vitruvius concludes his vindication of the importance of "commentaries" by stressing that these are not only useful to all peoples (*omnes gentes*) but directed, also, *ad mores corrigendos,* to the "correction" of *mores* or customs.[225] Judiciously exercised by Roman civilizers, architecture, the art of the geometrical footprint, was also a moral corrective.[226]

Caesar's refoundation of Corinth, Achaean port city of legendary decadence, the "squaring" of its territory, and its rebuilding under Augustus read like a paradigm of corrective renewal. Corinth, as discussed in chapter 3, is where Vitruvius situates the birth of the Corinthian capital in an etiology whose entire point is renewal.[227] The first city Augustus himself founded in Greece was Nikopolis, "city of victory," built on the site of his camp at Actium in order, says Suetonius, "to extend the fame of his victory and perpetuate its memory," and where, according to Dio Cassius, on the spot where he had had his tent he built a temple to Apollo "on a foundation of squared stones."[228] Populated with Greek colonists relocated from surrounding towns, Nikopolis was to have replaced Athens as the new center of the Greek world.[229]

Most astonishing among Augustan colonies in Greek Asia Minor was Antioch in Pisidia, refounded as the Latin-speaking city of Antioch Caesarea in 25 B.C. as an outpost of *romanitas* in the hills of the newly annexed province of Galatia.[230] The monumental focus of the city, dominating it from the highest point at its eastern edge, was a richly ornamented, west-facing, tetrastyle Corinthian Temple of Augustus. It was situated at the center of a deep, rock-cut hemicycle that extended the east side of the enclosed, nearly square temple precinct, whose plan closely resembles that of the Forum of Augustus at Rome, dedicated in the same year of 2 B.C.[231] The entrance to the temple precinct was through a triumphal gate to the west of it, on which, after his death, Augustus's *Res gestae,* his achievements, were inscribed in Latin.[232]

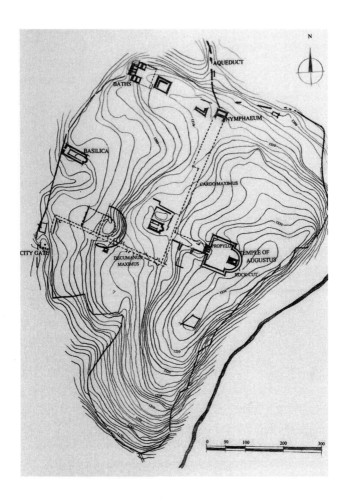

Plan of Pisidian Antioch in Galatia (Turkey).

·THE·TEMPLE·OF·AVGVSTVS·
ANTIOCH·OF·PISIDIA

CONJECTVRAL·RESTORATION·   ·FREDERICK·JAMES·WOOD

Reconstructed facade of the Temple of Augustus in Pisidian Antioch, dedicated 2 B.C., after Woodbridge. Kelsey Museum of Archaeology archive, Ann Arbor, Michigan (8.106).

A frieze of spiraling acanthus, virtually identical to those of contemporary temples of the imperial cult in other parts of the Roman world, ornamented the upper part of the temple's cella wall.[233] Large acanthus leaf acroteria sprouted on the gable ends and on the peak of the west pediment. The lush vegetation of the central acroterion, sculpted in marble and measuring over a meter and a half high, grows up around a small legless female figure at the center and nearly engulfs her. Her draped torso emerges from an acanthus leaf skirt—leafage which the lower part of her body in turn appears to generate along with the rest of the foliage that surrounds her. She wears a basketlike head-dress (a *calathos*) on which a large sun disk is balanced, like a host in a monstrance.[234] At dawn, when the sun rose behind the west-facing Temple of Augustus at Antioch Caesarea, the sun's own rays would have haloed the stone disk in the acroterion with its radiance.[235]

To a reader of Vitruvius, the image in the acroterion—the girl, the basket, the acanthus that grows up around it—looks almost like an iconic transcription of his story about the origin of the Corinthian capital.[236] Vitruvius does not mention the sun in his etiology, but he does say that the acanthus sprouted in the spring, and it goes without saying that sunlight made it sprout. And in book 9 he presents the sun's attractive power to draw plants upward toward itself as an argument for its cosmic hegemony.[237] Imagining the acroterion figure backlit at sunrise, one is also inevitably reminded of why it is, Vitruvius says, that temples ought to face west: so that "people undertaking vows will gaze at once upon the temple, on the sun rising in the eastern sky, and on the images themselves that also seem to rise in the east and gaze in turn upon those praying."[238]

Acroterion from the west pediment of the Temple of Augustus at Antioch in Pisidia, after Woodbridge. Kelsey Museum of Archaeology archive, Ann Arbor, Michigan.

In the Roman east, when the sun rose over Antioch Caesarea it rose over the Temple of Augustus, just as, at Rome, when it rose over the Forum Romanum it rose over the west-facing Temple of Divus Julius; or again just as when, in the west, it rose over Tarraco (Tarragona) in Spain, it rose over another west-facing Temple of Augustus—one that, according to Tacitus, "gave an example to all the provinces."[239] When the sun rose on the chest of the statue of Augustus from Prima Porta, it rose over the whole Roman world, binding east and west together in the body of the king. Together, temples like the ones just mentioned made the rhetoric of the statue a palpable matter of fact.

Even Greek cities that were not new foundations, or refoundations, acclaimed Augustus as *ktistês*, "founder"; Tralles, in Lydia, for instance, which he had rebuilt after an earthquake in 26 B.C., and also important cities such as Ephesus and Athens, whose civic centers, like those of most cities in the Greek east, underwent extensive construction or reconstruction initiated, once again, early in the Augustan principate.[240]

There is, in the conventional modern sense, no single identifiable master plan or standard blueprint to be extrapolated from these centers. Nevertheless, recent and ongoing archaeological research points, through analogous resemblances, to certain shared diagrammatic criteria (whose formal instantiation could, and did, vary greatly). These, loosely, are enclosure or limit, axiality—the "squaring" that was the schematic replication of *Roma quadrata*—and a hierarchization of spaces dominated by the *princeps* and/or his family, whose dynastic presence was the nexus of the spatial coherence that was the overriding aim of such interventions and for which enclosure and squaring, either independently or together, served as the formal means.[241]

The upper or "state" agora at Ephesus, developed on Hellenistic foundations in the Augustan period, is an important early example, one in which Pierre Gros has deciphered an organizational schema of relations with semantic (rather than strictly formal) equivalents not only in the Greek east but all over the Roman world.[242] These, as Gros and others have noted, are the same semantic relations that govern the forum and basilica at the Augustan veteran colony of Julia Fanestris (Fano) in northern Italy, whose building Vitruvius claims to have been charged with and which he describes in some detail in the first chapter of book 5, his book on "the arrangement of public places."[243]

In Athens, the squaring of the agora, where before Augustus virtually no building had ever stood at right angles to another, and where, even in Hellenistic times, the central space had never been encroached upon, was early and dramatic.[244] Fronted with a portico of Corinthian columns, the massive Odeon of Agrippa, built on a north-south axis at right angles to the middle stoa, and inaugurated in 15 B.C., penetrated the space to occupy over a third of the area west of the Panathenaic way.[245] A few years later, a fifth-century B.C. Doric temple of Ares (Mars, from whom Romans claimed descent through Romulus) was moved from a site thirteen kilometers away and reerected on an east-west axis in the northwest sector of the agora.[246] At the 90-degree intersection of the two invasively "corrective" lines introduced by the relocated temple and the huge new theater building stood Ares' altar, dedicated to Gaius Caesar (the "new Ares" who was Agrippa's son and Augustus's grandson and heir, also represented by the Amor at the feet of the Prima Porta Augustus) in a spatialization of *imperium* that gave the agora something it had never had before: a geometrical center,[247] one whose

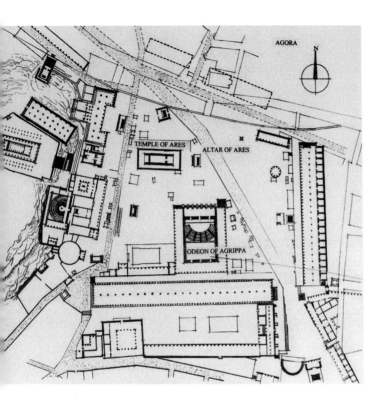

The Athenian agora in the second century A.D.

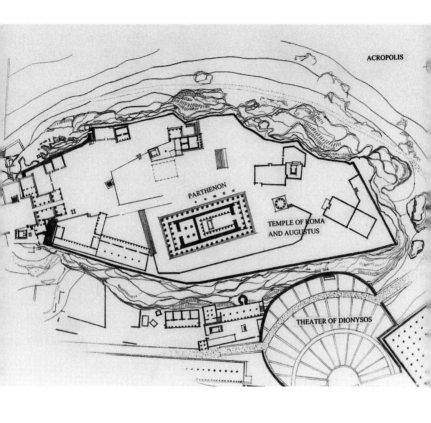

ACROPOLIS

PARTHENON

TEMPLE OF ROMA
AND AUGUSTUS

THEATER OF DIONYSOS

The Athenian Acropolis in the second century A.D.

dynastic referent related it at once to Rome and to all other analogous centers. Each to each, and all to all.

Far less intrusive, but in keeping with the same schema,
was the erection in about 20 B.C. of the circular monopteros
shrine on the Athenian Acropolis, dedicated "to the Goddess
Roma and Augustus Caesar by the people of Athens." Some
scholars now maintain that this monument was built in com-
memoration of the Parthians' return of the standards that was
also celebrated on the cuirass of the Prima Porta Augustus.[248] It
should be stressed that this intervention was the Athenians' own
initiative—one with parallels in countless similar local initia-
tives which, as Simon Price has argued, were the means
whereby Greeks represented Roman power to themselves in
terms they could understand.[249] The terms the Athenians chose
for its representation in the Temple of Roma and Augustus on
the Athenian Acropolis are worth reviewing.

Just under twenty-five meters from the east front of the
Parthenon, and located precisely on its east-west axis—an axiality that here, as in the agora, was without precedent—the
monopteral temple, built of Pentelic marble, consisted of a ring
of nine Ionic columns (one thinks of nine Muses) on a two-
stepped circular crepis.[250] Less precise, but close enough to appear deliberate, is its north-south axial relation with the Theater
of Dionysos on the south slope of the Acropolis below.[251] The
Temple of Roma and Augustus is sited at the intersection (nearly
ninety degrees) of these two axes, to determine the position of
which would have involved a conceptual flattening out of considerable vertical accidents of topography, to say the least. It would,
in other words, have entailed imagining the Acropolis strictly in
plan, with only two dimensions, instead of its rather obvious

three. Flat, one might recall, is how Vitruvius imagines the man he circles and then squares in the first chapter of book 3.

Urbanization in the western Roman provinces was carried out in fairly strict conformity with a similar two-dimensional view.[252] Coherence, for the Romans, appears to have been imaginable chiefly in terms of planar surfaces. The siting of the Temple of Roma and Augustus, which shows that the Athenians understood, and could if necessary adapt to, this kind of two-dimensional imagining, gave the southeast terrace of the Acropolis a new geometric and dynastic centrality.[253] A very few years later, the relation of the Temple of Roma and Augustus to the Theater of Dionysos and to the Parthenon—its relation to theater and temple—was to be precisely duplicated in the central position given to the altar of Ares dedicated to Gaius Caesar in the agora.

Inside the ring of the nine columns of the monopteros on the Acropolis and, since there was no cella, visible from all directions, cult statues of Roma and Augustus probably faced east, toward the wider intercolumniation between the two columns on that side. Although the temple was circular—twenty-five Attic feet in diameter at the top of the stylobate—it was built on a square foundation, into which a geison block from the Erechtheion was integrated. The Erechtheion, late fifth-century B.C. temple of Athena Polias, also supplied the model for the new temple's Ionic order.

The temple itself, the squaring that made it the focus of two of Athens's most important public monuments, and the circle-in-square geometry of its plan all belonged to Roma and Augustus for whom the shrine was built. Its materials, including especially its refined ornamental expression, were Greek, with direct references to the Erechtheion, the shrine that, more than any other Athenian temple, was a reliquary of the entire Athenian past whose civilizing torch, as the Athenians here publicly affirmed, had now passed to Rome.[254] When the sun rose in the east to illuminate Phidias's colossal gold-and-ivory statue of Athena in the cella of the Parthenon, it now rose over the Temple of Roma and Augustus.[255]

The enterprise is all too easily dismissed as servile flattery.[256] One might, less loftily, appreciate how perceptively, realistically, and even elegantly it expresses precisely what Romans would have wanted to hear in language they would have clearly understood: a graceful acknowledgment by the Athenians, who, as it turned out, had wrongly backed Mark Antony's losing side during the civil wars, that they stood "corrected."[257] One must above all appreciate that the Temple of Roma and Augustus inserted the Athenian Acropolis into the worldwide network of public places that made Roman *imperium* a *corpus* congruent with the king's. It is absurd, given the circumstances, to imagine wishfully that the Athenians might not have wanted to be part of that victorious imperial body or to censure adherence to it as sycophancy. If coherence was to be sustained, what alternative was there?

Of particular interest is the Athenians' early grasp of recognizably appropriate means for signifying their adherence. What it signals is schematic knowledge that seems to have been common both to Roman benefactors like Agrippa, builder of the Odeon in the agora, and to Pammenes, the Athenian "priest of the Goddess Roma and Augustus the Savior" under whose auspices the Temple of Roma and Augustus on the Acropolis was built.[258] Similar architectural knowledge was as familiar, appar-

The acroterion from the west pediment of the Temple of Augustus in Pisidian Antioch. Kelsey Museum of Archaeology archive, Ann Arbor, Michigan (Swain 7.1668).

ently, to the Roman veterans who built Pisidian Antioch as it was to ambitious Gauls who assisted in the urbanization of the western provinces or to Britons building *fora, templa,* and *theatra* in the newly conquered hinterland.[259] Marked by an overriding concern for coherence and continuity, this is the same knowledge that permeated Augustus's transformation of Rome from brick to marble,[260] in keeping, as Suetonius reports, with the "majesty of *imperium*"—a boast to which Dio Cassius gives the weight of famous last words. "I leave stony-skinned the Rome of earth I received as an inheritance," he has Augustus say on his deathbed. "In this," Dio glosses, "he was not exactly referring to the manner of building itself, but to the strength of his rule [*archē*]."[261] Had Dio Cassius been writing in Latin, he would have used the word *imperium.*

To encase *imperium* in a stony skin as permanent and impermeable as that of the cuirassed statue of Augustus from Prima Porta: that, ultimately, is the point of assembling and ordering the knowledge Vitruvius calls *architectura* into a complete *corpus.*[262] *De architectura,* the perfect body of empire.

CONCLUSION

Augustus's deathbed pronouncement on the stony skin of Roman *imperium* was, apparently, not quite his final word. According to Suetonius, the dying emperor asked for a mirror, "had his hair combed and falling jaws set straight," and then, as Dio Cassius also reports, requested applause like a comic actor about to leave the stage at the end of a farce.[1] Thus, adds Dio with a note of disapproval, "did he sum up in a single assessment the whole of men's lives."[2] The freedom to make such assessments—to let slip his mask and declare life a comedy—was the prerogative of a dying man. *Architectura,* the judiciously exercised knowledge of the architect, operated in the land of the living.

The evidence surveyed in the last chapter of this study leaves little room to doubt that there was a fit between the body of *De architectura* and the as-built body of Roman *imperium* that overlay the ancient world to constitute its stony skin of unchallengeable reality. This is not apparent at a small scale; in, for instance, the details of molding profiles, the proportions of column orders, or the architectural fantasies of late second style mural paintings Vitruvius objects to so strenuously.[3] The scholar who compares such practices to the *rationes* of *De architectura* is bound to find its author out of step. Vitruvius was looking at a rather larger picture, and so, to do him justice, should his readers.

This raises two issues I would like to address by way of conclusion. The first concerns the apparent exclusivity of the Roman world's architectural "mask." The second is the nature of the fit between the body of *De architectura* and the *corpus* of Roman *imperium*.

To begin with the mask. If Romans eventually came to view the entire world as the *princeps's temenos* (to recall the terms of Dio Cassius's fictitious debate), it was because of architecture.[4] Not architecture in the modern sense that, conventionally at least, limits its referents to building. It was, rather, because of the tripartite whole of Vitruvian *architectura*—building, gnomonics, and machines—that *imperium* could appear as a *corpus* ruled by the nod, the soul, and the mind of its king.[5]

This world-body was of course a Roman perception. It did not include territories inhabited by Chinese or Indians, or indeed those inhabited by any people living beyond the limits of Roman political and military control; peoples who, in turn, would never have described the world—their worlds—as Roman.[6] For Romans, as for Vitruvius, *omnes gentes* (all peoples) meant *omnes gentes subactae,* "all *subjected* peoples."[7]

Nor, within the confines of the empire, would peasants, bandits, slaves, or women have been likely to qualify themselves as adherents of Roman *imperium,* living as they did in marginal worlds incommensurate with its foursquare, kingly body.[8] My point here is that the "body of empire" was not only limited by the extent of Roman conquest. Within that extent, the *corpus* of *imperium* was almost entirely constituted by the network of cities newly built or rebuilt in the wake of conquest, where citizens (predominantly male) gathered in *fora,* sacrificed before *templa,* were entertained in *theatra,* and lived in keeping with imperial solar time.[9] The *corpus* of *imperium* was formed by the body of architecture whose naturally grounded *rationes,* delineated in *De architectura,* were in turn to forge the bonds of its lasting coherence.

The *corpus* of *architectura* was, reciprocally, shaped by the body of empire. Vitruvius's text circles the world on several occasions, but never once oversteps the boundaries of its specifically Augustan limits.[10] Even Britain remains unmentioned, although Caesar, and very possibly Vitruvius with him, campaigned there in 55 B.C.[11] But Caesar's British campaign was unsuccessful and Rome would only annex the province 88 years later. Vitruvius's complete delineation of all the *rationes* of his discipline is a body circumscribed by the extent of conquest, whose demonstration or "proof" he means architecture to be.[12] As the summation of learning, the discipline he calls a *summum templum* is as much a guarantee of empire as the great Temple of Jupiter on the Capitol at Rome, highest temple of the city and of the world.[13]

It goes without saying that no modern historian can comfortably view the world in such unwaveringly Romanocentric terms.[14] For most moderns there are many worlds, and the overwhelming trend in current scholarship has been to bypass master narratives and focus instead on the fragmentary, the subversive, the marginal, the feminine. But if the body of architecture Vitruvius wrote—a master narrative if ever there was one—was as much shaped by Romanocentricity as it was itself meant to create and maintain that shape, what is a modern historian to make of *architectura* so circumscribed? To what extent did (does) Vitruvius's originary delineation of it make the discipline itself a master narrative of master races? If the fundamental role of architecture is to make humans at home in the world, Vitruvius's narrative raises the question, in what world? And on whose terms? Similarly, if architecture is a body, a careful reader of Vitruvius is bound, now, to ask, whose?

This leads me to the question of fit and its implications. In order to perceive the fit between Vitruvius's book and the Augustan empire, one must, on the one hand, consider the *whole* of *De architectura* and, on the other, the *whole* of the as-built Roman world. It is a panoramic vision, certainly—not unlike the world-dominant Roman view, in fact.

The book, written for Augustus Caesar, and declared to be a body, is *about* architecture, which Vitruvius says is a whole consisting of three parts: building, *gnomonice,* and machines that include engines of war.[15] What we now call the Roman empire, also declared to be a body, was brought into being during the reign of Augustus *by* architecture: buildings, gnomonics, and machines. Viewed as wholes, each of these bodies, that of the book (*corpus architecturae*) and that of the world (*corpus imperii*), emerges as a tightly knit assembly of interrelated parts, made coherent through their common referent in the body of the king.

To show that, or exactly how, the Vitruvian diagram might have been used by Augustan architects and builders has not been my aim, nor has my point been to claim the existence of direct causal links between *De architectura* and the emergence of the Roman world-body during the early Empire. Indeed, as I have already suggested, if chains of causes there are, they lead as much from the Roman world-body to *De architectura* as in the other direction.

To reconstruct the precise role Vitruvius's text played in

determining the order of Roman architectural operations has not been my purpose either. Rather, I read the congruence of textual diagram and spatial reality less as evidence of the former's implementation than as an indispensable schema for understanding that spatial reality. The architectural reality of Roman *imperium* in turn provides the frame for assessing what Vitruvius meant to say in "writing the body of architecture."

Whether or not Vitruvius's contemporaries, his dedicatee in particular, saw the potential for this mutually entailing fit between book-body and world-body must remain speculation, although it is obvious to me that Vitruvius intended them to do so and it seems more than probable that many, especially Augustus, did. But the perception of this fit, shaped as it is by hindsight, is above all a historical perception, whose potential, likewise, is principally of historical value.

Whether, and on what terms, Vitruvius's medieval and Renaissance followers read his book as a diagram of the world, and (if they did) of *what* world they saw it as a diagram, suggests fertile ground for further study. So does the relation between the eventual superfluity of European kings and the virtually simultaneous degradation of the "body of architecture" that accompanied Vitruvius's loss of prestige in the eighteenth century. To reread Vitruvius, then, is to ask again what exactly his later followers and detractors read—or thought they were reading.

In sum, the fit between the Vitruvian body of architecture and the Augustan body of empire leads to the inevitable conclusion that architecture first acquired precise delineation as a discipline—as *the* discipline, the one that "demonstrates everything the other arts achieve"—in mutual dependence with the imperial project of fashioning the world as a single Roman body.[16] The Roman world, as most historians now view it, was neither single or complete. Nor, as critics have often pointed out, is *De architectura*. Both the book and the Roman world were, on the modern view, deliberate artifices; fictions, literally; things made. The study of culture, as of the discipline Vitruvius defends as *his,* the dominant culture's ultimate authorization, is in the end the study of such fictions. Less for the purpose of unmasking them than to try to understand what they mean: in the land of the living.

NOTES

ABBREVIATIONS

CIL   *Corpus inscriptionum latinarum.* Berlin, 1863–.

IG   *Inscriptiones graecae.* Berlin, 1873–.

LIMC   *Lexicon iconographicum mythologiae classicae.* Zurich, 1981–1997.

TLL   *Thesaurus linguae latinae.* Leipzig, 1900–.

INTRODUCTION

1 Perrault 1683, p. xviii.

2 The work may have been begun in the 30s but was probably not completed until the 20s. For recent views on the date and identity of Vitruvius and reviews of previous literature on the subject, Baldwin 1990; Fleury, Vitruvius 1990, pp. ix–xxiv. Romano 1987, pp. 17–20, argues that it was written between 27 and 23, with the prefaces to each of the ten books written later. Vitruvius 2.pref.4: "old age has spoiled my appearance, bad health has sapped my strength" (*faciem deformavit aetas, valetudo detraxit vires*). Romans considered old age to begin at forty-six (Cicero *De senectute* 60), so Vitruvius was probably in his fifties. His official position seems to have been that of *scriba armamentarius,* which made him a member of the *ordo apparitorum,* the class of Roman public servants situated between the equestrian order and the *plebs* (Gros 1994a, with Purcell 1983, Cohen 1984, Dumougin 1988, p. 706). Ruffel and Soubiran 1962, p. 142, give a succinct and plausible outline of Vitruvius's career. Numerological evidence has recently led Lionel March to speculate that Vitruvius and the late republican polymath Marcus Terentius Varro were one and the same person (March 1998, pp. 137–140).

3 The only other known ancient work on architecture, a thirty-page Byzantine *opusculum* of the first half of the sixth century A.D. written by one

Julian of Ascalon, deals with domestic construction in urban Palestine (Saliou 1994 and 1996; Hakim 2001). First comprehensive account of architecture: Vitruvius 4.pref. Germann 1991, pp. 214–236, dates the end of what he calls "Vitruvianism" to the eighteenth century and the work of Jean-Nicolas-Louis Durand. On Durand's functionalism as a historical watershed, Pérez-Gómez 1983, pp. 298–326.

4 In fact, the reception of Vitruvius was continuous throughout the Middle Ages: Koch 1951, p. 15; Ciapponi 1960, p. 98; Schuler 1999. The Harley manuscript (Harleianus 2767, now in the British Museum) is Carolingian and the oldest of the known Vitruvius manuscripts. On the manuscripts, Krinsky 1967, who documents seventy-eight of them; Sgarbi 1993.

5 For a complete listing of all known Vitruvius editions, translations, and major commentaries from the *editio princeps* of 1486 to 1915, see Ebhardt 1918. For an update to 1982, Callebat et al. 1984, pp. vii–xiii.

6 The *editio princeps* of *De re aedificatoria* appeared in 1485 but had already been circulating in manuscript for some time. On Alberti's as an "inaugural text," Choay 1988. Vitruvius's influence in the Renaissance is dealt with in Guillaume 1988; Germann 1991; Kruft 1994, pp. 66–72; Hart 1998; Payne 1999.

7 In the notes to his translation of *De architectura* (Perrault, Vitruvius 1673) and especially his *Ordonnance des cinq espèces de colonnes* (Perrault 1683, and McEwen 1998 with references).

8 Perrault 1683, p. xviii, cited in the epigraph above.

9 Recent scholarship has been reviewed twice by Pierre Gros: in his 1982 article in the *Aufsteig und Niedergang der römischen Welt*, and in his introduction to *Le projet de Vitruve* (1994).

10 See note 2 above.

11 Wesenberg 1983, 1984a, 1989, and 1994. Lothar Haselberger's discovery of 200 square meters of drawings etched onto the walls of the *adyton* of the Hellenistic Temple of Apollo at Didyma was another landmark

(Haselberger 1983 and 1984). See also the work of Knell 1985, Coulton 1989, and especially Wilson Jones 2000a.

12 Romano 1987. On Vitruvius's influences and intellectual milieu, see also Novara 1983 and 1994; Rawson 1985, passim.

13 Callebat 1982, 1992, and 1994. On Vitruvius's language, see also Corso and Romano, Vitruvius 1997, pp. lxxix–xcv.

14 Fleury 1993.

15 The first volume published was Book 9 (Soubiran, Vitruvius 1969). Books 1 (Fleury, 1990), 2 (Callebat et al., 1999), 3 and 4 (Gros, 1990 and 1992), 7 (Liou et al., 1995), 8 (Callebat, 1973), and 10 (Callebat and Fleury, 1986) are also now available. Books 5 and 6 are still in preparation.

16 This illustrated Italian edition has been published along with Rose's Latin text of 1867 (Corso and Romano, Vitruvius 1997; for the Latin, Rose and Müller-Strübing, Vitruvius 1867). It replaces Silvio Ferri's translation (Ferri, Vitruvius 1960) of Books 1 to 7 only. A more modest Italian translation appeared a year after the Corso and Romano edition (Bossalino, Vitruvius 1998).

17 Gros has dealt with questions as diverse as the philosophical foundations of Vitruvius's understanding of architectural harmony (1989a), his illustrations (1996b), and the rhetoric of architectural authority (1989b, 1991a), among other topics.

18 Gros 1971, 1973, 1975, and 1994a. On variety and inventiveness in Roman architecture, also Wilson Jones 2000a.

19 Gros 1994a and 1996b; Brown 1963.

20 For the terms, Sallmann 1984, p. 12. Cf. Gros 1994a, pp. 75–76.

21 He barely rates a mention in volumes IX and X, the relevant volumes of the new edition of the *Cambridge Ancient History,* for example. Rawson 1985 allows him a fair amount of attention in her study of intellectual life in the late republic, but finds him garrulous, pretentious, and inaccurate. MacMullen 2000, p. 128, also calls him pretentious.

22 Rowland and Howe, Vitruvius 1999, with Rowland's English translation and Howe's illustrated commentary.

23 McKay 1985. The book is only 88 pages long.

24 Vitruvius conferences include *Architecture et société*, Rome, 1980 (published 1983); *Bauplanung und Bautheorie der Antike*, Berlin, 1983 (1984); *Vitruv-Kolloquium Darmstadt*, Darmstadt, 1982 (1984); *Munus non ingratum*, Leiden 1987 (Geertman and de Jong 1989); *Le projet de Vitruve*, Rome 1993 (1994).

25 Rykwert's work runs from his early *On Adam's House in Paradise* (1981, first published 1972) to his recent *The Dancing Column* (1996), as well as countless articles (for a selection, Rykwert 1982). Other explorations of meaning in Vitruvius include Hersey 1966 and 1988 and Onians 1988. Pollitt 1974 draws heavily on Vitruvius in his work on ancient critical terms. For all of these scholars, including Wilson Jones 2000a which contains a chapter on Vitruvius, *De architectura* is only a part, not the focus, of the study.

26 The metaphor is the dominant theme of Rykwert 1996. A Rykwert *Festschrift* on the topic has recently appeared: George Dodds and Robert Tavernor, eds., *Body and Building* (Cambridge, Mass., and London, 2002).

27 On trees in *Natural History*, book 16, on painting in book 35, and on stones in book 36.

28 Frontinus *De aquis* 1.25.

29 See Plommer 1973.

30 Servius *Ad Aeneidem* 6.43.

31 Sidonius Apollinaris *Epistulae* 4.3.5. On the ancient reception of Vitruvius, Pellati 1921; Fleury, Vitruvius 1990, pp. ix–x.

32 On the epigraphic evidence, Thielscher 1961; Ruffel and Soubiran 1962.

33 "Corpus emendatum architecturae": Vitruvius 9.8.15. See also 2.1.8, 4.pref.1, 5.pref.5, 6.pref.7, 7.pref.10, 7.pref.14, 10.pref.4, 10.16.12.

34 Vitruvius 4.pref.1: "Cum animadvertissem, Imperator, plures de architectura praecepta voluminaque commentariorum non ordinata sed in-

cepta uti particulas errabundas reliquisse, dignam et utilissimam rem putavi tantae disciplinae corpus ad perfectam ordinationem perducere et praescriptas in singulis voluminibus singulorum generum qualitates explicare."

35 Gros, Vitruvius 1992, p. xiii. Vitruvius's mainly Greek sources are listed, for the most part, in the preface to book 7. On Vitruvius's originality, Gros 1975, p. 986; Gros 1994a, p. 90. See also Novara 1983, p. 288; Novara 1994, p. 57; Romano 1987, pp. 186–187; Callebat 1989; Kessissoglu 1993.

36 Vitruvius 6.pref.5: "Ideo notities parum est adsecuta."

37 Earl 1961, ch. 2; Knoche 1967; Brunt 1978, pp. 162, 183.

38 Epigraphic anonymity of architects: Gros 1983, pp. 427–428; Anderson 1997, pp. 68–75; Wilson Jones 2000a, pp. 19–20.

39 Vitruvius as *scriba armamentarius:* above, n. 2; lack of writing ability: Vitruvius 1.1.18. Recent reassessments, however, mitigate the poor view popular since the time of Alberti's unequivocal censure of Vitruvius's style in the fifteenth century (Alberti 1988, p. 154; Callebat 1982 and 1994). Vitruvius 6.pref.5: "Sed tamen his voluminibus editis, ut spero, etiam posteris ero notus"; 6.pref.7: "corpus architecturae rationesque eius putavi diligentissime conscribendas, opinans munus omnibus gentibus non ingratum futurum."

40 Cicero *De re publica* 5. "Originality" is an anachronistic term and would have no value in such a context. The Latin adjective *originalis* is postclassical and meant "primitive" (Lewis and Short 1962, s.v. *originalis*), which is something no civilized Roman would have aspired to.

41 Suetonius *Divus Augustus* 28.3; Gros 1994a, p. 89.

42 Novara 1983 and 1994.

43 Vitruvius 6.pref.7.

44 Vitruvius 4.pref.1; Novara 1994, p. 57.

45 Fensterbusch, Vitruvius 1964, translating 5.pref.5; Gros, Vitruvius 1992 for 4.pref.1; Soubiran, Vitruvius 1969 for 9.8.15; Corso and Romano, Vitruvius 1997 for 10.16.12; Granger, Vitruvius 1931 for 2.1.8.

Exceptionally, Ingrid Rowland (Rowland and Howe, Vitruvius 1999) renders 2.1.8 (*cum corpus architecturae scriberem*) "when I set out to write about the whole body of architecture," using the literal English equivalent of Vitruvius's "corpus" in her translation. But she reverts to "the whole of the discipline" and its "comprehensive account" at other points where Vitruvius writes *corpus* (4.pref.1, 9.1.15).

46 *TLL* IV, s.v. *corpus*, 1020–1021. Cicero *Ad Quintum fratrem* 2.11.4 and *Ad familiares* 5.12.4.

47 Age of Vitruvius's cultural formation: Schrijvers 1989a; Rawson 1985, p. vii. Cicero and Varro named: Vitruvius 9.pref.17. Vitruvius as part of the "encyclopedic" movement: Callebat 1989.

48 Moatti 1988, pp. 405–406; Moatti 1991; and Moatti 1997, pp. 109–124.

49 *TLL* IV, s.v. *corpus*, 1020–1021.

50 Romano 1987, ch. 1: "Vitruvio augusteo."

51 Vitruvius 1.pref.2. Given the Roman distaste for the title, Augustus was not called king (*rex*) at Rome. That he was *understood* as a king in virtually every other part of the Roman world, and this almost immediately after his defeat of Mark Antony in 31 B.C., has been demonstrated by Millar 1984. Cf. Dio Cassius 52.1.1. Modern literature on the period, beginning with Syme 1939, is abundant. Besides the new editions of volumes IX and X of the *Cambridge Ancient History,* with their exhaustive bibliographies, two useful collections of essays are Millar and Segal 1984 and Raaflaub and Toher 1990. The exhibition catalogue *Kaiser Augustus und die verlorene Republik* (Hofter et al. 1988) surveys the time of transition through the art and architecture of the period, as do Simon 1986 and most especially Zanker 1988.

52 Ramage 1987, p. 63; Vitruvius 1.pref.1: "Cum divina tua mens et numen, Imperator Caesar, imperio potiretur orbis terrarum invictaque virtute cunctis hostibus stratis." See also Grenade 1961, pp. 106–107, 149–151; Millar 1973, p. 66.

53 Augustus *Res gestae* 34.2; Ovid *Fasti* 1.607–616; Suetonius *Divus Augustus* 7.2, drawing on the Augustan writer Verrius Flaccus; Florus

Epitome 2.34.66; Dio Cassius 53.16.4. On the title Augustus, Gagé 1930; Erkell 1952; Dumézil 1957; Pollini 1993, pp. 262–263; Galinsky 1996, pp. 12–21; Price 1996, p. 822.

54 Kienast 1982a, pp. 336–365; Ovid *Tristia* 2.226. Cf. Béranger 1953, pp. 218–252; Kienast 1982b, who cites Ovid's as the first use of the phrase (p. 5); Richardson 1991.

55 Vitruvius 1.pref.2: *haec tibi scribere coepi*, "I began to write this work *for you*," i.e., Augustus.

56 *Angelos* (whence "angel") is the Greek word for messenger.

1 THE ANGELIC BODY

1 Vitruvius 4.pref.1.

2 On the omnipresence of writing in the Roman city, Corbier 1987.

3 Cicero *Academica* 1.9. Cf. Moatti 1988, 1991, and 1997, pp. 109–120; Beard 1991. On Varro, Skydsgaard 1968; Rawson 1985, passim; Griffin 1994, pp. 703–708; Tarver 1997.

4 Gordon 1990b, pp. 184–191. Cf. Beard 1991, pp. 54–55; Frézouls 1989, p. 234.

5 Goody 1977, pp. 52–111. Cf. Moatti 1988, p. 422; Beard 1991, p. 55.

6 Vitruvius 1.1.3.: "litteratus sit, peritus graphidos, eruditus geometria, historias complures noverit, philosophos diligenter audierit, musicam scierit, medicinae non sit ingnarus, responsa iurisconsultorum noverit, astrologiam caelique rationes cognitas habeat." According to Cornelius Nepos, a minor historian of the first century B.C. contemporary with Vitruvius, "the term *literatus* is commonly applied to those who can speak or write about anything judiciously, knowledgeably and with insight" (Suetonius *De grammaticis* 4). That Vitruvius has writing specifically in mind is born out by his ensuing account of what, for an architect, being *literatus* entails.

7 Vitruvius 1.1.4: "Litteras architectum scire oportet uti commentariis memoriam firmiorem efficere possit."

8 See Fleury, Vitruvius 1990, pp. 71–72, where the various options are reviewed.

9 Lewis and Short 1962, s.v. *firmus.*

10 Livy *Ab urbe condita* 6.1.2. Cf. Jaeger 1993, whose translation (p. 363) is cited here.

11 Vitruvius 1.1.4. See also 1.1.12, 2.8.8, 4.pref.1, 7.pref.1, 7.pref.14, 7.pref.17. Cf. Fleury, Vitruvius 1990, pp. 94–95.

12 Vitruvius 7.pref.1.

13 Vitruvius 7.pref.2.

14 Bömer 1953; Rüpke 1992. See also Skydsgaard 1968, pp. 110–121; Nicolet 1991, p. 101; De Laine 1996, p. 118.

15 The inscription, dating from the time of Marcus Aurelius (late second century A.D.), was first published in Seston and Euzennat 1971. For full documentation, Sherwin-White 1973. Cf. Millar 1984, p. 50.

16 Aulus Gellius *Noctes atticae* 14.7.2.

17 Aulus Gellius *Noctes atticae* 14.7.3. Cf. Moatti 1988, p. 424; Moatti 1991, p. 34.

18 Aulus Gellius *Noctes atticae* 14.7.4.

19 The *officium* of architecture: Vitruvius 2.pref.5, 2.1.8.

20 Frontinus *De aquis* 1.25; pref.2. De Laine 1996.

21 Sallmann 1984; Gros 1994a and 1996b. But see De Laine 1996.

22 Read in connection with the reference in Frontinus (*De aquis* 1.25), Vitruvius's book 8, on water, appears to reflect a period of service to Agrippa who was in charge of Rome's water supply from 33 B.C. Callebat, Vitruvius 1973, p. x; Fleury, Vitruvius 1990, p. xiv.

23 Frontinus *De aquis* 2.99.

24 Pliny *Natural History* 3.17. On Agrippa's map and its commentary, see especially Nicolet 1991, ch. 5. Also Roddaz 1984, pp. 291–293 and 572–587; Rüpke 1992, p. 213; Wiseman 1992. Fragments of the commentary are collected in Klotz 1931, pp. 386–486. On the *urbis-orbis* trope, which first became current in the late republic, Bréguet 1969.

25 The two sources are Julius Honorius and a so-called Aethicus, both of the late fourth or early fifth century A.D. For Julius Honorius, Riese 1878, pp. 21–55; for "Aethicus," Riese, pp. 71–103. Nicolet and Gautier-Dalché 1986; Purcell 1990; Nicolet 1991, p. 96; Wiseman 1992, p. 26.

26 Nicolet 1991, pp. 111–113.

27 Wiseman 1992, p. 41.

28 "Aethicus" in Riese 1878, pp. 71–72. Cf. Nicolet and Gautier-Dalché 1986, pp. 192–194; Wiseman 1992. The translation follows Wiseman (p. 26).

29 Vitruvius 1.pref.1: "When your divine mind and power, Imperator Caesar, were seizing command of the world, and all your enemies had been crushed by your invincible strength and citizens were glorying in your triumph and victory; when all subjected peoples awaited your nod and the Senate and the Roman people, now free of fear, were being guided by your most noble thoughts and counsels . . . in the midst of such great preoccupations, and fearing to vex you by intruding at a bad time, I did not dare to bring forth the writings on architecture I had developed with much deliberation." ("Cum divina tua mens et numen, Imperator Caesar, imperio potiretur orbis terrarum invictaque virtute cunctis hostibus stratis triumpho victoriaque tua cives gloriarentur et gentes omnes subactae tuum spectarent nutum populusque romanus et senatus liberatus timore amplissimis tuis cogitationibus consiliisque gubernaretur, non audebam, tantis occupationibus, de architectura scripta et magnis cogitationibus explicata edere, metuens ne, non apto tempore interpellans, subirem tui animi offensionem.")

30 Vitruvius 8.2.6. Cf. Fensterbusch, Vitruvius 1964, p. 565; Callebat, Vitruvius 1973, pp. 73–74. The map was installed at Rome in 13 A.D., twenty-five years after Agrippa's death (R. Hanslik, in Pauly 1894–1980, 9A.1, 1270, s.v. *Agrippa*).

31 Herodotus 2.16.1, 4.42.1.

32 Agrippa, fr. 1 (Klotz 1931, p. 386).

33 Nicolet 1991, pp. 101–108; Wiseman 1992, p. 40.

34 Caesar *Bellum gallicum* 1.1: "Gallia est omnis divisa in partes tres."

35 For an incisive account, Brunt 1978, pp. 178–183.

36 An eighth book was added later by Aulus Hirtius, one of Caesar's officers.

37 Götte 1964; Rüpke 1992, p. 217.

38 Strabo 2.5.11.

39 See for example Livy *Ab urbe condita* 41.12.2–10, 45.41.1–7; Caesar *Bellum gallicum* 2.35.4, 5.47.4, 5.49.3. Rüpke 1992, p. 217; Vasaly 1993, p. 151. *Litterae laureatae:* Caesar *Bellum gallicum* 2.35, 4.38, 7.90.

40 Weinstock 1971, pp. 60–79.

41 Cicero *Brutus* 262: "Commentarii [Caesaris] nudi sunt, recti et venusti." Cf. Rüpke 1992, p. 206.

42 Caesar *Bellum gallicum* 8.1: "Omnia Gallia devicta."

43 Caesar *Bellum gallicum* 1.2.

44 Aristotle *Poetics* 1450b27.

45 Burkert 1972, pp. 474–475.

46 Theon of Smyrna, as cited in Bulmer-Thomas 1939–1941, I, p. 87. Theon was a Greek mathematician of the early second century A.D.

47 Varro *Antiquitates rerum divinarum,* as quoted in Augustine *City of God* 7.28. Cf. Boyancé 1975, p. 102. Georges Dumézil accounts for the Capitoline triad in terms of the "tri-functional ideology" he saw at the root of all of Indo-European culture (Dumézil 1987, pp. 160–290). See Beard, North, and Price 1998, I, pp. 14–16, for a succinct summary of Dumézil's position.

48 Tripartite soul (reason, spirit, appetite) in Plato: *Republic* IV 443d6–7 and passim. Triadic systematization of doctrines was a common feature of Stoic thought (Fuhrmann 1960, pp. 147–148).

49 Rawson 1985, p. 260, wishes she had a map but says there is no sign that one was ever included.

50 Rüpke 1992, who (p. 213) cites four examples besides Caesar, all of which are later in date. Interestingly, he does not mention Vitruvius.

51 Frontinus *De aquis* 1.4.

52 That Vitruvius was in his twenties during the Gallic wars assumes he was in his fifties when *De architectura* appeared in the mid 20s B.C. Vitruvius 1.pref.2 and above, introduction, n. 2. His detailed description (2.9.15) of Caesar's construction of a siege tower while campaigning in the Alps at the beginning of the Gallic wars, probably in 59–58 B.C., bears all the marks of a firsthand account (Callebat et al., Vitruvius 1999, pp. 172–173), as does his description (10.16.11–12) of the siege of Marseilles in 49 B.C., at the beginning of the civil war that immediately followed the Gallic wars. These two descriptions clearly imply that Vitruvius's attachment to Caesar covered the intervening ten years. See also Callebat and Fleury, Vitruvius 1986, pp. 289–293.

53 Vitruvius 1.3.1: "Partes ipsius architecturae sunt tres: aedificatio, gnomonice, machinatio." Written not long before *De architectura* in 34–33 B.C., Varro's now lost work on the nine disciplines included a book on architecture, which Vitruvius mentions (7.pref.14), and could conceivably have made a similar division. Of the 74 works Varro wrote, only two survive, one on agriculture (*Libri tres rerum rusticarum*) and one on the Latin language (*De lingua latina*). Skydsgaard 1968; Rawson 1985, passim; Griffin 1994, p. 703; Liou et al., Vitruvius 1995, pp. 74–75.

54 Discussed in book 10, chapters 10 to 12.

55 Callebat, Vitruvius 1973, pp. ix–x and 165–167.

56 In his commentaries, Caesar discusses many of the same war machines as Vitruvius does in the last chapters of book 10 (Fleury 1993, pp. 230–231).

57 Vitruvius 9.pref.3: "Cum ergo tanta munera ab scriptorum prudentia privatim publiceque fuerint hominibus praeparata, non solum arbitror palmas et coronas his tribui oportere, sed etiam decerni triumphos et inter deorum sedes eos dedicandos iudicari."

58 Soubiran, Vitruvius 1969, p. xx, cites Xenophanes and Euripides. The view was also articulated in Vitruvius's own time by Athenodorus of Tarsus, one of Augustus's Greek philosophical advisors (Seneca *De tranquillitate animi* 3.1). Cf. Grimal 1946, p. 72.

59 Caesar's Gallic triumph in 46 B.C. was followed by three more, which celebrated his victories in Alexandria, Pontus, and Africa. Dio Cassius 43.19.1; Suetonius *Divus Julius* 37. Cf. Weinstock 1971, pp. 76–79.

60 He was proclaimed a god by the Senate on or about January 1 of 42 B.C. (Weinstock 1971, p. 386). Vitruvius 1.pref.2.

61 The third-century B.C. Greek geographer and polymath Eratosthenes (also mentioned by Vitruvius in the preface to book 9) was known as *pentathlos*, the pentathlete, because of the breadth of his learning (Jacob 1992).

62 Suetonius *Divus Julius* 56.5.

63 Cited in Pliny the Elder *Natural History* 7.117. Cf. Hendrickson 1906, p. 118; Griffin 1994, p. 715.

64 Seneca *Epistulae* 59.7. Cf. Lana 1953; Grimal 1978, pp. 254–258.

65 Vitruvius 1.1.2: "At qui utrumque perdidicerunt [*fabrica* and *ratiocinatio*], uti omnibus armis ornati, citius cum auctoritate quod fuit propositum sunt adsecuti."

66 Caesar *Bellum gallicum* 2.3, 5.51, 6.3, and most famously the "Veni, vidi, vici" of his Pontic victory of 47 B.C. Appian *Bellum civile* 2.81.384; Dio Cassius 42.48.1; Suetonius *Divus Julius* 35.2. Cf. Westall 1996, p. 115.

67 Vitruvius 1.1.11: "his gradibus disciplinarum scandendo scientia plerarumque litterarum et artium nutriti pervenerint ad summum templum architecturae." Similarly, in the first chapter of book 2, primitive humans, advancing *gradatim*, "step by step," from the construction of buildings to the other arts and disciplines, are led from their brutish existence in the wilderness to gentle *humanitas* (2.1.6). The step-climbing metaphor reappears, without overt mention of the "temple of architecture," at 7.pref.1 where the knowledge transmitted by writings builds up *gradatim*, step by step, *ad summam doctrinarum subtilitatem*. It also occurs at 9.pref.14 as the steps of men's memories (*gradibus memoriarum*) whereby great minds are raised up to heaven.

68 The archaic Temple of Jupiter burned down in 83 B.C. Rebuilding on the same, nearly square foundations (62.25 by 53.50 meters: over 200 by 170

feet) was begun by Sulla and completed by the consul Q. Lutatius Catulus, who dedicated it in 76 (Steinby 1993–2000, s.v. *Iuppiter Optimus Maximus, Aedes*). Gilded bronze roof tiles: Seneca the Elder *Controversiae* 1.6.4, 2.1.1; Pliny *Natural History* 33.57. Vitruvius stipulates elsewhere (1.7.1) that the tutelary deities of a city—Jupiter, Juno, and Minerva—are to be housed in a temple located *in excelsissimo loco,* in the very highest place: clearly an evocation of the Capitoline temple with its triple cella, which served as a model for Roman colonial foundations from the time of Caesar on (Gros 1987b, p. 356; Gros 1990; Price 1996, p. 844). The expression *in summo templo* also occurs at 3.4.3 with reference to the odd number of steps that are to front a temple so that the right foot with which one begins one's ascent is also the one placed *in summo templo,* on the temple platform at the top. Fleury, Vitruvius 1990, p. 93, notes that climbing the steps of a temple was a solemn and sacred matter. It certainly would have been for a *triumphator* at the moment of his apotheosis.

69 Dio Cassius 43.21.2.

70 Tacitus *Historiae* 3.72. Cf. Edwards 1996, p. 80. Tacitus, writing at the end of the first century B.C., was voicing an opinion that had been commonplace for some time.

71 No one has done so before, to the best of my present knowledge.

72 Festus, Lindsay edition 34. The relation between architecture and augury is to a large degree the theme of Rykwert 1988. The "temple" of *summum templum architecturae* is the *tempio* of Elisa Romano's *La capanna e il tempio* (Romano 1987, especially p. 193).

73 Succinctly, Rawson 1985, p. 288: "It was an article of faith with the Romans that they were the most religious of all peoples, and that this was the reason for their success." On Roman religion, recently, Beard, North, and Price 1998, and below, chapter 3.

74 The three divinities in the triple cella of the Capitoline temple were sometimes known as the *summi imperatores,* supreme commanders (Degrassi 1957–1963, 192, with commentary; cf. Crawford 1974, p. 363). Where would such *summi imperatores* live but in a *summum templum?*

75 See further below, chapter 2, pp. 145–148.

76 Vitruvius 1.1.5.

77 Vitruvius 1.1.5: "oppido capto, viris interfectis, civitate deleta, matronas eorum in servitutem abduxerunt nec sunt passi stolas neque ornatus matronales deponere uti non una triumpho ducerentur, sed aeterno servitutis exemplo."

78 The Persians burned down all the buildings on the Athenian Acropolis just before the battle of Salamis. The monuments of the Periclean Acropolis eventually replaced them. On the Athenian victory over the Persians at Salamis as the chief and perennial informant of its architecture, most recently Hurwit 1999.

79 The whole caryatid controversy, with citations and bibliography, is reviewed in Fleury, Vitruvius 1990, pp. 74–80. See also Vickers 1985; Rykwert 1996, pp. 129–138; King 1998.

80 Feeney 1998, p. 128, is illuminating: "Modern readers . . . tend to think of aetiology as bad history, a botched recovery of the past, although it is of course not that at all but rather the ancients' way of doing theory."

81 Rambaud 1953; Rüpke 1992.

82 Suetonius *Divus Augustus* 29.2; Ovid *Fasti* 5.569–578. The forum's octastyle Corinthian temple, built entirely of Luna marble, the largest Roman temple to date and considered the most beautiful, was not dedicated until 2 B.C.

83 Zanker 1968; Zanker 1988, pp. 201–204; Anderson 1984, pp. 65–100; La Rocca 1995; Galinsky 1996; Kellum 1996.

84 Zanker 1968, pp. 12–13, takes Vitruvius's story as pointing to the caryatids in the Forum of Augustus as a symbolic representation of the peoples humiliated by Augustus. Wesenberg 1984b disagrees, but admits that Vitruvius was probably aware of their inclusion in the project. On fifth-century B.C. Athens as the classical ideal emulated in Augustan art see Zanker 1988, pp. 269–283; Maderna-Lauter 1990. On the Forum of Augustus caryatids as part of that project of emulation, La Rocca 1995, p. 77.

85 Fleury, Vitruvius 1990, pp. lxii–lxvii; Carpo 1998, pp. 163–164; and Carpo 2001, chapter 2.

86 Gros 1995 and 1996b.

87 Carpo 2001, ch. 2, attributes the scarcity of drawings to Vitruvius's awareness of their futility at a time (before the age of printing) when their accurate reproduction in manuscript copies would have been impossible.

88 Vitruvius I.I.I: "Architecti est scientia pluribus disciplinis et variis eruditionibus ornata cuius iudicio probantur omnia quae ab ceteris artibus perficiuntur opera. Ea nascitur ex fabrica et ratiocinatione. Fabrica est continuata ac trita usus meditatio quae manibus perficitur e materia cuiuscumque generis opus est ad propositum deformationis. Ratiocinatio autem est quae res fabricatas sollertiae ac rationis pro portione demonstrare atque explicare potest." Since my translation of the first sentence deviates slightly from most modern ones, grammatical justification is in order. I have taken *cuius* as referring to the knowledge of the architect, not to the architect himself, since *scientia* is the subject of the sentence. *Judicio*, in my view, means "with or by discernment, discretion, good judgement" in this context (Lewis and Short 1962, s.v. *judicium* II C). I have taken *probantur* in the sense of "make (a thing) credible, show, prove, demonstrate" (Lewis and Short 1962, s.v. *probo* III B). Thus, literally, "the architect's knowledge . . . by the good judgment of which all the works that are brought to completion by the other arts are proven." In other words, the knowledge of the architect, judiciously exercised, demonstrates or proves (makes palpably credible, *shows*) the achievements of the other arts. This reading is entirely in keeping with Vitruvius's view of *architectura* as the summation of learning (*summum templum architecturae,* I.I.II) and bypasses the conventional, somewhat problematic construction that the architect judges the achievements of the other arts. See Fleury, Vitruvius 1990, pp. 65–66. Granger's text and translation of this passage (Vitruvius 1931) are no longer accepted.

89 It is usual to translate *ratiocinatio* as "theory," but see Schrijvers 1989b whom I have followed in this matter. Moreover, at 5.12.7 writing and "ratiocination" are used as equivalent terms: "Quae necessaria ad utilitatem in civitatibus publicorum locorum securrere . . . in hoc volumine scripsi . . . privatorum autem aedificiorum utilitates . . . in sequenti volumine ratiocinabor."

90 Vitruvius 1.1.2: "Itaque architecti qui sine litteris contenderant ut manibus essent exercitati non potuerunt efficere ut haberent pro laboribus auctoritatem; qui autem ratiocinationibus et litteris solis confisi fuerunt umbram non rem persecuti videntur. At qui utrumque perdidicerunt, uti omnibus armis ornati, citius cum auctoritate quod fuit propositum sunt adsecuti."

91 On the term in general, Heinze 1925; Pollitt 1974; Galinsky 1996, pp. 10–41. On Vitruvius and *auctoritas,* Gros 1989b.

92 Heinze 1925, p. 351.

93 Cicero *Topica* 73. Cf. Galinsky 1996, p. 15.

94 Cicero *De officiis* 3.103; Livy *Ab urbe condita* 1.21.3–4; Dionysius of Halicarnassus *Antiquitates romanae* 2.75.3; Dio Cassius 45.17.3; Plutarch *Numa* 16.1.

95 Pollitt 1974, p. 315.

96 Religious dimension of "Augustus": above, introduction. Relation to *augeo:* Suetonius *Divus Augustus* 7.2.

97 Galinsky 1996, pp. 10–41; Crook 1996, pp. 117–123.

98 Augustus *Res gestae* 34.3.

99 Corbier 1987 (p. 44: "l'écrit légitime"); Hopkins 1991.

100 Galsterer 1990, p. 10; Woolf 1996, p. 22. See also MacMullen 1982; Meyer 1990.

101 Suetonius *Divus Augustus* 84.1–2.

102 Dio Cassius 55.3.3.

103 Dio Cassius 55.4.1.

104 Above, p. 19; Millar 1984, p. 50.

105 Millar 1973. On Aphrodisias, see especially Erim 1986 and an ongoing series of conference papers, most recently Roueché and Smith 1996.

106 Price 1984 gives a subtle reading of the imperial cult in Asia Minor as an appropriate (not necessarily obsequious) thing to do. Inscriptions of imperial correspondence at Aphrodisias and elsewhere could be understood in similar terms.

107 Vitruvius 1.pref.2: "Cum vero adtenderem te non solum de vita communi omnium curam publicaeque rei constitutione habere, sed etiam de opportunitate publicorum aedificiorum ut civitas per te non solum provinciis esset aucta verum etiam ut maiestas imperii publicorum aedificiorum egregias haberet auctoritates, non putavi praetermittendum quin primo quoque tempore de his rebus ea tibi ederem, ideo quod primum parenti tuo de eo fueram notus et eius virtutis studiosus." On the relation of this passage to the ideology of the principate, see Grenade 1961, pp. 106–107 and 149. My reading both of this passage and of Vitruvian *auctoritas* in general owes a great deal to Gros 1989b.

108 Ruffel and Soubiran 1962, p. 145; Gros 1976a, p. 55. Cf. Fleury, Vitruvius 1990, pp. 56–57.

109 *Imperator Caesar:* 1.pref.1; *Imperator:* 2.pref.4, 3.pref.4, 10.pref.4; *Caesar:* 1.1.18, 6.pref.5, 7.pref.10, 9.pref.18. The prefaces to books 4 and 5 have both, opening with *Imperator* (4.pref.1, 5.pref.1) and invoking *Caesar* a little further on (4.pref.1, 5.pref.5). Cf. Fleury, Vitruvius 1990, pp. 51–52. Only the preface to book 8 has neither, on which see Callebat, Vitruvius 1973, p. viii, and below, at the end of this chapter. Until Octavian adopted "Imperator" as an official name in 29 B.C. and made it a permanent part of his identity, *Imperator,* a strictly temporary title, was the acclamation of a general (*imperator,* lower case) by his troops after a victory, and was one of the conditions for the award of a triumph (Dio Cassius 52.41.3; Suetonius *Divus Julius* 76; cf. Syme 1958, p. 176). It was never, until Augustus, a permanent name or title. See also Combès 1966 and further below, chapter 4, pp. 277–278.

110 Fleury, Vitruvius 1990, p. 52.

111 "Augustus" was added to it after 27 B.C. For epigraphic evidence, *TLL* VII.1, s.v. *imperator,* 558; for numismatic evidence, the reverse types of two *denarii* in the British Museum, dating from between 29 and 27 B.C.: 096494 and 195155, for example (cf. Pollini 1990, figs. 15 and 17).

112 Vitruvius 5.pref.1.

113 Vitruvius 5.pref.2: "ut memoriae tradantur, breviter exponam."

114 Gros 1989b, p. 126.

115 On *cura,* "care" for the public good, as an aspect of imperial ideology, Béranger 1953, pp. 169–217.

116 Cf. Suetonius *Divus Augustus* 28 (the brick-to-marble passage): "Urbem neque pro maiestate imperii ornatam … ut iure sit gloriatus marmoream se relinquere quam latericiam accepisset." On the relation between *maiestas* and *monumenta* as the agents of *consensus,* Gonzalez 1984; Gros 1990, pp. 56–58.

117 Cicero *De oratore* 3.5; cf. Gros 1989b, p. 127. Dio Cassius (55.3.4–5), writing in Greek about Augustus's Senate activities in 9 B.C., has difficulty with *auctoritas,* which he does not translate but simply transliterates, "for such is the general force of this word, to translate it into Greek by a term that will always be applicable is impossible." In the passage in question *auctoritas,* clearly an un-Greek notion, is also matter of written record.

118 Vitruvius 7.pref.17 (increased spending, greater richness of materials); 3.3.6, 3.3.8 (grander spaces); 3.3.9 (heightened contrast of light and shadow); 5.1.10 (bigger columns); 7.pref.17 (more columns).

119 Gros and Sauron 1988, pp. 51–56; Zanker 1988, pp. 5–78.

120 Vitruvius 1.pref.1.

121 Vitruvius 1.pref.2: "his rebus."

122 Vitruvius 1.1.18: "De artis vero potestate quaeque insunt in ea ratiocinationes, polliceor, uti spero, his voluminibus non modo aedificantibus, sed etiam omnibus sapientibus cum maxima auctoritate me sine dubio praestaturum."

123 Callebat 1989, p. 37.

124 Vitruvius 10.16.12: "Quas potui de machinis expedire rationes pacis bellique temporibus et utilissimas putavi in hoc volumine perfeci. In prioribus vero novem de singulis generibus et partibus conparavi, uti totum corpus omnia architecturae membra in decem voluminibus haberet explicata."

125 On ancient books and the relevance of their physical constitution, Small 1997, pp. 11–25.

126 Fensterbusch, Vitruvius 1964.

127 Exceptionally, each of the ten books of the Budé edition is being published as a separate volume, although the Budé volumes are codices, of course, not scrolls.

128 Vitruvius 7.pref.18.

129 Vitruvius 4.pref.1.

130 Vitruvius 5.pref.5. Similarly, 1.7.2.

131 Vitruvius 1.2.1: "Architectura autem constat ex ordinatione. . . ."

132 Vitruvius 1.2.2: "Ordinatio est modica membrorum operis commoditas separatim universeque proportionis ad symmetriaram comparatio. Haec componitur ex quantitate, quae graece *posotês* dicitur."

133 Vitruvius 9.pref.17; Varro *De re rustica* 5.3, *De lingua latina* 5.11–12. Cf. Skydsgaard 1968, pp. 12–13. It is precisely this obsession with quantities that has led Lionel March (March 1998, pp. 137–140) to speculate that Vitruvius and Varro were one and the same person.

134 Tarver 1997, p. 137.

135 Augustine *City of God* 6.3.

136 Aulus Gellius *Noctes atticae* 3.10.1. According to Pliny (*Natural History* 35.160), Varro was buried in the "Pythagorean way" in leaves of myrtle, olive, and black poplar. Cicero, in the Pythagorean *Somnium Scipionis*, calls seven "a number which is the key of almost everything" (*De republica* 6.18).

137 On Pythagoreanism in the late republic, Rawson 1985, pp. 291–295; Griffin 1994, pp. 707–710. There was a particular fascination with Plato's *Timaeus*, the most Pythagorean of his dialogues, parts of which

Cicero translated into Latin, and which contains, among other things, a full account of the cosmic role of the number four.

138 Cicero *De oratore* 2.154, *Republic* 2.28; cf. Griffin 1994, p. 707. A statue of Pythagoras that had stood next to the *comitium* in the Forum Romanum since the fourth century B.C. was removed by Sulla when he modified the area in the 80s B.C. (Cicero *Disputationes tusculanae* 4.2–5; Pliny *Natural History* 34.26). Plutarch (*Roman Questions* 2.25, 72, 95, 102, 112) draws many parallels between Roman and Pythagorean customs. Cf. Coleman 1964.

139 Vitruvius 5.pref.3: "cybicus rationibus"; 5.pref.5: "Cum ergo haec naturali modo sint a maioribus observata." On the fifth preface, Kessissoglu 1993; on cubical principles and Vitruvius in the Renaissance, Hersey 1966.

140 Vitruvius 5.pref.4.

141 My account of scrolls follows Clark 1901, pp. 27–30.

142 Above, p. 25.

143 On the lengths of the different books, Fleury, Vitruvius 1990, pp. xxiv–xxv. On the structure of books 3 and 4, Gros 1975 and Gros, Vitruvius 1990, pp. x–xvi.

144 For lopsidedness, see the diagram in Fleury, Vitruvius 1990, p. 121.

145 Vitruvius 3.1.5: "Nec minus mensurarum rationes, quae in omnibus operibus videntur ncessariae esse, ex corporis membris collegerunt, uti digitum, palmum, pedem, cubitum, et eas distribuerunt in perfectum numerum quem Graeci teleon dicunt. Perfectum autem antiqui instituerunt numerum qui decem dicitur; namque ex manibus digitorum numero [ab palmo pes] est inventus. Si autem in utrisque palmis ex articulis ab natura decem sunt perfecti, etiam Platoni placuit esse eum numerum ea re perfectum quod ex singularibus rebus, quae monades apud Graecos dicuntur, perficitur decusis. Quae simul autem undecim aut duodecim sunt factae, quod superaverint, non possunt esse perfectae, donec ad alterum decusim perveniant; singulares enim res particulae sunt eius numeri."

146 On ancient metrology in general, Fernie 1978 and 1996; Hecht 1979; Zöllner 1987, pp. 23–34; Rykwert 1996, passim; Wilson Jones 2000a, pp. 71–84. On ancient metrological reliefs that illustrate the bodily basis for ancient measurement discussed by Vitruvius here and also at 1.2.4, Wesenberg 1975–1976; Fernie 1981; Ben-Menahem and Hecht 1985; Dekoulakou-Sideris 1990; Wilson Jones 2000b.

147 Vitruvius 1.1.1: "Fabrica est continuata ac trita usus meditatio quae manibus perficitur e materia."

148 Vitruvius 2.1.2: "habentes ab natura praemium praeter reliqua animalia . . . manibus et articulis quam vellent rem faciliter tractarent."

149 Vitruvius 1.1.1, 1.1.15.

150 John Lydus *De mensibus* 3.4 (below, p. 47).

151 Aristotle *Metaphysics* 1092b; Theophrastus *Metaphysics* 3.

152 Raven 1951; Pollitt 1974, pp. 18–20 and 413–414; Gros 1989a, p. 17.

153 Vitruvius 1.1.4.

154 Lucian *Vitarum auctio* 4. Lucian was a literary figure of the mid second century A.D. See also Martianus Capella *De nuptiis Philologiae et Mercurii* 2.96, cited Lücke 1991, p. 81.

155 Sextus Empiricus *Adversus mathematicos* 7.95 (= *Against the Logicians* 1.95 in the Loeb edition). Sextus Empiricus, to whom we owe much of our understanding of ancient Stoicism, was a skeptic philosopher of the end of the second century A.D.

156 The Pythagoreans understood both 4 and 10 to be the keys of the order of nature (Iamblichus *Theologoumena arithmeticae* 22.60).

157 Lucian *De lapsu in salutando* 5.

158 West 1992, pp. 233–236.

159 Philolaus, as cited in Kessissoglu 1993, p. 101, n. 218.

160 Iamblichus *Theologoumena arithmeticae* 82.12 (Bulmer-Thomas 1939–1941, I, p. 77). Cf. Aristotle *Metaphysics* 986a8: "ten is thought to be perfect and to comprise the whole nature of number." See further Kessissoglu 1993, p. 102. Kessissoglu also links the perfection of ten to the ten books of *De architectura*.

161 John Lydus *De mensibus* 1.15 and 3.4. The source for John Lydus's Pythagoreanism is thought to have been a compendium of the first century A.D.; see Robbins 1921, pp. 97–112; Maas 1992, pp. 58–61.

162 John Lydus *De mensibus* 1.15. Trans. by author.

163 John Lydus *De mensibus* 3.4.

164 Vitruvius 1.4.5.

165 Vitruvius 2.1.9, for example.

166 Vitruvius 3.1.1.

167 Vitruvius 5.6.1: "quibus etiam in duodecim signorum caelestium astrologia ex musica convenientia astrorum ratiocinantur." Fensterbusch (Vitruvius 1964) takes this qualification as an interpolation, and suppresses it in his Latin text. Following Gros 1994b, pp. 59–64, on this matter, I have therefore exceptionally translated the text of the Harley manuscript here (Granger, Vitruvius 1931). On the texts followed, see the preface, above.

168 Vitruvius 8.3.26.

169 Plato *Timaeus* 38c. Cf. Griffin 1994, p. 709.

170 Vitruvius 10.1.4: "Omnis autem est machinatio rerum natura procreata ac praeceptrice et magistra mundi versatione instituta."

171 Striker 1991, pp. 2–13.

172 Cicero *De finibus* 3.74. Cf. Long 1971a, p. 103. For a general account of Stoicism, Long 1986, pp. 107–209.

173 Mainly in books 4, 6, and 8. All the surviving fragments of Varro's *Antiquitates rerum divinarum* have been collected in Cardauns 1976.

174 Augustine *City of God* 6.5. On Varro's theology, Boyancé 1955a and 1975, Pépin 1956; Lieberg 1973; Cardauns 1976 and 1978.

175 Varro in Augustine *City of God* 6.5. See further Cicero *De natura deorum* 2.37–39.

176 Vitruvius 2.2.1–2. Cf. Cicero *De finibus* 3.73. Long 1996, pp. 202–223, relates living according to nature—the "harmonics of stoic virtue"— to number (four in particular) and to ancient musical theory. See also Striker 1991, pp. 2–13.

177 Vitruvius 3.1.6. Mathematically, six was perfect because it was the sum of its factors: $1 + 2 + 3 = 6$; $1 \times 2 \times 3 = 6$. See Theon of Smyrna (ed. Hiller 45.9–46.19; as cited in Bulmer-Thomas 1939–1941, I, pp. 85–86) who also discusses three and twenty-eight, and Augustine *City of God* 11.30. Cf. Gros, Vitruvius 1990, pp. 73–74. Vitruvius seems to think that the "divisions" (*partitiones*) of six mean not only one, two, and three but also four and five. $1 + 2 + 3 + 4 + 5$ do *not* add up to six, and this, no doubt, is why he adds the qualification "according to their calculations," deferring to an authority he has not fully understood.

178 See further Varro *De lingua latina* 5.171–173.

179 Crawford 1974; Hornblower and Spawforth 1996, s.v. *coinage, Roman*.

180 Vitruvius 3.1.8: "Postea autem quam animadverterunt utrosque numeros esse perfectos et sex et decem, utrosque in unum coiecerunt et fecerunt perfectissimum decusis sexis. Huis autem rei auctorem invenerunt pedem; e cubito enim cum dempti sunt palmi duo, relinquitur pes quattuor palmorum, palmus autem habet quattuor digitos. Ita efficitur uti habeat pes sedecim digitos et totidem asses aeracius denarius."

181 My thanks to Joseph Rykwert who pointed this out to me. See also March 1998, pp. 28–30.

182 Below, chapter 3, pp. 162–183.

183 Cicero *De divinatione* 1.3 (divination from the Etruscans); 2.70 (divination as a service to the commonwealth); *De divinatione* 2.42, and Pliny *Natural History* 2.138 (sixteen-part sky). Cf. Vitruvius 1.4.9. It is probable that Varro divided his *Antiquitates rerum divinarum* into sixteen books for precisely this reason. See also Thulin 1905–1909; Weinstock 1946.

184 Vitruvius 1.pref.3. Crook 1996 has called this the frankest known statement of the quid pro quo of Augustan patronage (p. 142).

185 Millar 1984, p. 44. Cf. Levick 1982; Wallace-Hadrill 1986; Pollini 1990.

186 Wallace-Hadrill 1986, p. 70. Until that time the "head," if there was one, was usually that of a god.

187 Hornblower and Spawforth 1996, s.v. *coinage, Roman*. Cf. Kienast 1982a, p. 416; Millar 1984, p. 44.

188 The relation between monetary units and units of measurement, insisted upon by Vitruvius at 3.1.7, was an ancient one: Dörpfeld 1887; cf. Gros, Vitruvius 1990, p. 76. A short work on metrology by L. Volusius Maecianus, written in the second century A.D., dealt with *res pecuniariae* in terms both of coinage and of measurement (Nicolet, introduction to Nicolet and Gros 1996, p. 4).

189 Arrian *Anabasis* 7.1.5–6. Cf. Purcell 1990.

190 Footprints, divine and human, carved into the pavements of many Graeco-Roman monuments left lasting visible trace of a supplicant's fleeting encounter with divinity (Dunbabin 1990).

191 Ptolemy and Aristobulus, whose writings Arrian claims were his sources (*Anabasis* 1.1.1).

192 Caesar's commentaries are discussed earlier in this chapter. Augustus's testament, the *Res gestae,* could also be considered a *commentarius.* Written specifically for public inscription (Suetonius *Divus Augustus* 101.1–4), its gaunt style makes Caesar look verbose by comparison.

193 Vitruvius 1.2.2: "The forms of arrangement, called 'ideas' in Greek, are these: *ichnographia, orthographia, scaenographia.*" ("Species dispositionis, quae graece dicuntur *ideai,* sunt hae: ichnographia, orthographia, scaenographia.") *Orthographia* is usually taken to be the elevation of a building. *Scaenographia,* a controversial term, is often taken to refer to perspective representation. For a review of the various interpretations, Fleury, Vitruvius 1990, pp. 110–112.

194 *Ichnos:* "track, footstep"; *graphia:* "drawing, delineation" (Liddell and Scott 1968, s.v. *ichnographia*). Vitruvius 1.2.2: "Ichnographia est circini regulaeque modice continens usus e qua capiuntur formarum in solis arearum descriptiones."

195 Varro *De lingua latina* 5.95. G. P. Goold, the Loeb translator, has noted that there is no etymological relation between *pes* and *pecunia.* But see above, n. 188.

196 Below, chapter 3, pp. 183–198.

197 Augustus *Res gestae* 19–21, on which especially Elsner 1996. Cf. Suetonius *Divus Augustus* 29.1–3; Gros 1976a.

198 Aupert 1985, pp. 256–257; Knell 1985, pp. 35–37.

199 Theology of victory: Gagé 1933; Picard 1957; Fears 1981.

200 Lewis and Short 1962 (s.v. *ratio*) gives these as the primary English equivalents. *Ratio* is derived from the verb *reor* (past participle *ratus*), "reckon, calculate" and, by extension, "believe, think, imagine, judge."

201 Callebat et al. 1984. *Locus,* used 295 times, is the next most frequent.

202 The best general account of Pythagoreanism remains Burkert 1972.

203 Vitruvius 1.2.2. Above, n. 132 for the Latin.

204 Vitruvius 1.2.2: "Dispositio autem est rerum apta conlocatio elegansque compositionibus effectus operis cum qualitate."

205 Cicero *Academica* 1.25. See also Cicero *De natura deorum* 2.94.

206 Cicero *Academica* 1.24–28.

207 Above, pp. 33–34.

208 The term *divina mens* is a favorite with Cicero, who uses it 23 times in his philosophical works (Pease 1920, p. 102; cf. Soubiran, Vitruvius 1969, p. 70).

209 Vitruvius 8.pref.3, 9.1.1, 9.5.4. Vitruvius 6.1.11: "Ita divina mens civitatem populi romani egregia temperataque regione conlocavit, uti orbis terrarum imperii potiretur."

210 Vitruvius 1.pref.1. Above, n. 29 for the Latin.

211 Chrysippus, in Arnim 1903–1924, II, 911 (cf. Lapidge 1978, pp. 168–169); Cicero *De natura deorum* 2.29. See also Long 1986, pp. 171–172.

212 Long 1996, p. 228.

213 These definitions evolved from the related Stoic classification of mixtures, also tripartite, initially formulated by Chrysippus in the third century B.C. and given its fullest surviving account by Alexander of Aphrodisias in his *De mixtione* of the late second century A.D. (Todd 1976). They eventually made their way into the sixth-century A.D. compendium of Roman law known as the *Digest* of Justinian.

214 Sextus Empiricus *Adversus mathematicos* 9.78–80 (= Arnim 1903–1924, II, 1013; = *Against the Physicists* 1.78–80 in the Loeb edition). Cf. Long 1996, ch. 10, especially pp. 229ff.

215 Seneca *Epistulae* 102.6–7.

216 Pomponius *Digest* 41.3.30.

217 Cicero *De finibus* 3.74.

218 On Stoic influences in Vitruvius, Watzinger 1909; Rykwert 1981; Romano 1987; Gros 1989a. Book 2 of Cicero's *De natura deorum* can be read as representative of late republican Stoicism.

219 Sextus Empiricus *Adversus mathematicos* 7.38–42 (= Arnim 1903–1924, II, 132; = *Against the Logicians* 1.38–42 in the Loeb edition); cf. *Outlines of Pyrrhonism* 2.80–83. Cf. Long 1971a, pp. 98–106.

220 On *lekta,* Bréhier 1970; Long 1971a.

221 Vitruvius 2.1.8.

222 Compare Vitruvius 1.1.1: "The knowledge of the architect is furnished with many disciplines and various kinds of learning" (above, n. 88 for the Latin); and 2.1.8: "In order to write the body of architecture, I decided to set out in the first scroll with what disciplines and kinds of learning it should be furnished" ("Cum corpus architecturae scriberem, primo volumine putavi quibus eruditionibus et disciplinis esset ornata"). Since Vitruvius qualifies the "knowledge of the architect [*architecti scientia*]" and the "body of architecture [*corpus architecturae*]" with precisely the same terms, he clearly considered them equivalent.

223 Cicero *De oratore* 1.188: "quae rem dissolutam divulsamque conglutinaret, et ratione quadam constringeret." Compare Vitruvius 4.pref.1 (cited above, introduction). Cf. Gros 1989a, p. 15; Novara 1983, pp. 287–290. *De oratore* was one of Vitruvius's sources (9.pref.17).

224 Vitruvius 2.pref.5, 2.1.8.

225 Cicero *De officiis* 1.53–55. See also Brunt 1975, p. 12.

226 Romano 1987, pp. 143–161, and Romano 1994.

227 Cicero *Ad Atticum* 16.11.4 and 16.14.3. *Kathêkô:* "it is meet" (Liddell and Scott 1968, s.v.). Cicero based his *De officiis* on the Stoic Panaetius's *Peri kathêkonta.* Cf. Powell 1995, p. xvi.

228 Diogenes Laertius 7.107.

229 Pomponius *Digest* 41.3.30; Seneca *Epistulae* 102.6.

230 Law as bond: Cicero *De republica* 1.49 and passim; *De legibus* passim. *Corpus rei publicae: De inventione* 2.168; *Pro Murena* 51; *Philippics* 8.15; *De officiis* 1.85, 3.22, 3.32.

231 Cicero *Philippics* 8.15; *De officiis* 3.32. See also Nestle 1926–1927.

232 Suetonius *Divus Julius* 77. Caesar's Epicureanism: Mulgan 1978–1979; Rawson 1989, p. 242.

233 Vitruvius 1.1.12: "At fortasse mirum videbitur inperitis hominibus posse naturam tantum numerum doctrinarum perdiscere et memoria continere. Cum autem animadverterint omnes disciplinas inter se coniunctionem rerum et communicationem habere, fieri posse faciliter credent; encyclios enim disciplina uti corpus unum ex his membris est composita." Cf. Cicero *Pro Archia* 1.2; *De oratore* 3.21.

234 Vitruvius 1.1.1.

235 Vitruvius 1.1.15–16: "ex duabus rebus singulas artes esse compositas, ex opere et eius ratiocinatione, ex his autem unum proprium esse eorum qui singulis rebus sunt exercitati: id est operis effectus, alterum commune cum omnibus doctis: id est rationem; uti medicis et musicis est de venarum rythmo et [ad] pedum motus. . . . Similiter cum astrologis et musicis est disputatio communis de sympathia stellarum et symphoniarum . . . ceterisque omnibus doctrinis multae res vel omnes communes sunt dumtaxat ad disputandum."

236 Vitruvius identifies learned men as "philologi" at 6.pref.4, 6.7.7, 9.pref.17. See Kuck 1965, who argues that the Greek term *philologos* ("lover of *logos*") meant precisely those who practiced their learning through discussion.

237 Long 1971a; Long 1986, pp. 124–125, 175; Long 1996, p. 246: "The central insight of the Stoics [is that] the human soul is a capacity for living as

a language animal." "Connection" or "sequence" (*akolouthia* in Greek): Sextus Empiricus *Adversus mathematicos* 8.275ff. (= *Against the Logicians* 2.275ff. in the Loeb edition).

238 Gros 1996b.

239 Vitruvius 1.1.1–2.

240 Vitruvius 1.1.1: "Fabrica est continuata ac trita usus meditatio quae manibus perficitur e materia cuiuscumque generis opus est ad propositum deformationis." The terms *continuata, trita, usus,* and *meditatio* all stress—to the point of redundancy—the *habitual* nature of *fabrica* as shaped by repeated activity.

241 Aristotle *Nicomachean Ethics* 1140a9–10. Cf. Pollitt 1974, pp. 32–37.

242 Aristotle *Nicomachean Ethics* 1106b36. Cf. Pollitt 1974, p. 50.

243 Diogenes Laertius 7.98.

244 Sextus Empiricus *Adversus mathematicos* 9.78 (above, p. 56).

245 Diogenes Laertius 7.138–139. Cf. Long 1996, p. 233.

246 Argued in detail by Long 1996, pp. 224–249, whose discussion forms the basis for my understanding of the question.

247 Lapidge 1978, pp. 168–175; Hays 1983, p. 44.

248 Long 1996, pp. 230–231.

249 Vitruvius 1.4.5: "Namque e principiis, quae Graeci *stoicheia* appellant, ut omnia corpora sunt composita, id est e calore et umore, terreno et aere, et ita mixtionibus naturali temperatura figurantur omnium animalium in mundo generatim qualitates." Cf. Pellati 1951 and Fleury, Vitruvius 1990, p. 128, who trace the theory to Empedocles and the pre-Socratics, as indeed Vitruvius himself does at 2.2.1.

250 Vitruvius 1.4.3, 1.4.4.

251 Vitruvius 1.4.6: "Item si umor occupavit corporum venas inparesque eas fecit, cetera principia, ut a liquido corrupta, diluuntur et dissolvuntur compositionibus virtutes."

252 Vitruvius 1.4.7. The theory as articulated here is in complete contradiction with that of Aristotle (*Historia animalium, De partibus animalium, De respiratione*), who seems to have believed that the health of animals

depended on their having more, not less, of their native element in their bodies. In Aristotle's view, fish were full of water, for instance. Cf. Fleury, *Vitruvius* 1990, p. 129. Vitruvius favors a symbiotic rather than a sympathetic relation of the animal with its habitat, a view which in turn is coherent with his account of the behavior of building materials in the following book, and may indeed have been adopted for that very reason.

253 Vitruvius 1.4.8: "Ergo si haec ita videntur quemadmodum proposuimus et e principiis animalium corpora composita sensu percipimus et e superationibus aut defectionibus ea laborare dissolvique iudicamus, non dubitamus quin diligentius quaeri oporteat uti temperatissimas caeli regiones eligamus cum quaerenda fuerit in moenium conlocationibus salubritas." Choosing "the most temperate regions of the sky" refers to the proper orientation of a city.

254 Vitruvius 6.1.10–11. Cf. 9.1.16. See also Cicero *De natura deorum* 2.119; Pliny *Natural History* 2.34, 3.39.

255 Vitruvius 2.9.10: "permanet inmortalis ad aeternitatem."

256 Vitruvius 1.2.2. See above, nn. 132, 204 for the Latin.

257 Vitruvius 1.2.3: "Eurythmia est venusta species commodusque in compositionibus membrorum aspectus."

258 Vitruvius 1.2.4: "Item symmetria est ex ipsius operis membris conveniens consensus ex partibusque separatis ad universae figurae speciem ratae partis responsus. Uti in hominis corpore e cubito, pede, palmo, digito ceterisque particulis symmetros est eurythmiae qualitas, sic est in operum perfectionibus." See also 1.2.2, 3.1.1, 3.1.3, 3.1.4, 3.1.9, and below, chapter 3, pp. 195–200, where the question is discussed more fully.

259 Pliny *Natural History* 34.65. The Latin *symmetria* is a transliteration of the Greek word. See especially Pollitt 1974, pp. 14–22 and 256–258.

260 For example, 3.1.1, 6.2.1.

261 Vitruvius 1.2.4.

262 Chrysippus in Galen *De placitis Hippocratis et Platonis* 5.2.32–33: "Health in the body is a kind of good blend and symmetry [*eukrasia kai symmetria*] of the elements . . . *symmetria* or lack of it in the sinews is strength or

weakness, firmness or softness; *symmetria* or lack of it in the limbs is beauty or ugliness." A few paragraphs later (5.3.14), Galen comments, "For he distinguished them [health and beauty] accurately in the case of the body, placing health in the *symmetria* of the elements, and beauty in the *symmetria* of the members." Cf. Raven 1951, pp. 149–150; Pollitt 1974, pp. 14ff.; Rykwert 1996, p. 109.

263 Métraux 1995 has argued that the sculptors of early classical Greece were attempting to make health visible.

264 Vitruvius 6.2.1: "detractionibus aut adiectionibus"; see also 3.3.13.

265 Vitruvius 5.6.7: "Nec tamen in omnibus theatris symmetriae ad omnes rationes et effectus possunt respondere, sed oportet architectum animadvertere quibus proportionibus necesse sit sequi symmetriam et quibus ad loci naturam aut magnitudinem operis temperari."

266 Moatti 1988, 1991; and 1997, ch. 3.

267 For the dating, see introduction, n. 2.

268 Horace *Odes* 1.2. Cf. Bickerman 1961; Nisbet and Hubbard 1970, pp. 34–36; Farnoux 1981, pp. 486–500.

269 Horace *Odes* 1.2.41–44: "sive mutata iuvenem figura / ales in terris imitaris almae / filius Maiae, patiens vocari / Caesaris ultor." Trans. by author.

270 Dessau 1892–1916, 2.1.3200: "Lucri repertor atque sermonis dator." Trans. by author.

271 Ovid *Fasti* 5.663–692; Farnoux 1981, pp. 466–467. On the iconography of Mercury, *LIMC* V, 500–554. Stoic accounts of Hermes appear in chapter 16 of Cornutus's *Epitome* and chapter 72 of Heraclitus Homericus's *Homêrica Problêmata*, both of the first century A.D.

272 Farnoux 1981, pp. 492–493, and *LIMC* V, s.v. *Mercurius*, no. 187.

273 For example, London, British Museum 195154. Cf. Pollini 1990, fig. 14, where the coin is illustrated.

274 For a particularly incisive discussion of *logos* and money, Nimis 1988. Cf. Carson 1993. On the intertwining of the use and operation of money and writing in the Roman empire, Hopkins 1991, p. 157.

275 Hill 1989; cf. Elsner 1996, p. 41. Hill says that the first appearance of a monument on a coin appears to have been in around 135 B.C. (p. 7). The practice became common from the reign of Augustus on. For example, see the coins illustrated on p. 193 in this volume.

276 See Gros and Sauron 1988, pp. 58–59.

277 Vitruvius 1.pref.3.

278 Vitruvius 1.pref.3: "conscripsi praescriptiones terminatas ut eas adtendens et ante facta et futura qualia sint opera per te posses nota habere; namque his voluminibus aperui omnes disciplinae rationes."

279 Use of *Imperator* and *Caesar:* above, n. 109.

280 Augustine *City of God* 7.14.

281 Henry Bettenson, translator of the Penguin edition (*City of God,* p. 272, n. 36), has called the etymology "fantastic." Mercurius is connected with *merx*, as the Augustan *philologus* Verrius Flaccus noted. Cf. Farnoux 1981, pp. 465–466.

282 Suetonius *Divus Julius* 77; Pliny the Elder *Natural History* 7.117.

283 On Caesar's *De analogia*, Hendrickson 1906. Cf. Rawson 1985, pp. 121–129; Griffin 1994, pp. 703–704.

284 Varro *De lingua latina* 10.2.

285 Vitruvius 9.pref.17.

286 Varro *De lingua latina* 9.2–3. See also 9.113–114 and 10.1.

287 ". . . nisi si non est homo ex anima, quod est ex corpore et anima."

288 Varro *De lingua latina* 9.79.

289 The practice of changing the heads of statues was quite common in antiquity (below, chapter 2, pp. 127–128).

290 Varro *De lingua latina* 9.40.

291 Dahlmann 1932, pp. 10–14; Lloyd 1971, pp. 61–62.

292 Vitruvius 3.1.1: "Ea autem paritur a proportione, quae graece *analogia* dicitur." Cf. Varro *De lingua latina* 10.37: "What is the *ratio* that is *pro portione?* This is called *ana logon* in Greek, from which comes *analogia.*" The question of proportion will be treated more fully below in chapter 3.

293 Vitruvius 1.1.3: "Cum in omnibus enim rebus tum maxime etiam in architectura haec duo insunt: quod significatur et quod significat. Significatur proposita res de qua dicitur; hanc autem significat demonstratio rationibus doctrinarum explicata."

294 Callebat 1994, p. 35. See Fleury, Vitruvius 1990, pp. 69–70 for a review of opinions to date.

295 Sackur 1925, p. 155; Boëthius 1939, p. 116; MacDonald 1982, pp. 10–11. Wilson Jones 2000a, pp. 34–38, gives a useful summary of the traditionally alleged failings of *De architectura*.

296 Scheid 1986.

297 Vernant 1985, pp. 325–338. The archaic *kolossos* was not a giant statue but a stele, which was not an image or even very large, and was planted in the ground. The *kolossos* only became a giant statue in Hellenistic times with the colossos of Rhodes, at the beginning of the fourth century B.C. See also Benveniste 1932; Roux 1960.

298 Augustine *City of God* 6.9.2.

299 Beard 1994.

300 On semiotics in classical antiquity, Manetti 1993.

301 Ferri, Vitruvius 1960, pp. 34–35; Cf. Gros 1995, p. 174; Gros 1996b, p. 27.

302 Cicero *De finibus* 3.74 (cited above, p. 48).

303 Sextus Empiricus *Adversus mathematicos* 8.11–12 (= *Against the Logicians* 2.11–12 in the Loeb edition). Cf. Long 1971a, p. 76. Diogenes Laertius 7.62–63 attributes the theory to Chrysippus (third century B.C.).

304 On the Stoic theory of incorporeals, Bréhier 1970.

305 Long 1971a, p. 79.

306 Long 1971a, p. 97.

307 Long 1996, pp. 284–285.

308 Vitruvius 1.1.4. Above, n. 7 for the Latin.

309 Seneca *Epistulae* 117.13.

310 Quintilian *Institutio oratoria* 3.5.1. Cf. Ferri, Vitruvius 1960, p. 35; Callebat 1994, p. 35. At 3.6.37, Quintilian attributes the distinction to the Stoic Posidonius (ca. 135–50 B.C.). Watzinger 1909, pp. 206–207.

311 Vitruvius 1.1.1: "ea nascitur ex fabrica et ratiocinatione"; 1.1.2: "At qui utrumque [*fabrica* and *ratiocinatio*] perdidicerunt, uti omnibus armis ornati, citius cum auctoritate quod fuit propositum sunt adsecuti."

312 Vitruvius 1.1.3.

313 Vitruvius 1.1.3.

314 *De architectura* and rhetoric: Brown 1963; Gros 1979; André 1987; Callebat 1994. Mention of *De oratore:* Vitruvius 9.pref.17.

315 Callebat 1994, p. 45.

316 *Inventio, distributio, elocutio, memoria,* and *actio* are the five parts of classical rhetoric, dealt with in Roman treatises such as the *Rhetorica ad Herennium,* Cicero's *De oratore,* and Quintilian's *Institutio oratoria.* Cicero's *De partitione oratoria,* a short work written for his son, gives an especially succinct account. On memory in general: Yates 1966; Blum 1969; Rouveret 1989, pp. 303–336; Carruthers 1990; Vasaly 1993, pp. 89–104; Small 1997; and especially Onians 1999, pp. 162–216. Specific studies of texts and monuments which take the art of memory as their reference: Bergmann 1994; McEwen 1994 and 1995; Elsner 1996; Jaeger 1997; Güven 1998.

317 *Rhetorica ad Herennium* 3.28–40 (written ca. 85 B.C.); Cicero *De oratore* 2.350–361; Quintilian *Institutio oratoria* 11.2.1–51. Cf. especially Yates 1966, ch. 1; Small 1997.

318 Cicero *De oratore* 2.359.

319 Cicero *De oratore* 2.353. This key principle was discovered by Simonides of Ceos (556–468 B.C.) when he was able to give names to mangled corpses, crushed beyond recognition in the course of a banquet by a collapsed ceiling, because he remembered who had been sitting where and in what order before the accident (*De oratore* 2.351–353; Quintilian *Institutio oratoria* 11.2.11–16).

320 *Rhetorica ad Herennium* 3.39; Cicero *De oratore* 2.359.

321 Cicero *De oratore* 2.358. See Plato *Timaeus* 52B. Plato's view was that place (*chôra*) ideally, or as an object of thought, preexists the things that occupy it. For the Stoics who followed Aristotle on this, place—incorporeal, like *lekta*—coexisted with bodies, just as *lekta* coexist with their signifiers on whose existence their *sub*sistence depends. Bréhier 1970, pp. 37–44.

322 Small 1997, pp. 95–116 and 239.

323 Small 1997, p. 94.

324 *Rhetorica ad Herennium* 3.16.

325 Quintilian *Institutio oratoria* 11.2.21.

326 Vitruvius 2.1.5: "Item in Capitolio commonefacere potest et significare mores vetustatis Romuli casa."

327 Cicero *De re publica* 5.1.

328 There was another, far better documented and probably older hut of Romulus on the Palatine. See further below, chapter 2, pp. 146–148 and notes.

329 *Rhetorica ad Herennium* 3.30. Cf. Cicero *De oratore* 2.354 and 2.360; Quintilian *Institutio oratoria* 11.2.21.

330 Quintilian *Institutio oratoria* 11.2.26.

331 Quintilian *Institutio oratoria* 11.2.10.

332 Jaeger 1997, ch. 1. Livy *Ab urbe condita* pref.3.

333 Marking each fifth *locus*: *Rhetorica ad Herennium* 3.31; Jaeger 1997, pp. 20–21.

334 Vasaly 1993, p. 77, with specific reference to Cicero *In Catalinam* 3.

335 Cicero *Pro rege Deiotaro* 6. Cf. Vasaly 1993, p. 34.

336 Cicero *De finibus* 5.2. Cf. Vasaly 1993, p. 88.

337 Wiseman 1984, p. 122. See also Grimal 1948.

338 Vitruvius 5.pref.1: "Non enim de architectura sic scribitur uti historia aut poemata." For a detailed study of this preface, Kessissoglu 1993.

339 On the difficulty of signifying or "grasping" architecture in writing, see also Vitruvius 4.8.7 and 10.11.9.

340 On *amplificatio*, see *Rhetorica ad Herennium* 2.20; Cicero *Partitiones oratoriae* 15; Quintilian *Institutio oratoria* 2.5.9.

341 Vitruvius 5.pref.2: "Itaque occultas nominationes commensusque e membris operum pronuntians, ut memoriae tradantur, breviter exponam; sic enim expeditius ea recipere poterunt mentes."

342 Vitruvius 5.pref.4: "inmotam efficiat ibi memoriae stabilitatem."

343 After describing cubical principles (216 lines per *conscriptio*), Vitruvius writes (5.pref.5), "Therefore . . . I have decided to write in short scrolls, so that [their matter] might reach the minds of readers more easily, and so be readily understood." ("Ergo . . . quo facilius ad sensus legentium pervenire possint, brevibus voluminibus iudicavi scribere; ita enim expedita erunt ad intellegendum.") The implication of the "therefore" is obviously that brevity is also (in principle at least) "cubical."

344 Vitruvius 5.pref.5: "I set up their [the scroll's] order so that people looking for explanations need not gather them piecemeal, but can obtain them from a single body with separate scrolls for the different subjects." ("Eorum ordinationes institui, uti non sint quaerentibus separatim colligenda, sed e corpore uno et in singulis voluminibus generum haberent explicationes.")

345 My emphasis. Vitruvius 7.pref.5: "qui summo studio summaque diligentia cotidie omnes libros ex ordine perlegeret." Oder 1899, p. 185, n. 186, argued that Varro, who wrote a book called *De bibliothecis*, is the source for the anecdote, as does Frazer 1970, p. 117.

346 Vitruvius 7.pref.7: "fretus memoria e certis armariis infinita volumina eduxit . . .".

347 Thus, typically, concluding the preface to book 5 (5.pref.5), "Therefore, Caesar, I have set out the principles of temples in the third and fourth scrolls, and in this book I will treat the arrangement of public places." ("Itaque, Caesar, tertio et quarto volumine aedium sacrarum rationes exposui, hoc libro publicorum locorum expediam dispositiones.")

348 Vitruvius 4.pref.1. For the Latin, above, introduction, n. 34.

349 Vitruvius 1.pref.3: "et publicorum et privatorum aedificiorum pro amplitudine rerum gestarum ut posteris memoriae traderentur curam habiturum, conscripsi praescriptiones terminatas ut eas adtendens et ante

facta et futura qualia sint opera per te posses nota habere; namque his voluminibus aperui omnes disciplinae rationes."

350 Augustus's *Res gestae,* his autobiography in which particular stress is laid on his built works, was in fact later inscribed, in Latin and Greek, on the walls of the Temple of Roma and Augustus at Ankara in the Roman province of Galatia (Elsner 1996; Güven 1998). The two other surviving copies of the *Res gestae* were also found in Galatia, one as a Greek inscription, in Apollonia; the other as a Latin one, in the Roman colony of Antioch in Pisidia (Ramsay and von Premerstein 1927; Güven 1998, pp. 32–34; Mitchell and Waelkens 1998, pp. 148–150). Augustus meant the work for inscription, not literary publication, from the outset, stating in his will that it was to be inscribed on two bronze pillars in front of his mausoleum at Rome (Suetonius *Divus Augustus* 101.1–4).

351 Callebat, Vitruvius 1973, p. viii.

352 Heraclitus fr. 12; cf. Kirk, Raven, and Schofield 1983, pp. 194–197.

353 Vitruvius 8.pref.4, 8.1.1.

354 Vernant 1959; Illich 1985.

2 THE HERCULEAN BODY

1 Vitruvius 2.pref.1: "Dinocrates architectus cogitationibus et sollertia fretus, cum Alexander rerum potiretur, profectus est e Macedonia ad exercitum regiae cupidus commendationis. Is e patria a propinquis et amicis tulit ad primos ordines et purpuratos litteras, ut aditus haberet faciliores."

2 Vitruvius 2.pref.1–3: "Fuerat enim amplissima statura, facie grata, forma dignitateque summa. His igitur naturae muneribus confisus vestimenta posuit in hospitio et oleo corpus perunxit caputque coronavit populae fronde, laevum umerum pelle leonina texit dextraque clavam tenens incessit contra tribunal regis ius dicentis. Novitas populum cum avertisset, conspexit eum Alexander. Admirans, ei iussit locum dari ut accederet, interrogavitque quis esset. At ille: 'Dinocrates,' inquit, 'architectus

Macedo, qui ad te cogitationes et formas adfero dignas tuae claritati. Namque Athon montem formavi in statuae virilis figuram, cuius manu laeva designavi civitatis amplissimae moenia, dextra pateram quae exciperet omnium fluminum quae sunt in eo monte, aquam, ut inde in mare profunderetur.' Delectatus Alexander ratione formae statim quaesiit si essent agri circa qui possent frumentaria ratione eam civitatem tueri. Cum invenisset non posse nisi transmarinis subvectionibus: 'Dinocrates,' inquit, 'attendo egregiam formae compositionem et ea delector, sed animadverto si qui deduxerit eo loco coloniam, fore ut iudicium eius vituperetur.'"

3 Vitruvius 2.pref.3–4: "'Itaque quemadmodum formationem puto probandum, sic iudico locum inprobandum. Teque volo esse mecum, quod tua opera sum usurus.' Ex eo Dinocrates ab rege non discessit et in Aegyptum est eum persecutus. Ibi Alexander cum animadvertisset portum naturaliter tutum, emporium egregium, campos circa totam Aegyptum frumentarios, inmanis fluminis Nili magnas utilitates, iussit eum suo nomine civitatem Alexandriam constituere.

Ita Dinocrates a facie dignitateque corporis commendatus ad eam nobilitatem pervenit. Mihi autem, imperator, staturam non tribuit natura, faciem deformavit aetas, valetudo detraxit vires. Itaque quoniam ab his praesidiis sum desertus, per auxilia scientiae scriptaque, ut spero, perveniam ad commendationem."

4 The preface contains only one further paragraph, which repeats the concluding paragraph of book 1 (1.7.2).

5 The Aristippus story that opens the preface to book 6 is the only comparable one, but the story takes up only one short paragraph before the moralizing, which goes on for a further six, begins.

6 Varro as the source: Oder 1899, p. 365, n. 186; Frazer 1970, p. 117. The names given to Alexander's architect vary enormously. See Mansuelli 1983, pp. 87–90, for the onomastic tradition, and further Fabricius, in Pauly 1894–1980, s.v. *Deinocrates* (6); Frazer 1972, II, p. 4, n. 12; Traina

1988, pp. 311–316; Tomlinson 1996; Pierre Gros in Callebat et al., Vitruvius 1999, pp. 55–56.

7 The five architects named are Archimedes, Chersiphron, Philo, Ctesibius, Dinochares (Pliny *Natural History* 38.125); foundation of Alexandria: *Natural History* 5.62 and 7.125.

8 Ausonius *Mosella* 300–317: Daedalus, Philo, Archimedes, Menecrates, Chersiphron, Ictinus, Dinochares. There is no known architect called Menecrates, although a doctor called Menecrates is reported to have been active during the reign of Alexander's father, Philip of Macedon (Athenaeus *Deipnosophistai* 7.289; cf. Meyer 1986, p. 24). On Varro's now lost *Hebdomades*, above, chapter 1, p. 40.

9 Ausonius *Mosella* 311–317: "Dinochares" gets the longest notice of the seven architects named. When the sun is at a certain altitude, a pyramid "devours its own shadow" ("ipsa suas consumit pyramis umbras") because the shadow of the apex falls within the area of its square base (cf. Ammianus Marcellinus 22.15.29, and Hugh G. Evelyn White's note in the Loeb edition of Ausonius). Pliny (*Natural History* 34.148) makes "Timochares" the architect of the Temple of Arsinoë, deified sister and bride of Ptolemy Philadelphus, second of the Ptolemaic kings of Egypt.

10 Strabo 17.1.6, 14.1.23; Solinus 40.5.

11 Pseudo-Callisthenes 1.31 as cited by Fabricius, in Pauly 1894–1980, s.v. *Deinocrates* (6).

12 Plutarch *Alexander* 72.3, Plutarch *Fortune of Alexander, Moralia* 335c–e. Lucian, Plutarch's near contemporary of the second century A.D., also writes about the Mount Athos project, but he does not name its architect (*Pro imaginibus* 9; *Quomodo historia conscribenda sit* 12). On Alexander and Hephaestion see, inter alia, Hammond 1989, p. 16; Green 1991, p. 167.

13 Valerius Maximus 1.4.7, for which one manuscript reads "Dimocrates." Cf. Frazer 1972, II, p. 4, n. 12. Ammianus Marcellinus 22.16.7; Julius Valerius 1.25.

14 Vitruvius's prefaces and the relation of architects to power: Romano 1987, pp. 43–48.

15 Liddell and Scott 1968, s.v. *kratos*.

16 Iamblichus *Theologoumena arithmeticae* 59. The Pythagoreans gave names to all the numbers. One, for example, was *nous* and *ousia;* two, *doxa,* and so on. Cf. Burkert 1972, pp. 467–468.

17 Liddell and Scott 1968, s.v. *dinos*.

18 Clement of Alexandria *Stromateis* 2.14 as cited in Liddell and Scott, s.v. *dinos;* Vitruvius 9.1.2, 10.1.4.

19 *Deinos* appears to be a way of describing people endowed with the cunning the Greeks called *metis* (Detienne and Vernant 1978).

20 Sophocles *Philoctetes* 440; Plato *Protagoras* 341a.

21 *Fabrica* and *ratiocinatio:* Vitruvius 1.1.1.

22 Sextus Empiricus *Adversus mathematicos* 7.38–42 (= Arnim 1903–1924, II, 132; = *Against the Logicians* 1.38–42 in the Loeb edition); cf. *Outlines of Pyrrhonism* 2.80–83. Long 1971a, pp. 98–106; and above, chapter 1, pp. 57–58.

23 In an effort to reconcile Vitruvius's Macedonian architect with the Dinocrates the other sources say is from Rhodes, Traina 1988, p. 316, suggests Dinocrates' claim to be a Macedonian simply means that he was part of Alexander's following. Vitruvius places far too much emphasis on the architect's Macedonian origin for this to be plausible. See also Pierre Gros's commentary in Callebat et al., Vitruvius 1999, p. 56.

24 The first of these (p. 93 in this volume) is Conservatori Museums 1265: gilded bronze, height 2.41 meters; *LIMC* IV, s.v. *Herakles* no. 372; cf. Palagia 1990 with bibliography. The second is Vatican 252, gilded bronze, height 3.83 meters: *LIMC* IV, no. 302; Pietrangeli 1949–1950, pp. 37–52 and figs. 4–7. The Conservatori bronze is missing its lion skin but is thought to have had one originally. The statue was probably quite prominent in Vitruvius's Rome. Usually dated to the second or first century B.C. (Palagia dates it later), it was originally located in the Forum Boarium, where the cult of Hercules was concentrated. The Vatican bronze, from the sanctuary of Venus Victrix, is dated to 150–200 A.D. Vitruvius was a Roman writer, and I am therefore using the Latin

"Hercules" throughout, except in quotations where the version of the text cited is reproduced.

25 Unequivocally, Plutarch *Alexander* 1.2: "As for the lineage of Alexander, on his father's side he was a descendent of Heracles through Caranus . . . this is accepted without any question." See also Anderson 1928, pp. 12–29; Hammond 1989, passim; Green 1991, passim. Coins issued by Alexander from Sidon after its submission in 332 B.C. show Alexander wearing Hercules' traditional lion skin, trophy of his first labor, as a helmet; so does the famous marble Alexander Sarcophagus, also from Sidon, now in the Istanbul Archaeological Museum (inv. 370), of the late fourth century B.C. (p. 99 in this volume). For a catalogue of Alexander portraits, Bieber 1964. On Hercules in ruler portraiture, Palagia 1986.

26 See, for example, Arrian *Anabasis* 4.8.2–3, 5.29.1. Cf. Hammond 1989, pp. 219–220; Green 1991, p. 361.

27 Hammond 1989, p. 239 and passim; Green 1991, p. 129 and passim.

28 Arrian *Anabasis* 2.181–182; Plutarch *Alexander* 24.3; cf. Green 1991, p. 251.

29 Vitruvius 2.pref.2. Above, n. 2 for the Latin. Oechslin 1982 surveys the various interpretations of the Mount Athos project, from Francesco di Giorgio in the fifteenth century down to the twentieth. See also Meyer 1986.

30 Plutarch *Fortune of Alexander, Moralia* 335c–e.

31 Many interpreters, influenced perhaps by Plutarch's version, have assumed that Vitruvius means Alexander. Körte 1937; Oechslin 1982; Meyer 1986.

32 Anderson 1928, p. 9; Galinsky 1972, ch. 5 and passim; Pauly 1894–1980, supp. III, s.v. *Heracles*, 1010.37–1013.9. On the Roman Hercules as civilizer, Beard 1996, pp. 90–95.

33 Isocrates *Letter to Philip* 109–114. Cf. Galinsky 1972, p. 106; Green 1991, p. 49.

34 Xenophon *Memorabilia* 2.1.20–34. Cf. Galinsky 1972, p. 102. Cicero retells the fable in *De officiis* 1.118.

35 Apollodorus *Bibliotheca* 2.4.12; Diodorus Siculus 4.9.5, 4.24.2.

36 For example, Cicero *De finibus* 3.66, *De officiis* 5.25, *Pro Sestio* 143, *Disputationes tusculanae* 1.32. Cf. Galinsky 1972, p. 150, n. 9.

37 Vitruvius 2.pref.4. Above, n. 3 for the Latin.

38 Above, chapter 1, p. 74.

39 Ovid *Fasti* 5.64; Quintilian *Institutio oratoria* 1.6.33; Servius *Ad Aeneidem* 1.426; cf. Maltby 1991, s.v. *senatus*. Cicero *De senectute* 60.

40 Cicero *De senectute* 61: "Apex est autem senectutis auctoritas."

41 Cicero *De senectute* 62.

42 On the authority conferred by age, Grimal 1945, pp. 269–270.

43 Vitruvius 9.pref.17: "Item plures post nostram memoriam nascentes cum Lucretio videbuntur velut coram de rerum natura disputare, de arte vero rhetorica cum Cicerone, multi posterorum cum Varrone conferent sermonem de lingua latina, non minus etiam plures philologi, cum Graecorum sapientibus multa deliberantes, secretos cum his videbuntur habere sermones; et ad summam, sapientium scriptorum sententiae, corporibus absentibus vetustate florentes … maiores habent quam praesentium sunt auctoritates omnes."

44 Marble copy, probably of the third century A.D., 3.17 meters high, of a bronze by the fourth-century B.C. Greek sculptor Lysippus, found at the Baths of Caracalla and now in the Naples Archaeological Museum. See further Beard 1996.

45 Lucian *Hercules* 1, trans. H. G. Fowler and F. G. Fowler. Cf. Galinsky 1972, p. 108.

46 Lucian *Hercules* 4–5.

47 Benoit 1969, fig. 76: coin of the Aulerci Cenomeni tribe from a region of western Gaul roughly corresponding to modern Normandy (Paris, Bibliothèque nationale). A similar image also appears on a Lucanian *askos* of the third century B.C. (Reggio Museum, Calabria, cf. Benoit 1952, p. 104).

48 Caesar *Bellum gallicum* 6.17. On the complex relation between Gallic and Greco-Roman gods, Benoit 1952, 1969.

49 Crawford 1974, 348.6. On the basis of epigraphic evidence, Hepnig 1907, p. 268, says both were gods of the palaestra. This is corroborated by Athenaeus *Deipnosophistae* 561d and Cornutus *Epidrome* 16.11 (see below).

50 On Janus, especially Holland 1961 and Dumézil 1987, pp. 333–342.

51 Janiform herms which couple Hercules with another god, sometimes Hermes (*LIMC* IV, s.v. *Herakles,* nos. 1205–1207), are thought to be an invention of the first century A.D. (*LIMC* IV, p. 795). The pairing on the republican coin appears to be unique in Roman coinage.

52 On the caduceus, Farnoux 1981, pp. 474–478; Kellum 1990, p. 288.

53 BMC Tib. 116 (p. 106 in this volume). Cf. *LIMC* IV, s.v. *Herakles,* no. 739; Vermeule 1957, pls. 1.4–6; Pekary 1966–1967; Gasparri 1979, figs. 5–6; Kellum 1990, fig. 2. On the temple itself, also Rebert and Marceau 1925 and Steinby 1993–2000, s.v. *Concordia, aedes.*

54 On the importance of such anniversaries and the case of the Temple of Concord in particular, Gros 1976a, pp. 28–34. Ovid *Fasti* 1.637–638 gives a date of 10 A.D., whereas Suetonius *Tiberius* 20 says the temple was consecrated in 12 A.D. My thanks to Jane Francis for pointing out this discrepancy. Whichever the year, the day (January 16) is not disputed. See further Degrassi 1963, pp. 398–400.

55 The Temple of Divus Julius, built at the eastern end of the Forum, had been vowed in 42 B.C. and was dedicated in August of 29. Gros 1976a, pp. 85–92 and 207–210, and below chapter 3, pp. 175–178. On the Augustan transformation of the Forum, especially Zanker 1972.

56 Rebert and Marceau 1925, p. 73.

57 For a detailed reading, based on Manilius, of the temple in astrological terms, Kellum 1990.

58 Earlier temples of Concord: the first was dedicated by Camillus in 367 B.C. to celebrate the reconciliation of the plebeians with the patricians after a long period of discord. The second, after the death of Gracchus in 121 B.C., by L. Opimius. Rebert and Marceau 1925, pp. 53–54; Gasparri 1979, pp. 11–13; Steinby 1993–2000, s.v. *Concordia, aedes.*

59 The terms were taken up again inside the temple, where Mercury was paired with Mars, the god of war (Kellum 1990, p. 287). An ancient identification of Mars and Hercules is explained by Macrobius (*Saturnalia* 3.12.1–10). Commerce and the peaceful unity of empire: Suetonius *Divus Augustus* 93.2.

60 Pliny *Natural History* 34.33. Among the achievements in which Augustus took special pride was the closing of the Temple of Janus, decreed by the *maiores* "when victories had secured peace by land and sea throughout the whole empire of the Roman people" (Augustus *Res gestae* 13, trans. Brunt and Moore). On the connection between *pax, concordia,* and the cult of Janus, with specific reference to Augustus, Richard 1963; Turcan 1981, pp. 376–380.

61 Athenaeus *Deipnosophistae* 561d; cf. Schofield 1991, p. 49. Athenaeus dates from the late second century A.D. The point about Eros's being "far from anything ignoble" is that the Stoic Eros who upholds the safety of cities is not lust but friendship. Schofield 1991, pp. 28–46; and below, chapter 3, pp. 210–211.

62 Cornutus *Epidrome* 16.11, trans. Robert Stephen Hays. The *Epidrome* was a compilation from works of earlier philosophers. See Hays 1983, introduction, and Most 1989, p. 2016, who gives Apollodorus of Athens (second century B.C.) as the most likely source.

63 Heraclitus Homericus *Homerica Problêmata* 33.9. Like Cornutus, with whom he shares many similarities, Heraclitus is thought to have used Apollodorus of Athens as a source. See Buffière, introduction to the French edition of Heraclitus, pp. xxxi–xxxii. This Heraclitus has nothing to do with the better-known "obscure" Heraclitus of sixth-century B.C. Ephesus.

64 Heraclitus Homericus *Homerica Problêmata* 34.2.

65 Plutarch *De E delphico, Moralia* 387d.

66 Cornutus *Epidrome* 31.1.

67 Iamblichus *De vita pythagorica* 155; cf. Detienne 1960, p. 43. On the Pythagorean Hercules, also Carcopino 1943.

68 Iamblichus *De vita pythagorica* 50; cf. Detienne 1960, p. 22.

69 On natural theology in the context of Varro's tripartite classification, above, chapter 1, p. 49.

70 Above, chapter 1, p. 62.

71 Varro in Augustine *City of God* 7.7.

72 Kellum 1990.

73 Manilius *Astronomica* 2.453–484, 4.701–710, 4.744–817.

74 For further evidence of Manilius's Stoicism, *Astronomica* 1.247–254, 2.60–135, 3.48–55, 4.866–935.

75 Walsh 1958, among others.

76 Grimal 1945–1946; Lana 1953, pp. 9–12; Yavetz 1990, p. 33.

77 Dio Cassius 51.16.3–4; cf. Plutarch *Moralia* 814d, *Antony* 80. Kahn 1983, p. 6; Brad Inwood in Goulet 1989–, I, pp. 345–347; Hahm 1990, pp. 3035–3047. On Roman rulers and philosophical advisors in general, Rawson 1989.

78 The largest fragments survive in Stobaeus's *Anthologium* of the fifth century A.D. On Arius and the *Epitome*, Fortenbaugh 1983; Brad Inwood in Goulet 1989–, I, p. 346; Hahm 1990. An abridgment like Arius's *Epitome*—perhaps even the work itself—was almost certainly the source for many of Vitruvius's philosophical notions.

79 Rawson 1989, p. 245.

80 Suetonius *Divus Augustus* 85.1.

81 Yavetz 1984, p. 24, and p. 35 n. 201 for a partial list.

82 Athenaeus *Deipnosophistae* 561d.

83 Vitruvius 1.1.1: "Ea nascitur ex fabrica et rationcinatione."

84 See p. 106 in this volume and Vermeule 1957, who discusses the representation as a certain statue type.

85 Palagia 1990, p. 55, and n. 24 above. See p. 93 in this volume.

86 Vitruvius 9.pref.1.

87 Vitruvius 2.pref.1.

88 Virgil *Eclogues* 7.61, *Georgics* 2.66, *Aeneid* 8.276; Ovid *Heroïdes* 9.64; Pliny *Natural History* 12.3.

89 Pausanias *Description of Greece* 5.14.2. Cf. Becatti 1968, p. 4. See also Cicero *Disputationes tusculanae* 1.48; Varro *De lingua latina* 7.6; and Lucretius 3.978–1023 for whom Acheron is the underworld itself.

90 Virgil *Aeneid* 8.33–65.

91 Virgil *Aeneid* 8.51–54.

92 Forum Boarium in general: Coarelli 1988. Rite of the *ara maxima:* Latte 1960, pp. 213–215; Dumézil 1987, pp. 443–448. Just behind the *ara maxima Herculis invicti,* to the east, stood a Tuscan-style Aedes Herculis Invicti, also known as the Aedes Herculis Pompeiani from Pompey's restoration of it in the first century B.C. Vitruvius 3.3.5 mentions it along with the Capitoline Temple of Jupiter as an example of an areostyle temple. To the north of the altar was a round Aedes Aemiliana Herculis (also possibly "Hercules Victor") dedicated perhaps by Scipio Aemilianus in 142 B.C. Its remains were destroyed by Pope Sixtus IV at the end of the fifteenth century. The surviving round Temple of Hercules Victor (also known as Hercules Olivarius) "ad Portam Trigeminam" was not in the Forum Boarium proper, standing as it did next to the Forum just outside the Servian wall. Palagia 1990, pp. 51–54, gives a clear summary of the somewhat confusing evidence. On the surviving round temple, Rakob and Heilmeyer 1973, and Ziolkowski 1988 who argues that it was dedicated in 142 B.C. by the Roman general Mummius as a victory monument celebrating the destruction of Corinth in 146. On all of these temples, Steinby 1993–2000, s.v.

93 Virgil *Aeneid* 8.175–178.

94 Cacus and Evander as good and evil: Carcopino 1943, p. 179; Béranger 1953, p. 181; Fuchs 1973, p. 21.

95 Virgil *Aeneid* 8.184–267.

96 Virgil *Aeneid* 8.268–269.

97 Virgil *Aeneid* 8.274–305.

98 Prodicus's fable: Xenophon *Memorabilia* 2.1.20–34, and above, pp. 101–102.

99 Dumézil 1987, p. 434; Levi 1997, p. 31.

100 Carcopino 1943, pp. 182–183, notes that there were at least four locations in the area which bore the name "Cacus," one of which was the Forum Boarium itself (Aethicus *Varia Historia*, p. 83 Riese).

101 Steinby 1993–2000, s.v. *Hercules Musarum, Aedes*. The other temple, the older of the two, was dedicated to Hercules Custos, the protector, in the late third century B.C. (Steinby 1993–2000, s.v. *Hercules Custos, Aedes*). For a summary of the scholarship on the Ambracia Muses, Ridgway 1990, pp. 246–252.

102 On Pythagoreanism, Hercules, and the Muses, see Boyancé 1937 and 1955b; Dugas 1944; Detienne 1960; Sauron 1994, pp. 84–90. The cult statue of the temple—Hercules wearing a lion skin and playing the lyre, his club in front of him—appears on the reverse of a denarius of Q. Pomponius Musa of 66 B.C. (Crawford 1974, 410.1, and p. 119 in this volume). The obverse type is a head of Apollo, the more traditional *musagetes*, whose function Hercules here doubles.

103 Cicero *Pro Archia* 27. See also Eumenius *Panegyrici latini* 9.7.3 (cf. Boyancé 1955b, p. 175).

104 Plutarch *Roman Questions* 59. Juba was a historian contemporary with Vitruvius.

105 Plutarch *On the Signs of Socrates, Moralia* 579.

106 Fabius Pictor, as cited on a fragmentary inscription discovered at Taormina in 1969 (cf. Manganaro 1974, pp. 394–395). Livy *Ab urbe condita* 1.7.8: "miraculo litterarum."

107 In his *Bibliotheca* of the second century B.C., Apollodorus of Athens relates that the Pythian priestess at Delphi initially imposed ten labors on Hercules (2.4.12) but explains that there ended up being twelve of them because Eurystheus discounted two on technical grounds (2.5.5). Diodorus Siculus says twelve labors were imposed originally (4.9.5) but then contradicts himself later (4.24.2) saying that Hercules' immortality was to be the reward for ten.

108 Propertius *Elegies* 4.9.17: "labor ultime clavae."

109 Virgil *Aeneid* 8.288–304.

110 Diodorus Siculus 4.21.3; Dionysius of Halicarnassus *Antiquitates romanae* 1.40.6; Plutarch *Roman Questions* 18. Sulla offered a tenth of the spoils of his Greek victories to Hercules when he triumphed in 82 B.C. (Plutarch *Sulla* 35.1).

111 Besides Virgil, Livy *Ab urbe condita* 1.7.3–15; Propertius *Elegies* 4.9; Ovid *Fasti* 1.543–586. Among Greek writers, Diodorus Siculus (who completed his *Bibliothêkê* at Rome between 56 and 30 B.C.) 4.21.1–4; Dionysius of Halicarnassus (living in Rome and contemporary with Vitruvius) *Antiquitates romanae* 1.39; Strabo (late Augustan) 5.3.3. Cf. Winter 1910, pp. 171–273; Bayet 1926, pp. 127–128.

112 Macrobius *Saturnalia* 3.12.1–5, who cites Varro as his source. Cf. Coarelli 1988, p. 165.

113 Women were in fact barred from the rite of the *ara maxima:* Plutarch *Roman Questions* 60; Propertius *Elegies* 4.9.52–72; Macrobius *Saturnalia* 1.12.28.

114 Livy *Ab urbe condita* 1.7.15. Similarly Cicero, citing Ennius (*Disputationes tusculanae* 1.28; cf. Anderson 1928, pp. 29–30).

115 *CIL* VI, 312–319; Grimal 1951, p. 52 and n. 2; Degrassi 1963, p. 493; Dumézil 1987, p. 437; Palmer 1990, p. 235, n. 5. Coarelli (1988, pp. 61–77) and others have identified a platform of large tufa blocks under the rear of the church of Santa Maria in Cosmedin as the remains of the *ara maxima.*

116 *CIL* I.2, 180; Macrobius *Saturnalia* 1.12.3–5; cf. Grimal 1951, p. 53.

117 The feast of Hercules was also the date of Pompey's dedication of the Temple of Hercules Invictus in the Forum Boarium (Grimal 1951, p. 54).

118 Virgil deliberately makes Aeneas Herculean from the beginning, with Aeneas setting out from Troy with a lion's skin slung over his shoulders (*Aeneid* 2.721–723). Cf. Galinsky 1972, pp. 143–145.

119 Virgil *Aeneid* 8.626–731.

120 Grimal 1951, p. 60: "Auguste est bien le seul Hercule pacificateur et triomphant."

121 Anderson 1928, pp. 44–58; Béranger 1953, pp. 180–182; Galinsky 1972, pp. 128ff.

122 Suetonius *Divus Augustus* 57.2; cf. Schilling 1942; Jaczynowska 1981, pp. 634–635. Cult of Hercules and Augustus at Tibur: *CIL* XIV, 3665, 3681, 3679, 3679a. Similarly in southern Italy at Grumentum: *CIL* X, 320; cf. Anderson 1928, p. 45.

123 Virgil *Aeneid* 6.791–807.

124 Norden 1899; cf. Anderson 1928, p. 53; Kienast 1969, p. 436; Schwarzenberg 1975, p. 241; Vidal-Naquet 1984, p. 339.

125 Weinstock 1957; Michel 1967. For a list of statues dedicated to Hercules by republican generals, Latte 1960, pp. 219–220.

126 Anderson 1928, pp. 31–58; Weinstock 1957; Michel 1967.

127 Suetonius *Divus Augustus* 18.1; cf. Dio Cassius 51.16.3–15. Instinsky 1962, p. 33; Vidal-Naquet 1984, p. 339.

128 Suetonius *Divus Augustus* 50; Pliny *Natural History* 37.10; Dio Cassius 51.3.4. On Augustus's seal, Instinsky 1962; cf. Kienast 1969, pp. 435–436.

129 Dio Cassius 47.41.2. Cf. Instinsky 1962, p. 24.

130 Instinsky 1962, p. 33 and plate 4; Bieber 1964, p. 72 and fig. 62.

131 Vitruvius 1.pref.1. Above, chapter 1, n. 29 for the Latin.

132 Vitruvius 1.pref.1 and the triple triumph: Grenade 1961, p. 106; Fleury, Vitruvius 1990, p. 52; Corso and Romano, Vitruvius 1997, p. 59. The triumphal route: Coarelli 1988, pp. 365–414. Hercules *triumphalis:* Pliny *Natural History* 34.33; Bayet 1926, pp. 308, 328, 353; Versnel 1970, p. 90; Coarelli 1988, pp. 17, 165.

133 Vitruvius 1.pref.2. Above, chapter 1, n. 107 for the Latin.

134 Coarelli 1988, pp. 74–76, 150. In 22 B.C., after the floods and famines of the previous year, Augustus accepted the *cura annonae,* not held by any single man since Pompey in 56 B.C. (Rilkman 1980, pp. 58–62). Unofficially Augustus had been making distributions of grain and money since 44 (Rilkman, p. 179). Such distributions, "made at [his] own cost and by [his] own efforts [*impensa et cura mea*]," figure largely in his *Res gestae* (5.2, 15, 18; trans. Brunt and Moore). See also Berchem 1975.

135 Augustus *Res gestae* 27: "I added Egypt to the empire of the Roman people" (trans. Brunt and Moore).

136 Gauer 1974, p. 130; Coarelli 1988, p. 197. The *annona* relief, so-called, appears in the middle level on the right-hand side of the city facade of the arch. See also Simon 1981, p. 8.

137 Coarelli 1988, pp. 197–200.

138 Becatti 1968, pp. 9–10; Coarelli 1988, p. 199.

139 He does not mention this particular temple, but he does mention the Temple of Hercules Invictus (or Pompeianus) which stood nearby (Vitruvius 3.3.5).

140 Both of Hercules' hands are now missing, but what remains of the club rests on his right shoulder, so he must have been grasping it in his raised right hand.

141 *LIMC* IV, s.v. *Herakles*. Poplar-crowned statues include the so-called "Cook" Hercules (Museo Nazionale Romano, 182596; *LIMC* IV, no. 574) to which Becatti 1968, p. 10, gives the same approximate date as the Hercules Victor represented on Trajan's arch. The Hadrianic Hope Hercules in the Getty Museum (*LIMC* IV, no. 319) and a number of herms, also of the second century A.D., are also crowned with poplar.

142 Statius *Silvae* 1.1.86; Pliny *Natural History* 35.4. Weinstock 1957, p. 233; Schwarzenberg 1975, p. 258; Schilling 1982, p. 310.

143 Pliny *Natural History* 35.92–94. Cf. Anderson 1928, p. 55. On changing the heads of statues, see also Suetonius *Divus Gaius* (*Caligula*) 22. The head of the Hope Hercules (above, n. 141) is the portrait head of a deceased young man.

144 Varro *De lingua latina* 9.79; above, chapter 1, p. 72–73. The cast of characters in Varro's linguistic demonstration is uncannily close to that of Vitruvius's second preface (he mentions *Hercules* as an example of an anomalous nominative).

145 *De lingua latina* is mentioned by name at Vitruvius 9.pref.17.

146 Lewis and Short 1962, s.v. *potior.*

147 Hornblower and Spawforth 1996, s.v. *imperium.*

148 Above, chapter 1, pp. 41 and 45.

149 Vitruvius 2.pref.2.

150 Vitruvius 2.pref.3.

151 Vitruvius 1.pref.2–3.

152 On the role of votive tablets which named both the dedicator and the god invoked, Beard 1991, pp. 45–46: "Inscribed votive texts enacted that crucial conversion of an *occasional* sacrifice into a *permanent* relationship" (her emphasis).

153 Dionysius of Halicarnassus *Antiquitates romanae* 1.39–40.

154 Dionysius of Halicarnassus *Antiquitates romanae* 1.41.1. Alexander was also especially concerned with mingling barbarians with Greeks. On his concern for *homonoia* and the partnership between Macedonians and Persians, Arrian *Anabasis* 7.4.4–8, 7.7.8–9.

155 Vitruvius 1.3.1: "Partes ipsius architecturae sunt tres: aedificatio, gnomonice, machinatio." On book 10, Fleury 1993.

156 Diodorus Siculus 1.19.1–4: "Consequently certain of the Greek poets worked the incident into a myth, to the effect that Heracles had killed the eagle which was devouring the liver of Prometheus." Cf. Galinsky 1972, p. 129. Diodorus Siculus also makes Hercules a road builder (4.22.1–2).

157 On Euhemerism, Voegelin 1974, pp. 101–113; Price 1984, pp. 38–46; Feeney 1991, pp. 120–128.

158 Vitruvius 9.pref.16.

159 On this question Novara 1983 and 1994; Gros 1994a.

160 Vitruvius 6.pref.5, 6.pref.7. Above, introduction, n. 39 for the Latin.

161 Vitruvius 9.pref.1: "qui infinitas utilitates aevo perpetuo omnibus gentibus praestant." Cf. Novara 1983, p. 297; Novara 1994, p. 60.

162 Vitruvius 9.pref.2: "non solum suis civibus, sed etiam omnibus gentes."

163 Seneca *De tranquillitate animi* 3.1. Cf. Grimal 1946, p. 70; Goguey 1978, p. 105.

164 Zeno, cited in Plutarch *The Virtue of Alexander* (*Moralia* 329a), is the earliest source on universal brotherhood. Verbeke 1973, pp. 4–5.

165 Vitruvius 1.pref.1. Above, chapter 1, n. 29 for the Latin.

166 *TLL* VI.2, s.v. *gens,* 1848–1850.

167 *Rhetorica ad Herennium* 4.9.13. It is worth stressing that the author presents this kind of thing as standard and exemplary.

168 Cicero *Pro Balbo* 16, *In Pisonem* 34.

169 Cicero *Philippics* 6.19. See also *Epistulae ad familiares* 11.5.3, *De oratore* 1.14, *Pro Milone* 19.

170 Cicero *In Catalinam* 4.2.

171 Cicero *De lege agraria* 1.18.

172 Martial *Epigrams* 61.3–5: "orbe cantor et legor toto . . . spargor per omnes Roma quas tenet gentes."

173 Vitruvius 6.1.11. Above, chapter 1, n. 209 for the Latin. For a similar view, Strabo 2.5.26.

174 Pliny *Natural History* 3.5.39; cf. Dionysius of Halicarnassus *Antiquitates romanae* 1.41.1, cited above.

175 Vitruvius 9.pref.2. On Croton's attack on Sybaris and Milo's disguise, Diodorus Siculus 12.9.2; cf. Detienne 1960, pp. 20–21.

176 Vitruvius 9.pref.2: "instituunt civitatibus humanitatis mores, aequa iura, leges, quibus absentibus nulla potest esse civitas incolumis."

177 Vitruvius 9.pref.3–7.

178 Clavel-Levêque 1992. See also Guillaumin 1994.

179 Vitruvius 9.pref.15: "non solum ad mores corrigendos, sed etiam ad omnium utilitatem perpetuo sunt praeparata."

180 Vitruvius 6.pref.1: "Aristippus philosophus Socraticus, naufragio cum eiectus ad Rhodiensium litus animadvertisset geometrica schemata descripta, exclamavisse ad comites ita dicitur: 'bene speremus! hominum enim vestigia video.' Statimque in oppidum Rhodum contendit et recta gymnasium devenit, ibique de philosophia disputans muneribus est donatus, ut non tantum se ornaret, set etiam eis, qui una fuerunt, et vestitum et cetera, quae opus essent ad victum, praestaret. Cum autem eius comites in patriam reverti voluissent interrogarentque eum, quidnam vellet domum renuntiari, tunc ita mandavit dicere: eiusmodi

possessiones et viatica liberis oportere parari, quae etiam e naufragio una possent enatare."

181 Vitruvius 6.pref.2: "doctum ex omnibus solum neque in alienis locis peregrinum neque amissis familiaribus et necessariis inopem amicorum, sed in omni civitate esse civem difficiliesque fortunae sine timore posse despicere casus."

182 Vitruvius 6.pref.4: "[ars] . . . quae non potest probata sine litteratura encyclioque doctrinarum omnium disciplina." Compare Vitruvius 1.1.1.

183 Cicero *De republica* 1.28–29. In Cicero, the place of the shipwreck is unspecified. Varro might have been a common source (Oder 1899, p. 365; Frazer 1970, p. 117). Other versions of the story appear in later works (Corso and Romano, Vitruvius 1997, p. 860). On the Aristippus story in later interpretations, Oechslin 1981.

184 Diogenes Laertius 2.70, citing Aristippus: "Better to be a beggar than uneducated: the first lacks money; the second humanity [*anthrôpismos*]." Aristippus would indeed seem to be the best match for Cicero's shipwrecked philosopher.

185 Cicero *De republica* 1.35.

186 Vasaly 1993, p. 134. The idea of Stoic world citizenship as a possible political reality toward which the Roman imperial project was directed only came to fruition during the reign of Augustus (Wright 1995).

187 Vitruvius 6.1.1, 6.1.11.

188 Vitruvius 8.3.

189 Vitruvius 8.3.13. Silphium was a rare herb valued both as a condiment and a medicine. Callebat, Vitruvius 1973, pp. 105–108.

190 Vitruvius 9.1.1: "Ea autem sunt divina mente comparata habentque admirationem magnam considerantibus, quod umbra gnomonis aequinoctialis alia magnitudine est Athenis, alia Alexandriae, alia Romae."

191 Vitruvius 9.1.1: "*Analêmma* est ratio conquista solis cursu et umbrae crescentis ad brumam observatione inventa, e qua per rationes architectonicas circinique descriptiones est inventus effectus in mundo."

192 Vitruvius 1.2.2. Above, chapter 1, n. 194 for the Latin.

193 Vitruvius 1.1.4: "Geometria . . . ex euthygrammis circini tradit usum, e quo maxime facilius aedificiorum in areis expediuntur descriptiones normarumque et librationum et linearum directiones . . . difficilesque symmetriarum quaestiones geometricis rationibus et methodis inveniuntur."

194 Vitruvius 1.6.

195 Vitruvius 1.6.6–8, 1.6.12–13.

196 Millar 1984, p. 50.

197 Vitruvius 2.pref.3: "I note that if someone were to lead a colony there, his choice of site would be condemned." Above, n. 2 for the Latin.

198 Hyginus Gromaticus *De condicionibus agrorum* and *Constitutio limitum*, in Thulin 1971, pp. 82–83 and 165–166, respectively. Cf. Millar 1984, p. 50. See also Millar 1977, pp. 263–264.

199 According to Diogenes Laertius (2.60), Aristippus was the first philosopher to charge for his teaching, a practice that elicited nothing but scorn from Socrates, his avowed mentor.

200 Canfora 1992, p. 50. On Alexandria, Frazer 1972; Canfora 1991 (particularly on the library, which he argues was identical with the museum).

201 Strabo 9.2.2. Rawson 1985, pp. 321–325; Wallace-Hadrill 1988. For a similar view, Cicero *Ad Quintum fratrem* 1.1.27, cited below, n. 203 (cf. Woolf 1994, p. 119).

202 Strabo 9.2.2. The Boeotians must have had something of a reputation for philistinism. Plutarch, writing of the education of Hercules in *De E delphico* (*Moralia* 387d), asserts that in his youth, before acquiring wisdom, Hercules despised dialectic and syllogistic reasoning, "like a real Boeotian." Cf. Dugas 1944, p. 68.

203 Strabo 9.2.2. Compare Cicero *Ad Quintum fratrem* 1.1.27: "But seeing that we are governing that race of mankind [i.e., the Greeks] in which not only do we find real civilization, but from which it is also supposed to have spread to others, it is at any rate our duty to bestow upon them, above all things, just that which they have bestowed upon us."

204 Wallace-Hadrill 1988, p. 232.

205 Moatti 1988, 1991, and 1997.

206 Cicero *De republica* 1, passim; Cicero *Pro Sestio* 6.1.5: "naufragium rei publicae"; Horace *Odes* 1.14 (interpreted by Quintilian in *Institutio oratoria* 8.6.44). Schäfer 1972; Blumenberg 1997, pp. 10–17.

207 Virgil *Aeneid* 1.132–156.

208 Most recently by Galinsky 1996, pp. 21–23. An intaglio in the Boston Museum of Fine Arts (inv. 27.733) similarly pictures Augustus as Neptune, riding over the waves in a chariot drawn by hippocamps. Zanker 1988, pp. 96–97.

209 Cicero *Academica* 1.32; *De oratore* 1.13: "summa dicendi vis."

210 Cicero *De oratore* 1.13–16, 1.186–188. *De oratore* as a source, Vitruvius 9.pref.17.

211 Novara 1983, pp. 287–290; André 1987; Romano 1987, pp. 57–59, 68–75; Gros 1989a, pp. 13–15; Callebat 1994.

212 Brown 1963.

213 Gros 1994a.

214 Vitruvius 1.1.18. On the protocol of building in the republic, and the profound changes that took place from the early to mid first century B.C. and culminated with Augustus's sole charge of public construction, Gros and Sauron 1988. *De architectura* as a brief: Gros 1994a, p. 89. See also Novara 1983 and 1994.

215 Cicero *De oratore* 1.32.

216 Above, chapter 1, pp. 60–61.

217 Cicero *De oratore* 1.32.

218 Cicero *De oratore* 1.33.

219 Cicero *De inventione* 1.2. See also Quintilian *Institutio oratoria* 2.16.9.

220 Vitruvius 2.pref.5. Rykwert 1981, with its exploration of the notion of the primitive hut throughout history, remains fundamental; on Vitruvius's chapter, pp. 105–140. See also Romano 1987, pp. 108–124; and most recently Pierre Gros's commentary in Callebat et al., Vitruvius 1999, pp. 64–78. The "primitive hut" of Vitruvius 2.1.1 is the *capanna* of Elisa Romano's *La capanna e il tempio* (the *tempio* is *architectura*).

221 Vitruvius 2.pref.5. Lucretius (*De rerum natura* 5.925–1104) as a source: Merrill 1904; Rykwert 1981, pp. 112–113; Romano 1987, p. 111. Varro's now lost *Antiquitates rerum humanarum* would almost certainly have included a similar account. Such accounts of the origins of civilization have been traced to the fifth-century B.C. Greek atomist Democritus (Cole 1967; Burford 1972, p. 186).

222 Vitruvius 2.1.1: "Homines vetere more ut ferae in silvis et speluncis et nemoribus nascebantur ciboque agresti vescendo vitam exigebant."

223 Vitruvius 2.1.2: "Ergo cum propter ignis inventionem conventus initio apud homines et concilium et convictus esset natus, et in unum locum plures convenirent habentes ab natura praemium praeter reliqua animalia ut non proni, sed erecti ambularent mundique et astrorum magnificentiam aspicerent, item manibus et articulis quam vellent rem faciliter tractarent, coeperunt in eo coetu . . . facere tecta."

224 Vitruvius 2.1.5. I have taken Hispania Lusitania not as two separate regions but as the single Augustan province that had included what is now western Spain and Portugal until its southernmost part, Lusitania, was founded as a separate province between 16 and 13 B.C. (Hornblower and Spawforth 1996, s.v. *Lusitania;* Alarcão and Etienne 1979, p. 878). Origin of civilization at Rome: Gordon 1990c, p. 235; Feeney 1991, p. 119.

225 Cicero *De lege agraria* 1.18. Cf. Vasaly 1993, p. 36.

226 Pensabene 1990–1991. See Callebat et al., Vitruvius 1999, p. 73, for the numerous citations referring to the Palatine hut which begin, chronologically, with Varro (*De lingua latina* 5.54). Also, especially, Edwards 1996, pp. 32–43. Balland 1984, pp. 73–74, thinks the hut on the Capitol was built in the early part of Augustus's reign, probably during the reconstruction of the *area Capitolina* in 26–20 B.C. The writers who refer to the Capitoline hut are all Augustan or later. Among them is Virgil who includes it in his description of Aeneas's shield (*Aeneid* 8.654), whose images, including the hut, chronicle Rome's past as prophecy of its present greatness under Augustus (Edwards 1996, pp. 35–36). Valerius Max-

imus, who wrote under Tiberius, Augustus's successor, calls the small hut "the column of the whole world" (2.8).

227 Lucretius *De rerum natura* 5.1011–1014.

228 He does speculate how fire may first have been discovered (a storm, tree branches rubbing together, and so on: 1.897–903, 5.1091–1111), using terms that Vitruvius has interpolated into his version. But for Lucretius, the discovery of fire is in no way *the* key to the beginning of civilization.

229 Cicero *De inventione* 1.2.

230 Zeno, in Arnim 1903–1924, 1.34; cf. Long 1986, pp. 154–156.

231 Cicero *De natura deorum* 2.118.

232 Arius Didymus in Eusebius *Evangelicae praeparationis* 15.14.

233 Varro *Antiquitates rerum divinarum* fr. 23.15–16 (Cardauns 1976), cited by Tertullian *Ad nationes* 2.2.19. Cf. Pépin 1956, p. 268. Varro *De lingua latina* 5.70 (*ignis* derived from *gnasci*).

234 Degrassi 1957–1963, 452; cf. Beard, North, and Price 1998, I, pp. 189–191.

235 Lapidge 1978, p. 162, paraphrasing Posidonius fr. 186 (Edelstein and Kidd 1972).

236 Vitruvius 3.1.5. Above, chapter 1, p. 44.

237 See also Cicero *De republica* 1.40–41.

238 Cicero *De officiis* 1.153, *De republica* 1.25. Cf. Schofield 1995, p. 67: in Cicero "there is no logical space for the idea of a state or commonwealth distinct from people or community."

239 Cicero *Pro Sestio* 143.

240 Vitruvius 2.1.6: "Cum . . . natura non solum sensibus ornavisset gentes quemadmodum reliqua animalia, sed etiam cogitaionibus et consiliis armavisset mentes et subiecisset cetera animalia sub potestate, tunc vero ex fabricationibus aedificiorum gradatim progressi ad ceteras artes et disciplinas, e fera agrestique vita ad mansuetam perduxerunt humanitatem."

241 Vitruvius 2.1.7: "deinde observationibus studiorum e vagantibus iudiciis et incertis ad certas symmetriarum perduxerunt rationes."

242 Disciplines of the architect: Vitruvius 1.1.11. Above, chapter 1, n. 67 for the Latin.

243 On "summum templum architecturae" as a trope for the Temple of Jupiter Capitolinus, guarantee of Roman *imperium,* above, chapter 1, pp. 28–29.

244 Seneca the Elder *Controversiae* 1.6.4. Cf. Edwards 1996, p. 38, whose translation I have followed. When the Temple of Jupiter was rebuilt in the early part of the first century B.C., it was, apparently, roofed with gilded bronze tiles: Seneca the Elder *Controversiae* 2.1.1; Pliny *Natural History* 33.57.

245 Virgil *Aeneid* 8.414, 423, 628, 710. Virgil's use of the epithet appears to be unique (*TLL,* s.v. *ignipotens*).

246 Virgil *Aeneid* 8.562–564.

247 Virgil *Aeneid* 8.675.

248 Virgil *Aeneid* 8.722–723.

249 *Gentes omnes subactae:* Vitruvius 1.pref.1. Homer *Iliad* 18.607–608; Virgil *Aeneid* 8.724–729. It is more than a little painful to recognize in Virgil's parade of captives his parallel for Homer's *choros,* "Ariadne's dance," with which the latter concludes his description of Achilles' shield (*Iliad* 18.590–606) and sums up its cosmic significance.

250 Vitruvius 4.pref.1: "tantae disciplinae corpus." Vitruvius also insists on the greatness of his discipline, which "overflows" with the ornaments of different kinds of learning at 1.1.11, opening the sentence that concludes with the ascent to "summum templum architecturae," an abundance that does indeed recall the Temple of Jupiter itself, with its gold roof and other magnificent materials and ornaments, which included gilded acroteria (Cicero *Ad Verrem* 2.68–69; Ovid *Ars amatoria* 3.115; Dionysius of Halicarnassus *Antiquitates romanae* 4.61.4).

251 Vitruvius 4.pref.1.

252 Vitruvius 1.1.1. Above, chapter 1, n. 88 for the Latin, and a justification of my slightly unconventional reading.

253 For example, Cicero *De oratore* 1.20. See also Vasaly 1993, p. 187.

254 Homer *Odyssey* 9.124–129, 17.381–384, with McEwen 1993, p. 73.

255 Arius Didymus in Stobaeus *Anthologium*, II, pp. 103.24–104.9 (cf. Schofield 1991, p. 137).

256 Cicero *Pro Roscio Amerino* 120ff.; *De oratore* 2.40 (cf. Ramage 1973, p. 56).

257 Simonides of Ceos (556–468 B.C.), eleg. 25 (cf. Ramage 1973, pp. 158–159).

258 Ramage 1973, pp. 14–19. On the idea that only the "humane" man can appreciate beauty, Varro *De lingua latina* 8.31 (cf. Novara 1983, p. 306).

259 Ramage 1973, p. 18, referring specifically to the Hellenistic context. One might recall that the lovers of Ovid's late Augustan *Ars amatoria* all disport themselves exclusively in the Roman *urbs*.

260 Vitruvius 2.1.1.

261 Aulus Gellius *Noctes atticae* 13.17, citing Varro and Cicero on the question of *humanitas, philanthropia,* and *paideia.* Among secondary sources, Rieks 1967; Ramage 1973; Schadewalt 1973. For a summary, and a discussion of *humanitas* as the badge of elite superiority, Gordon 1990c, pp. 235–238. See also Veyne 1993. On the dissemination of *humanitas* as the justification for world conquest, Brunt 1978; Gabba 1982 and 1984; Erskine 1990, pp. 192–100; Woolf 1994; Woolf 1998, pp. 54–71. The *locus classicus* for the latter is the passage from Pliny's *Natural History* (3.5.39) cited above.

262 Julius Caesar (*Bellum gallicum* 1.1.3) was also aware of the dangerously feminizing potential of *humanitas* (cf. Veyne 1993, p. 343).

263 Vitruvius 2.8.12: "Ita singillatim decurrentes et ad coetus convenientes e duro feroque more commutati in Graecorum consuetudinem et suavitatem sua voluntate reducebantur. Ergo ea aqua non inpudico morbi vitio, sed humanitatis dulcedine mollitis animis barbarorum eam famam est adepta."

264 Strabo 9.2.2. Cf. Cicero *Ad Quintum fratrem* 1.1.27 and above, p. 140.

265 On the nomad as the ultimate barbaric type in classical thought, Shaw 1982 (cf. Woolf 1998, p. 106).

266 Virgil *Aeneid* 6.851–853: "Tu regere imperio populos, Romane, me-
mento / (hae tibi erunt artes) pacique imponere morem, / parcere sub-
iectis et debellare superbos."

267 Tacitus *Agricola* 21.2. The translation follows Woolf 1998, p. 69, for the
first part; Beard and North, introduction to Gordon 1990c, for the second.

268 Tacitus *Annals* 16.28.

269 Veyne 1993, p. 368.

270 Ovid *Fasti* 2.684. Bréguet 1969, pp. 143–145, cites all the occurrences beginning with Cicero's Catalinarian orations of 63 B.C. See also Nicolet
1991, pp. 111–114; Romm 1992, pp. 46–48; Edwards 1996, pp. 99–100.

271 The translation is Edwards's (1996, p. 100), who glosses that "Rome extends through the whole world and at the same time all the world is concentrated in Rome."

272 Varro *De lingua latina* 5.143; Servius *Ad Aeneidem* 1.12: "urbs dicta est ab
orbe" (cf. Maltby 1991, s.v. *urbs*).

273 Vitruvius 1.1.12: "encyclios enim disciplina uti corpus unum ex his
membris est composita." Compare Cicero *Pro Archia* 1.2; *De oratore* 3.21.

274 Vitruvius 6.pref.4.

275 Vitruvius 1.1.18. Above, chapter 1, n. 122 for the Latin.

3 THE BODY BEAUTIFUL

1 Vitruvius 3.1.3: "Similiter vero sacrarum aedium membra ad universam
totius magnitudinis summam ex partibus singulis convenientissimum
debent habere commensus responsum. Item corporis centrum medium
naturaliter est umbilicus; namque si homo conlocatus fuerit supinus
manibus et pedibus pansis circinique conlocatum centrum in umbilico
eius, circumagendo rotundationem utrarumque manuum et pedum digiti linea tangentur. Non minus quemadmodum schema rotundationis in
corpore efficitur, item quadrata designatio in eo invenietur; nam si a pedibus imis ad summum caput mensum erit eaque mensura relata fuerit

ad manus pansas, invenietur eadem latitudo uti altitudo, quemadmodum areae, quae ad normam sunt quadratae."

2 On Leonardo's drawing (Accademia, Venice, no. 228), dated between 1476 and 1490, see, among others, Pedretti 1977, I, pp. 224–251; Pedretti 1988, pp. 160–162; Zöllner 1987, pp. 77–87; Rykwert 1996, pp. 86–90, 97–99. On the drawing and the passage just cited, see now especially Gros 2001. Fra Giocondo's is the first illustrated Vitruvius edition (Giocondo, Vitruvius 1511, fols. 22r and v for Vitruvian man, reproduced on pp. 158–159 in this volume).

3 Fleury, Vitruvius 1990, pp. lxii–lxiii.

4 Above, chapter 1, pp. 16–18, 32–34.

5 Entasis: Vitruvius 3.3.13; Ionic volutes: Vitruvius 3.5.8. Cf. Fleury, Vitruvius 1990, pp. lxiii–lxiv.

6 This is true not only of the Leonardo and Fra Giocondo images mentioned above in note 2, but of all their subsequent iterations as well. My point here is not that Leonardo and his successors got it wrong, but rather to stress how easily the images can obscure the text and, more importantly, the historical specificity of its signified matter.

7 Man without thickness: Gros, Vitruvius 1990, p. 66, who notes that for the diagram to work, fingers and toes would have to be in the same plane. See also Gros 2001.

8 Cicero De natura deorum 2.47. Cf. Plato Timaeus 33b. Cicero translated parts of the Timaeus.

9 Cicero De natura deorum 2.48.

10 Cicero De natura deorum 2.84. The view that the universe is governed by two kinds of motion, circular and rectilinear, can be traced to Aristotle (De caelo 1.1–2; cf. Lapidge 1978, pp. 177–178).

11 Cicero De natura deorum 2.90.

12 On the vogue for astronomy/astrology in the early principate, Barton 1994, pp. 47–54. Soubiran, Vitruvius 1969, p. lv, notes that Vitruvius was one of its earliest exponents.

13 Manilius *Astronomica* 1.206, 211–212. The discussion of circularity continues to 1.750, with particular emphasis in 565ff.

14 Manilius *Astronomica* 1.247. Cf. 1.134, 148, 807; 2.705.

15 Manilius *Astronomica* 1.147–173.

16 Manilius *Astronomica* 1.663–665.

17 Manilius *Astronomica* 4.587–589.

18 Cicero *De divinatione* 2.92. Manilius makes the same observation (*Astronomica* 1.661–662).

19 See above, chapter 1, pp. 45–46.

20 John Lydus *De mensibus* 3.4. See above, chapter 1, p. 47.

21 Raven 1951, pp. 151–152.

22 Musti 1975; Traina 1988, p. 337.

23 Varro *De lingua latina* 5.143.

24 Varro in Solinus 1.18: "dictaque primum est Roma quadrata, quod ad aequilibrium foret posita." Cf. Rykwert 1988, p. 98.

25 Solinus 1.18.

26 Ox. pap. XVII, 1927, 2088.14–17, as restored by Piganiol 1937, p. 347. Trans. by author. Castagnoli 1951, pp. 394–395; Wiseman 1987, p. 401. Thomsen 1980, pp. 12–17, has an alternative restoration of the text, as well as a discussion of the complete fragment.

27 Festus 310–312l. The passage has also been taken as referring exclusively to a specific Augustan monument (Zanker 1983, p. 21; Rykwert 1988, p. 98; Richardson 1992, s.v. *Roma Quadrata*). My reading follows Wiseman 1987, p. 401, which leads me to suspect that Festus was locating the putative Romulean foundation in reference to, or *in terms of,* the Augustan monument—which, no doubt, was the intention. See further Gagé 1930 on Augustus as a second Romulus; Timpanaro 1950 for additional discussion of Festus's text.

28 Cicero *De divinatione* 1.30. Cf. Valerius Maximus 1.1; Livy *Ab urbe condita* 5.41; Plutarch *Camillus* 32.

29 Steinby 1993–2000, s.v. *Apollo Palatinus, aedes.*

30 Virgil *Aeneid* 6.69; Servius *Ad Aeneidem* 8.720. The only other Augustan temple so constructed was the Temple of Jupiter Tonans on the Capitol (Pliny *Natural History* 36.50). Cf. Gros 1976a, p. 73.

31 Vitruvius 2.7.1, 2.8.5–7, 4.4.4.

32 Above, chapter 2, pp. 143–148.

33 Suetonius *Divus Augustus* 29.3.

34 Ovid *Fasti* 4.951–954.

35 Pensabene 1997, pp. 151, 159, 163–168.

36 Le Glay 1991, p. 123; Rey-Coquais 1991; *TLL* II, s.v. *Augustus,* 1415–1419.

37 Suetonius *Divus Augustus* 7.2, drawing on the Augustan writer Verrius Flaccus. For the bibliography on the term "Augustus," above, introduction, n. 53.

38 On augury in general, Linderski 1986; Gargola 1995, pp. 25–50. See also Rykwert 1988, pp. 44–49; Beard, North, and Price 1998, I, pp. 22–23.

39 Szabo 1938 and 1956. Cf. Castagnoli 1951, p. 397; Musti 1975, p. 307; Rykwert 1988, pp. 97–100.

40 Cicero *De legibus* 2.21.

41 Varro *De lingua latina* 7.7; cf. Rykwert 1988, pp. 45–49.

42 Cicero *De divinatione* 1.31; cf. Szabo 1956, p. 261.

43 Cicero *De divinatione* 1.30.

44 Gordon 1990a, p. 179; Beard, North, and Price 1998, I, pp. 21–24, 27–28.

45 On the various kinds of *templum,* Linderski 1986, pp. 2256–2296. Not all temples (*aedes*) were *templa,* in the augural sense, as for example the circular Temple of Vesta in the Forum. Nor, clearly, were all *templa* temples, in the sense of shrines dedicated to a deity, since a military camp or a public building such as the Curia Julia were also *templa.*

46 Cicero *De legibus* 2.31.

47 Gagé 1930; Vierneisel and Zanker 1979 for a catalogue of portraits; Zanker 1988, pp. 126–127; Price 1996, pp. 824–825. On the *Gemma augustea,* for example (p. 147 in this volume), Augustus holds a *lituus.*

48 On the setting up of Roman military camps: Hyginus Gromaticus *De munitionibus castrorum;* Polybius 6.26–32. For the *augurale,* Tacitus *Agricola* 2.13, 15.30; Quintilian *Institutio oratoria* 8.2.8. Hyginus (*De munitionibus castrorum* 11, cited Gargola 1995, p. 28) gives particularly clear instructions for the placing of the *auguratorium* of a military camp.

49 Gagé 1930, pp. 160–162.

50 Dio Cassius 51.1.3. Cf. Suetonius *Divus Augustus* 18.2.

51 Horace *Odes* 1.3.32. In Horace's *Carmen saeculare* 5.61–62, Apollo is specifically the Apollo of the Palatine temple. The Delphic Apollo as the Greek city founder's authority: Malkin 1987, ch. 1. See also Gagé 1955, p. 111; Wiseman 1981 and 1987.

52 Vitruvius 1.4.9.

53 Scheid 1993, p. 116. On Varro's tripartite theology—natural, civil, and poetic—above, chapter 1, p. 51.

54 Vitruvius 9.pref.3–8.

55 Vitruvius 1.6.6–8 and 1.6.12–13. On the sixteen-part sky, Cicero *De divinatione* 2.42; Pliny *Natural History* 2.138.

56 Vitruvius 9.4.1, 9.4.6.

57 Soubiran, Vitruvius 1969, pp. 143–145, referring in particular to Cuillandre 1944, pp. 185–228. On left and right in general, Needham 1973.

58 Virgil *Georgics* 1.235–236; Ovid *Metamorphoses* 1.45; Manilius *Astronomica* 3.183–185; Vitruvius 9.4.1 and 9.4.6. Cf. Soubiran, Vitruvius 1969, p. 144.

59 Frontinus *De limitibus,* in Thulin 1971, pp. 10–11. Trans. by author. Cf. Hyginus Gromaticus *Constitutio limitum,* in Thulin 1971, pp. 131–134, where an almost identical description appears. See also Gargola 1995, pp. 41–50. Hyginus Gromaticus is variously dated between the second and fourth centuries A.D. (Hornblower and Spawforth 1996, s.v.); Frontinus is late first century A.D. Either both used the same source (Hyginus does not mention Varro), or Hyginus followed Frontinus.

60 On Roman surveying, Dilke 1971.

61 Frontinus *De limitibus,* in Thulin 1971, p. 14. Trans. by author.

62 Varro *De lingua latina* 7.7. See also Livy *Ab urbe condita* 1.18.6–7. Cf. Rykwert 1988, pp. 46–49; Beard, North, and Price 1998, II, pp. 86–87.

63 Varro in Festus 434l. Cf. Ferri, Vitruvius 1960, p. 170.

64 See also, at greater length, Hyginus Gromaticus *Constitutio limitum*, in Thulin 1971, p. 134.

65 Since Frontinus is one of the few ancient authors to mention Vitruvius by name (*De aquis* 1.25), his source is almost certainly *De architectura*.

66 Vitruvius 4.5.1: "Regiones autem quas debent spectare aedes sacrae deorum inmortalium sic erunt constituendae uti, si nulla ratio inpedierit liberaque fuerit potestas, aedis signumque quod erit in cella conlocatum spectet ad vespertinam caeli regionem uti qui adierint ad aram immolantes aut sacrificia facientes spectent ad partem caeli orientis et simulacrum quod erit in aede, et ita vota suscipientes contueantur aedem et orientem caelum ipsaque simulacra videantur exorientia contueri supplicantes et sacrificantes, quod aras omnes deorum necesse esse videatur ad orientem spectare."

67 Gros, Vitruvius 1992, p. 157.

68 West-facing Hellenistic temples: Gros, Vitruvius 1992, pp. 152–157. Vitruvius on the *aedes Ephesi Dianae:* 7.pref.16.

69 Nissen 1869, p. 162, lists 53 east-facing Greek temples as opposed to 3 that face north, 5 that face south, and 5 west. Cf. Ferri, Vitruvius 1960, p. 170.

70 Vitruvius 4.9.1. The Ara Pacis Augustae, the altar of Augustan Peace in the Campus Martius, dedicated in 9 B.C., faced east and was directly linked to the course of the sun by its location next to the Horologium Augusti, Augustus's sun clock, just west of it (on the latter, below, chapter 4, pp. 244–246). The principal entrance of the altar's encompassing screen wall faced west.

71 Gros 1976a, pp. 151–152.

72 Virgil *Aeneid* 8.714–716.

73 On the temples built or restored by Augustus, including the Temple of Divus Julius, Augustus *Res gestae* 19–21; Suetonius *Divus Augustus* 29.

On the dedication of the temple on August 18 of 29 B.C., and the games that celebrated it, Dio Cassius 51.22.2 and 4–9. On Caesar's divinity, Weinstock 1971 (pp. 385–401 on the temple). For an updated assessment, Beard, North, and Price 1998, I, pp. 140–149.

74 Steinby 1993–2000, s.v. *Iulius, Divus, aedes.*

75 Pycnostyle intercolumniation: Vitruvius 3.3.2.

76 Wide door: Statius *Silvae* 1.1.22–24. Cf. Gros 1976a, p. 86.

77 Gros 1976a, p. 86. The temple appears on the reverses of an aureus and a sestertius of 36 B.C., with a bearded Octavian on the obverse, stamped IMP.CAESAR.DIVI.F. ("Imperator Caesar, son of the god"). Crawford 1974, 540.1–2. The aureus is illustrated on p. 176 of this volume.

78 Gros 1976a, p. 152, links the orientation to Caesar's birthday, which was July 13.

79 Augustus's birth on September 23 linked it to the autumnal equinox, but Capricorn, the sun's birth sign under which Augustus would have been conceived, was much more frequent in the iconography of the Augustan principate (see pp. 180 and 263 in this volume). Dwyer 1973; Pollini 1993, pp. 280–284; Barton 1994, pp. 40–47. Vitruvius 9.6.2 mentions an Achinopolus (or Athenodorus), expert in Chaldean "arts," who "left detailed rules for casting nativities based not on the time of birth but of conception [*qui etiam non e nascentia, sed ex conceptione genethialogiae rationes explicatas reliquit*]." Augustus was not only conceived under Capricorn; the moon was in Capricorn at the time of his birth in September (Pollini 1993, p. 281). On Augustus's relation to the sun, further below, chapter 4, pp. 237–239, 288–290.

80 On the evidence of the coins described in n. 77 above.

81 Significantly, in view of how Vitruvius explains the need for west-facing temples, Virgil has Aeneas gaze at the rising sun when he prays at dawn on the day he first sets foot on the future site of Rome (*Aeneid* 8.68–70).

82 Vitruvius 4.5.1.

83 For a partial list of such monuments, below, chapter 4, n. 239.

84 On the restructuring of the Forum, Zanker 1972; Gros 1976a, pp. 85–92; Coarelli 1983–1985, II, pp. 233–334; Gros and Sauron 1988, pp. 60–63; Simon 1986, pp. 84–91.

85 On fora as augural spaces, Gros 1990, pp. 32–34; Gros 1996a, pp. 207–209.

86 As already noted, you cannot argue with buildings; the sole recourse is their destruction. The storming of the Bastille, for instance, or the bombing of Dresden. The attacks on the World Trade Center were devastating proof of the signifying power of buildings.

87 See Gros, Vitruvius 1990, pp. 66–70; Gros 2001. It is fairly common to invoke, as Gros does, the age-old mathematical problem of squaring the circle as latent in Vitruvius's description, but there seems to me to be little contextual justification for this.

88 Vitruvius 3.1.3. Above, n. 1 for the Latin.

89 Vitruvius 3.1.3.

90 Vitruvius 1.2.2. Above, chapter 1, n. 194 for the Latin.

91 Vitruvius 1.1.4. Above, chapter 2, n. 193 for the Latin.

92 Festus 11l. Trans. by author.

93 Florus *Digesta* 50.16.211, as cited *TLL*, s.v. *area*, 496.78–79.

94 Varro *De lingua latina* 5.38.

95 Vitruvius 1.4.12, 1.6.1, 1.7.1, 2.pref.5.

96 Vitruvius 1.6.6–8 and 1.6.12–13.

97 Vitruvius 3.pref.4: "Nunc in tertio de deorum inmortalium aedibus sacris dicam." See also 1.7.2, 2.10.3, 4.pref.1, 4.8.7, 4.9.1, 5.pref.5, where Vitruvius identifies book 3 in the same way. Cf. Gros, Vitruvius 1990, p. vii.

98 Vitruvius 1.3.1: "Publicorum autem distributiones sunt tres, e quibus est una defensionis, altera religionis, tertia opportunitatis."

99 Vitruvius 1.3.1: "religionis deorum inmortalium fanorum aediumque sacrarum conlocatio."

100 On belief, Feeney 1998, pp. 12–46, and especially Price 1984, p. 10: "'Belief' as a religious term is profoundly Christian in its implications; it was forged out of the experience which the Apostles and Saint Paul had

of the Risen Lord. The emphasis which 'belief' gives to spiritual commitment has no necessary place in the analysis of other cultures." My discussion of Roman religion draws heavily on the recent assessments of Beard, North, and Price 1998 and Feeney 1998. For earlier studies see, among others, Latte 1960, Scheid 1985, and Dumézil 1987.

101 "The 'ancient' religions of the Romans, Greeks, Hittites, and Aztecs . . . remember no founder, seek no converts, and aim not at the salvation of the individual in a future life but at the preservation and growth of the community in this one." Feeney 1998, p. 13, citing Pettazoni 1972, pp. 28–29.

102 Augustine *City of God* I.pref. and passim.

103 Succinctly, Dupont 1986, p. 233: "À Rome la religion consiste en pratiques, non en théories."

104 Beard, North, and Price 1998, I, p. 216, with relevant citations.

105 Festus 424l, citing one Aelius Gallus who wrote in the early Augustan period. Trans. by author. See also Cicero *De domo sua* 127; Gaius *Institutes* 2.6. Cf. Scheid 1985, p. 54.

106 On *religio* and *superstitio,* Beard, North, and Price 1998, I, pp. 215–244. See also Grodzynkski 1974; Gordon 1990c, pp. 237–240; Scheid 1985, pp. 129–147; Sachot 1991. Grodzynski (p. 59) concludes with a useful chronological summary of how the meaning of *superstitio* changed over time.

107 Cicero *De natura deorum* 2.70, 3.92; *De domo sua* 105; *De divinatione* 1.7, 2.19, 2.125. Cf. Grodzynski 1974, p. 41.

108 Beard, North, and Price 1988, I, pp. 225–227.

109 Seneca *De clementia* 2.5.1. Cf. Beard, North, and Price 1998, I, p. 216.

110 Brunt 1978, p. 162; Harris 1979, pp. 117–130; Scheid 1985, p. 120; Woolf 1998, p. 48.

111 Vitruvius 6.1.11.

112 On the signifying power of architecture, Vitruvius 1.1.3, and above, chapter 1, pp. 71–88.

113 Beard, North, and Price 1998, I, p. 359: "It is hard now to appreciate that Jesus' claim in the Gospels (Matthew 22.15–22; Mark 12.13–17; Luke 20.20–6) that one should give unto Caesar that which is Caesar's and give unto God that which is God's was, in the context of the first century A.D., utterly startling."

114 Horace *Odes* 3.6.1–6. The translation follows Galinsky 1996, pp. 290–291. See also Gros 1976a, p. 25.

115 Decay of religion: Cicero *De legibus* 2.33, *De natura deorum* 2.7, 2.9, *De divinatione* 1.25, 1.27–28, 2.71; Dionysius of Halicarnassus *Antiquitates romanae* 2.62; Pliny *Natural History* 10.20. Cf. Beard 1994; Galinsky 1996, p. 422.

116 Horace in the ode just cited (3.6), as well as in his other Roman odes, frequently points to the failure of *religio* as the reason for Rome's recent near collapse. Cf. Gros 1976a, p. 25.

117 Decay of temples: Cicero *De natura deorum* 1.82; Livy *Ab urbe condita* 4.20.7; Propertius *Elegies* 2.6.35–36, 3.13.47; Tacitus *Annales* 2.49.1. Cf. Gros 1976a, p. 21.

118 Zanker 1988, pp. 65–71; Beard, North, and Price 1998, I, pp. 120–125.

119 Beard, North, and Price 1998, I, pp. 31–41. "Roman writers represent communication between men and gods primarily through the medium of ritualized exchange and interpretation of signs—not through intervention, inspiration or incubation" (p. 31). See also Scheid 1985, pp. 51–55; Scheid 1986.

120 Virgil *Aeneid* 8.714–716.

121 Horace *Odes* 1.2, and above, chapter 1, pp. 67–69.

122 Livy *Ab urbe condita* 4.20.7. Cf. Edwards 1996, p. 49.

123 Ovid *Fasti* 2.59–64. The translation follows Beard, North, and Price 1998, I, p. 197.

124 On Augustan temples in Rome, Gros 1976a; Zanker 1988, pp. 65–71, 102–118, 135–156; Beard, North, and Price 1998, I, pp. 196–201; Purcell 1996.

125 Augustus *Res gestae* 19–21. Cf. Suetonius *Divus Augustus* 29; Elsner 1996.

126 Accumulation of priesthoods: Beard, North, and Price 1998, I, pp. 186–189.

127 Cicero *De domo sua* 1. The translation follows Beard, North, and Price 1998, I, p. 115. See also Beard 1994, pp. 729–734.

128 Beard 1990, 1994.

129 As, for example, the Temple of Hercules Musarum built by Fulvius Nobilior discussed above in chapter 2.

130 Beard 1990, p. 31; Beard 1994, pp. 731–732.

131 Augustus *Res gestae* 34.3 (trans. Brunt and Moore).

132 Speyer 1986; Beard 1990, p. 48; Gordon 1990a, b, c; Scheid 1993; Price 1996; Beard, North, and Price 1998, I, pp. 182–210.

133 Gros 1976a, pp. 31–35. The Circus Flaminius was where the spoils of war were displayed on the days preceding the triumphs that set out from there.

134 Livy *Ab urbe condita* 1.10.4–7, 4.20.3–7; Dionysius of Halicarnassus *Antiquitates romanae* 2.34.4; Augustus *Res gestae* 19. Steinby 1993–2000, s.v. *Iuppiter Feretrius, Aedes*; Richardson 1992, s.v. *Iuppiter Feretrius, Aedes*; Gagé 1930, pp. 141–142; Gros 1976a, p. 26.

135 Tacitus *Historiae* 3.72: "pignus imperii." Cf. Edwards 1996, p. 80.

136 Augustus *Res gestae* 20.

137 Suetonius *Divus Augustus* 29.3. Cantabria is in northwestern Spain.

138 Suetonius *Divus Augustus* 90.

139 Seneca *Natural Questions* 2.31–41, 47–51; Pliny *Natural History* 2.137–146. Cf. Thulin 1905–1909, I; Weinstock 1951; Latte 1960, pp. 159–160; Dumézil 1987, pp. 624–635.

140 Servius *Ad Aeneidem* 2.649. Cf. Dumézil 1987, p. 625.

141 Festus 389l. Cf. Dumézil 1987, p. 625.

142 Dionysius of Halicarnassus *Antiquitates romanae* 2.5.1–2.

143 Suetonius *Divus Augustus* 29.3.

144 Suetonius *Divus Augustus* 94.2.

145 Solid marble Temple of Apollo: Virgil *Aeneid* 6.69 and Servius *Ad Aeneidem* 8.720; *opus quadratum* Temple of Jupiter Tonans: Pliny *Natural History* 36.50. Cf. Gros 1976a, pp. 73–74, 100.

146 Hexastyle Corinthian: the reverse types of a number of Augustan coins (both *aurei* and *denarii*) minted around 19 B.C., as illustrated on p. 193. See also Steinby 1993–2000, s.v. *Iuppiter Tonans, Aedes;* Richardson 1992, s.v.

147 Suetonius *Divus Augustus* 91.2.

148 Suetonius *Divus Augustus* 91.2; Dio Cassius 54.4.2–4.

149 Gros 1976a, pp. 15–52.

150 Incorrect transmission: Wesenberg 1983, Coulton 1989, among others; not applied: Alberti onward—recently Wilson Jones 2000a, pp. 33–38.

151 Pliny *Natural History* 34.65. The Latin *symmetria* is a transliteration of the Greek word. Pollitt 1974, pp. 256–258, who catalogues far more citations from Vitruvius than from anyone else but includes the term in his Greek (not Latin) lexicon, assumes that all the authors he cites are referring to a single, more or less constant principle of ancient Greek aesthetics.

152 Vitruvius 3.1.1: "Aedium compositio constat ex symmetria, cuius rationem diligentissime architecti tenere debent. Ea autem paritur a proportione, quae graece *analogia* dicitur. Proportio est ratae partis membrorum in omni opere totoque commodulatio, ex qua ratio efficitur symmetriarum. Namque non potest aedis ulla sine symmetria atque proportione rationem habere compositionis, nisi uti [ad] hominis bene figurati membrorum habuerit exactam rationem."

153 The principle is usually referred to today as modular construction, but it does not in fact appear to have been the method Greek and Roman architects used when they designed their buildings (Coulton 1989; Wilson Jones 1989 and 2000a).

154 Vitruvius 1.2.2, 1.2.4, 3.1.1, 3.1.3, 3.1.4, 3.1.9. Cf. Gros, Vitruvius 1990, pp. 57–61, 65–66.

155 Vitruvius 3.1.2. The literature on Polykleitos is vast. Among recent works, two useful collections of essays are Moon 1995 and *Polyklet* 1990, in which Caterina Maderna-Lauter's "Polyklet in Rom" is particularly relevant. Link with Vitruvius: Raven 1951; Gros, Vitruvius 1990, pp. 61–65; Rykwert 1996, pp. 97–110.

156 Galen *De placitis Hippocratis et Platonis* 5.3.15–16, a report of Chrysippus's view that beauty lies in the "symmetry of . . . members [of the body], of finger to finger, obviously, and of all the fingers to the palm and wrist and of these to the forearm and the forearm to the arm and of every part to the whole, *as it is written in the Kanon of Polykleitos*" (trans. Phillip de Lacy; my emphasis). Cf. Galen *De temperamentis* 1.566 (cited in Stewart 1978a, p. 125) and Pollitt 1974, pp. 14–15. The relationship of body parts to each other and to the configuration of the whole, said here to have been itemized in Polykleitos's *Canon*, is so close to how Vitruvius presents the principle of architectural symmetry that a Polykleitan source for the latter is almost certain.

157 Vitruvius 3.1.3. Above, n. 1 for the Latin.

158 Rykwert 1996, passim.

159 Vitruvius 3.1.4, 3.1.9.

160 Cicero's *Laws*, for instance, is modeled on Plato's but its substance is entirely Roman.

161 Suetonius *Divus Augustus* 79.1–2.

162 As, for example, the coins with the Temple of Jupiter Tonans on them, illustrated on p. 193.

163 Ovid *Tristia* 2.287; cf. Edwards 1996, p. 24.

164 Vitruvius 1.2.3: "Eurythmia est venusta species commodusque in compositionibus membrorum aspectus." On eurythmy (*eurhythmia*, in Greek; literally, "well-shapedness"), Pollitt 1974, pp. 169–181; Bek 1985.

165 Vitruvius 3.3.13, 6.2.5, 6.3.11. On "tempering," above, chapter 1, pp. 63–66.

166 Vitruvius 1.2.1. Rhetoric and *De architectura:* André 1987; Brown 1963; Callebat 1994; Gros 1989a, pp. 13–15; Novara 1983, pp. 287–290; Romano 1987, pp. 57–59, 68–75.

167 "In unum locum": Cicero *De inventione* 1.2, *De oratore* 1.33; Vitruvius 2.1.2; and above, chapter 2, pp. 141–148.

168 Cicero *De oratore* 1.17. Similarly Aristotle: "A statement [*logos*] is persuasive . . . because there is someone whom it persuades" (*Rhetoric* 1356b27–28).

169 Cicero *Brutus* 185.

170 Plutarch *On Listening to Lectures, Moralia* 45e. Cf. Lucian *Heracles* (above, chapter 2, pp. 103–104); Fleury, Vitruvius 1990, p. 112; Callebat 1994, p. 40.

171 *Eurhythmia* as the "well-shapedness" of a speech: Isocrates *Letter to Philip* 27. Plato writes that a good speech should be put together like a well-shaped man, with all its parts "adapted to one another and to the whole" (*Phaedrus* 264c).

172 Vitruvius 1.2.4 (cited above, chapter 1, n. 258). In fact, eurythmy comes before symmetry in book 1, chapter 2, where Vitruvius lists the principles on which he says architecture depends.

173 Vitruvius 1.2.2 and above, chapter 1, pp. 54–55.

174 Vitruvius 1.3.2: "Haec autem ita fieri debent ut habeatur ratio firmitatis, utilitatis, venustatis."

175 Vitruvius 1.3.2: "venustatis vero cum fuerit operis species grata et elegans membrorumque commensus iustas habeat symmetriarum ratiocinationes."

176 Vitruvius 6.8.9: "Cum vero venuste proportionibus et symmetriis [opus] habuerit auctoritatem, tunc fuerit gloria [aria] architecti." The Fensterbusch text (Fensterbusch, Vitruvius 1964) followed for book 6 suppresses the problematic *aria,* an unknown word in Latin, whose inclusion may be due to faulty transcription. On the texts followed, above, preface.

177 Vitruvius 6.8.10.

178 Callebat et al. 1984.

179 Pollitt 1974, p. 448; Pliny *Natural History* 35.79 (cited and translated Pollitt, p. 298).

180 Vitruvius 3.3.13. Cicero also couples *venustas* with *voluptas* when writing of the beauty of a ship (*De oratore* 3.180). At *De officiis* 1.130, Cicero distinguishes two kinds of *pulchritudo: venustas,* which he says is feminine beauty, and *dignitas,* which is masculine.

181 Cicero *De natura deorum* 2.69.

182 Varro *De lingua latina* 5.61–62, cited below, chapter 4, pp. 255–256. As already noted, Vitruvius names *De lingua latina* at 9.pref.17.

183 Varro *De lingua latina* 5.63: "The poets, in that they say that the fiery seed fell from the Sky into the sea and Venus was born 'from the foam masses,' through the conjunction of fire and moisture, are indicating that the *vis*, 'force' which they have is that of Venus. Those born of this *vis* have what is called *vita*, 'life.'"

184 Plutarch *On the Face of the Moon* (*Moralia* 926e–927). Cf. Schilling 1982, pp. 197–198.

185 Lucretius *De rerum natura* 1.1–23. *De rerum natura* is mentioned by name at Vitruvius 9.pref.17.

186 Hesiod *Theogony* 154–206, which dates from about 700 B.C., is the earliest.

187 Schilling 1982, pp. 197–200.

188 Schilling 1982, pp. 85–88, 234–254. The epithet *genetrix* first appears in Ennius's *Annales* (52v) of ca. 200 B.C. (Weinstock 1971, p. 23).

189 With certain reservations, the following discussion of the Roman Venus draws principally on Schilling 1982, which remains the only monograph devoted to the topic. Schilling tries to keep her religious and juridical or political aspects separate, which, as we have seen, is a misunderstanding.

190 Schilling 1982, p. 85.

191 *Venus*/charm: Schilling 1982, pp. 31–32; personalization: Schilling, pp. 84–86.

192 Schilling 1982, pp. 37–38.

193 Virgil *Georgics* 1.338.

194 Cicero *De natura deorum* 2.72. Another view has *religio* derived from *religare*, "to tie" or "to bind," but the source—the Christian apologist Lactantius (*Divinae institutiones* 4.28.12) of the third century A.D.—is rather late. On the whole question, Sachot 1991, pp. 364–367.

195 Vitruvius 1.3.2. Above, n. 175 for the Latin.

196 Schilling 1982, pp. 39–42.

197 Reciprocity—the exchange of favors—is also the nub of the Greek *charis* for which, as noted earlier, *venustas* was the Latin translation. Carson 1999, pp. 19–21.

198 Schilling 1982, pp. 273–296; Beard, North, and Price 1998, I, pp. 144–145.

199 Pompey's theater and the Temple of Venus Victrix: Aulus Gellius *Noctes atticae* 10.1.6–7; Pliny *Natural History* 8.20; Hanson 1959, pp. 43–55; Coarelli 1971–1972; Gros 1987a; Richardson 1987; Sauron 1987.

200 Schilling 1982, pp. 275, 280 (Sulla); p. 297 (Pompey).

201 Schilling 1982, pp. 303–304.

202 Venus Genetrix and the Forum Julium: Steinby 1993–2000, s.v. *Venus Genetrix, aedes;* Weinstock 1971, pp. 80–87; Amici 1991; Westall 1996.

203 Dio Cassius 43.43.3: "bloom of youth," *anthos ti hôras.* Cf. Weinstock 1971, pp. 18, 23–26. On Caesar's good looks, Cicero *Brutus* 261; Suetonius *Divus Julius* 45; Velleius Paterculus 2.41.3; Plutarch *Caesar* 17.2.

204 Suetonius *Divus Julius* 49, citing Cicero. Cf. Weinstock 1971, p. 18.

205 Murray 1965; Grimal 1966; Gigante 1995, ch. 4. The charred fragments of this and other works by Philodemus, now in the archaeological museum in Naples, were discovered at the Villa of the Papyri at Herculaneum in the eighteenth century.

206 Philodemus *On the Good King According to Homer* cols. xix–xxi, as cited Murray 1965, p. 171. An edition of Philodemus's works has yet to be published.

207 Lucretius *De rerum natura* 5.1110–1113; cf. Grimal 1966, p. 270.

208 Diotogenes in Stobaeus *Anthologium* IV, p. 267.11, cited and translated Chesnut 1978, p. 1317. The treatise is either Hellenistic or imperial Roman, probably of the second century A.D.

209 Venus Anadyomene in the Temple of Divus Julius: Pliny *Natural History* 35.91; Strabo 14.2.19. Binding power of Venus: Varro *De lingua latina* 5.63.

210 Pliny *Natural History* 35.79. On Apelles in general: 35.79–98.

211 Strabo 14.2.19.

212 For ancient descriptions, see Overbeck 1959, nos. 1847–1866, and the commentary on Pliny *Natural History* 35.91 in Sellers 1896, p. 127.

213 Leonidas of Tarentum, in *The Greek Anthology* 16.182 (vol. 5 in the Loeb edition; Overbeck 1959, no. 1852). See further *The Greek Anthology* 16.178–181.

214 Ovid *Ars amatoria* 3.389–402, in the context, interestingly enough, of a rumination on the signifying power of various Augustan monuments.

215 Strabo 14.2.19.

216 Schilling 1982, pp. 311–313. The statue was sculpted by the Greek sculptor Arcesilaus.

217 Suetonius *Divus Julius* 88; Dio Cassius 45.7.1; Pliny *Natural History* 2.94.

218 Star in pediment: Crawford 1974, 540.1–2, illustrated on p. 176 above.

219 Link between comet and the planet Venus: Weinstock 1971, pp. 370–384; Schilling 1982, pp. 316–323. Vitruvius notes that the planet Venus (*Veneris stella*) had two names, Vesperugo as the evening star and, as the morning star, Lucifer (9.1.7).

220 Vitruvius 3.1.

221 See, for example, Vitruvius 3.3.11, 3.3.13, 6.2.11.

222 Zeno, fourth-century B.C. founder of the Stoic school, claimed in his now lost *Republic* that "Eros is a god who stands ready to help in furthering the safety of the city" (Athenaeus *Deipnosophistai* 561d; cf. Schofield 1991, p. 49). On the whole question of love and the Stoic city, Babut 1963; Schofield 1991, especially chs. 2 and 3.

223 Arius Didymus in Stobaeus *Anthologium* II, p. 115.1–2, trans. Malcolm Schofield. Schofield 1991, p. 29, has called this the official school definition. Similarly, Arius Didymus in Stobaeus *Anthologium* II, p. 66.11–13 and p. 91.15–16.

224 Arius Didymus, in Stobaeus *Anthologium* II, p. 123.7–12. Trans. in Görgemanns 1983, p. 171.

225 Diogenes Laertius 7.130. Cf. Schofield 1991, p. 29.

226 Cicero *Disputationes tusculanae* 4.72. Pollitt 1974, p. 448.

227 For Vitruvius, *venustas* is invariably a question of appearance: 1.2.3, 1.3.2, 2.3.4, 3.3.6 (twice), 3.3.11, 3.3.13, 3.5.11, 4.2.2, 4.3.1, 5.1.10, 6.3.11. The highest concentration of occurrences (7 out of 12) is in the two books (3 and 4) on temples.

228 Vitruvius 3.1.

229 Suetonius *Divus Augustus* 79.1–2.

230 Suetonius *Divus Augustus* 79–83.

231 Zanker 1988, pp. 98–100.

232 Vitruvius 3.3.13.

233 Sextus Empiricus *Adversus mathematicos* 7.239 (= *Against the Logicians* 1.239 in the Loeb edition). Cf. Schofield 1991, p. 114.

234 Corinthianization: Gros 1976a, pp. 197–242; Gros and Sauron 1988, p. 68; Onians 1988, pp. 41–58; Sauron 1988; Gans 1992; Wilson Jones 2000a, pp. 138–140. Examples of acanthus flourishing on flat surfaces include the frieze of the Temple of Venus Genetrix at Rome; the frieze of the Temple of Divus Julius at Rome; the frieze of the Maison Carrée at Nîmes; and the friezes on many temples dedicated to the imperial cult in other parts of the Roman world (Hänlein-Schäfer 1985, plates).

235 Sauron 1988, and especially Castriota 1995, pp. 58–73, among others.

236 Vitruvius 4.1.9–10: "Eius autem capituli prima inventio sic memoratur esse facta. Virgo civis Corinthia, iam matura nuptiis inplicata morbo decessit. Post sepulturam eius, quibus ea virgo viva poculis delectabatur, nutrix collecta et conposita in calatho pertulit ad monumentum et in summo conlocavit et, uti ea permanerent diutius sub divo, tegula texit. Is calathus fortuito supra acanthi radicem fuerat conlocatus. Interim pondere pressa radix acanthi media folia et cauliculos circum vernum tempus profudit, cuius cauliculi secundum calathi latera crescentes et ab angulis tegulae ponderis necessitate expressi flexuras in extremas partes volutarum facere sunt coacti.

Tunc Callimachus, qui propter elegantiam et subtilitatem artis marmoreae ab Atheniensibus Catatexitechnos fuerat nominatus, praete-

riens hoc monumentum animadvertit eum calathum et circa foliorum
nascentum teneritatem, delectatusque genere et formae novitate ad id
exemplar columnas apud Corinthios fecit symmetriasque constituit. Ex
eo in operis perfectionibus Corinthii generis distribuit rationes."

237 Other references are imperial Roman and later: Strabo 4.4.6; Pliny *Natural History* 34.13; Pausanias 8.45.4. Athenaeus's *Deipnosophistae* (5.205c)
of the late second century A.D. cites Callixenes of Rhodes (second century B.C.) saying that the capitals of Ptolemy IV's floating palace were *ko-
rinthiourgeis*, "of Corinthian work," but this is more likely to refer to
Corinthian craftsmanship (which was famed in antiquity) than to the actual form of the capital. Roux 1961, pp. 359–362; Gros, Vitruvius 1992,
pp. 50–51.

238 For a review, Gros, Vitruvius 1992, pp. 75–90, to which must be added
Rykwert 1996, pp. 317–349, and Wilson Jones 2000a, pp. 136–138.

239 The floppy-leafed *Acanthus mollis* (bear's-foot) is the kind Vitruvius means,
not the prickly *spinosus* variety. For the distinction between the two vari-
eties, Pliny *Natural History* 22.76. Not native to Corinthia: Baumann
1984, pp. 188–189; cf. Gros, Vitruvius 1992, pp. 76–77.

240 Homolle 1916; Roux 1961, p. 196; Rykwert 1996, pp. 321–327. See also
Kempter 1934; Schauenburg 1957, pp. 198–204; cf. Gros, Vitruvius
1992, p. 77.

241 Mallwitz 1981, pp. 318–321 (capital used to support Phidias's colossal
statue of Athena in the Parthenon); Pedersen 1989 (capitals of the interior columns of the west room of the Parthenon); cf. Gros, Vitruvius
1992, p. 79.

242 For more details than those enumerated here, Gros 1976a, pp. 197–234;
Lawrence 1983, passim; Roux 1961, pp. 359–380; Rykwert 1996,
pp. 338–349.

243 The temple was first excavated in the early nineteenth century. Shortly
after, the Corinthian capital that was discovered there mysteriously disappeared, but not before it was recorded in the drawings of the British architect C. R. Cockerell who was part of the expedition. Cockerell 1860;

Roux 1961, pp. 362–367; Lawrence 1983, pp. 230–234; Beard and Henderson 1995, pp. 10–12; Rykwert 1996, pp. 338–340.

244 Roux 1961, pp. 367–369; Lawrence 1983, pp. 242–244; Rykwert 1996, p. 343.

245 Called "normal" by German scholars because it is like the capital Vitruvius describes, and is the recognizable model for the one that the Romans adopted. Heilmeyer 1970; Bauer 1973; Frazer 1990, pp. 171–189.

246 Antiochus's temple was never finished. Begun as a Doric temple under the Peisistratids in the late sixth century B.C., the Temple of Zeus Olympios was not completed until the reign of Hadrian in the thirties of the second century A.D. According to Pliny (*Natural History* 34.65), Sulla brought some of its columns to Rome for use in the restoration of the Roman Capitol at the beginning of the first century B.C. There had been an Augustan project for the temple's completion as a shrine dedicated to Augustus's *genius* (Suetonius *Divus Augustus* 60), which never came to fruition. Cossutius and the Temple of Zeus Olympios: Vitruvius 7.pref.15; cf. Liou et al., Vitruvius 1995, pp. 74–77.

247 Strabo 8.6.20. See also Salomon 1984, pp. 398–401; Williams 1986.

248 Williams 1986.

249 Aristophanes *Frogs* 354.

250 Strabo 8.6.20.

251 Roman obsession with morals: Edwards 1993 (pp. 5–6 on luxury and lust as cognate vices). Conquest as a moral corrective: Woolf 1994, pp. 119–125; Woolf 1998, p. 71. See also Petrochilos 1974.

252 Cicero *Ad familiares* 4.5.4; *Disputationes tusculanae* 3.53; Pausanias 7.16.7–8; Plutarch *Caesar* 57.8; Polybius 39.2; Strabo 8.6.23; Velleius Paterculus 1.13.1. Cf. Wiseman 1979, pp. 491–495.

253 *CIL* I.2, 616 = *CIL* VI, 331 = Degrassi 1957–1963, 122. Ziolkowski 1988 argues that, although the inscription was found on the Caelian Hill at some distance from the Forum Boarium, the temple Mummius dedicated to Hercules is the round temple that still stands on the bank of the Tiber. Coarelli 1988, pp. 185–186, disagrees, claiming that the latter's sty-

listic features give it a later date than the 140s B.C. of Mummius's dedication. The temple is in any case Corinthian, the earliest Corinthian
temple in Rome. If Ziolkowski is right, this first use of the order at Rome
would tie it directly to the sack of Corinth, and corroborate my reading of
Vitruvius's story (see below).

254 Strabo 8.6.23.

255 Cicero *De lege agraria* 1.5. Cf. Wiseman 1979, p. 493.

256 Appian *Punica* 136 as cited in Wiseman 1979, p. 497, n. 2; Dio Cassius
43.50.33. On the name and the epigraphic evidence for it, Broneer 1941;
cf. Wiseman 1979, pp. 497–498. See also Williams 1987; Hoskins Walbank 1996.

257 Centuriation of the site: Romano 1993. Rebuilding of Corinth: Musti
and Torelli 1986, pp. 217–220; Williams 1987, 1993; Gros 1990, pp. 50–
52; Ward-Perkins 1994, pp. 255–263; Hoskins Walbank 1996.

258 Basilica at Fano: Vitruvius 5.1; cf. Gros 1990, p. 50.

259 Gaius and Lucius, who were to have been Augustus's heirs, died in 2 and
4 B.C. The group, now in the Corinth museum, dates from the late Augustan period. The ever-youthful Augustus, togate and *capite velato*, is
much better-looking than and appears even younger than the two nude
youths who were his grandsons. Vierneisel and Zanker 1979, p. 47.

260 Williams 1987, p. 32; Hoskins Walbank 1996. Cf. Vitruvius 4.5.1.

261 There was a famous Corinthian prostitute, Lais, whose grave was still an
attraction in the second century A.D. (Pausanias 2.2.4). Antipater of
Sidon (*The Greek Anthology* 7.218, vol. 2 in the Loeb edition) immortal-
ized her in an epitaph not long after the city was sacked: "I contain her
who in Love's company luxuriated in gold and purple, / more delicate
than tender Cypris / Lais, citizen of sea-girt Corinth . . .". Lais, the beautiful dead courtesan, is an evocative metaphor for the ruined city and suggests a possible anchor for Vitruvius's allegory of it. Like Vitruvius,
Antipater calls her a "citizen of Corinth" and emphasizes her delicacy
and tenderness. Cf. Engels 1990, p. 98.

262 Ziolkowski 1993.

263 Vitruvius 7.pref.15; Suetonius *Divus Augustus* 60.

264 Vitruvius 4.1.11–12.

265 Ionic: Vitruvius 3.5.1–15; Doric: 4.3.1–10.

266 For the Ionic order, and indeed much of book 3, one source is the Hellenistic architect Hermogenes of Alabanda (late second century B.C.), whom Vitruvius admires greatly: Vitruvius 3.2.6, 3.3.8, 3.3.9 (cf. Gros 1978; Akurgal 1985, pp. 20–25). Pythias, who designed the Ionic Temple of Athena at Priene, is another. See 7.pref.12, where other sources are listed, including those for the Doric order and an otherwise unknown Arcesius on the Corinthian (cf. Liou et al., Vitruvius 1995, pp. 62–69).

267 Vitruvius 4.1.1: "Columnae corinthiae praeter capitula omnes symmetrias habent uti ionicae."

268 Vitruvius 4.1.1. According to Vitruvius, the Ionic capital is a third of a column diameter high; the Corinthian a full diameter.

269 Vitruvius 4.1.2.

270 On Vitruvius's failure to recognize the development of a distinctive Corinthian entablature in the architecture of late republican Rome, Gros 1976a, pp. 197–234, especially pp. 200–201. According to Gros, the fully developed Roman Corinthian order, with its own proper entablature, first appears in the Temple of Mars Ultor in the Forum of Augustus, begun around 25 B.C. and dedicated in 2 B.C. See also Wilson Jones 2000a, pp. 140–147.

271 In fact, being able to fit in anywhere—although not for the reason Vitruvius gives—makes the Corinthian order easier to use than the Doric or the Ionic. The Doric and the Ionic orders both present formal difficulties when it comes to turning corners: the Doric because of the triglyphs of its entablature, the Ionic because the capital is frontal. Since all four fronts of the Corinthian capital are identical, and since there are no triglyphs in its entablature, the Corinthian order presents no such difficulties. On the ease of using the Corinthian order and the method of its design in Roman architecture, Wilson Jones 1989; 2000a, pp. 136–156.

272 Vitruvius 4.1.3: "Ita e generibus duobus capitulo interposito tertium genus in operibus est procreatum." One might recall that Aristophanes used *korinthiazomai* for "fornicate" (above, n. 249).

273 Vitruvius 4.1.6–7. Cf. Rykwert 1996, pp. 171–216.

274 Rykwert 1996, p. 317, has read Vitruvius 4.1.3 (cited above) as intimating that the Corinthian order is the child of the Doric and the Ionic.

275 The symbolic fruitfulness of acanthus in the phenomenon known as Corinthianization is most spectacularly deployed, with specific references to Venus, in the frieze on the screen wall of the Ara Pacis Augustae, consecrated in 9 B.C. (Castriota 1995, pp. 58–73).

276 Varro *De lingua latina* 5.61–62 (cited below, chapter 4, pp. 255–256).

277 Vitruvius 4.1.8: "Tertium vero, quod corinthium dicitur, virginalis habet gracilitatis imitationem, quod virgines propter aetatis teneritatem gracilioribus membris figuratae effectus recipiunt in ornatu venustiores."

278 Vitruvius 4.1.10. Cf. Vitruvius 1.2.5, where he also stresses the youthful tenderness of the Corinthian order.

4 THE BODY OF THE KING

1 De facto monarchy: Millar 1984, and above, introduction, n. 51.

2 Cicero *De natura deorum* 2.118; Arius Didymus in Eusebius *Evangelicae praeparationis* 15.14. Long 1986, pp. 154–155, and above, chapter 2, pp. 143–144.

3 Varro *De lingua latina* 5.70.

4 Vitruvius 2.1.2. Above, chapter 2, n. 223 for the Latin.

5 Vitruvius 1.pref.2. Above, chapter 1, n. 107 for the Latin.

6 Vitruvius 1.1.1. For the Latin, above, chapter 1, n. 88, which also sets out the grammatical justification for this reading.

7 The debate appears in book 52 of Dio Cassius's *Roman History*. Cf. Vitruvius 1.pref.1.

8 Dio Cassius 52.35.5.

9 It was in a centrally located sanctuary in the forum of the Roman colony of Arles that the best-preserved marble copy of the *clipeus virtutis*, "shield of virtue," whose gold original had been conferred on Augustus by the Senate in January 27 B.C. along with his new name, was enshrined only a year later to acquire what Pierre Gros has called "une valeur fondatrice" (Gros 1987b, p. 436). There were four virtues inscribed on the shield, other copies of which were almost certainly enshrined elsewhere: *virtus, clementia, iustitia, pietas.* See further Wallace-Hadrill 1981.

10 Béranger 1953, pp. 218–252; Kienast 1982b; Richardson 1991; Mac-Mullen 2000; Ando 2000.

11 Kantorowicz 1957. See also Dupont 1986, and especially Ando 2000, pp. 336–405.

12 Kantorowicz 1957, pp. 3–7. The book explores the notion from its first explicit formulations in the early Middle Ages to the eighteenth century.

13 Above, chapter 1.

14 Vitruvius 1.pref.3. Above, chapter 1, n. 278 for the Latin.

15 Vitruvius 2.pref.4.

16 Vitruvius 9.pref.17. Above, chapter 2, n. 43 for the Latin.

17 Vitruvius 7.5.3–7. For commentary and references, Liou et al., Vitruvius 1995, pp. 139–149.

18 Vitruvius 7.5.4: "Haec autem nec sunt nec fieri possunt nec fuerunt." Similarly, with respect to the necessity of grounding the ordering of the Doric entablature in the "reality" or "truth" of wood construction, Vitruvius 4.2.5: "Therefore they [the Greeks] thought that what cannot be done in reality could have no valid reason for being done in images." ("Ita quod non potest in veritate fieri, id non putaverunt in imaginibus factum posse certam rationem habere.")

19 Vitruvius 1.3.1: "Partes ipsius architecturae sunt tres: aedificatio, gnomonice, machinatio."

20 Fleury 1993, pp. 22–25 and table 1, p. 17.

21 Soubiran, Vitruvius 1969, pp. ix–xi.

22 Soubiran, Vitruvius 1969, p. lxx. On ancient sundials, with a catalogue of surviving ones, Gibbs 1976.

23 Pliny *Natural History* 36.72. On the Horologium Augusti, begun in 13 B.C., below, pp. 244–250.

24 McEwen 1993, pp. 32–38.

25 Liddell and Scott 1968, s.v. *gnomon;* Lewis and Short 1962, s.v. *norma.*

26 Gnomons and sundials: Vitruvius 9 passim; gnomons and the laying out of cities: Vitruvius 1.6. Upright posture: Vitruvius 2.1.2.

27 Kubitschek 1928, pp. 180–182; Neugebauer 1975, II, pp. 736–738.

28 Apollodorus *Bibliotheca* 3.5.8.

29 Vitruvius 9.pref.2–14.

30 Vitruvius 9.pref.3–7. Clavel-Levêque 1992; Guillaumin 1994.

31 Varro in Frontinus *De limitibus,* in Thulin 1971, p. 10. Centuriation's foundation in Greek science: Clavel-Levêque 1992, Guillaumin 1994. See especially Gargola 1995, pp. 41–50.

32 Varro *De lingua latina* 7.7–10.

33 Livy *Ab urbe condita* 1.18.6–7. Augury and ritual quartering of the sky, Rykwert 1988, pp. 45–47; Gargola 1995, pp. 41–50; and above, chapter 3, pp. 166–167.

34 Cicero *De legibus* 2.21; Polybius 6.26.

35 Frontinus *De limitibus,* in Thulin 1971, pp. 10–11.

36 Vitruvius 4.5.1; Frontinus *De limitibus,* in Thulin 1971, p. 11; and above, chapter 3, pp. 172–175.

37 Frontinus *De limitibus,* in Thulin 1971, p. 14.

38 Cicero *Academica* 2.126. Cleanthes (331–232 B.C.) was a student of Zeno and his successor as head of the Stoa.

39 Cicero *De republica* 6.17.

40 Above, chapter 3, pp. 210–212. The work in question is his *Epitome,* an abridgment of mainly Stoic philosophy which survives only in fragmentary form, mainly in the fifth-century A.D. *Anthologium* of Stobaeus. Fortenbaugh 1983; Hahm 1990.

41 Arius Didymus in Eusebius *Evangelicae praeparationis* 15.15.7 (Arnim 1903–1924, I, 499). Trans. by author. See also Diogenes Laertius 7.139; Censorinus 1.4; Aëtius 2.4.16 (the latter two as cited in Arnim 1903–1924, I, 499).

42 Cicero *Academica* 2.126.

43 Lewis and Short 1962, s.v. *potior*.

44 Vitruvius 1.pref.1. Above, chapter 1, n. 29 for the Latin.

45 Vitruvius 2.pref.1: "cum Alexander rerum potiretur."

46 Vitruvius 6.1.11. Above, chapter 1, n. 209 for the Latin.

47 See further Cicero *De natura deorum* 2.29: "I use the term 'ruling principle' [*principatum*] as the equivalent of the Greek *hêgemonikon*, meaning that part of anything which must and ought to have supremacy . . . that which contains the ruling principle of the whole of nature must also be the most excellent of all things and the most deserving of authority and sovereignty over all things [*omnium rerum potestate dominatuque*]."

48 The other four sources (Cicero, Aëtius, Censorinus, Diogenes Laertius: above, nn. 41 and 42) simply state Cleanthes' opinion that the sun is the world's *hêgemonikon* and leave it at that.

49 Cicero (*De natura deorum* 2.29) defines the *hêgemonikon* as that which "holds the whole universe together and preserves it."

50 Vitruvius 9.pref.18: "in hoc de gnomonicis rationibus, quemadmodum de radiis solis in mundo sunt per umbras gnomonis inventae, quibusque rationibus dilatentur aut contrahantur explicabo."

51 Vitruvius 9.1.1, 9.6.1.

52 *IG* XII, 8.240. Trans. by author. Dunst and Buchner 1973, p. 129; Buchner 1976, p. 319; Gibbs 1976, no. 8008.

53 Vitruvius 9.7.1–2.

54 Vitruvius 9.1.1: "*Analêmma* est ratio conquista solis cursu et umbrae crescentis ad brumam observatione inventa, e qua per rationes architectonicas circinique descriptiones est inventus effectus in mundo."

55 Vitruvius 9.1.2: "Mundus autem est omnium naturae rerum conceptio summa. . . . Id volvitur continenter circum terram atque mare per axis

cardines extremos. Namque in his locis naturalis potestas ita architectata est."

56 Vitruvius 10.1.2.

57 Fascination with *Timaeus:* Griffin 1994, p. 709.

58 Cicero *De natura deorum* 2.90.2.

59 Vitruvius 4.pref.

60 Cicero *De republica* 6.17: "dux et princeps et moderator."

61 Vitruvius 9.3.1, 9.3.3. With each period between sunrise and sunset divided into twelve hours no matter what the season, ancient hours were shorter in winter than in summer. Only at the equinoxes (under Aries and Libra) did the day consist of twelve 60-minute hours. Kubitschek 1928, pp. 182–183; cf. Soubiran, Vitruvius 1969, p. 143. On ancient chronology in general, Samuel 1972.

62 Vitruvius 9.1.11. Cf. Cicero *De republica* 6.17, where the sun "fills and reveals all things [in the universe] with its light"; similarly *De natura deorum* 2.119.

63 Vitruvius 9.1.12: "ut etiam fructus e terra surgentes in altitudinem per calorem videmus, non minus aquae vapores a fontibus ad nubes per arcus excitari, eadem ratione solis impetus vehemens . . . insequentes stellas ad se perducit, et ante currentes veluti refrenando retinendoque non patitur progredi . . . sed ad se regredi."

64 Pliny *Natural History* 2.69–72. Cf. Soubiran, Vitruvius 1969, pp. 106–107.

65 Arius Didymus in Eusebius *Evangelicae praeparationis* 15.15.7 (Arnim 1903–1924, I, 499), cited above.

66 Beard 1986, p. 34, claims that "Cicero was the first, or among the first, fully to integrate Hellenizing philosophy with traditional Roman practice."

67 On Varro's tripartite theology, Boyancé 1955a and 1975; Pépin 1956; Lieberg 1973; Cardauns 1976 and 1978; and above, chapter 1, p. 49.

68 Varro in Augustine *City of God* 6.5.

69 Vitruvius 6.1.3–11.

70 West-facing temples: Vitruvius 4.5.1. Capricorn: pp. 180 and 193, above.

71 Macrobius *Saturnalia* 1.13.1–5 on Numa's alleged institution of a lunar civil year of 354 days. On the republican calendar up to the time of Caesar's reform, Samuel 1972, pp. 159–170; on the Julian calendar, pp. 155–158.

72 Macrobius *Saturnalia* 1.16.39. Dio Cassius 43.26.2: "He got this improvement [the calendar reform] from his stay in Alexandria." Caesar was in Egypt in 48–47 B.C. (Dio Cassius 42.7–46).

73 Macrobius *Saturnalia* 1.14.3, trans. Percival Vaughan Davies. Pliny *Natural History* 18.211–212 says he did this with the help of one Sosigenes, an Alexandrian (cf. Rawson 1985, p. 112). See also Suetonius *Divus Julius* 40; Dio Cassius 43.26.1–3.

74 Samuel 1972, pp. 12–18.

75 Samuel 1972, p. 153.

76 Samuel 1972, pp. 145–146.

77 Weinstock 1971, pp. 381–384 (quotation from p. 384).

78 Hellenistic kings and radiate crowns: Weinstock 1971, pp. 381–382. Record of victories: Appian *Bellum civile* 2.106.442; birthday: Dio Cassius 44.4.4, 47.18.4. Change of Quintilis to Julius in 44 B.C.: Appian *Bellum civile* 2.106.44; Dio Cassius 44.5.2, 4; Macrobius *Saturnalia* 1.12.34 (cf. Weinstock 1971, pp. 197, 155–158; Samuel 1972, p. 155).

79 Macrobius *Saturnalia* 1.14.15. The fine tuning involved correcting the priests' error of intercalating an extra day every three years instead of every four (Macrobius 1.14.14).

80 Censorinus 22.16; Macrobius *Saturnalia* 1.12.35; Dio Cassius 55.6; Suetonius *Divus Augustus* 31.2 (cf. Samuel 1972, p. 155).

81 Divine kingship in Egypt: (recently) Silverman 1991, especially pp. 58–87. The Egyptian king's relation to time: Jordan 1998, p. 92.

82 Grenier 1995, pp. 3185, 3187–3191. See also Millar 1984, pp. 38–39.

83 Strocka 1980.

84 On Heliopolis (just north of modern Cairo), Lesko 1991, pp. 91–93. Dedication of obelisks at Heliopolis: Pliny *Natural History* 36.64–65. See also Iverson 1968–, I, pp. 11–13; Habachi 1977, pp. 4–6.

85 Pliny *Natural History* 36.69–71; Strabo 17.1.27 (cf. Grenier 1995, p. 3182).

86 On the removal and reappropriation of obelisks over the centuries, Iverson 1968–; Habachi 1977.

87 Iverson 1968–, II, pp. 90–91; Habachi 1977, p. 165.

88 Pliny *Natural History* 36.69. Merriam 1884; Iverson 1968–, II, pp. 91–92; Habachi 1977, pp. 164–167. One of the pair ("Cleopatra's needle") now stands on the Thames embankment in London. The other is in Central Park in New York City.

89 Two of these crabs are now in the Metropolitan Museum, New York. The inscription on one of them credits one Pontius with having "architected" the work (Merriam 1884).

90 Pliny *Natural History* 36.71, who confuses this obelisk with the one set up in the Campus Martius (see below). Richardson 1992, s.v. *Sol et Luna, Aedes.*

91 Propertius *Elegies* 2.31.11. Augustus dedicated the Temple of Apollo in 28 B.C. Association of Sol and Apollo in the Augustan period: Gagé 1955, pp. 629–637. Relation of Augustus's Palatine *domus* and the Temple of Apollo to the Circus Maximus: Gros 1996d, pp. 238–239. See also Zanker 1983, pp. 32–33.

92 Tertullian *De spectaculis* 8.

93 Tertullian *De spectaculis* 8–9. Vitruvius 9.1.12.

94 *CIL* VI, 701: IMP. CAESAR. DIVI. F. / AUGUSTUS / PONTIFEX. MAXIMUS. / IMP. XII. COS. XI. TRIB. POT. XIV / AEGVPTO. IN. POTESTATEM / POPULI. ROMANI. REDACTA / SOLI. DONUM. DEDIT. This obelisk is now in the Piazza del Popolo in Rome. Iversen 1968–, I, pp. 65–75. Cf. Augustus *Res gestae* 27.1: "Aegyptum imperio populi romani adieci [I added Egypt to the empire of the Roman people]."

95 *CIL* VI, 702, partially illustrated on pp. 37 and 242 above.

96 Both an hour indicator (*horologium*) and calendar (*solarium*): Buchner 1976. Buchner 1983, pp. 499–500, judges the clock to have been half as big as St. Peter's square, and the whole complex, including the Ara Pacis

and the mausoleum, twice as big. (Buchner 1983 provides a convenient summary of Buchner 1982.) The reconstruction of the Ara Pacis on view in Rome today is not located on the site of the original, which stood several hundred meters southeast of Augustus's mausoleum, at the site of the present Palazzo Fiano. The gnomon-obelisk now stands in front of the Palazzo Montecitorio, where it was raised in 1792. See also Bandini 1750; Iversen 1968–, I, pp. 142–160.

97 Buchner 1982 and reviews by Gros (1984a) and Wallace-Hadrill (1985, pp. 246–247; 1987, pp. 224–227).

98 Schutz 1990, who has questioned a number of Buchner's conclusions.

99 Pliny *Natural History* 36.72 and above, chapter 3, n. 79.

100 Vitruvius 9.7.2.

101 Adoption of Augustus's birthday as the beginning of the new year in 9 B.C.: Sherk 1969, pp. 335–336. Era of Actium: Magie 1950, p. 1289, n. 37. See also Price 1984, pp. 106–107.

102 Wilhelm Dittenberger, ed., *Orientis graeci inscriptiones selectae* (Leipzig, 1903), 458; Ehrenberg and Jones 1972, no. 98; Sherk 1969, pp. 328–337, with commentary; Braund 1985, C29 (for a translation).

103 Fragments of copies from five cities survive (Sherk 1969, p. 328). The assembly of Asian cities not only accepted the proposed calendar change but also decreed that Paulus Fabius Maximus be awarded a crown for having suggested such a unique way of honoring Augustus (Sherk, p. 334).

104 Pliny *Natural History* 36.64: "Radiorum eius argumentum in effigie est."

105 Pliny *Natural History* 36.64: "et ita significatur nomine Aegyptio."

106 Ausonius *Mosella* 313; Ammianus Marcellinus 22.15.29.

107 Ausonius *Mosella* 313, and above, chapter 2, p. 95.

108 Pliny *Natural History* 36.72: "vertice umbra colligeretur in se ipsam."

109 Pliny *Natural History* 36.72.

110 Pliny *Natural History* 36.72: "ratione, ut ferunt, a capite hominis intellecta." Buchner (1976, p. 330 and plate 110.2) claims that the gilded bronze ball in question is one of two now in the Palazzo dei Conservatori

in Rome. The other is from the Vatican obelisk. See also Buchner 1988, and cat. no. 110 in Hofter et al. 1988.

111 Buchner, for instance, relies entirely on Vitruvius.

112 Parian marble: Pollini and Herz 1992; findspot: Pollini 1987–1988. The statue is now in the Vatican museums (Braccio Nuovo, inv. 2290). When I examined it in May of 1998, the statue was temporarily in a laboratory for cleaning and study, where, thanks to the kind assistance of Dott. Paolo Liverani, I was able to make a thorough photographic survey of it. For a recent bibliography of work on the statue, see the notes to Pollini 1995, and more recently still Galinsky 1996, pp. 24–28.

113 For a survey of opinions on the dating, Brommer 1980, who himself supports a date of 19 B.C. See also Hölscher 1988 (17 B.C.); Zanker 1988, pp. 189–192 (soon after 20 B.C.); Pollini 1995 (20 B.C. or soon thereafter).

114 Vitruvius 1.pref.1.

115 That of Crassus in 53 B.C., of Saxa in 40, and of Antony in 36. Parthia was in Asia Minor, just east of the Euphrates.

116 Dio Cassius 54.8.2.

117 A cosmic-imperial narrative, similar in many respects to that of the Prima Porta statue (although not imbricated into the king's body), is deployed in the Gemma Augustea, the famous late Augustan sardonyx cameo now in the Kunsthistorisches Museum in Vienna (illustrated on p. 147 above), on which see especially Pollini 1993.

118 Tiberius sent to recover the standards: Suetonius *Tiberius* 9.1; Florus *Epitome* 2.34.63; Dio Cassius 54.8.1. Cf. Brilliant 1963, p. 66, who, with other scholars, identifies the figure on the cuirass as Tiberius and argues further that his appearance there contributes to evidence for dating the statue after Augustus's death.

119 Vitruvius 4.5.1.

120 On Venus, the morning and evening star, Vitruvius 9.1.7.

121 Varro *De lingua latina* 5.61–62.

122 The identification of the figure below the *imperator*'s left breast as an
eastern Celt from the recently annexed province of Galatia (rather than,
as has been more usual, a western Gaul) follows Hölscher 1988. For a review of the iconology, Pollini 1978, pp. 8–74.

123 Cicero *De natura deorum* 2.164; Varro in Augustine *City of God* 7.8; Pliny
the Younger *Panegyricus* 32.

124 Very much in the spirit of the Tellus Mater of the large relief to the left of
the west-facing entrance of the Ara Pacis Augustae.

125 Apollo on griffin: *LIMC* II.1, pp. 229–230.

126 Artemis/Diana: *LIMC* II.1, s.v.

127 Suetonius *Divus Augustus* 7.2.

128 Above, chapter 3, pp. 156–183.

129 Coins (both aurei and denarii), stamped with the legend *signis receptis*
("standards recovered"), were issued in celebration of the event all over
the Roman world: in the east (Mattingly 1968, I, nos. 17, 46, 47, 48), in
the west (Mattingly I, nos. 256, 302, 303, 304, 305), and at Rome itself
(Mattingly I, nos. 98, 99, 100). See also p. 263 below and Dio Cassius
54.8.2.

130 Chrysippus, in Arnim 1903–1924, II, 911; Cicero *De natura deorum* 2.29.
Lapidge 1978, pp. 168–169; Long 1986, pp. 171–172.

131 Varro *De lingua latina* 5.59.

132 Seneca *De clementia* 2.2.1 (cf. Kienast 1982b, p. 11).

133 Fragments of works on kingship by three Pythagorean authors of uncertain date survive in a chapter of the fifth-century A.D. anthology of Stobaeus (*Anthologium* 4.7, "Advice about Kings"). The authors (Diotogenes,
Sthenidas, and Ecphantus—all apparently pseudonymous) share a common understanding of divine rulership in which the king as *logos empsy-
chos*, the animate or living *logos*, ruled on earth as God rules the heavens.
Scholars make the three authors in question either Hellenistic, placing
them in the third century B.C., or imperial Roman, with a date in the second century A.D. See Goodenough 1928; Delatte 1942; Dvornik 1966,
chs. 5 and 8; Chesnut 1978 (a good summary). Whether the kingship

theory predates or postdates Augustan ideology, its resonance with the rhetoric of the Prima Porta Augustus is unmistakable. Ecphantus even writes of the "light of majesty" in which legitimate kings are bathed, comparing them to eagles who, according to legend, were the only animals who could look straight into the sun without blinking (Stobaeus *Anthologium* IV, p. 273.2, cf. Chesnut 1978, p. 1319), recalling in this the relation between Sol and the Roman eagle of the Prima Porta cuirass.

134 Above, chapter 3, pp. 188–194.

135 Béranger 1953, pp. 246–248; Chesnut 1978, pp. 1326–1329; Grimal 1979.

136 Cicero *De republica* 1.56–60.

137 Vitruvius 1.pref.1. Above, chapter 1, n. 29 for the Latin.

138 Pollini 1995, pp. 265–266. Kähler 1959, pp. 12–13, gave him a laurel branch. Ingholt 1969, who places the bronze original of the marble statue in the sanctuary of Athena at Pergamon, gives him a spear, as does Simon 1986, p. 56.

139 Brilliant 1963, p. 67; Pollini 1995, pp. 265–266, with n. 24, p. 277; Galinsky 1996, p. 24.

140 Pollini 1995, p. 266.

141 See above, chapter 1, pp. 60–61.

142 Cicero *De inventione* 1.2, *De oratore* 1.32–33, and above, chapter 2, pp. 141–142.

143 Vitruvius 2.1, and above, chapter 2, pp. 142–150.

144 Vitruvius 1.pref.1. See also Virgil *Aeneid* 8.722–729.

145 On the Doryphoros as model, most recently Lahusen 1990, who stresses its ideological significance; Galinsky 1996, pp. 24–27; and especially Pollini 1995, with references to earlier literature. Of the two copies of the Doryphoros considered to be the best, one, from the Samnite Palaestra at Pompeii, is now in Naples (Museo Nazionale 6011). The other, whose provenance is uncertain, is judged to be of even higher quality than the Naples statue and is now in the Minneapolis Institute of Arts (Maderna-Lauter 1990, pp. 331–336; Meyer 1995; Hallett 1995). The acquisition of

the latter occasioned the detailed studies published in Moon 1995. In general, see also Lorenz 1972; *Polyklet* 1990.

146 Height of statues: Meyer 1995, pp. 73, 86; Pollini 1995, p. 266.

147 The proportions of the Doryphoros: Tobin 1975; Berger 1990. On the difficulty of establishing such proportions, Stewart 1978a. There are no similar studies of the Prima Porta statue.

148 See Pollini 1995.

149 Stewart 1995, pp. 252–253, citing Hallett 1986, p. 82.

150 Stewart 1995. That Polykleitos was especially known for his muscled torsos is echoed by the reference to the "Polykleitan chest" (*pectus Polycletium*) as a type in the *Rhetorica ad Herennium* (4.9). Cf. Pollini 1995, p. 277. See also Maderna-Lauter 1990, pp. 345–350.

151 The Doryphoros as Canon: Pliny *Natural History* 34.55; Cicero *Brutus* 70; Quintilian *Institutio oratoria* 5.12.21. Cf. Leftwich 1995, p. 50, n. 1; Rykwert 1996, pp. 104–110. See also Galen *De placitis Hippocratis et Platonis* 5.3.26, *De temperamentis* 1.566; and Stewart 1978a, pp. 124–125, where these and other sources on the Canon are cited with translations.

152 Pliny *Natural History* 34.55.

153 Pliny *Natural History* 34.55; Galen *De placitis Hippocratis et Platonis* 5.3.15 (trans. Phillip de Lacy). Cf. Galen *De temperamentis* 1.566 (cited in Stewart 1978a, p. 125) and Pollitt 1974, pp. 14–15.

154 At the end of the first century A.D., Quintilian (*Institutio oratoria* 5.12.21) singled out the Doryphoros—who, in fact, represents an athlete and/or warrior, perhaps Achilles (Pliny *Natural History* 34.18)—as a model for public speakers. Galinsky 1996, pp. 24–25, interprets this as pointing to Quintilian's reading the Doryphoros *through* the Prima Porta statue, of which it is assumed there were countless copies. See also Lahusen 1990; Maderna-Lauter 1990, pp. 331–336; Pollini 1995, pp. 267–273.

155 Philo *Mechanicus* iv 1.49.20; Galen *De placitis Hippocratis et Platonis* 5.3.15; Plutarch *Moralia* 45c. See Stewart 1978a, pp. 124–125, for the citations.

156 Cicero *Brutus* 70: "pulchiora etiam Polycliti [signa] et plane perfecta."

157 Pliny *Natural History* 34.56. See further *Natural History* 34.65, where Pliny writes that Lysippus also cultivated symmetry but "altered the square builds [*quadratas staturas*] used by the older sculptors." One assumes that by the latter Pliny means Polykleitos and his imitators.

158 Stewart 1978b, p. 167; Hurwit 1995, p. 12.

159 Varro in Solinus 1.18: "dictaque primum est Roma quadrata, quod ad aequilibrium foret posita."

160 Simonides in Plato *Protagoras* 339a. Cf. Ferri 1940; Pollitt 1974, pp. 247–248; Stewart 1978b, p. 167.

161 Hurwit 1995, p. 12, for instance, tries to distinguish metaphorical from descriptive squaredness. But see Maderna-Lauter 1990, who concludes (pp. 381–385) that it was, precisely, the ethical content of the Polykleitan ideal that made it the preferred vehicle for promoting the monarchy at Rome.

162 Diogenes Laertius 7.100. Cf. Long 1996, p. 211, whose translation I have followed.

163 Pollini 1995, p. 266.

164 Above, chapter 3, pp. 210–212.

165 Dio Cassius 54.8.5. Gaius represented in the Amor of the Prima Porta statue: Simon 1986, pp. 55–56. Gaius and his younger brother Lucius (sons of Augustus's daughter Julia and of Agrippa) were adopted as the *princeps*'s heirs three years later in 17 B.C.

166 Galen *De placitis Hippocratis et Platonis* 5.3.26.

167 Vitruvius 1.1.13: "Non enim debet nec potest esse architectus . . . plastes quemadmodum Myron seu Polyclitus, sed rationis plasticae non ignarus."

168 Vitruvius 3.pref.2.

169 Relation to the Polykleitan canon: Raven 1951; Zöllner 1987, pp. 23–35; Gros, Vitruvius 1990, pp. 64–65; Rykwert 1996, pp. 97–110, among others. Vitruvius 3.1.2: "Reliqua quoque membra suas habent commensus proportiones, quibus etiam antiqui pictores et statuarii nobiles usi

magnas et infinitas laudes sunt adsecuti." On Vitruvian man, Vitruvius 3.1.3 and above, chapter 3.

170 Scholars almost invariably *assume* that they did, attributing the missing evidence to Vitruvius's lost sources.

171 Plato *Phaedrus* 264c: "Every discourse ought to be a living creature, having a body of its own and a head and feet; there should be a middle, beginning and end, adapted to one another and to the whole." Cf. Cicero *De oratore* 3.171–172, *Orator* 149, *De officiis* 1.98. Quintilian's similar referent (*Institutio oratoria* 5.12.21) is not just any well-shaped man; it is the Doryphoros statue itself. Cf. Gros, Vitruvius 1990, pp. 55–56; Lahusen 1990, p. 394; Maderna-Lauter 1990, pp. 380–381; Callebat 1994, pp. 43–44; Pollini 1995, p. 270.

172 Vitruvius 3.1.1: "Aedium compositio constat ex symmetria."

173 Cicero *De inventione* 2.168, *Pro Murena* 51, *Philippics* 8.15, *De officiis* 1.85, 3.22, 3.32. Caesar cited in Suetonius *Divus Julius* 77.

174 Dionysius of Halicarnassus *Antiquitates romanae* 6.86; Livy *Ab urbe condita* 2.32 (cf. Nestle 1926–1927).

175 For example, four fingers = one palm, four palms = one foot. Proportionally, finger is to palm as palm is to foot: mathematically, 1:4::4:16 (cf. Vitruvius 3.1.8). For references on ancient metrology, above, chapter 1, n. 146.

176 Vitruvius 3.1.5, and above, chapter 1, pp. 39–54.

177 Aristotle *Metaphysics* 986a8; Iamblichus *Theologoumena arithmeticae* 82.12; John Lydus *De mensibus* 1.15.

178 Lucian *Vitarum auctio* 4.

179 Vitruvius 3.1.8.

180 Raven 1951, p. 151.

181 On the difficulty of extrapolating a canon from a statue, or even of establishing that any given statue is canonic, Stewart 1978a. The Prima Porta statue's resemblance to the Doryphoros would have been more than enough to persuade any viewer familiar with both statues that the portrait of the *princeps* was canonic.

182 The Doryphoros is not a portrait (above, n. 154).

183 Cicero *De oratore* 1.188: "quae rem dissolutam divulsamque conglutinaret, et ratione quadam constringeret." Compare Vitruvius 4.pref.1.

184 Dio Cassius 54.8.5.

185 Dio Cassius 54.8.4.

186 Steinby 1993–2000, s.v. *Miliarium aureum,* with references. There appears to be no evidence to support the tradition that the milestone recorded the names of the most important cities in the Roman world and their distances from Rome.

187 Kienast 1982a, pp. 415–417; Ando 2000, pp. 336–405.

188 Kienast 1982a, p. 418; Kienast 1982b. See also Béranger 1953, pp. 218–252.

189 Ovid *Tristia* 2.213–230. Lucius and Gaius Caesar were Augustus's heirs until their deaths in 2 and 4 A.D. respectively. After this, he adopted Tiberius, his wife Livia's son by a previous marriage.

190 Ovid *Tristia* 2.231–232: "denique, ut in tanto, quantum non extitit umquam / corpore pars nulla est, quae labet, imperii" (cf. Kienast 1982b, p. 5; Richardson 1991, p. 7). See also Ovid *Fasti* 4.857–863.

191 For citations, Béranger 1953, pp. 218–252; Kienast 1982b.

192 Florus *Epitome* 2.14.5–6. Cf. Béranger 1953, p. 228.

193 Kienast 1961, 1982b; Combès 1966; Lintott 1981, and especially Richardson 1991. On the indissolubility of politics and religion, above, chapter 3, pp. 183–198.

194 Richardson 1991, p. 4.

195 Lewis and Short 1962, s.v. *provincia,* for which the original meaning still held in the first century B.C. (Levick 1967, p. 21).

196 Vasaly 1993, p. 134; Ando 2000, pp. 277–335.

197 Virgil *Aeneid* 1.279.

198 Dio Cassius 52.41.3; Suetonius *Divus Julius* 76. Syme 1958, p. 176, says Augustus was already using the name in 38 B.C. See also Combès 1966.

199 Vitruvius 2.9.15 has excellent examples of common usage.

200 On the acclamation, Kienast 1961, pp. 403–404; Combès 1966, p. 2.

201 Syme 1958, p. 182. See also Gagé 1933: "L'empire romain est une monarchie militaire . . . l'empire se résume en un *Imperator* chef des armées" (p. 1).

202 Vitruvius 1.pref.2. Above, chapter 1, n. 107 for the Latin.

203 Compare Suetonius *Divus Augustus* 28.3, the famous brick-to-marble passage: "Urbem neque pro maiestate imperii ornatum . . .". On *auctoritates* as "guarantees," above, chapter 1, pp. 35–38.

204 Vitruvius 1.pref.3.

205 Vitruvius 1.pref.2–3.

206 Ovid *Tristia* 2.232 (see above). On the mnemonic dimension of *De architectura*, above, chapter 1, pp. 79–88.

207 Augustus *Res gestae* 28. See also Suetonius *Divus Augustus* 46; Kienast 1982a, pp. 336–365 and pp. 391–406, where the colonies founded in these places are listed; Millar 1984, p. 50; Fear 1996; Woolf 1998.

208 Augustus *Res gestae* 28; Kienast 1982a, p. 399.

209 Aulus Gellius *Noctes atticae* 16.13.8–9 (cf. Fear 1996, p. 63).

210 Hyginus Gromaticus *Constitutio limitum*, in Thulin 1971, pp. 140–141.

211 Woolf 1998, pp. 106–168. Vitruvius's attachment to Caesar: 1.pref.2, and above, chapter 1, n. 52.

212 Urbanization and *humanitas:* Woolf 1998, pp. 106–113, and above, chapter 2, pp. 149–154.

213 Woolf 1998, pp. 114–115.

214 Goudineau 1980, p. 267, stresses "la volonté de cohérence" as the driving force behind the imposition of grids, whose large module could not be applied to a topographically varied landscape which hence required leveling. Coherence needed a flat surface. See also Woolf 1998, pp. 116–120.

215 Woolf 1998, pp. 120–122. On the urbanization of Gaul as Augustan in inception, Gros 1987b, 1991b; Goudineau 1991; Le Glay 1991; Aupert and Sablayrolles 1992.

216 Woolf 1998, p. 122.

217 Woolf 1998, p. 124; Vitruvius 2.8.20, 2.1.3–4.

218 Woolf 1998, pp. 123–124; wall paintings: pp. 203–204.

219 Vitruvius 2.1.7.

220 Among recent studies, Alarcâo and Étienne 1976, 1979; Fishwick 1987–1992; Mierse 1990; Étienne 1996; Fear 1996; MacMullen 2000, pp. 57–67. Cf. Tacitus *Agricola* 21.

221 On Conimbriga, Alarcâo and Étienne 1979, who claim that the initial layout of the Augustan city follows Vitruvius. Cf. Kienast 1982a, p. 405.

222 Vitruvius 2.8.12; Tacitus *Agricola* 21 (above, chapter 2, pp. 151–152). Étienne 1958, pp. 75–80; Fishwick 1996, p. 184; Woolf 1998, pp. 124–125; MacMullen 2000, pp. 124–138.

223 Étienne 1958, 1996; Fishwick 1987–1992, 1996; Gros 1987b, 1991b; Mierse 1990, pp. 322–324; Le Glay 1991. Ten Gallic cities had *Augusta* attached to their names (Goudineau, Février, and Fixot 1980, p. 99).

224 Cicero *Ad Quintum fratrem* 1.1.27. Woolf 1994, pp. 119–124.

225 Vitruvius 9.pref.15. On *omnes gentes,* above, chapter 2, pp. 131–134. For a different assessment of *ad mores corrigendos* and the ethical dimension of architecture in Vitruvius, Romano 1987, pp. 143–171.

226 Vitruvius 6.pref.1, and above, chapter 2, pp. 136–139.

227 Vitruvius 4.1.9–10.

228 Suetonius *Divus Augustus* 18.2 (compare Vitruvius 1.pref.3); Dio Cassius 51.1.3.

229 Kienast 1982a, p. 373, with nn. 25, 26 for the sources.

230 On Pisidian Antioch, most recently Mitchell and Waelkens 1998.

231 Mitchell and Waelkens 1998, pp. 113–141. The dedicatory inscription on the gate to the temple precinct is dated to 2/1 B.C. (Mitchell and Waelkens, pp. 147 and 167), which means the temple was built earlier.

232 They were inscribed on the interior walls of the central archway of this gate and also in two other known locations, both in Galatia: one, in both Greek and Latin, in the pronaos of the Ionic pseudodipteral Temple of Roma and Augustus at Ankara, built in about 20 B.C., and another, in Greek, on the base of a dynastic statuary group in Apollonia which represented the imperial family. On the Antiochian inscription, Ramsay and

von Premerstein 1927. Cf. Elsner 1996; Güven 1998; Mitchell and Waelkens 1998, pp. 147–150 and 163.

233 Frieze on Antioch temple: Mitchell and Waelkens 1998, pp. 123–127. Similar friezes appear on the Corinthian Temple of Roma and Augustus at Pola in northern Italy and on the Maison Carrée at Nîmes, also Corinthian, which was dedicated to Augustus's heirs, Gaius and Lucius Caesar. Temple at Pola: Zanker 1988, pp. 312–313; Maison Carrée: Amy and Gros 1979. For additional examples, Hänlein-Schäfer 1985.

234 Robinson 1926–1927, p. 17; cf. Mitchell and Waelkens 1998, p. 171, and pp. 287, 289, and 297 in this volume.

235 On the sun disk in Augustan iconography, notably the one that appears on the late Augustan sardonyx cameo known as the Gemma Augustea, Pollini 1993, pp. 280–282.

236 Vitruvius 4.1.9 and above, chapter 3, pp. 212–224. A generically similar (although not quite as literal) kind of figure—a winged young woman with lush acanthus foliage spiraling out from under her skirt—appeared on the frieze of the Temple of Divus Julius at Rome (illustrated Galinsky 1996, p. 154), a temple whose westward orientation seems to have been exactly duplicated in the Antioch temple.

237 Vitruvius 9.1.12.

238 Vitruvius 4.5.1, above, chapter 3, n. 66 for the Latin.

239 Tacitus *Annals* 1.78: "datum in omnes provincias exemplum." The temple at Tarraco was built in 15 A.D., just after the death of Augustus. Cf. Hänlein-Schäfer 1985, A 56 and plate 61a, which locates the temple at the eastern edge of the city. Plans of Pisidian Antioch strongly suggest that the temple there, which faced west-northwest like the Temple of Divus Julius at Rome, was, like the Roman temple, oriented in mimetic sympathy with the dawn of the winter solstice and the "birth" of the sun in Capricorn. For plans, Mitchell and Waelkens 1998, fig. 18; Robinson 1926–1927, fig. 2; and p. 286 of this volume. Sculptural reliefs on the propylon of the temple precinct included an image of Capricorn (Mitchell and Waelkens, plate 115; Robinson, fig. 54). On the Temple of

Divus Julius, above, chapter 3, pp. 175–178. Other west-facing dynastic monuments include both the Julian basilica and the dynastic temple of the *gens Julia* at Corinth; and, in Asia Minor, the Temple of Roma and Augustus at Ankara, the Temple of Roma and Augustus at Pessinus in Phrygia, and the Sebasteion in Carian Aphrodisias. The enclosure of the Ara Pacis Augustae in the Campus Martius at Rome had a west-facing main entrance, while the altar itself faced east, in keeping with Vitruvius's dual prescription (4.5.1, 4.9.1).

240 Kienast 1982a, p. 355.

241 Price 1984, pp. 135–162; Lyttleton 1987; Gros and Sauron 1988, pp. 66–67; Gros 1991b, 1996c.

242 Gros 1991b, pp. 127–129. See also Price 1984, pp. 135–162; Gros 1996c.

243 Vitruvius 5.pref.5: "hoc libro publicorum locorum expediam dispositiones." Forum and basilica: Vitruvius 5.1; David 1983; Gros 1984b; Gros 1990, pp. 47–62; Gros 1991b; Gros 1996c, p. 116; Price 1984, p. 143.

244 On Augustan interventions in the Athenian agora in general: Gros and Sauron 1988, pp. 66–67; Gros 1991b, pp. 129–131.

245 Thompson 1950; Roddaz 1984, pp. 435–439; Ward-Perkins 1994, pp. 265–268.

246 McAllister 1959; Thompson 1962.

247 Gaius Caesar as a new Ares: *IG* II.2, 3250; Gros 1991b, p. 131.

248 Inscription on epistyle: *IG* II.2, 3173. On the Athenian Temple of Roma and Augustus in general: Binder 1969; Travlos 1971, p. 494; Hoff 1996, pp. 185–194; Hurwit 1999, pp. 279–280 and 317. Vitruvius introduces his account of circular temples with a discussion of monopteroi (4.8.1). Dedicated in 19 B.C. to commemorate return of the standards: Hoff 1996, pp. 92–93; Hurwit 1999, p. 279.

249 Price 1984.

250 The nine columns of the Augustan monopteros are without precedent or sequel in the circular temples of classical antiquity (Binder 1969, p. 193), leading one to suspect that their number had some specific point. Evocation of the Muses would make Augustus a *musagetes*, the "leader of the

Muses" at the origin of civilization, like Hercules (above, chapter 2, pp. 115–118) or Apollo. Two-stepped crepis: Hoff 1996, p. 188, who differs with previous studies which give it three.

251 The axial relation to the Theater of Dionysos does not appear to have been previously noted, although the more obvious one to the Parthenon is stressed by all scholars who have dealt with the Temple of Roma and Augustus (n. 248 above).

252 Goudineau 1980, p. 267; Woolf 1998, pp. 116–120.

253 Polybius's (6.42) comparison of the very different approaches Greeks and Romans took when they laid out their military camps is instructive in this respect.

254 On the Erechtheion, most recently Hurwit 1999, pp. 200–209 and 316, who stresses its reliquary status.

255 Korres 1994, p. 140, says that at a height of about 10 meters and a distance of some 25 meters from the front of the Parthenon, the monopteros would have been too low to prevent the light of the rising sun from entering the cella of the former (cf. Hurwit 1999, p. 279).

256 Price 1984 is a first, important counterargument to this kind of dismissal.

257 Antony and Athens: Plutarch *Antony* 23.2–3, 33.4; Dio Cassius 48.39.2. According to Dio (50.15.2), the statues of Antony and Cleopatra that the Athenians had placed on the Acropolis were prophetically "hurled down into the theater" by thunderbolts on the eve of Actium. Since Dio can only mean the Theater of Dionysos (there was no other theater near the Acropolis at the time), the statues in question must have stood on the same southeastern terrace overlooking it as those of Roma and Augustus that later replaced them. On Athens's troubled relations with Augustus in the first years of the principate, Hoff 1989.

258 Pammenes: *IG* II.2, 3173.

259 Pisidian Antioch: above, pp. 285–290. Urbanization of Gaul: pp. 282–283. Building in Britain: Tacitus *Agricola* 21, and above, chapter 2, p. 151.

260 "Sans solution de continuité" ("with no break in continuity") is the phrase Pierre Gros (1976a) uses repeatedly to describe Augustus's urban projects at Rome: his reconstruction of the Circus Flaminius (pp. 81–84), his transformation of the Forum Romanum (pp. 85–92), and his building of the Forum of Augustus (pp. 92–95). Brick to marble: Suetonius *Divus Augustus* 28.3.

261 Dio Cassius 56.30.3–4 (trans. by author).

262 Vitruvius 4.pref.1.

CONCLUSION

1 Suetonius *Divus Augustus* 99.1. Dio Cassius 56.30.4.

2 Dio Cassius 56.30.4 (trans. by author).

3 Vitruvius 7.5.3–7.

4 Dio Cassius 52.35.5, and above, chapter 4, pp. 226–227.

5 Florus *Epitome* 2.14.5–6. Compare Vitruvius 1.pref.1 and 4.pref.1.

6 Woolf 1998, p. 18: "It was a peculiarity of Roman imperial culture that it was so closely linked to the fact of empire that it never extended beyond the limits of the territory under Roman political and military control." See further Ando 2000, ch. 8.

7 Vitruvius 1.pref.1.

8 On Romanization and its limits, Gordon 1990c; MacMullen 1990, 2000; Woolf 1998, pp. 135–169; Ando 2000.

9 On the imperial role of a sundial donated by a Roman citizen to the town of Igaeditani in Lusitania in 16 B.C., Étienne 1992. In general, above, chapter 4, pp. 229–250.

10 For instance, Vitruvius 2.1.4–5 (catalogue of primitive huts); 6.1.1 (adapting architecture to local climate); 8.3 (encomium on water); 9.1.1 and 9.7.1 (varying lengths of the equinoctial shadows of gnomons).

11 Vitruvius's attachment to Caesar: 1.pref.2 and above, chapter 1, n. 52.

12 Vitruvius 1.pref.3, 1.1.1, and above, chapter 1, n. 88.

13 *Summum templum architecturae:* Vitruvius 1.1.11; Temple of Jupiter as "guarantee of empire": Tacitus *Historiae* 3.72, and above, chapter 1, pp. 28–30, and chapter 2, pp. 145–148.

14 The *locus classicus* in *De architectura* is Vitruvius 6.1.4–11.

15 Vitruvius 1.3.1.

16 Vitruvius 1.1.1, and above, chapter 1, n. 88.

BIBLIOGRAPHY

ABBREVIATIONS

AJA   *American Journal of Archaeology*

ANRW   *Aufstieg und Niedergang der römischen Welt*. Ed. Hildegard
           Temporini. Berlin, 1972–.

JRA   *Journal of Roman Archaeology*

JRS   *Journal of Roman Studies*

MDAI   *Mitteilungen des deutschen archäologischen Instituts. (A):*
           Athenische Abteilung; (R): Römische Abteilung

MÉFRA   *Mélanges d'archéologie et d'histoire de l'École française de*
           Rome

REA   *Revue des études anciennes*

EDITIONS OF VITRUVIUS CITED

Bossalino, Vitruvius 1998. *De architectura libri X*, Marco Vitruvio Pol-
lione. A cura di Franca Bossalino. Traduzione di Franca Bossalino e
Vilma Nazzi. Rome. Italian.

Callebat, Vitruvius 1973. *Vitruve. De l'architecture. Livre VIII*. Texte établi,
traduit et commenté par Louis Callebat. Collection des universités de
France. Paris. Book 8. Latin and French.

Callebat and Fleury, Vitruvius 1986. *Vitruve. De l'architecture. Livre X*.
Texte établi, traduit et commenté par Louis Callebat. Avec la collabora-
tion pour le commentaire de Philippe Fleury. Collection des universités
de France. Paris. Book 10. Latin and French.

Callebat et al., Vitruvius 1999. *Vitruve. De l'architecture. Livre II.* Texte établi et traduit par Louis Callebat. Introduit et commenté par Pierre Gros. Recherche sur les manuscrits et apparat critique par Catherine Jacquemard. Collection des universités de France. Paris. Book 2. Latin and French.

Corso and Romano, Vitruvius 1997. *Vitruvio. De architectura.* A cura di Pierre Gros. Traduzione et commento di Antonio Corso e Elisa Romano. Turin. 2 vols. Illustrated. Latin and Italian.

Fensterbusch, Vitruvius 1964. *Vitruv. Zehn Bücher über Architektur.* Übersetzt und mit Anmerkungen versehen von Dr. Curt Fensterbusch. Darmstadt. Latin and German.

Ferri, Vitruvius 1960. *Vitruvio. Architettura (dai libri I–VII).* Recensione del testo, traduzione e note di Silvio Ferri. Rome. Books 1 to 7. Latin and Italian.

Fleury, Vitruvius 1990. *Vitruve. De l'architecture. Livre 1.* Texte établi, traduit et commenté par Philippe Fleury. Collection des universités de France. Paris. Book 1. Latin and French.

Giocondo, Vitruvius 1511. *M. Vitruvius per Iocundum solito castigatur factus cum figuris et tabula utiam legi et intellegi posit.* Fra Giocondo, ed. Venice. Illustrated. Latin.

Granger, Vitruvius 1931. *Vitruvius. On Architecture.* Edited from the Harleian manuscript 2767 and translated into English by Frank Granger. Loeb Classical Library. Cambridge, Mass., and London. 2 vols. Latin and English.

Gros, Vitruvius 1990. *Vitruve. De l'architecture. Livre III.* Texte établi, traduit et commenté par Pierre Gros. Collection des universités de France. Paris. Book 3. Latin and French.

Gros, Vitruvius 1992. *Vitruve. De l'architecture. Livre IV.* Texte établi, traduit et commenté par Pierre Gros. Collection des universités de France. Paris. Book 4. Latin and French.

Liou et al., Vitruvius 1995. *Vitruve. De l'architecture. Livre VII.* Texte établi et traduit par Bernard Liou et Michel Zuinghedau. Commenté par Marie-Thérèse Cam. Collection des universités de France. Paris. Book 7. Latin and French.

Morgan, Vitruvius 1914. *Vitruvius. The Ten Books on Architecture.* Translated by Morris Hicky Morgan. With illustrations and original designs prepared under the direction of Herbert Langford Warren. Cambridge, Mass. Illustrated. English.

Perrault, Vitruvius 1673. *Les dix livres d'architecture de Vitruve.* Corrigez et traduits nouvellement en François, avec des Notes & des Figures. Claude Perrault, trans. Paris. Illustrated. French.

Rose and Müller-Strübing, Vitruvius 1867. *Vitruvii de architectura libri decem. Ad antiquissimos codices nunc primum ediderunt.* Valentin Rose and Hermann Müller-Strübing, eds. Bibliotheca Teubneriana. Leipzig. Latin.

Rowland and Howe, Vitruvius 1999. *Vitruvius. Ten Books on Architecture.* Translation by Ingrid D. Rowland. Commentary and illustrations by Thomas Noble Howe, with additional commentary by Ingrid D. Rowland and Michael J. Dewar. Cambridge, U.K., and New York. English.

Soubiran, Vitruvius 1969. *Vitruve. De l'architecture. Livre IX.* Texte établi, traduit et commenté par Jean Soubiran. Collection des universités de France. Paris. Book 9. Latin and French.

EDITIONS OF OTHER CLASSICAL AUTHORS CITED

Aethicus. In Riese 1878 (modern authors, below). Latin.

Ammianus Marcellinus. *Ammianus Marcellinus.* Trans. John C. Rolfe. Revised ed. Loeb Classical Library. 3 vols. Cambridge, Mass., and London, 1950–1952. Latin and English.

Apollodorus *Bibliotheca. Apollodorus. The Library.* Trans. Sir James G. Frazer. Loeb Classical Library. 2 vols. Cambridge, Mass., and London, 1976. Greek and English.

Appian *Bellum civile. The Civil Wars.* Trans. John Carter. Harmondsworth, 1996. English.

Arrian *Anabasis. Arrian. Anabasis Alexandri.* Trans. E. Iliff Robson. Loeb Classical Library. 2 vols. Cambridge, Mass., and London, 1967. Greek and English.

Augustine *City of God. The City of God against the Pagans.* Various trans. Loeb Classical Library. 7 vols. Cambridge, Mass., 1957–1972. Latin and English.

Augustus *Res gestae. Res gestae Divi Augusti / The Achievements of the Divine Augustus.* Trans. P. A. Brunt and J. M. Moore. Oxford, 1967. Latin and English.

Aulus Gellius *Noctes atticae. The Attic Nights of Aulus Gellius.* Trans. John C. Rolfe. Loeb Classical Library. 3 vols. London and New York, 1927–1928. Latin and English.

Ausonius *Mosella. Ausonius.* Trans. Hugh G. Evelyn White. Loeb Classical Library. 2 vols. Cambridge, Mass., and London, 1961. Latin and English.

Caesar *Bellum gallicum. Caesar. The Gallic War.* Trans. H. J. Edwards. Loeb Classical Library. Cambridge, Mass., and London, 1958. Latin and English.

Cicero (all works cited). Various trans. Loeb Classical Library. Cambridge, Mass., London, and New York, 1912–1999. Latin and English.

Cornutus *Epidrome.* In Hays 1983 (modern authors, below). Greek and English.

Dio Cassius. *Dio's Roman History.* Trans. Ernest Cary. Loeb Classical Library. 9 vols. Cambridge, Mass., and London, 1914–1927. Greek and English.

Diodorus Siculus. *Diodorus of Sicily.* Trans. C. H. Oldfather. Loeb Classical Library. 12 vols. London and New York, 1933–1967. Greek and English.

Diogenes Laertius. *Lives of the Eminent Philosophers.* Trans. R. D. Hicks. Loeb Classical Library. 2 vols. London and New York, 1925. Greek and English.

Dionysius of Halicarnassus *Antiquitates romanae. The Roman Antiquities of Dionysius of Halicarnassus.* Trans. Ernest Cary. Loeb Classical Library. 7 vols. London, 1937–1950. Greek and English.

Ennius *Annals. Remains of Old Latin.* Trans. E. H. Warmington. Loeb Classical Library. 4 vols. Cambridge, Mass., and London, 1967. Latin and English.

Eumenius *Panegyrici latini. In Praise of Later Roman Emperors (The Panegyrici Latini).* Trans. C. E. V. Nixon and Barbara Saylor Rodgers. Los Angeles and Oxford, 1994. Latin and English.

Eusebius *Evangelicae praeparationis. Eusebii Pamphili Evangelicae praeparationis libri XV.* Ed. Thomas Gaisford. 4 vols. Oxford, 1843. Greek.

Festus. *Sexti Pompei Festi. De verborum significatu quae supersunt cum Pauli Epitome.* Ed. Wallace M. Lindsay. Bibliotheca Teubneriana. Leipzig, 1913. Latin.

Florus *Epitome. Lucius Annaeus Florus. Epitome of Roman History.* Trans. Edward Seymour Forster. Loeb Classical Library. Cambridge, Mass., and London, 1984. Latin and English.

Frontinus *De aquis. Sextus Julius Frontinus. The Stratagems and the Aqueducts of Rome.* Trans. Charles E. Bennett. Loeb Classical Library. London, 1925. Latin and English.

Frontinus *De limitibus.* In Thulin 1971 (modern authors, below). Latin.

Galen *De placitis Hippocratis et Platonis. Galen. On the Doctrines of Hippocrates and Plato.* Trans. Phillip de Lacy. 2d ed. 2 vols. Berlin, 1981. Greek and English.

Greek Anthology. *The Greek Anthology*. Trans. W. R. Paton. Loeb Classical Library. 5 vols. London, 1916–1918. Greek and English.

Heraclitus Homericus. *Héraclite. Allégories d'Homère*. Trans. Félix Buffière. Collection des universités de France. Paris, 1962. Latin and French.

Horace *Odes. Horace. The Odes and Epodes*. Trans. C. E. Bennett. Loeb Classical Library. Cambridge, Mass., and London, 1968. Latin and English.

Hyginus Gromaticus *Constitutio limitum, De condicionibus agrorum*. In Thulin 1971 (modern authors, below). Latin.

Hyginus Gromaticus *De munitionibus castrorum. Liber de munitionibus castrorum*. Ed. A. von Domaszewski. Leipzig, 1887. Latin.

Iamblichus *De vita pythagorica. On the Pythagorean Way of Life*. Trans. John Dillon and Jackson Hershbell. Atlanta, 1991. Greek and English.

Iamblichus *Theologoumena arithmeticae. Iamblichus. Theologumena arithmeticae*. Ed. Vittorio de Falco. Bibliotheca Teubneriana. Leipzig, 1922. Greek.

Isocrates *Letter to Philip. Isocrates*. Trans. George Norlin. Loeb Classical Library. 3 vols. Cambridge, Mass., and London, 1966. Greek and English.

John Lydus *De mensibus. Liber de mensibus*. Ed. Richard Wuensch. Bibliotheca Teubneriana. Leipzig, 1898. Rpt. 1967. Greek.

Julius Honorius. In Riese 1878 (modern authors, below). Latin.

Livy *Ab urbe condita*. Livy. *Ab urbe condita*. Trans. B. Foster et al. Loeb Classical Library. 14 vols. London, 1919–1959. Latin and English.

Livy *Periochae*. *Abrégés des livres de l'histoire romaine de Tite-Live*. Trans. Paul Jal. Collections des universités de France. Paris, 1984. Latin and French.

Lucian (all works cited). *The Works of Lucian of Samosata*. Trans. H. W. Fowler and F. G. Fowler. 4 vols. Oxford, 1905. English.

Lucretius. *Lucretius. De rerum natura*. Trans. W. H. D. Rouse. Rev. 2d ed., ed. Martin Ferguson Smith. Loeb Classical Library. Cambridge, Mass., and London, 1982. Latin and English.

Macrobius *Saturnalia*. Text: *Macrobius. Works*. 2d ed., ed. Jacob Willis. Bibliotheca Teubneriana. 2 vols. Stuttgart and Leipzig, 1994. Latin. Translation: *Macrobius. Saturnalia*. Trans. Percival Vaughan Davies. New York, 1969. English.

Manilius *Astronomica*. *Manilius. Astronomica*. Trans. G. P. Goold. Loeb Classical Library. Cambridge, Mass., and London, 1977. Latin and English.

Martial *Epigrams*. *Martial. Epigrams*. Trans. D. R. Shackleton Bailey. Loeb Classical Library. 3 vols. Cambridge, Mass., 1993. Latin and English.

Martianus Capella *De nuptiis Philologiae et Mercurii*. *Martianus Capella*. Ed. Adolphus Dick and Jean Preaux. 2d ed. Bibliotheca Teubneriana. Stuttgart, 1978. Latin.

Ovid *Ars amatoria. The Art of Love and Other Poems.* Trans. J. H. Mozley. 2d ed. Loeb Classical Library. Cambridge, Mass., 1979. Latin and English.

Ovid *Fasti. Ovid's Fasti.* Trans. Sir James George Frazer. Loeb Classical Library. London and New York, 1931. Latin and English.

Ovid *Metamorphoses.* Trans. Frank Justus Miller. 3d ed. Loeb Classical Library. 2 vols. Cambridge, Mass., 1977. Latin and English.

Ovid *Tristia. Ovid. Tristia. Ex Ponto.* Trans Arthur Leslie Wheeler. 2d ed. Loeb Classical Library. Cambridge, Mass., and London, 1988. Latin and English.

Pausanias. *Pausanias. Description of Greece.* Trans. W. H. S. Jones. Loeb Classical Library. 5 vols. Cambridge, Mass., and London, 1966. Greek and English.

Plato (all works cited). *Plato.* Trans. H. N. Fowler and W. R. M. Lamb. Loeb Classical Library. 14 vols. London and New York, 1914–1967. Greek and English.

Pliny *Natural History. Pliny. Natural History.* Trans. H. Rackham. Loeb Classical Library. 10 vols. Cambridge, Mass., and London, 1938–1963. Latin and English.

Pliny the Younger *Panegyricus. Pliny. Letters and Panegyricus.* Trans. Betty Radice. Loeb Classical Library. 2 vols. Cambridge, Mass., and London, 1969. Latin and English.

Plutarch *Antony, Caesar,* etc. *Plutarch's Lives.* Trans. Bernadette Perrin. Loeb Classical Library. 11 vols. London, 1914–1926. Greek and English.

Plutarch *Moralia. Plutarch. Moralia*. Trans. Frank Cole Babbitt. Loeb Classical Library. 15 vols. Cambridge, Mass., and London, 1959–. Greek and English.

Plutarch *Roman Questions. The Roman Questions of Plutarch*. Trans. H. J. Rose. Oxford, 1924. English.

Pomponius *Digest. The Digest of Justinian*. Ed. Theodor Mommsen and Paul Krueger. Trans. Alan Watson. 4 vols. Philadelphia, 1985–. Latin and English.

Posidonius. In Edelstein and Kidd 1972 (modern authors, below). Greek and English.

Propertius *Elegies. Propertius. Elegies*. Trans. G. P. Goold. Loeb Classical Library. Cambridge, Mass., and London, 1990. Latin and English.

Quintilian *Institutio oratoria. Quintilian. De institutione oratoria*. Trans. H. E. Butler. Loeb Classical Library. 4 vols. London, 1920–1922. Latin and English.

Rhetorica ad Herennium. Ad C. Herennium de ratione dicendi (Rhetorica ad Herennium). Trans. Harry Caplan. Loeb Classical Library. Cambridge, Mass., and London, 1954. Latin and English.

Seneca the Elder *Controversiae. The Elder Seneca. Declamations*. Trans. M. Winterbottom. Loeb Classical Library. 2 vols. Cambridge, Mass., 1974. Latin and English.

Seneca *De clementia. Sénèque. De la clémence*. Trans. François Préchac. Collection des universités de France. Paris, 1967. Latin and French.

Seneca *De tranquillitate animi*. In Seneca, *Four Dialogues*. Ed. C. D. N. Costa. Warminster, U.K., 1994. Latin and English.

Seneca *Epistulae. Ad Lucilium epistulae morales*. Trans. Richard M. Gummere. Loeb Classical Library. 3 vols. Cambridge, Mass., and London, 1961–1962. Latin and English.

Servius *Ad Aeneidem. Servii Grammatici qui feruntur in Vergilii carmini commentarii*. Ed. Georg Thilo and Hermann Hagen. Hildesheim, 1961. Latin.

Sextus Empiricus. *Sextus Empiricus*. Trans. R. G. Bury. Loeb Classical Library. 4 vols. London and New York, 1933–1949. Greek and English.

Simonides. *Greek Lyric III: Stesichorus, Ibycus, Simonides and Others*. Trans. David A. Campbell. Loeb Classical Library. Cambridge, Mass., and London, 1991. Greek and English.

Solinus. *C. Julii Solini. Collectanea rerum memorabilium*. Ed. Theodor Mommsen. Berlin, 1864. Latin.

Statius *Silvae. Statius*. Trans. J. H. Mozley. Loeb Classical Library. 2 vols. London, 1928. Latin and English.

Stobaeus *Anthologium. Ioannis Stobaei Anthologii*. Ed. Kurt Wachsmuth and Otto Hense. 4 vols. Berlin, 1884–1909. Greek.

Strabo. *The Geography of Strabo*. Trans. Horace Leonard Jones. Loeb Classical Library. 8 vols. London, 1917–1933. Greek and English.

Suetonius (all works cited). *Suetonius*. Trans. John C. Rolfe. Rev. ed. Loeb Classical Library. 2 vols. London, 1950–1960. Latin and English.

Tacitus (all works cited). *Tacitus in Five Volumes.* Various trans. Loeb Classical Library. 5 vols. Cambridge, Mass., and London, 1925–1980. Latin and English.

Tertullian *De spectaculis. Tertullian. Apology. De spectaculis.* Trans. T. R. Glover. Loeb Classical Library. London and New York, 1931. Latin and English.

Valerius Maximus. *Valerii Maximi factorum et dictorum memorabilium libri novem.* Ed. Karl Kempf. Berlin, 1854. Latin.

Varro *De lingua latina. Varro. On the Latin Language.* Trans. Roland G. Kent. Rev. ed. Loeb Classical Library. 2 vols. Cambridge, Mass., and London, 1951. Latin and English.

Varro *De re rustica. Marcus Porcius Cato, On Agriculture; Marcus Terentius Varro, On Agriculture.* Trans. William Davis Hooper and Harrison Boyd Ash. Cambridge, Mass., and London, 1934. Latin and English.

Velleius Paterculus. *Velleius Paterculus. Histoire Romaine.* Trans. Joseph Hellegouarc'h. Collection des universités de France. Paris, 1962. Latin and French.

Virgil (all works cited). *Virgil in Two Volumes.* Trans. H. Rushton Fairclough. Rev. ed. Loeb Classical Library. 2 vols. Cambridge, Mass., and London, 1935. Latin and English.

Xenophon *Memorabilia. Xenophon. Memorabilia and Oeconomicus.* Trans. O. J. Todd. Loeb Classical Library. 7 vols. Cambridge, Mass., and London, 1979. Greek and English.

Akurgal, Ekrem. 1985. Ancient civilisations and Ruins of Turkey. 6th ed. Ankara.

Alarcâo, J., and R. Étienne. 1976. "Le Portugal à l'époque augustéenne." *Symposium de ciudades augusteas. Bimilenario de la colonia Caesaraugusta*, pp. 171–187. Saragossa.

Alarcâo, J., and R. Étienne. 1979. "Conimbriga, ville de Lusitanie." *Latomus* 38, pp. 877–890.

Alberti, Leon Battista. 1988. *On the Art of Building in Ten Books*. Trans. Joseph Rykwert, Neil Leach, and Robert Tavernor. Cambridge, Mass., and London.

Alexandre le Grand, image et réalité. 1976. Fondation Hardt, Entretiens sur l'antiquité. Geneva.

Amici, C. M. 1991. *Il Foro di Cesare*. Rome.

Amy, R., and P. Gros. 1979. *La Maison Carrée de Nîmes*. 2 vols. *Gallia*, suppl. 38. Paris.

Anderson, A. R. 1928. "Heracles and His Successors: A Study of a Heroic Ideal and the Recurrence of a Heroic Type." *Harvard Studies in Classical Philology* 39, pp. 7–58.

Anderson, J. C. 1984. *The Historical Topography of the Imperial Fora*. Brussels.

Anderson, J. C. 1997. *Roman Architecture and Society*. Baltimore.

Ando, Clifford. 2000. *Imperial Ideology and Provincial Loyalty in the Roman Empire*. Berkeley.

André, J. M., ed. 1978. *Recherches sur les artes à Rome*. Paris.

André, J. M. 1987. "La rhétorique des préfaces de Vitruve. Le statut culturel de la science." *Filologia e forme letterarie, studi offerti a Franceso della Corte*, III, pp. 265–289. Urbino.

Architecture et société. 1983. Actes du colloque international organisé par le C.N.R.S. / École française de Rome. Rome.

Arnim, Hans Friedrich August von. *Stoicorum veterum fragmenta*. 4 vols. Leipzig, 1903–1924.

Aupert, P. 1985. "Remarques sur le dessin d'architecture et le tracé d'implantation dans la Grèce d'époque impériale." *Le dessin d'architecture dans les sociétés antiques; actes du colloque de Strasbourg*, pp. 255–268. Leiden.

Aupert, P., and R. Sablayrolles. 1992. "Villes d'Aquitaine, centres civiques et religieux." *Villes et agglomérations urbaines antiques du sudouest de la Gaule. Aquitania*, suppl. 6, pp. 283–290. Bordeaux.

Babut, D. 1963. "Les stoïciens et l'amour." *Revue des études grecques* 76, pp. 55–63.

Baldwin, Barry. 1990. "The Date, Identity and Career of Vitruvius." *Latomus* 49, pp. 425–434.

Balland, André. 1984. "La *casa Romuli* au Palatin et au Capitole." *Revue des études latines* 62, pp. 58–80.

Bandini, Angelo Maria. 1750. *De obelisco Caesaris Augusti e Campi Martii ruderibus nuper eruto commentarius.* Rome.

Barnes, Jonathan, and Miriam Griffin, eds. 1997. *Philosophia Togata II: Plato and Aristotle at Rome.* Oxford.

Barton, Tamsyn S. 1994. *Power and Knowledge: Astrology, Physiognomics and Medicine under the Roman Empire.* Ann Arbor, Mich.

Bauer, H. 1973. *Korintische Kapitelle des 4. und 3. Jahrhunderts v. Chr.* Berlin.

Baumann, H. 1984. *Le bouquet d'Athéna. Les plantes dans la mythologie et l'art grec.* Paris.

Bauplanung und Bautheorie der Antike. 1984. Berlin.

Bayet, J. 1926. *Les origines de l'Hercule romain.* Paris.

Beard, Mary. 1986. "Cicero and Divination: The Formation of a Latin Discourse." *JRS* 76, pp. 33–46.

Beard, Mary. 1990. "Priesthood in the Roman Republic." Beard and North 1990, pp. 17–48.

Beard, Mary. 1991. "Writing and Religion: Ancient Literacy and the Function of the Written Word in the Roman World." Humphrey 1991, pp. 35–58.

Beard, Mary. 1994. "Religion." *Cambridge Ancient History* IX, pp. 729–768. Cambridge, U.K.

Beard, Mary. 1996. "Le mythe (grec) à Rome: Hercule aux bains." Trans. Valérie Huet. Stella Georgoudi and Jean-Pierre Vernant, eds., *Mythes grecs au figuré: de l'antiquité au baroque*, pp. 81–104. Paris.

Beard, Mary, and John Henderson. 1995. *Classics, a Very Short Introduction*. Oxford.

Beard, Mary, and John North, eds. 1990. *Pagan Priests: Religion and Power in the Ancient World*. London.

Beard, Mary, John North, and Simon Price. 1998. *Religions of Rome*. 2 vols. Cambridge, U.K.

Becatti, G. 1968. "Una statua di Ercole con cornucopia." *Bollettino d'arte* 53, pp. 1–11.

Bek, Lise. 1980. *Towards Paradise on Earth: Modern Space Conception in Architecture, a Creation of Renaissance Humanism. Analecta Romana Instituti Danici*, suppl. 9. Odense.

Bek, Lise. 1985. "*Venusta Species:* A Hellenistic Rhetorical Concept as the Aesthetic Principle in Roman Townscape." *Analecta Romana Instituti Danici* 14, pp. 142–143.

Ben-Menahem, Hanina, and Neil S. Hecht. 1985. "A Modest Addendum to the Greek Metrological Relief at Oxford." *Antiquaries Journal* 65, pp. 139–140.

Benoit, Fernand. 1952. "Le thême hellénistique de l'enchaînement d'Ogmios." *Comptes rendus des séances: Académie des inscriptions*, January–March, pp. 103–114.

Benoit, Fernand. 1969. *Art et dieux de la Gaule*. Paris.

Benveniste, E. 1932. "Le sense du mot *kolossos* et les noms grecs de la statue." *Revue de philologie*, pp. 118–135.

Béranger, Jean. 1953. *Recherches sur l'aspect idéologique du principat*. Basel.

Berchem, Denis van. 1975. *Les distributions de blé et d'argent à la plèbe romaine sous l'empire*. New York.

Berger, Ernst. 1990. "Zum Kanon des Polyklet." *Polyklet*, pp. 156–184. Mainz-am-Rhein.

Bergmann, Bettina. 1994. "The Roman House as Memory Theater: The House of the Tragic Poet in Pompeii." *Art Bulletin* 76.2, pp. 225–256.

Bickerman, E. J. 1961. "*Filius Maiae* (Horace, *Odes* 1.2.43)." *Parola del passato* 16, pp. 5–19.

Bieber, M. 1964. *Alexander the Great in Greek and Roman Art*. Chicago.

Binder, W. 1969. *Der Roma-Augustus Monopteros auf der Acropolis in Athen und sein typologischer Ort*. Stuttgart.

Blegen, Carl, et al. 1930. *Corinth, Vol. III, Part I: Acrocorinth, Excavations in 1926*. Cambridge, Mass.

Blum, H. 1969. *Die antike Mnemotechnik*. Hildesheim.

Blumenberg, Hans. 1997. *Shipwreck with Spectator: Paradigm of a Metaphor for Existence*. Trans. Steven Rendall. Cambridge, Mass., and London.

Boëthius, Axel. 1939. "Vitruvius and the Roman Architecture of His Age." *Dragma, Festschrift M. P. Nilsson. Acta Inst. Rom. Regni Sueciae* 1, pp. 114–143. Lund.

Bömer, F. 1953. "Der Commentarius." *Hermes* 88, pp. 211–250.

Bonnefond, M. 1987. "Transfert de fonction et mutation idéologique: le Capitole et le Forum d'Auguste." *L'urbs: espace urbain et histoire*, pp. 251–278. Rome.

Boyancé, P. 1937. *Le culte des muses chez les philosophes grecs.* 2d ed. 1972, rpt. 1993. Paris.

Boyancé, P. 1955a. "Sur la théologie de Varron." *REA* 57, pp. 57–84.

Boyancé, P. 1955b. "Fulvius Nobilior et le dieu ineffable." *Revue de philologie* 29, pp. 172–192.

Boyancé, P. 1975. "Etymologie et théologie chez Varron." *Revue des études latines* 53, pp. 99–115.

Braudy, Leo. 1986. *The Frenzy of Renown: Fame and Its History.* New York.

Braund, David. 1985. *Augustus to Nero: A Sourcebook on Roman History 31 B.C.–A.D. 68.* Beckenham, Kent.

Bréguet, E. 1969. "*Urbi et orbi:* un cliché et un thème." J. Bibauw, ed., *Hommages à M. Renard I*, pp. 140–152. Brussels.

Bréhier, Émile. 1914. "Poseidonios d'Apamée, théoricien de la géométrie." *Revue des études grecques* 27, pp. 44–58.

Bréhier, Émile. 1970. *La théorie des incorporels dans l'ancien stoïcisme.* 4th ed. Paris.

Brilliant, Richard. 1963. *Gesture and Rank in Roman Art.* New Haven.

British Museum Catalogue of Coins of the Roman Empire. 1923–. London.

Brommer, F., 1980. "Zur Datierung des Augustus von Prima Porta." *Eikones: Studien zum griechischen und römischen Bildnis. Antike Kunst,* suppl. 12, pp. 78–80. Bern.

Broneer, Oscar. 1941. "Colonia Laus Julia Corinthiensis." *Hesperia* 10, pp. 388–390.

Brown, F. E. 1963. "Vitruvius and the Liberal Art of Architecture." *Bucknell Review* 11.4, pp. 99–107.

Brunt, P. A. 1975. "Stoicism and the Principate." *Proceedings of the British School at Rome* 43, pp. 7–35.

Brunt, P. A. 1978. "Laus Imperii." P. D. A. Garnsey and C. R. Whittaker, eds., *Imperialism in the Ancient World,* pp. 159–191. Cambridge, U.K. (Rpt. in Brunt 1990).

Brunt, P. A. 1990. *Roman Imperial Themes.* Oxford.

Buchner, Edmund. 1976. "Solarium Augusti und Ara Pacis." *MDAI (R)* 83, pp. 319–376.

Buchner, Edmund. 1980. "Horologium Solarium Augusti." *MDAI (R)* 87, pp. 320–369.

Buchner, Edmund. 1982. *Die Sonnenuhr des Augustus*. Mainz.

Buchner, Edmund. 1983. "Horologium Augusti." *Gymnasium* 90, pp. 494–508.

Buchner, Edmund. 1988. "Horologium Solarium Augusti." Hofter et al. 1988, pp. 240–247.

Bulmer-Thomas, Ivor, ed. 1939–1941. *Selections Illustrating the History of Greek Mathematics*. Loeb Classical Library. 2 vols. Cambridge, Mass.

Burford, A. 1972. *Craftsmen in Greek and Roman Society*. London.

Burkert, Walter. 1972. *Lore and Science of Ancient Pythagoreanism*. Trans. Edwin J. Minor, Jr. Cambridge, Mass.

Callebat, Louis. 1982. "La prose du *De architectura* de Vitruve." *ANRW* II 30.1, pp. 696–722.

Callebat, Louis. 1989. "Organisation et structure du *De architectura* de Vitruve." Geertman and de Jong 1989, pp. 34–38.

Callebat, Louis. 1992. "Problèmes formels de la vulgarisation scientifique et technique." *Latin vulgaire, latin tardif. Actes du IIIe Colloque international sur le latin vulgaire et tardif*, pp. 63–70. Tübingen.

Callebat, Louis. 1994. "Rhétorique et architecture dans le *De architectura* de Vitruve." *Le projet de Vitruve*, pp. 31–46. Rome.

Callebat, L., P. Bouet, Ph. Fleury, and M. Zuinghedau. 1984. *Vitruve. De architectura. Concordance*. Hildesheim.

Cambridge Ancient History, The. 1961–. 2d ed. Cambridge.

Canfora, Luciano. 1991. *The Vanished Library.* London.

Canfora, Luciano. 1992. "Le monde en rouleaux." Jacob and de Polignac 1992, pp. 49–62.

Caropino, Jérôme. 1943. "Les origines pythagoriciennes de l'Hercule romain." *Aspects mystiques de la Rome païenne,* pp. 173–206. Paris.

Cardauns, Burkhart. 1976. *M. Terentius Varro, Antiquitates rerum divinarum.* Wiesbaden.

Cardauns, Burkhart. 1978. "Varro und die römische Religion. Zur Theologie, Wirkungsgeschichte und Leistung der *Antiquitates rerum divinarum.*" *ANRW* II 16.1, pp. 80–103.

Carettoni, G. 1983. *Das Haus des Augustus auf dem Palatin.* Mainz am Rhein.

Carpo, Mario. 1998. "The Making of the Typographical Architect." Hart 1998, pp. 158–169.

Carpo, Mario. 2001. *Architecture in the Age of Printing.* Cambridge, Mass., and London.

Carruthers, Mary. 1990. *The Book of Memory: A Study of Memory in Medieval Culture.* Cambridge, U.K.

Carson, Anne. 1993. "Your Money or Your Life." *Yale Journal of Criticism* 6.1, pp. 75–91.

Carson, Anne. 1999. *Economy of the Unlost*. Princeton.

Carson, Anne. 2001. *The Beauty of the Husband*. New York.

Castagnoli, F. 1951. "Roma Quadrata." George E. Mylonas, ed., *Studies Presented to David Moore Robinson on His Seventieth Birthday*, pp. 389–399. St. Louis.

Castriota, David. 1995. *The Ara Pacis Augustae and the Imagery of Abundance in Later Greek and Early Roman Imperial Art*. Princeton.

Chesnut, G. F. 1978. "The Ruler and the *Logos* in Neo Pythagorean, Middle Platonic and Late Stoic Political Philosophy." *ANRW* II 16.2, pp. 1310–1332.

Choay, Françoise. 1988. "Le *De re aedificatoria* comme texte inaugural." Guillaume 1988, pp. 83–90.

Ciapponi, Lucia A. 1960. "Il *De architectura* di Vitruvio nel primo umanismo." *Italia medioevale e umanistica* 3, pp. 59–99.

Clark, John Willis. 1901. *The Care of Books: An Essay on the Development of Libraries and Their Fittings*. Cambridge, U.K.

Clarke, John R. 1991. *The Houses of Roman Italy, 100 B.C.–A.D. 250: Ritual, Space and Decoration*. Berkeley.

Clavel-Levêque, Monique. 1992. "Centuriation, géométrie et harmonie: le cas du Biterrois." Jean-Yves Guillaumin, ed., *Mathématiques dans l'antiquité*, pp. 161–177. Saint-Étienne.

Coarelli, Filippo. 1971–1972. "Il complesso pompeiano del Campo Marzio e la sua decorazione scultorea." *Rendiconti della Pontificia Accademia Romana di Archeologia* 44, pp. 99–122.

Coarelli, Filippo. 1983–1985. *Il Foro Romano*. Rome.

Coarelli, Filippo. 1988. *Il Foro Boario*. Rome.

Coarelli, Filippo. 1989. "La casa dell'aristocrazia romana." Geertman and de Jong 1989, pp. 178–187.

Cockerell, C. R. 1860. *The Temples of Jupiter Panhellenius at Aegina and of Apollo Epicurus at Bassae*. London.

Cohen, Benjamin. 1975. "La notion d'*ordo* dans la Rome antique." *Bulletin de l'Association Guillaume Budé*, pp. 259–282.

Cohen, Benjamin. 1984. "Some Neglected *Ordines:* The Apparitorial Status-Group." *Des ordres à Rome*, pp. 23–60. Paris.

Cole, T. 1967. *Democritus and Sources of Greek Anthropology*. Cleveland.

Coleman, R. G. G. 1964. "The Dream of Cicero." *Proceedings of the Cambridge Philological Society* 10, pp. 1–14.

Combès, Robert. 1966. *Imperator*. Paris.

Corbier, Mireille. 1987. "L'écriture dans l'espace public romain." *L'urbs: espace urbain et histoire*, pp. 27–60. Rome.

Corpus inscriptionum latinarum. Berlin, 1863–.

Coulton, J. J. 1989. "Modules and Measurement in Ancient Design." Geertman and de Jong 1989, pp. 85–89.

Crawford, Michael H. 1974. *Roman Republican Coinage*. 2 vols. London.

Crook, J. A. 1996. "Augustus: Power, Authority, Achievement." *Cambridge Ancient History* X, pp. 113–146.

Cuillandre, J. 1944. *La droite et la gauche dans les poèmes homériques*. Paris.

Dahlmann, H. 1932. *Varro und die hellenistische Sprachtheorie*. Berlin.

David, Jean Michel. 1983. "Le tribunal dans la basilique: évolution fonctionelle et symbolique de la république à l'empire." *Architecture et société de l'archaïsme grec à la fin de la République*, pp. 219–241. Rome.

Degrassi, Attilio. 1963. *Fasti anni Numani et Iuliani* (*Inscriptiones Italiae, 3.2*). Rome.

Degrassi, Attilio. 1957–1963. *Inscriptiones latinae liberae rei publicae*. 2 vols. Florence.

Dekoulakou-Sideris, I. 1990. "A Metrological Relief from Salamis." *AJA* 94, pp. 445–451.

De Laine, Janet. 1996. "'*De Aquis Suis*'? The *Commentarius* of Frontinus." Nicolet and Gros 1996, pp. 117–139.

Delatte, Louis. 1942. *Les traités de la royauté d'Ecphante, Diotogène et Sthenidas*. Paris and Liège.

Dessau, Hermann, ed. 1892–1916. *Inscriptiones latinae selectae*. Berlin.

Detienne, Marcel. 1960. "Héraclès, héros pythagoricien." *Revue de l'histoire des religions* 158, pp. 19–53.

Detienne, Marcel, and Jean-Pierre Vernant. 1978. *Cunning Intelligence in Greek Culture and Society*. Trans. Janet Lloyd. Atlantic Highlands, N.J.

Dilke, O. A. W. 1971. *The Roman Land Surveyors: An Introduction to the Agrimensores*. Newton Abbot.

Dinsmoor, William Bell. 1950. *The Architecture of Ancient Greece*. 3d ed. London.

Dörpfeld, W. 1887. "Der römische und der italische Fuss." *Hermes* 22, pp. 79–85.

Dugas, C. 1944. "Héraclès Musikos." *Revue des études grecques* 57, pp. 61–70.

Dumézil, Georges. 1957. "Augur." *Revue des études latines* 35, pp. 121–151. Rpt. in Dumézil, *Idées romaines* (Paris, 1969), pp. 79–102.

Dumézil, Georges. 1987. *La religion romaine archaïque*. 2d ed. Paris. (1st ed. trans. Philip Krapp as *Archaic Roman Religion*. 2 vols. Chicago, 1970.)

Dumougin, S. 1988. *L'ordre équestre sous les Julio-Claudiens*. Rome.

Dunbabin, Katherine M. D. 1990. "*Ipsae Deae Vestigia* . . . Footprints Divine and Human on Graeco-Roman Monuments." *JRA* 3, pp. 85–109.

Dunst, Günter, and Edmund Buchner. 1973. "Aristamenes-Uhren in Samos." *Chiron* 3, pp. 119–129.

Dupont, Florence. 1986. "L'autre corps de l'empereur-dieu." *Le temps de la réflexion* 7: *Corps des dieux*, pp. 231–252. Paris. Trans. as "The Emperor God's Other Body." *Fragments for a History of the Human Body* III (New York, 1989), pp. 396–419.

Dvornik, Francis. 1966. *Early Christian and Byzantine Political Philosophy: Origins and Background.* 2 vols. Washington, D.C.

Dwyer, Eugene J. 1973. "Augustus and the Capricorn." *MDAI (R)* 80, pp. 59–67.

Earl, Donald C. 1961. *The Political Thought of Sallust.* Cambridge, U.K.

Ebhardt, B. 1918. *Vitruvius. Die zehn Bücher der Architektur des Vitruv und ihre Herausgeber.* Berlin. Rpt. New York, 1962.

Edelstein, L., and I. G. Kidd, eds. 1972. *Posidonius.* 2 vols. Cambridge, U.K.

Edwards, Catharine. 1993. *The Politics of Immorality in Ancient Rome.* Cambridge, U.K.

Edwards, Catharine. 1996. *Writing Rome: Textual Approaches to the City.* Cambridge, U.K.

Ehrenberg, V., and A. H. M. Jones. 1972. *Documents Illustrating the Reigns of Augustus and Tiberius.* 2d ed. Oxford.

Elsner, Jaś. 1996. "Inventing Imperium: Texts and the Propaganda of Monuments in Augustan Rome." Elsner, ed., *Art and Text in Roman Culture*, pp. 32–53. Cambridge, U.K.

Engels, Donald W. 1990. *Roman Corinth: An Alternative Model for the Classical City*. Chicago.

Erim, K. T. 1986. *Aphrodisias: City of Venus Aphrodite*. London and New York.

Erkell, H. 1952. *Augustus, Felicitas, Fortuna. Lateinische Wortstudien*. Göteborg.

Erskine, A. 1990. *The Hellenistic Stoa: Political Thought and Action*. London.

Étienne, R. 1958. *Le culte impérial dans la peninsule ibérique d'Augsute à Dioclétien*. Paris.

Étienne, R. 1992. "L'horloge de la *civitas Igaeditanorum* et la création de la province de Lusitanie." REA 94, pp. 355–362.

Étienne, R. 1996. "Du nouveau sur les débuts du culte impérial dans la peninsule ibérique." Small 1996, pp. 153–163.

Farnoux, B. C. 1981. "Mercure romain, les 'Mercuriales' et l'institution du culte impériale sous le Principat augustéen." *ANRW* II 17.1, pp. 458–501.

Fear, A. T. 1996. *Rome and Baetica: Urbanization in Southern Spain*. Oxford.

Fears, J. Rufus. 1981. "The Theology of Victory at Rome: Approaches and Problems." *ANRW* II 17.2, pp. 736–826.

Feeney, D. C. 1991. *The Gods in Epic: Poets and Critics of the Classical Tradition*. Oxford.

Feeney, D. C. 1998. *Literature and Religion at Rome: Cultures, Contexts and Beliefs*. Cambridge, U.K.

Ferguson, J. 1990. "Epicureanism under the Roman Empire." *ANRW* II 36.4, pp. 2257–2327.

Fernie, Eric. 1978. "Historical Metrology and Architectural History." *Art History* 1.4, pp. 383–399. Rpt. in Fernie 1996.

Fernie, Eric. 1981. "The Metrological Relief in Oxford." *Antiquaries Journal* 61, pp. 265–263.

Fernie, Eric. 1996. *Romanesque Architecture: Design, Meaning and Metrology*. London.

Ferri, Silvio. 1940. "Nuovi contributi esegeti al 'canone' della scultura greca." *Rivista del Reale Istituto d'Archeologia e Storia dell'Arte* 7, pp. 117–152.

Février, P. A., M. Fixot, C. Goudineau, and V. Kruta. 1980. *L'histoire de la France urbaine I: La ville antique*. Paris.

Fishwick, D. 1987–1992. *The Imperial Cult in the Latin West*. Leiden, New York, and Cologne.

Fishwick, D. 1996. "Four Temples at Tarraco." Small 1996, pp. 165–184.

Fittschen, K. 1976. "Zur Panzerstatue in Cherchel." *Jahrbuch des Deutschen archäologischen Instituts* 91, pp. 203–208.

Fleury, Philippe. 1993. *La mécanique de Vitruve*. Caen.

Fortenbaugh, William W., ed. 1983. *On Stoic and Peripatetic Ethics: The Work of Arius Didymus*. New Brunswick, N.J.

Frazer, A., ed. 1990. *Samothrace 10: The Propylon of Ptolemy II*. Princeton.

Frazer, P. M. 1970. "Aristophanes of Byzantion and Zoilos Homero-mastix in Vitruvius: A Note on Vitruvius VII, praef. 4–9." *Eranos* 68, pp. 115–122.

Frazer, P. M. 1972. *Ptolemaic Alexandria*. 3 vols. Oxford.

Frézouls, E. 1989. "Fondements scientifiques, armature conceptuel et praxis dans le *De architectura*." Geertman and de Jong 1989, pp. 39–48.

Fuchs, Harald. 1973. *Augustin und der antike Friedensgedanke*. Rpt. of 1926 ed. New York.

Fuhrmann, Manfred. 1960. *Das systematische Lehrbuch; ein Beitrag zur Geschichte der Wissenschaften im der Antike*. Göttingen.

Gabba, Emilio. 1982. "Political and Cultural Aspects of the Classical Revival in the Augustan Age." *Classical Antiquity* 1, pp. 43–65.

Gabba, Emilio. 1984. "The Historians and Augustus." Millar and Segal 1984, pp. 61–88.

Gagé, Jean. 1930. "Romulus-Augustus." *MÉFRA* 47, pp. 138–181.

Gagé, Jean. 1933. "La théologie de la victoire impériale." *Revue historique* 171, pp. 1–43.

Gagé, Jean. 1955. *Apollon romain.* Paris.

Galinsky, Karl. 1972. *The Herakles Theme.* Oxford.

Galinsky, Karl. 1996. *Augustan Culture, an Interpretive Introduction.* Princeton.

Galsterer, H. 1990. "A Man, a Book, and a Method: Sir Ronald Syme's *Roman Revolution* after Fifty Years." Raaflaub and Toher 1990, pp. 1–20.

Gans, U. W. 1992. *Korinthisierende Kapitelle der römischen Kaiserzeit.* Cologne, Weimar, and Vienna.

Gargola, D. J. 1995. *Lands, Laws and Gods: Magistrates and Ceremony in the Regulation of Public Lands in Republican Rome.* Chapel Hill, N.C., and London.

Gasparri, C. 1979. *Aedes Concordiae Augustae.* Rome.

Gauer, W. 1974. "Zum Bildprogramm des Trajansbogens von Benevent." *Jahrbuch des Deutschen archäologischen Instituts* 89, pp. 308–335.

Geertman, H., and J. J. de Jong, eds. 1989. *Munus Non Ingratum: Proceedings of the International Symposium on Vitruvius' De Architectura and the Hellenistic and Republican Architecture.* Leiden.

Germann, Georg. 1991. *Vitruve et le vitruvianisme.* Trans. Michèle Zaugg and Jacques Gubler. Lausanne.

Gibbs, Sharon L. 1976. *Greek and Roman Sundials*. New Haven and London.

Gigante, Marcello. 1995. *Philodemus in Italy: The Book from Herculaneum*. Trans. Dirk Obbink. Ann Arbor, Mich.

Goguey, D. 1978. "La formation de l'architecte: culture et technique." André 1978, pp. 100–115.

Gonzalez, J. 1984. "Tabula siarensis, fortunales siarensis." *Zeitschrift für Papyrologie und Epigraphik,* pp. 55–100.

Goodenough, E. R. 1928. "The Political Philosophy of Hellenistic Kingship." *Yale Classical Studies* 1, pp. 55–102.

Goody, Jack. 1977. *The Domestication of the Savage Mind*. Cambridge, U.K.

Gordon, Richard. 1990a. "From Republic to Principate: Priesthood, Religion and Ideology." Beard and North 1990, pp. 179–198.

Gordon, Richard. 1990b. "The Veil of Power: Emperors, Sacrificers and Benefactors." Beard and North 1990, pp. 199–232.

Gordon, Richard. 1990c. "Religion in the Roman Empire: The Civic Compromise and Its Limits." Beard and North 1990, pp. 233–255.

Görgemanns, H. 1983. "*Oikeiosis* in Arius Didymus with comments by B. Inwod." Fortenbaugh 1983, pp. 165–201.

Götte, G. 1964. "Die Frage der geographischen Interpretation in Caesars *Bellum gallicum*." Diss. Marburg.

Goudineau, C. 1980. "Les villes de la paix romaine." Février et al. 1980, pp. 237–391.

Goudineau, C. 1991. Introduction to Goudineau and Rebourg 1991, pp. 7–15.

Goudineau, C., P. A. Février, and M. Fixot. 1980. "Le réseau urbain." Février et al. 1980, pp. 71–109.

Goudineau, C., and A. Rebourg, eds. 1991. *Les villes augusténnes de Gaule.* Autun.

Goulet, Richard, ed. 1989–. *Dictionnaire des philosophes antiques.* Paris.

Graf, F., ed. 1993. *Mythos in mythenloser Gesellschaft: Das Paradigma Roms.* Colloquium Rauricum 3. Stuttgart and Leipzig.

Green, Peter. 1991. *Alexander of Macedon, 356–323 B.C.* Berkeley and Los Angeles.

Gregory, Timothy E., ed. 1993. *The Corinthia in the Roman Period. JRA,* suppl 8. Ann Arbor, Mich.

Grenade, P. 1961. *Essai sur les origines du principat.* Paris.

Grenier, Jean-Claude. 1995. "L'empereur et le pharaon." *ANRW* II 18.5, pp. 3181–3194.

Griffin, Miriam. 1994. "The Intellectual Developments of the Ciceronian Age." *Cambridge Ancient History* IX, pp. 689–728.

Griffin, Miriam, and Jonathan Barnes, eds. 1989. *Philosophia Togata.* 2d ed. with updated bibliography, 1996. Oxford.

Grimal, P. 1945–1946. "Auguste et Athénodore de Tarse." *REA* 47 (1945), pp. 261–273; 48 (1946), pp. 62–79.

Grimal, P. 1948. "La promenade d'Évandre et d'Énée à la lumière des fouilles récentes." *REA* 50, pp. 348–351.

Grimal, P. 1951. "Énée à Rome et le triomphe d'Octave." *REA* 53, pp. 51–61.

Grimal, P. 1966. "Le bon roi de Philodème et la royauté de César." *Revue des études latines* 44, pp. 254–285.

Grimal, P. 1978. *Sénèque ou la conscience de l'empire.* Paris.

Grimal, P. 1979. "Du *De republica* au *De clementia:* reflexions sur l'évolution de l'idée monarchique à Rome." *MÉFRA* 91, pp. 671–691.

Grodzynski, D. 1974. "Superstitio." *REA* 76, pp. 36–60.

Gros, Pierre. 1971. Review of Soubiran, Vitruvius 1969. *REA* 73, pp. 464–467.

Gros, Pierre. 1973. "Hermodorus et Vitruve." *MÉFRA* 85, pp. 158–165.

Gros, Pierre. 1975. "Structures et limites de la compilation vitruvienne dans les livres III et IV du *De architectura.*" *Latomus* 34, pp. 986–1009.

Gros, Pierre. 1976a. *Aurea Templa: Recherches sur l'architecture religieuse de Rome à l'époque d'Auguste.* Paris.

Gros, Pierre. 1976b. "Les premières générations d'architectes hellénis-
tiques à Rome." *Mélanges Heurgon: l'Italie préromaine et la Rome républi-
caine* I, pp. 387–410. Paris and Rome.

Gros, Pierre. 1978. "Le dossier vitruvien d'Hermogénès." *MÉFRA* 90,
pp. 687–703.

Gros, Pierre. 1979. "La rhétorique des ordres dans l'architecture clas-
sique." *Colloque sur la rhétorique (Calliope I)*, pp. 333–347. Paris.

Gros, Pierre. 1982. "Vitruve: l'architecture et sa théorie à la lumière des
études récentes." *ANRW* II 30.1, pp. 659–695.

Gros, Pierre. 1983. "Statut social et rôle culturel des architectes (période
hellénistique et augustéenne)." *Architecture et société*, pp. 425–452.

Gros, Pierre. 1984a. Review of Buchner 1982. *Revue archéologique*,
pp. 374–376.

Gros, Pierre. 1984b. "La basilique du forum selon Vitruve 5.1." *Bauplanung und Bautheorie der Antike*, pp. 49–69.

Gros, Pierre. 1987a. "La fonction symbolique des édifices théâtraux dans
le paysage urbain de la Rome augustéenne." *L'urbs: espace urbain et histoire*, pp. 319–346. Rome.

Gros, Pierre. 1987b. "Un programme augustéen: le centre monumental
de la colonie d'Arles." *Jahrbuch des Deutschen archäologischen Instituts*
102, pp. 339–363.

Gros, Pierre. 1989a. "Les fondements philosophiques de l'harmonie architecturale selon Vitruve." *Journal of the Faculty of Letters of the University of Tokyo: Aesthetics* XIV, pp. 13–22.

Gros, Pierre. 1989b. "L'*auctoritas* chez Vitruve: contribution à l'étude de la sémantique des ordres dans le *De architectura.*" Geertman and de Jong 1989, pp. 126–133.

Gros, Pierre. 1990. "Les étapes de l'aménagement monumental du forum." *La città nell'Italia settentrionale in età romana*, pp. 29–68. Rome.

Gros, Pierre. 1991a. "De la rhétorique à l'architecture: l'ambiguïté de l'*asperitas.*" *Voces* 2, pp. 73–79.

Gros, Pierre. 1991b. "Nouveau paysage urbain et cultes dynastiques: remarques sur l'idéologie de la ville augustéenne à partir des centres monumentaux d'Athènes, Thasos, Arles et Nîmes." Goudineau and Rebourg 1991, pp. 127–140.

Gros, Pierre. 1994a. "*Munus non ingratum:* le traité vitruvien et la notion de service." *Le projet de Vitruve*, pp. 75–90. Rome.

Gros, Pierre. 1994b. "Le schéma vitruvien du théâtre latin et sa signification dans le schéma normatif du *De architectura.*" *Revue archéologique*, pp. 57–80.

Gros, Pierre. 1995. "Les mots et les choses dans le *De architectura.*" *Alla signorina: Mélanges offerts à Noëlle de la Blanchardière*, pp. 167–174. Rome.

Gros, Pierre. 1996a. *L'architecture romaine du début du IIIe s. av. J-C à la fin du haut-empire.* Paris.

Gros, Pierre. 1996b. "Les illustrations du *De architectura* de Vitruve: histoire d'un malentendu." Nicolet and Gros 1996, pp. 19–36.

Gros, Pierre. 1996c. "Les nouveaux espaces civiques du début de l'Empire en Asie Mineure: les exemples d'Ephèse, Iasos et Aphrodisias." Roueché and Smith 1996, pp. 111–120.

Gros, Pierre. 1996d. "Le palais hellénistique et l'architecture augustéenne: l'exemple du complexe du Palatin." W. Hoepfner and G. Brands, eds., *Basileia. Die Paläste der hellenistischen Könige*, pp. 234–239. Mainz-am-Rhein.

Gros, Pierre. 2001. "La géométrie platonicienne de la notice vitruvienne sur l'homme parfait (*De architectura* III, 1, 2–3)." *Annali di architettura* 13, pp. 15–32.

Gros, Pierre, and Gilles Sauron. 1988. "Das politische Programm der öffentlichen Bauten." Hofter et al. 1988, pp. 48–58.

Guillaume, Jean, ed. 1988. *Les traités d'architecture de la renaissance.* Paris.

Guillaumin, J. Y. 1994. "Géométrie grecque et agrimensorique romaine; la science comme justification d'une idéologie." *Dialogues d'histoire ancienne* 20, pp. 279–295.

Güven, Suna. 1998. "Displaying the *Res Gestae* of Augustus." *Journal of the Society of Architectural Historians* 57.1, pp. 30–45.

Habachi, Labib. 1977. *The Obelisks of Egypt: Skyscrapers of the Past.* New York.

Hahm, D. 1990. "The Ethical Doxography of Arius Didymus." *ANRW* II 36.4, pp. 2935–3055.

Hakim, Besim S. 2001. "Julian of Ascalon's Treatise of Construction and Design Rules from Sixth-Century Palestine." *Journal of the Society of Architectural Historians* 60.1, pp. 4–25.

Hallett, C. H. 1986. "The Origins of the Classical Style in Sculpture." *Journal of Hellenic Studies* 106, pp. 71–84.

Hallett, C. H. 1995. "The Replica of Polykleitos' Doryphoros in the Minneapolis Institute of Arts: An Archaeological Description." Moon 1995, pp. 116–120.

Hammond, N. G. L. 1989. *Alexander the Great.* 2d ed. Bristol.

Hänlein-Schäfer, Heidi. 1985. *Veneratio Augusti: Studien zu den Tempeln des ersten römischen Kaisers.* Rome.

Hanson, J. A. 1959. *Roman Theater Temples.* Princeton.

Harris, William V. 1979. *War and Imperialism in Republican Rome, 327–70 B.C.* Oxford.

Hart, Vaughan, ed. 1998. *Paper Palaces: The Rise of the Renaissance Architectural Treatise.* New Haven and London.

Haselberger, L. 1983. "Bericht über die Arbeit am jüngeren Apollontempel von Didyma." *Istanbuler Mitteilungen* 33, pp. 91–123.

Haselberger, L. 1984. "Die Werkzeichnungen des Niaskos im Apollontempel von Didyma." *Bauplanung und Bautheorie der Antike,* pp. 111–119.
Berlin.

Hays, Robert Stephen. 1983. "Lucius Annaeus Cornutus' *Epidrome:* Introduction, Translation and Notes." Diss. U. of Texas, Austin.

Hecht, K. 1979. "Zum römischen Fuss." *Abhandlungen der Braun-
schweigischen wissenschaftlichen Gesellschaft* 30, pp. 1–31.

Heilmeyer, W. D. 1970. *Korinthische Normalkapitelle.* Heidelberg.

Heinze, R. 1925. "Auctoritas." *Hermes* 60, pp. 348–366.

Hendrickson, G. L. 1906. "The *De Analogia* of Julius Caesar." *Classical
Philology* 1.2, pp. 97–120.

Hepnig, H. 1907. "Die Arbeiten zu Pergamon 1904–1905." *MDAI (A),*
pp. 241–377.

Hersey, George L. 1966. *Pythagorean Palaces: Magic and Architecture in
the Italian Renaissance.* Ithaca, N.Y.

Hersey, George L. 1988. *The Lost Meaning of Classical Architecture.* Cambridge, Mass., and London.

Hill, P. V. 1989. *The Monuments of Ancient Rome as Coin Types.* London.

Hinrichs, F. T. 1989. *Histoire des institutions gromatiques.* Trans. D. Mi-
nary. Paris.

Hoff, M. C. 1989. "Civil Disobedience and Unrest in Augustan Athens." *Hesperia* 58, pp. 267–276.

Hoff, M. C. 1996. "The Politics and Culture of the Athenian Imperial Cult." Small 1996, pp. 185–200.

Hofter, Mathias, et al., eds. 1988. *Kaiser Augustus und die verlorene Republik*. Exh. cat. Berlin.

Holland, L. A. 1961. *Janus and the Bridge*. Rome.

Hölscher, T. 1988. "Historische Reliefs." Hofter et al. 1988, pp. 386–387.

Homolle, T. 1916. "L'origine du chapiteau corinthien." *Revue archéologique* 2, pp. 17–60.

Hopkins, Keith. 1991. "Conquest by the Book." Humphrey 1991, pp. 133–158.

Hornblower, Simon, and Antony Spawforth, eds. 1996. *The Oxford Classical Dictionary*. 3d ed. Oxford.

Hoskins Walbank, Mary E. 1996. "Evidence for the Imperial Cult in Julio-Claudian Corinth." Small 1996, pp. 201–213.

Humphrey, S., ed. 1991. *Literacy in the Roman World*. Ann Arbor, Mich.

Hurwit, Jeffrey M. 1995. "The Doryphoros: Looking Backward." Moon 1995, pp. 3–18.

Hurwit, Jeffrey M. 1999. *The Athenian Acropolis: History, Mythology, and Archaeology*. Cambridge, U.K.

Illich, Ivan. 1985. *H₂O and the Waters of Forgetfulness*. Dallas.

Ingholt, Herald. 1969. "The Prima Porta Statue of Augustus." *Archaeology* 22, pp. 176–187 and 304–318.

Inscriptiones graecae. Berlin, 1873–.

Instinsky, H. U. 1962. *Die Siegel des Kaisers Augustus*. Baden-Baden.

Iversen, Erik. 1968–. *Obelisks in Exile*. Copenhagen.

Jacob, Christian. 1992. "Un athlète du savior: Eratosthène." Jacob and de Polignac 1992, pp. 113–124.

Jacob, Christian, and François de Polignac, eds. 1992. *Alexandrie. IIIᵉ siècle av. J.-C. Tous les savoirs du monde ou le rêve d'universalité des Ptolémées*. Paris.

Jaczynowska, Maria. 1981. "Le culte de l'Hercule romain au temps du haut-empire." *ANRW* II 17.2, pp. 631–661.

Jaeger, Mary. 1993. "*Custodiae Fidelis Memoriae:* Livy's Story of M. Manlius Capitolinus." *Latomus* 52, pp. 350–363.

Jaeger, Mary. 1997. *Livy's Written Rome*. Ann Arbor, Mich.

Jordan, Paul. 1998. *Riddles of the Sphinx*. New York.

Kähler, H. 1959. *Die Augustusstatue von Primaporta*. Cologne.

Kahn, Charles H. 1983. "Arius as Doxographer." Fortenbaugh 1983, pp. 3–13.

Kantorowicz, Ernst H. 1957. *The King's Two Bodies: A Study in Medieval Political Theology.* Princeton.

Kellum, Barbara. 1990. "The City Adorned: Programmatic Display at the *Aedes Concordiae Augustae.*" Raaflaub and Toher 1990, pp. 276–307.

Kellum, Barbara. 1994. "The Construction of Landscape in Augustan Rome: The Garden Room at the Villa *ad Galinas.*" *Art Bulletin* 76.2, pp. 212–224.

Kellum, Barbara. 1996. "The Phallus as Signifier: The Forum of Augustus and Rituals of Masculinity." Natalie Boymel Campen, ed., *Sexuality in Ancient Art,* pp. 170–179. Cambridge, U.K.

Kempter, F. 1934. *Akanthus, die Entstehung eines Ornamentmotivs.* Leipzig.

Kessissoglu, Alexander. 1993. *Die fünfte Vorrede in Vitruvs De architectura.* Frankfurt.

Kienast, Dietmar. 1961. "Imperator." *Zeitschrift für die Rechtsgeschichte* 91, pp. 403–421.

Kienast, Dietmar. 1969. "Augustus und Alexander." *Gymnasium* 76, pp. 430–456.

Kienast, Dietmar. 1982a. *Augustus, Princeps und Monarch.* Darmstadt.

Kienast, Dietmar. 1982b. "Corpus imperii." G. Wirth et al., eds., *Romanitas, Christianitas. Untersuchungen zur Geschichte und Literatur der römischen Kaiserzeit. Johannes Straub zum 70. Geburtstag,* pp. 1–17. Berlin.

King, Dorothy. 1998. "Figured Supports: Vitruvius' Caryatids and Atlantes." *Quaderni ticinesi di numismatica e antichità classiche* 26, pp. 275–305.

Kirk, G. S., J. E. Raven, and M. Schofield. 1983. *The Presocratic Philosophers.* 2d ed. Cambridge, U.K.

Klotz, A. 1931. "Die geographischen commentarii des Agrippa und ihre Überreste." *Klio* 24, pp. 38–58 and 386–466.

Knell, Heiner. 1985. *Vitruvs Architekturtheorie: Versuch einer Interpretation.* Darmstadt.

Knoche, U. 1967. "Der römische Ruhmesgedanke." H. Oppermann, ed., *Römische Wertbegriffe,* pp. 420–445. Darmstadt.

Koch, Herbert. 1951. *Vom Nachleben Vitruvs.* Baden-Baden.

Korres, M. 1994. "The Parthenon from Antiquity to the 19th Century." Tournikiotis 1994, pp. 137–161.

Körte, W. 1937. "Dinocrates und die barock Phantasie." *Antike* 13, pp. 289–312.

Krinsky, C. H. 1967. "Seventy-eight Vitruvius Manuscripts." *Journal of the Warburg Institute* 30, pp. 36–70.

Kruft, Hanno-Walter. 1994. *A History of Architectural Theory.* Trans. Ronald Taylor, Elsi Callander, and Antony Wood. London and New York.

Kubitschek, W. 1928. *Grundriss der antiken Zeitrechnung.* Munich.

Kuck, H. 1965. *Philologos*. Berlin.

Lahusen, Götz. 1990. "Polyklet und Augustus." *Polyklet,* pp. 393–396. Mainz-am-Rhein.

Lana, I. 1953. "Sextiorum nova et Romani roboris secta." *Rivista di filologia e di istruzione classica* 31, pp. 1–26 and 209–233.

Lapidge, M. 1978. "Stoic Cosmology." Rist 1978, pp. 161–186.

La Rocca, E. 1995. "Il programma figurativa del Foro di Augusto." *I luoghi del consenso imperiale,* pp. 74–87. Rome.

Latte, Kurt. 1960. *Römische Religionsgeschichte*. Munich.

Lawrence, A. W. 1983. *Greek Architecture*. Revised with additions by R. A. Tomlinson. Harmondsworth.

Leftwich, Gregory V. 1995. "Polykleitos and Hippocratic Medicine." Moon 1995, pp. 38–51.

Le Glay, M. 1991. "Le culte d'Auguste dans les villes augustéennes." Goudineau and Rebourg 1991, pp. 117–126.

Lesko, Leonard H. 1991. "Ancient Egyptian Cosmogonies and Cosmology." Byron E. Shafer, ed., *Religion in Ancient Egypt*, pp. 88–122. Ithaca and London.

Levi, Mario Attilio. 1997. *Ercole e Roma*. Rome.

Levick, B. 1967. *Roman Colonies in Southern Asia Minor*. Oxford.

Levick, B. 1982. "Propaganda and Imperial Coinage." *Antichthon* 16, pp. 104–116.

Lewis, Charlton T., and Charles Short. 1962. *A Latin Dictionary Founded on Andrews' Edition of Freund's Latin Dictionary*. Oxford.

Lexicon iconographicum mythologiae classicae. Zurich, 1981–1997.

Liddell, Henry George, and Robert Scott. 1968. *A Greek-English Lexicon*. Rev. Sir Henry Stuart Jones et al. Oxford.

Lieberg, Godo. 1973. "Die *theologia tripertita* in Forschung und Bezeugung." *ANRW* I 4, pp. 63–116.

Linderski, J. 1986. "The Augural Law." *ANRW* II 16.3, pp. 2146–2312.

Lintott, A. W. 1981. "What Was the 'Imperium Romanum'?" *Greece and Rome* 28, pp. 53–67.

Lloyd, A. C. 1971. "Grammar and Metaphysics in the Stoa." Long 1971b, pp. 58–74.

Long, A. A. 1971a. "Language and Thought in Stoicism." Long 1971b, pp. 75–112.

Long, A. A., ed. 1971b. *Problems in Stoicism*. London.

Long, A. A. 1986. *Hellenistic Philosophy*. 2d ed. London.

Long, A. A. 1996. *Stoic Studies*. New York.

Lorenz, Thuri. 1972. *Polyklet*. Wiesbaden.

Lücke, Hans-Karl. 1991. "*Mercurius Quadratus:* Anmerkungen zur An-
thropometrie bei Cesariano." *Mitteilungen des Kunsthistorischen Institutes
in Florenz* 35.1, pp. 61–84.

Lyttleton, Margaret. 1987. "The Design and Planning of Temples and
Sanctuaries in Asia Minor in the Roman Imperial Period." Macready and
Thompson 1987, pp. 38–49.

Maas, M. 1992. *John Lydus and the Roman Past.* London.

MacDonald, William L. 1982. *The Architecture of the Roman Empire. Volume I: An Introductory Study.* Rev. ed. New Haven and London.

MacDonald, William L. 1986. *The Architecture of the Roman Empire. Volume II: An Urban Appraisal.* New Haven and London.

MacMullen, Ramsey. 1982. "The Epigraphic Habit in the Roman Empire." *American Journal of Philology* 103, pp. 233–246.

MacMullen, Ramsey. 1990. "Notes on Romanization." R. MacMullen,
Changes in the Roman Empire: Essays in the Ordinary, pp. 56–66. Princeton.

MacMullen, Ramsey. 2000. *Romanization in the Time of Augustus.* New
Haven and London.

Macready, S., and F. H. Thompson, eds. 1987. *Roman Architecture in the
Greek World.* Society of Antiquaries Occasional Papers. New Series 10.
London.

Maderna-Lauter, Caterina. 1990. "Polyklet in Rom." *Polyklet*, pp. 328–
392. Mainz-am-Rhein.

Magie, David. 1950. *Roman Rule in Asia Minor.* 2 vols. Princeton.

Malkin, Irad. 1987. *Religion and Colonization in Ancient Greece.* Leiden.

Manetti, Giovanni. 1993. *Theories of the Sign in Classical Antiquity.* Trans. C. Richardson. Bloomington and Indianapolis.

Mallwitz, A. 1981. "Ein Kapitell aus gebranten Ton, oder zur Genesis des korinthischen Kapitells." *X. Bericht über die Ausgrabungen in Olympia,* pp. 318–352. Berlin.

Maltby, R. 1991. *A Lexicon of Ancient Latin Etymologies.* Leeds.

Manganaro, G. 1974. "Una biblioteca storica nel ginnasio di Tauromenion." *Parola del passato* 29, pp. 389–409.

Mansuelli, G. A. 1983. "Contributo a Deinokrates in Alessandria e il mondo ellenistico-romano." *Studi in onore di Achille Adriani,* pp. 78–90. Rome.

March, Lionel. 1998. *Architectonics of Humanism.* Chichester, U.K.

Mattingly, Harold. 1968. *The Roman Imperial Coinage.* 10 vols. London.

McAllister, M. H. 1959. "The Temple of Ares at Athens: A Review of the Evidence." *Hesperia* 28, pp. 1–64.

McEwen, Indra K. 1993. *Socrates' Ancestor: An Essay on Architectural Beginnings.* Cambridge, Mass., and London.

McEwen, Indra K. 1994. "Hadrian's Rhetoric II: *Thesaurus Eloquentiae,* the Villa at Tivoli." *Res* 25, pp. 51–60.

McEwen, Indra K. 1995. "Housing Fame: In the Tuscan Villa of Pliny the Younger." *Res* 27, pp. 11–24.

McEwen, Indra K. 1998. "Claude Perrault: Modernising Vitruvius." Hart 1998, pp. 320–337.

McKay, Alexander Gordon. 1985. *Vitruvius, Architect and Engineer: Buildings and Building Techniques in Augustan Rome.* Bristol.

Merriam, Augustus C. 1884. *The Greek and Latin Inscriptions on the Obelisk-Crab in the Metropolitan Museum.* New York.

Merrill, W. A. 1904. "Notes on the Influence of Lucretius on Vitruvius." *Transactions of the American Philological Association* 35, pp. 16–21.

Métraux, Guy. 1995. *Sculptors and Physicians in Fifth-Century Greece.* Montreal.

Meyer, Elizabeth A. 1990. "Explaining the Epigraphic Habit in the Roman Empire: The Evidence of Epitaphs." *JRS* 80, pp. 74–96.

Meyer, Hugo. 1986. "Der Berg Athos als Alexander. Zu den realen Grundlagen der Vision des Dinocrates." *Rivista di Archeologia*, pp. 22–30.

Meyer, Hugo. 1995. "A Roman Masterpiece: The Minneapolis Doryphoros." Moon 1995, pp. 65–115.

Michel, Dorothea. 1967. *Alexander als Vorbild für Pompeius, Caesar und Marcus Antonius: archaeologische Untersuchungen.* Brussels.

Mierse, W. 1990. "Augustan Building Programs in the Western Provinces." Raaflaub and Toher 1990, pp. 308–333.

Millar, Fergus. 1973. "Triumvirate and Principate." *JRS* 63, pp. 50–67.

Millar, Fergus. 1977. *The Emperor in the Roman World: 31 B.C.–A.D. 337.* London.

Millar, Fergus. 1984. "The Impact of the Monarchy." Millar and Segal 1984, pp. 37–60.

Millar, Fergus, and Erich Segal, eds. 1984. *Caesar Augustus: Seven Aspects.* Oxford.

Mitchell, Stephen, and Marc Waelkens. 1998. *Pisidian Antioch: The Site and Its Monuments.* Swansea.

Moatti, C. 1988. "Tradition et raison chez Cicéron." *MÉFRA* 100, pp. 385–430.

Moatti, C. 1991. "La crise de la tradition à la fin de la république romaine à travers la littérature juridique et la science des antiquaires." M. Pani, ed., *Continuità e trasformazione fra repubblica e principato*, pp. 30–45. Bari.

Moatti, C. 1997. *La raison de Rome: naissance de l'esprit critique à la fin de la république.* Paris.

Moon, Warren G., ed. 1995. *Polykleitos, the Doryphoros and Tradition.* Madison, Wisc.

Morgan, Morris Hicky. 1909. "The Preface of Vitruvius." *Proceedings of the American Academy of Arts and Sciences* 44, pp. 149–175.

Most, Glenn W. 1989. "Cornutus and Stoic Allegories: A Preliminary Report." *ANRW* II 36.3, pp. 2014–2065.

Mulgan, R. G. 1978–1979. "Was Caesar an Epicurean?" *Classical World* 72, pp. 337–339.

Murray, Oswyn. 1965. "Philodemus on the Good King According to Homer." *JRS* 55, pp. 161–182.

Musti, Domenico. 1975. "Varrone nell'insieme delle tradizioni su Roma Quadrata." *Studi urbinati di storia, filosofia e letteratura*. Nuova serie B.1, pp. 297–318.

Musti, Domenico, and Mario Torelli. 1986. *Pausania. Guida della Grecia II, La Corinzia e l'Argolide*. Milan.

Naredi-Rainer, P. V. 1982. *Architektur und Harmonie*. Cologne.

Needham, Rodney, ed. 1973. *Right and Left: Essays on Dual Symbolic Classification*. Chicago.

Nenci, G. 1958. "L'*imitatio Alexandri* nelle *Res gestae Divi Augusti*." *Introduzione alle Guerre Persiane e altri saggi di storia antica*, pp. 285–308. Pisa.

Nestle, Wilhelm. 1926–1927. "Die Fabel des Menenius Agrippa." *Klio* 21, pp. 350–360.

Neugebauer, O. 1975. *A History of Ancient Mathematical Astronomy*. 3 vols. Berlin.

Nicolet, C. 1991. *Space, Geography and Politics in the Early Empire*. Ann Arbor, Mich.

Nicolet, C., and P. Gautier-Dalché. 1986. "Les quatres sages de Jules César et la mesure du monde de Jules César selon Julius Honorius." *Journal des savants,* pp. 157–218.

Nicolet, C., and P. Gros, eds. 1996. *Les littératures techniques dans l'antiquité.* Geneva.

Nimis, S. 1988. "Aristotle's Analogical Metaphor." *Arethusa* 21, pp. 215–226.

Nisbet, R. G. M., and M. Hubbard. 1970. *A Commentary on Horace, Odes, Book 1.* Oxford.

Nissen, H. 1869. *Das Templum: antiquarische Untersuchungen.* Berlin.

Norden, E. 1899. "Ein Panegyricus auf Augustus in Vergils Aeneis." *Rheinisches Museum für Philologie,* pp. 466–482.

Novara, Antoinette. 1983. "Les raisons d'écrire de Vitruve ou la revanche de l'architecte." *Bulletin de l'Association Guillaume Budé,* pp. 284–308.

Novara, Antoinette. 1994. "Faire oeuvre utile: la mesure de l'ambition chez Vitruve." *Le projet de Vitruve,* pp. 47–61. Rome.

Oder, E. 1899. "Ein angebliches Bruchstück Democrits über die Entdeckung unterirdischer Quellen." *Philologus,* Supplbd. 7, pp. 229–384.

Oechslin, Werner. 1981. "Geometry and Line: The Vitruvian Science of Architectural Drawing." *Daidalos* 1, pp. 20–35.

Oechslin, Werner. 1982. "Dinocrates and the Myth of the Megalomaniacal Institution of Architecture." *Daidalos* 4, pp. 7–26.

Onians, John. 1988. *Bearers of Meaning: The Classical Orders*. Princeton.

Onians, John. 1999. *Classical Art and the Cultures of Greece and Rome*. New Haven and London.

Overbeck, J. A. 1959. *Die antiken Schriftquellen zur Geschichte der bilden-den Kunst bei den Griechen*. (Rpt. of 1868 edition.) Hildesheim.

Palagia, Olga. 1986. "Imitation of Herakles in Ruler Portraiture: A Survey from Alexander to Maximius Daza." *Boreas: Münstersche Beiträge zur Archäologie* 9, pp. 137–151.

Palagia, Olga. 1990. "Two Statues of Hercules in the Forum Boarium in Rome." *Oxford Journal of Archaeology* 9.1, pp. 51–69.

Palmer, R. E. A. 1990. "Cults of Hercules, Apollo Caelispex and Fortuna in and around the Roman Cattle Market." *JRA* 3, pp. 234–244.

Pauly, August Friedrich von. 1894–1980. *Paulys Realencyclopädie der classischen Altertumswissenschaft*. Ed. Georg Wissowa, Wilhelm Kroll, et al. Stuttgart.

Payne, Alina. 1999. *The Architectural Treatise in the Italian Renaissance: Architectural Invention, Ornament and Literary Culture*. New York.

Pease, A. S., ed. 1920. *M. Tulli Ciceronis De divinatione: liber primus*. Urbana, Ill.

Pedersen, P. 1989. *The Parthenon and the Origin of the Corinthian Capital*. Odense.

Pedretti, Carlo. 1977. *The Literary Works of Leonardo da Vinci.* Oxford. (Reprint, with commentary by Pedretti, of *The Literary Works of Leonardo da Vinci,* ed. and comp. Jean Paul Richter. 2 vols. London, 1970.)

Pedretti, Carlo. 1988. *Leonardo architetto.* 2d ed. Milan.

Pekary, R. 1966–1967. "Tiberius und der Tempel der Concordia in Rom." *MDAI (R)* 73–74, pp. 103–133.

Pellati, F. 1921. "Vitruvio e la fortuna del suo trattato nel mondo antico." *Rivista di filologia e di istruzione classica,* pp. 305–335.

Pellati, F. 1927. "Quod significatur et quod significat." *Historia* 5.1, pp. 53–58.

Pellati, F. 1951. "La dottrina degli elementi nella fisica di Vitruvio." *Rinascimento* 2, pp. 241–259.

Pensabene, Patrizio. 1990–1991. "Casa Romuli sul Palatino." *Atti dell'Accademia nazionale dei Lincei,* pp. 115–162.

Pensabene, Patrizio. 1997. "Elementi architettonici dalla Casa di Augusto sul Palatino." *MDAI (R)* 104, pp. 149–192.

Pépin, Jean. 1956. "La théologie tripartite de Varron." *Revue des études augustiniennes* 2, pp. 265–294.

Pérez-Gómez, Alberto. 1983. *Architecture and the Crisis of Modern Science.* Cambridge, Mass., and London.

Perrault, Claude. 1683. *Ordonnance des cinq espèces de colonnes selon la méthode des anciens.* Paris. Trans. Indra K. McEwen as *Ordonnance for the*

Five Kinds of Columns after the Method of the Ancients. Santa Monica, Calif., 1993.

Petrochilos, N. 1974. *Roman Attitudes to the Greeks.* Athens.

Pettazoni, R. 1972. "On Common Religious Impulses." Walter H. Capps, ed., *Ways of Understanding Religion,* pp. 28–32. New York.

Picard, G. Ch. 1957. *Trophées romains.* Paris.

Pietrangeli, Carlo. 1949–1950. "*Bidentalia.*" *Rendiconti della Pontificia accademia romana di archeologia* 25, pp. 37–52.

Piganiol, André. 1937. "Le papyrus de Servius Tullius." *Scritti in onore di Bartolomeo Nogara,* pp. 373–389. Rome.

Plommer, H. 1973. *Vitruvius and Later Roman Building Manuals.* Cambridge, U.K.

Pollini, John. 1978. "Studies in Augustan Historical Reliefs." Diss. U. of California, Berkeley.

Pollini, John. 1987–1988. "The Findspot of the Statue of Augustus from Prima Porta." *Bullettino della Commissione archeologica comunale di Roma* 92, pp. 103–108.

Pollini, John. 1990. "Man or God: Divine Assimilation and Imitation in the Late Republic and Early Principate." Raaflaub and Toher 1990, pp. 334–363.

Pollini, John. 1993. "The Gemma Augustea: Ideology, Rhetorical Imagery, and the Construction of Dynastic Narrative." P. Holliday, ed., *Narrative and Event in Ancient Art*, pp. 258–298. Cambridge, U.K.

Pollini, John. 1995. "The Augustus from Prima Porta and the Transformation of the Heroic Ideal: The Rhetoric of Art." Moon 1995, pp. 262–281.

Pollini, J., and N. Herz. 1992. "The Marble Type of the Augustus from Prima Porta." *JRS* 5, pp. 203–208.

Pollitt, J. J. 1974. *The Ancient View of Greek Art*. New Haven.

Pollitt, J. J. 1995. "The *Canon* of Polykleitos and Other Canons." Moon 1995, pp. 19–24.

Polyklet: Der Bildhauer der griechischen Klassik. Ausstellung im Liebieghaus, Museum alter Plastik, Frankfurt am Main. 1990. Exh. Cat. Mainz-am-Rhein.

Powell, J. G. F., ed. 1995. *Cicero the Philosopher*. Oxford.

Price, S. R. F. 1984. *Rituals and Power: The Roman Imperial Cult in Asia Minor*. Cambridge, U.K.

Price, S. R. F. 1996. "The Place of Religion." *Cambridge Ancient History* X, pp. 812–847.

Le projet de Vitruve. Objet, destinataires et réception du De architectura. 1994. Actes du colloque internationale, École française de Rome. Rome.

Purcell, Nicolas. 1983. "The *Apparitores:* A Study in Social Mobility." *Papers of the British School at Rome* 51, pp. 125–173.

Purcell, Nicolas. 1990. "Maps, Lists, Money, Order and Power." *JRS* 80, pp. 178–182.

Purcell, Nicolas. 1992. "The City of Rome." Richard Jenkyns, ed., *The Legacy of Rome: A New Appraisal,* pp. 421–453. Oxford.

Purcell, Nicolas. 1996. "Rome and Its Development under Augustus and His Successors." *Cambridge Ancient History* X, pp. 782–811.

Raaflaub, Kurt A., and Mark Toher, eds. 1990. *Between Republic and Empire: Interpretations of Augustus and His Principate.* Berkeley and Los Angeles.

Rakob, F., and W. D. Heilmeyer. 1973. *Der Rundtempel am Tiber in Rom.* Mainz-am-Rhein.

Ramage, E. S. 1973. *Urbanitas: Ancient Sophistication and Refinement.* Norman, Okla.

Ramage, E. S. 1987. *The Nature and Purpose of Augustus' Res Gestae.* Stuttgart.

Rambaud, Michel. 1953. *L'art de la déformation historique dans les commentaires de César.* Annales de l'université de Lyon, Sér. 3. Lettres, Fasc. 23. Lyons.

Ramsay, W. M., and A. von Premerstein. 1927. *Das Monumentum Antiochenum. Klio,* Beiheft 19. Leipzig.

Raven, J. E. 1951. "Polyclitus and Pythagoreanism." *Classical Quarterly* 45, pp. 147–152.

Rawson, E. 1985. *Intellectual Life in the Late Roman Republic.* London.

Rawson, E. 1989. "Roman Rulers and the Philosophical Advisor." Griffin and Barnes 1989, pp. 233–258.

Rebert, H. F., and H. Marceau. 1925. "The Temple of Concord in the Roman Forum." *Memoirs of the American Academy in Rome* 5, pp. 53–75.

Rey-Coquais, Jean-Paul. 1991. "Villes augustéennes d'orient." Goudineau and Rebourg 1991, pp. 141–150.

Rich, John, and Graham Shipley, eds. 1993. *War and Society in the Roman World.* London and New York.

Richard, J.-Cl. 1963. "*Pax, Concordia* et la religion officielle de Janus." *MÉFRA* 75, pp. 303–386.

Richardson, J. S. 1991. "*Imperium Romanum:* Empire and the Language of Power." *JRS* 81, pp. 1–9.

Richardson, L., Jr. 1987. "A Note on the Architecture of the Theatrum Pompei in Rome." *AJA* 91, pp. 123–126.

Richardson, L., Jr. 1992. *A New Topographical Dictionary of Ancient Rome.* Baltimore.

Ridgway, B. S. 1990. *Hellenistic Sculpture I. The Styles of ca. 331–200.* Madison, Wisc.

Rieks, R. 1967. *Homo, humanus, humanitas.* Munich.

Riese, A., ed. 1878. *Geographi latini minores.* Heilbronn. Rpt. Hildesheim, 1964.

Rilkman, G. 1980. *The Corn Supply of Ancient Rome.* Oxford.

Rist, J. M. 1969. *Stoic Philosophy.* Cambridge, U.K.

Rist, J. M., ed. 1978. *The Stoics.* Berkeley and Los Angeles.

Robbins, F. E. 1921. "The Tradition of Greek Arithmology." *Classical Philology* 16.2, pp. 97–123.

Robinson, D. M. 1926–1927. "Roman Sculptures from Colonia Caesarea (Pisidian Antioch)." *Art Bulletin* 9, pp. 5–69.

Roddaz, J. M. 1984. *Marcus Agrippa.* Rome.

Romano, David Gilman. 1993. "Post 146 B.C. Land Use in Corinth and Planning of the Roman Colony of 44 B.C." Gregory 1993, pp. 9–30.

Romano, Elisa. 1987. *La capanna e il tempio: Vitruvio o dell'architettura.* Palermo.

Romano, Elisa. 1994. "Dal *De officiis* a Vitruvio, da Vitruvio a Orazio: il dibattito sul lusso edilizio." *Le projet de Vitruve,* pp. 63–93. Rome.

Romm, James S. 1992. *The Edges of the Earth in Ancient Thought.* Princeton.

Roueché, Charlotte, and R. R. R. Smith, eds. 1996. *Aphrodisias Papers 3. JRA,* suppl. 20. Ann Arbor, Mich.

Rouveret, Agnès. 1989. *Histoire et imaginaire de la peinture ancienne.* Paris and Rome.

Roux, Georges. 1960. "Qu'est-ce qu'un *kolossos?*" *REA,* pp. 5–40.

Roux, Georges. 1961. *L'architecture de l'Argolide aux IVe et IIIe siècles avant J.-C.* Paris.

Rowland, Ingrid. 1998. "Vitruvius in Print and in Vernacular Translation: Fra Giocondo, Bramante, Raphael and Cesare Cesariano." Hart 1998, pp. 105–121.

Royo, Manuel. 1991. "Du Palatin au *Palatium.*" M. Pani, ed., *Continuità e trasformazione fra repubblica e principato,* pp. 83–101. Bari.

Ruffel, P., and J. Soubiran. 1962. "Vitruve ou Mamurra?" *Pallas* 11.2, pp. 123–179.

Rüpke, Jörg. 1992. "Wer las Caesars *bella* als *commentarii?*" *Gymnasium* 99, pp. 201–226.

Rykwert, Joseph. 1981. *On Adam's House in Paradise.* 2d ed. Cambridge, Mass., and London.

Rykwert, Joseph. 1982. *The Necessity of Artifice: Ideas in Architecture.* New York.

Rykwert, Joseph. 1988. *The Idea of a Town.* 2d ed. Cambridge, Mass., and London.

Rykwert, Joseph. 1992. "Body and Building." *Daidalos* 45, pp. 100–109.

Rykwert, Joseph. 1996. *The Dancing Column: On Order in Architecture*. Cambridge, Mass., and London.

Sablayrolles, R. 1981. "Espace urbain et propagande politique: l'organisation du centre de Rome par Auguste (*Res gestae* 19 à 21)." *Pallas* 21, pp. 59–77.

Sachot, M. 1991. "*Religio/Superstitio:* histoire d'une subversion et d'un retournement." *Revue de l'histoire des religions* 108, pp. 355–394.

Sackur, Walter. 1925. *Vitruv und die Poliorketiker*. Berlin.

Saliou, Catherine. 1994. "*Iura quoque nota habeat oportet . . .* une autre façon de traiter de l'architecture: l'écrit de Julien d'Ascalon." *Le projet de Vitruve*, pp. 213–229. Rome.

Saliou, Catherine. 1996. *Le traité d'urbanisme de Julien d'Ascalon: droit et architecture en Palestine au VIe siècle*. Paris.

Sallmann, K. 1984. "Bildungsvorgaben des Fachschriftstellers. Bemerkungen zur Pädagogik Vitruvs." *Vitruv-Kolloquium Darmstadt*, pp. 11–26. Darmstadt.

Salomon, J. B. 1984. *Wealthy Corinth: A History of the City to 338 B.C.* Oxford.

Samuel, A. E. 1972. *Roman Chronology: Calendars and Years in Classical Antiquity*. Munich.

Sauron, Gilles. 1987. "Le complexe pompéien du Champ de Mars: nouveauté urbanistique à finalité idéologique." *L'urbs: espace urbain et histoire*, pp. 457–473. Rome.

Sauron, Gilles. 1988. "Le message esthétique des rinceaux de l'Ara Pacis Augustae." *Revue archéologique*, fasc. 1, pp. 3–40.

Sauron, Gilles. 1994. *Quis deum? L'expression plastique des idéologies politiques et religieuses à Rome à la fin de la République et au début de l'Empire*. Rome.

Schadewalt, W. 1973. "Humanitas romana." *ANRW* I 4, pp. 43–62.

Schäfer, Eckart. 1972. "Das Staatschiff. Zur Präzision eines Topos." P. Jehn, ed., *Toposforschung*, pp. 259–292. Frankfurt.

Schauenburg, K. 1957. *Zur Symbolik untenitalischer Rankenmotive. MDAI (R)* 64, pp. 198–221.

Scheid, John. 1985. *Religion et piété à Rome*. Paris.

Scheid, John. 1986. "Le flamine de Jupiter, les vestales et le général triomphant." *Le temps de la réflexion* 7: *Corps des dieux*, pp. 213–230. Paris.

Scheid, John. 1993. "Culte, mythes et politique au début de l'empire." Graf 1993, pp. 109–127.

Schilling, Robert. 1942. "L'Hercule romain en face de la réforme religieuse d'Auguste." *Revue de philologie* 68, pp. 31–57.

Schilling, Robert. 1982. *La religion romaine de Vénus*. 2d ed. Paris.

Schofield, Malcolm. 1991. *The Stoic Idea of the City*. Cambridge, U.K., and New York. Rpt. Chicago 1999, with a foreward by Martha C. Nussbaum.

Schofield, Malcolm. 1995. "Cicero's Definition of *Res Publica*." Powell 1995, pp. 63–83.

Schrijvers, P. H. 1989a. "Vitruve et la vie intellectuelle de son temps." Geertman and de Jong 1989, pp. 13–21.

Schrijvers, P. H. 1989b. "Vitruve 1.1.1: explication de texte." Geertman and de Jong 1989, pp. 49–54.

Schuler, Stefan. 1999. *Vitruv im Mittelalter: die Rezeption von* De architectura *von der Antike bis in die frühe Neuzeit.* Cologne.

Schutz, M. 1990. "Zur Sonnenuhr des Augustus auf dem Marsfeld." *Gymnasium* 97, pp. 432–457.

Schwarzenberg, Erkinger. 1975. "The Portraiture of Alexander." *Alexandre le Grand, image et réalité,* pp. 223–278. Geneva.

Sellers, E., ed. 1896. *The Elder Pliny's Chapters on the History of Art.* London.

Seston, W., and M. Euzennat. 1971. "Un dossier de la chancellerie romaine: la *Tabula Banasitana,* étude de diplomatique." *Comptes rendus de l'Académie des inscriptions et belles-lettres,* p. 468.

Sgarbi, Claudio. 1993. "A Newly Discovered Corpus of Vitruvian Images." *Res 23,* pp. 31–51.

Shaw, B. D. 1982. "'Eaters of Flesh, Drinkers of Milk': The Ancient Mediterranean Ideology of the Pastoral Nomad." *Ancient Society* 13, pp. 5–31.

Sherk, Robert K. 1969. *Roman Documents from the Greek East.* Baltimore.

Sherwin-White, A. N. 1973. "The *Tabula* of Banasa and the *Constitutio Antoniniana.*" *JRS* 63, pp. 86–97.

Silverman, David P. 1991. "Divinity and Deities in Ancient Egypt." Byron E. Shafer, ed., *Religion in Ancient Egypt*, pp. 7–87. Ithaca and London.

Simon, Erika. 1981. "Die Götter am Trajansbogen zu Benevent." *Trierer Winckelmannsprogramme* 1–2 (1979–1980). Mainz-am-Rhein.

Simon, Erika. 1986. *Augustus: Kunst und Leben in Rom um die Zeitenwende.* Munich.

Skydsgaard, J. E. 1968. *Varro the Scholar. Analecta Romana Instituti Danici*, suppl. 4. Copenhagen.

Small, A., ed. 1996. *Subject and Ruler: The Cult of the Ruling Power in Classical Antiquity. JRA*, suppl. 17. Ann Arbor, Mich.

Small, Jocelyn Penny. 1997. *Wax Tablets of the Mind: Cognitive Studies of Memory and Literacy in Classical Antiquity.* London.

Speyer, Wolfgang. 1986. "Das Verhältnis des Augustus zur Religion." *ANRW* II 16.3, pp. 1777–1805.

Steinby, Eva Margareta, ed. *Lexicon topographicum urbis Romae.* 6 vols. Rome, 1993–2000.

Steward, Andrew. 1978a. "The Canon of Polykleitos: A Question of Evidence." *Journal of Hellenic Studies* 98, pp. 122–131.

Stewart, Andrew. 1978b. "Lysippan Studies I: The Only Creator of Beauty." *AJA* 82, pp. 163–171.

Stewart, Andrew. 1995. "Notes on the Reception of the Polykleitan Style: Diomedes to Alexander." Moon 1995, pp. 246–261.

Striker, G. 1991. "Following Nature: A Study in Stoic Ethics." *Oxford Studies in Ancient Philosophy* 9, pp. 1–74.

Strocka, Volker Michael. 1980. "Augustus als Pharao." *Eikones: Studien zum griechischen und römischen Bildnis. Antike Kunst,* suppl. 12, pp. 177–180. Bern.

Sutherland, C. H. V., and R. A. G. Carson, eds. 1984. *The Roman Imperial Coinage.* Rev. ed. London.

Syme, Ronald. 1939. *The Roman Revolution.* Oxford.

Syme, Ronald. 1958. "Imperator Caesar: A Study in Nomenclature." *Historia* 7, pp. 172–188.

Szabo, Arpad. 1938. "Roma Quadrata." *Rheinisches Museum für Philologie* 87, pp. 160–168.

Szabo, Arpad. 1956. "Roma Quadrata." *Maia* 9, pp. 243–274.

Tarver, Thomas. 1997. "Varro and the Antiquarianism of Philosophy." Barnes and Griffin 1997, pp. 131–164.

Thesaurus linguae latinae. Leipzig, 1900–.

Thielscher, P. 1961. "Vitruvius." Pauly 1894–1980, 2d ser., IX.1, pp. 419–489.

Thompson, H. A. 1950. "The Odeion in the Athenian Agora." *Hesperia* 19, pp. 31–141.

Thompson, H. A. 1962. "Itinerant Temples of Attica." *AJA* 66, p. 200.

Thomsen, R. 1980. *King Servius Tullius*. Copenhagen.

Thulin, C. O. 1905–1909. *Die etruskische Disziplin*. 3 vols. Göteborg.

Thulin, C. O., ed. 1971. *Corpus agrimensorum romanorum*. Stuttgart. (Rpt. of 1908 ed.)

Timpanaro, S., Jr. 1950. "Romae regnare quadratae." *Maia* 3, pp. 26–32.

Tobin, R. 1975. "The Canon of Polykleitos." *AJA* 79, pp. 307–321.

Todd, Robert B. 1976. *Alexander of Aphrodisias: A Study of the De Mixtione, with Preliminary Essays, Text, Translation and Commentary*. Leiden.

Tomlinson, R. 1996. "Alexandria: The Hellenistic Arrangement." *Quaderni ticinesi di numismatica e antichità classiche* 25, pp. 155–164.

Tournikiotis, Panayotis, ed. 1996. *The Parthenon and Its Impact in Modern Times*. New York.

Traina, Giusto. 1988. "Da Dinocrate a Vitruvio." *Civiltà classica e cristiana* 9, pp. 303–349.

Travlos, John. 1971. *Pictorial Dictionary of Ancient Athens*. London.

Turcan, Robert. 1981. "Janus à l'époque impériale." *ANRW* II 17.1, pp. 374–402.

L'urbs: espace urbain et histoire (Ier siècle av. J.-C.–IIIe siècle ap. J.-C.). 1987. Collection de l'École française de Rome 98. Rome.

Vasaly, Ann. 1993. *Representations: Images of the World in Ciceronian Oratory.* Berkeley and Los Angeles.

Verbeke, Gerhard. 1973. "Le stoïcisme, une philosophie sans frontières." *ANRW* I 4, pp. 3–42.

Vermeule, C. C. 1957. "Herakles Crowning Himself: New Greek Statuary Types and Their Place in Hellenistic and Roman Art." *Journal of Hellenic Studies* 77, pp. 283–289.

Vernant, Jean-Pierre. 1959. "Aspects mythiques de la mémoire en Grèce." *Journal de psychologie*, pp. 1–29.

Vernant, Jean-Pierre. 1985. *Mythe et pensée chez les grecs.* 2d ed. Paris.

Versnel, H. S. 1970. *Triumphus.* Leiden.

Veyne, Paul. 1993. "*Humanitas:* Romans and Non-Romans." Andrea Giardina, ed., *The Romans,* trans. Lydia G. Cochrane, pp. 342–369. Chicago.

Vickers, Michael. 1985. "Persepolis, Vitruvius and the Erechtheum Caryatids: The Iconography of Medism and Servitude." *Revue archéologique,* pp. 3–28.

Vidal-Naquet, P. 1984. "Flavius Arrien entre deux mondes." Arrien, *Histoire d'Alexandre,* trans. Pierre Savinel, pp. 311–394. Paris.

Vierneisel, Klaus, and Paul Zanker, eds. 1979. *Die Bildnisse des Augustus.* Exh. cat. Munich.

Vitruv-Kolloquium Darmstadt. 1984. Darmstadt.

Voegelin, Eric. 1974. *The Ecumenic Age.* Baton Rouge, La.

Wagenvoort, H. 1947. *Roman Dynamism.* Oxford.

Walker, Susan. 1981. *The Image of Augustus.* London.

Wallace-Hadrill, Andrew. 1981. "The Emperor and His Virtues." *Historia* 30, pp. 298–323.

Wallace-Hadrill, Andrew. 1985. Review of Kienast 1982a, Buchner 1982, Carettoni 1983, and Millar and Segal 1984. *JRS* 75, pp. 245–250.

Wallace-Hadrill, Andrew. 1986. "Image and Authority in the Coinage of Augustus." *JRS* 76, pp. 66–87.

Wallace-Hadrill, Andrew. 1987. "Time for Augustus: Ovid, Augustus and the Fasti." P. Hardie and M. Whitby, eds., *Homo Viator: Classical Essays for John Bramble,* pp. 221–230. Bristol.

Wallace-Hadrill, Andrew. 1988. "Greek Knowledge, Roman Power." *Classical Philology* 83 (July), pp. 224–233.

Wallace-Hadrill, Andrew. 1994. *Houses and Society in Pompeii and Herculaneum.* Princeton.

Walsh, P. G. 1958. "Livy and Stoicism." *American Journal of Philology* 79, pp. 355–375.

Ward-Perkins, J. B. 1994. *Roman Imperial Architecture.* Rpt. of 2d ed. (1981). New Haven and London.

Watzinger, Carl. 1909. "Vitruvstudien." *Rheinisches Museum für Philologie* 44, pp. 203–223.

Weinstock, Stefan. 1946. "Martianus Capella and the Cosmic System of the Etruscans." *JRS* 36, pp. 101–129.

Weinstock, Stefan. 1951. "Libri Fulgurales." *Papers of the British School at Rome* 19, pp. 122–153.

Weinstock, Stefan. 1957. "*Victor* and *Invictus.*" *Harvard Theological Review* 50, pp. 211–247.

Weinstock, Stefan. 1971. *Divus Julius.* Oxford.

Wesenberg, Burkhardt. 1975–1976. "Zum metrologischen Relief in Oxford." *Marburger Winckelmann-programm*, pp. 15–22.

Wesenberg, Burkhardt. 1983. *Beiträge zur Rekonstruktion griechischer Architektur nach literarischen Quellen. MDAI (A)*, Beiheft 9. Berlin.

Wesenberg, Burkhardt. 1984a. "Zu den Schriften griechischer Architekten." *Bauplanung und Bautheorie der Antike*, pp. 39–48. Berlin.

Wesenberg, Burkhardt. 1984b. "Augustusforum und Akropolis." *Jahrbuch des Deutschen archäologischen Instituts* 99, pp. 161–185.

Wesenberg, Burkhardt. 1989. "Griechisches und Römisches in der vitruvianischen Architektur: ein Beitrag zur Quellenfrage." Geertman and de Jong 1989, pp. 76–84.

Wesenberg, Burkhardt. 1994. "Die Bedeutung des Modulus in der vitruvianischen Tempelarchitektur." *Le projet de Vitruve*, pp. 91–104. Rome.

West, Martin L. 1992. *Ancient Greek Music*. Oxford and New York.

Westall, Richard. 1996. "The *Forum Julium* as Representation of Imperator Caesar." *MDAI (R)* 103, pp. 83–118.

Williams, C. K., II. 1986. "Corinth and the Cult of Aphrodite." Mario A. Del Chiaro, ed., *Corinthiaca: Studies in Honor of David A. Amyx*, pp. 12–24. Columbia, Mo.

Williams, C. K., II. 1987. "The Refounding of Corinth: Some Roman Religious Attitudes." Macready and Thompson 1987, pp. 26–37.

Williams, C. K., II. 1993. "Roman Corinth as a Commercial Centre." Gregory 1993, pp. 31–46.

Wilson Jones, Mark. 1989. "Designing the Roman Corinthian Order." *JRA* 2, pp. 35–69.

Wilson Jones, Mark. 2000a. *Principles of Roman Architecture*. New Haven and London.

Wilson Jones, Mark. 2000b. "Doric Measure and Doric Design, I: The Evidence of the Relief from Salamis." *AJA* 104, pp. 73–93.

Winter, J. G. 1910. *The Myth of Hercules at Rome*. New York.

Wirth, G. 1976. "Alexander und Rom." *Alexandre le Grand, image et réalité*, pp. 181–210. Geneva.

Wiseman, J. 1979. "Corinth and Rome I: 228 B.C.–A.D. 267." *ANRW* II 7.1, pp. 438–548.

Wiseman, T. P. 1981. "The Temple of Victory on the Palatine." *Antiquaries Journal* 61, pp. 35–52.

Wiseman, T. P. 1984. "Cybele, Virgil and Augustus." A. J. Woodman and D. West, eds., *Poetry and Politics in the Age of Augustus*, pp. 117–128. Cambridge, U.K.

Wiseman, T. P. 1987. *"Conspicui Postes Tectaque Digna Deo:* The Public Image of Aristocratic and Imperial Houses in the Late Republic and Early Empire." *L'urbs: espace urbain et histoire,* pp. 393–413. Rome.

Wiseman, T. P. 1992. "Julius Caesar and the Mappa Mundi." T. P. Wiseman, *Talking to Virgil,* pp. 22–42. Exeter.

Woolf, Greg. 1993. "Roman Peace." Rich and Shipley 1993, pp. 171–194.

Woolf, Greg. 1994. "Becoming Roman, Staying Greek: Culture, Identity and the Civilizing Process in the Roman East." *Proceedings of the Cambridge Philological Society* 40, pp. 116–143.

Woolf, Greg. 1996. "Monumental Writing and the Expansion of Roman Society in the Early Empire." *JRS* 86, pp. 22–39.

Woolf, Greg. 1998. *Becoming Roman: The Origins of Provincial Civilization in Gaul.* Cambridge, U.K.

Wright, M. R. 1995. "Cicero on Self-Love and Love of Humanity in *De Finibus* 3." Powell 1995, pp. 171–195.

Yates, Frances A. 1966. *The Art of Memory.* Chicago.

Yavetz, Zvi. 1984. "The *Res Gestae* and Augustus' Public Image." Millar and Segal 1984, pp. 1–36.

Yavetz, Zvi. 1990. "The Personality of Augustus." Raaflaub and Toher 1990, pp. 21–41.

Zanker, P. 1968. *Forum Augustum.* Tübingen.

Zanker, P. 1972. *Forum Romanum.* Tübingen.

Zanker, P. 1983. "Der Apollontempel auf dem Palatin." *Città e architettura nella Roma imperiale. Analecta Romana Instituti Danici,* suppl. 10, pp. 21–40. Odense.

Zanker, P. 1988. *The Power of Images in the Age of Augustus.* Trans. Alan Shapiro. Ann Arbor, Mich.

Ziolkowski, A. 1988. "Mummius' Temple of Hercules Victor and the Round Temple on the Tiber." *Phoenix* 42, pp. 309–333.

Ziolkowski, A. 1993. "*Urbs Direpta,* or How the Romans Sacked Cities." Rich and Shipley 1993, pp. 69–91.

Zöllner, Frank. 1987. *Vitruvs Proportionsfigur: quellenkritische Studien zur Kunstliteratur im 15. und 16. Jahrhundert.* Worms.

ILLUSTRATION SOURCES

FRONTISPIECE   Photo by Richard-Max Tremblay,
courtesy Galerie René Blouin, Montréal.

PAGE 27   Photo by author.

PAGE 29   Plan redrawn by Sarah Balleux, after L. Cozza.

PAGE 37   Photo by author.

PAGE 41   Photo by Marianne McEwen.

PAGE 68   Photo by author.

PAGE 89   Photo by author.

PAGE 93   Photo by author.

PAGE 99   Photo courtesy the Istanbul Archaeological Museum.

PAGE 106   Photo courtesy the British Museum, London.

PAGE 108   Plan redrawn by Sarah Balleux, after P. Zanker.

PAGE 114   Plan redrawn by Sarah Balleux, after A. Vasaly.

PAGE 116   Photo by author.

PAGE 117   Plan redrawn by Sarah Balleux, after F. Coarelli.

PAGE 119   Photo courtesy the British Museum, London.

PAGE 123   Photo courtesy the Musée du Cinquantenaire, Brussels.

PAGE 126   Photo courtesy the Deutsches archäologisches
Institut, Rome. DAI neg. no. 72.2633.

PAGE 147   Photo courtesy the Kunsthistorisches Museum, Vienna.

PAGE 153   Photo by author.

PAGE 158   Photo courtesy Rare Books and Special Collections,
            McGill University.

PAGE 159   Photo courtesy Rare Books and Special Collections,
            McGill University.

PAGE 164   Plan redrawn by Sarah Balleux, after G. Carettoni.

PAGE 170   Photo courtesy the Bibliotheca Apostolica Vaticana.

PAGE 171   Photo courtesy the Herzog August Bibliothek,
            Wolfenbüttel.

PAGE 176   Photo courtesy the British Museum, London.

PAGE 179   Plan redrawn by Sarah Balleux, after P. Zanker.

PAGE 180   Photo courtesy the British Museum, London.

PAGE 193   Photos courtesy the British Museum, London.

PAGE 206   Photo by author.

PAGE 207   Photo © Jo Selsing, courtesy Ny Carlsberg Glyptotek,
            Copenhagen.

PAGE 214   Photo by author.

PAGE 219   Plan redrawn by Sarah Balleux, after Gros 1996a, fig. 291.

PAGE 221   Reprinted from Amy and Gros 1979 (II, pl. 17) by kind
            permission of Pierre Gros.

PAGE 223   Reprinted from Dinsmoor 1950, fig. 101.

PAGE 231   Photo by author.

PAGE 242   Photo courtesy Centre Canadien d'Architecture/Canadian
            Centre for Architecture, Montréal.

PAGE 243   Redrawn by Sarah Balleux, after E. Buchner.

PAGE 247   Photo by author.

PAGE 249   Photo courtesy Centre Canadien d'Architecture/Canadian
            Centre for Architecture, Montréal.

PAGE 252   Photo courtesy Alinari / Art Resource, New York.

PAGE 253   Photo by author.

PAGE 255   Photo by author.

PAGE 258   Photo by author.

PAGE 259   Photo by author.

PAGE 260   Photo by author.

PAGE 263   Photos courtesy the British Museum, London.

PAGE 265   Photo courtesy the Minneapolis Institute of Arts.

PAGE 267   Photo by author.

PAGE 271   Photo by author.

PAGE 281   Photo courtesy the Bibliotheca Apostolica Vaticana.

PAGE 286   Plan redrawn by Sarah Balleux, after Mitchell and
            Waelkens.

PAGE 287   Photo courtesy the Kelsey Museum of Archaeology
            archive, Ann Arbor, Michigan.

PAGE 289   Reprinted from Mitchell and Waelkens 1998, fig. 26.

PAGE 292   Plan redrawn by Sarah Balleux, after J. Travlos.

PAGE 293   Plan redrawn by Sarah Balleux, after J. Travlos.

PAGE 297   Photo courtesy the Kelsey Museum of Archaeology
            archive, Ann Arbor, Michigan.

Acanthus, 212–213, 215, 218, 224, 288

Achilles, shield of, 148

Actium, 67, 163, 168, 246, 256, 280

Aeneas, 31, 113, 120, 140, 201–202
 shield of, 146–148

Agricola, Gnaeus Julius, 151

Agrippa, Marcus Vipsanius, 20–22, 24–25, 227, 291, 296

Alberti, Leon Battista, 2

Alêtheia and *to alêthes* (truth and the true), 57–58, 97

Alexander the Great, 12, 18, 20, 52–53, 73, 92–97, 127–129, 142, 205
 and Augustus, 120–124
 and Hercules, 98–100

Alexandria, 84, 94–96, 122, 124, 127, 137, 139, 149, 241

Altars, 173–174, 182, 291
 ara maxima (altar of Hercules), Rome, 113–115, 120
 Ara Pacis Augustae (altar of Augustan peace), Rome, 213, 244–246

Ambracia, 115

Ammianus Marcellinus, 96

Amor, son of Venus, 209, 270

Amplification, 83

Analemma, 137–138, 235, 245

Analogia, 26, 71–72, 195

Angelos (messenger), 11

Anomalia, 71–72

Antioch in Pisidia (Antioch Caesarea), 285–290, 298

Antiochus IV Epiphanes, 216

Antony, Mark (Marcus Antonius, triumvir), 67, 163, 296

Apelles, 127, 205, 209

Aphrodisias, 34

Aphrodite, 201, 216. *See also* Venus

Apollo, 67, 165, 256
 temples of, 125, 162–165, 168, 285

Aquitania, 143, 146

Ara maxima, rite of, 113–115, 120

Architectura. See also Architecture
 as the agent of squaring, 246
 as the art of the geometrical footprint, 226
 as knowledge of the architect, 58, 100, 148, 299
 as proof of conquest, 151
 as summation of *humanitas,* 145–146, 152–154
 summum templum of, 28–30, 145–148, 301
 tripartite whole of, 25, 300, 302

Architecture. *See also Architectura; De architectura;* Vitruvius
 body of, 6, 9, 12, 57, 129, 227–229, 236, 250, 270, 274, 300–302
 Christian, 174
 and empire, 145–149, 193–195, 279–280
 factuality of, 186, 192
 and *humanitas,* 152–154
 as a moral corrective, 284–285
 and nature, 47–48, 128–129, 220
 power of, 38

and rhetoric, 79–82, 140–144,
    198–199, 264
signifying power of, 79–83,
    178, 227
Arch of Trajan, Beneventum, 125
Areas, 181–182, 217
Ares, 291
Aristippus, 135–138, 149
Aristophanes (Athenian play-
    wright), 216
Aristophanes of Byzantium, 84–85
Aristotle, 24, 26, 61, 132
Arius Didymus, 111, 144, 149, 210–
    211, 226, 233–235
Arrangement, 65
Ars, 58, 60, 275
Asia, 22, 246, 285
Athenodorus of Tarsus, 111, 132
Athens, 46, 137, 143, 215, 290
  Acropolis, 30, 294–296
  agora, 291–294
  Erechtheion, 30–31, 295–296
  Odeon of Agrippa, 291, 296
  Parthenon, 294–296
Athos, Mount, 92, 96, 100, 125,
    128–129, 139
Auctoritas (authority), 32–38,
    49, 103
Auguraculum (also *augurium*),
    30, 168
Augurale (also *auguratorium*), 168
Augurs, 167–168, 172, 232–233
Augury, auspices, 28–30, 165–177,
    191, 203–204, 209–210, 232–
    233, 238, 277. *See also* Divi-
    nation
Augustine, Saint, 40, 49, 70,
    75, 184

Augustus (Gaius Julius Caesar
    Octavianus), 1, 8, 10, 19,
    31, 34–35, 39, 51–53, 107, 139,
    193, 237
  autobiography (*Res gestae*),
    10, 285
  beauty of, 204–205, 211–212
  birthday, 177, 190, 198, 239, 245–
    246
  building programs, 10–12, 53, 87,
    226, 280–298
  control of religion, 189–190
  death, 298–299
  and Hercules, 120–124
  house of, Rome, 163–165, 167
  philosophical advisors, 111
  Prima Porta statue of, 250–275
  relation to the sun, 238–246, 250
  seal, 122
  and Stoicism, 111–112
  temples built by, 186–188, 190–
    193, 197–198
  triple triumph (29 B.C.), 120–
    124, 146–147, 175, 177, 186
Aurora, 254
Ausonius, Decimus Magnus, 95
Authority. *See Auctoritas*

Barbarians, 130, 139, 150,
Beard, Mary, 129, 189
Beauty, 12, 198–212. *See also Pul-
    chritudo*; *Venustas*
  of Augustus Caesar, 204–205,
    211–212
  of kings, 205
  of Polykleitos's statues, 268–269
  and the Stoic city, 210–212
  of young men, 210–212

Benefits
  of architecture, 130–154, 230
  of *De architectura*, 8
  of writing, 25–26
Body
  angelic, 11, 15–88, 228
  of architecture, 6, 9, 12, 57, 71,
    129, 227–229, 236, 250, 270,
    274
  beautiful, 12, 155–224
  defined by coherence, 55–58,
    195–197
  of empire, 10–11, 275–298, 300–
    301, 303
  Herculean, 11, 91–154, 193–195
  of the king, 12, 225–298, 300
  of knowledge, 60, 152–154
  and language, 72–73
  politic (*corpus rei publicae*), 59,
    272–273
  of truth, 57–58, 97
  unified, 11, 54–71
  of the world, 48, 56–57, 161, 181,
    234, 275
Boeotia, 139–140
Bonds, bonding, 63–66, 69, 88.
    See also Coherence
  and Venus, 200–201, 224, 254–
    256
Britain, 151, 298, 301
Brown, Frank E., 3, 141
Buchner, Edmund, 245
Building, 25, 43, 229–230

Cacus, 113–115
Caesar, Gaius Julius, 20, 28, 40,
    52, 59, 104, 127, 175
  Bellum gallicum, 22–25

De analogia, 26, 71
  reform of the Roman calendar,
    239–240
  refoundation of Corinth, 217
  temple of, Rome (Temple of Di-
    vus Julius), 175–179, 190, 205,
    209, 239, 290
  and Venus, 204–209
  and Vitruvius, 10, 25, 28, 35, 38,
    167, 218, 301
Callebat, Louis, 3, 79
Callimachus, 213, 215
Calpurnius Piso, Lucius, 205
Cancer (astrological sign), 244–
    245
Canfora, Luciano, 139
Canon, canonic, 196–197, 273
Cantabria, 191–192
Cappadocia, 10
Capricorn (astrological sign), 177,
    239, 245–246
Cardinal points, 161, 169, 172, 178,
    233. *See also* Four
Caryatids, 30–31
Cato the Younger (Marcus Porcius
    Cato Uticensis), 48, 76
Cetius Faventius, 5
Charis, 200–201, 205
Christianity, 174, 183–185
Chrysippus, 62–63
Cicero, Marcus Tullius, 9, 16, 25,
    51, 66–67, 82, 103, 133, 142–
    149, 199, 204, 228
  Academica, 54, 234
  on augury, 167
  on circles, 160–161
  on the *corpus rei publicae,* 59, 272
  De divinatione, 238

De finibus, 48
De inventione, 141–142
De natura deorum, 236
De officiis, 58–59
De oratore, 58, 79, 141
De republica, 136–137, 261
  on monarchy, 261–262
  on religion, 188–189, 202–203
Circle, 152–154, 197
  as source of coherence, 160
  and Vitruvian man, 160–183
Cities. *See also* Colonization
  foundation of, 163, 168–169,
    282–283
  humanitas and, 149–150, 282
  love and, 210–212
Civilization, 141, 143, 283, 296. *See
    also Humanitas*
Cleanthes, 110, 233–234
Cleopatra, 67, 163, 241
Clocks. *See Gnomonice*
Clodius Thrasea, 152
Coherence, 72, 200–201, 222, 251,
    282, 290, 296. *See also* Bonds,
    bonding
  brought about by *ratio,* 55–56,
    196, 261
  as defining condition of bodies,
    55–58, 210
  of the Roman world, 276–277,
    300
Coinage, 50–52, 69
Colonization, 138–139, 280–285
Commensurability, 65–66, 272.
    See also Proportion; Symmetry
Commentaries, 18–32, 34, 77
Commerce, 67–69
Conimbriga, 284

Corinth, 213, 215–220, 285
Corinthianization, 212–213
Corinthian order, 43, 212–224
  origin of capital, 213–215, 288
Cornutus, Lucius Annaeus, 109–
    110
Corpus, as *Gesamtwerk,* 8–9. *See
    also* Body
Corpus imperii, 11, 275–298, 302
Corpus rei publicae (Cicero), 59,
    272
Corso, Antonio, 3
Cosmic order, 46–47, 61, 73
  and hegemony of the sun, 235–
    237
Cossutius, 216

Daedalus, 95
De architectura. See also Vitruvius
  benefits of, 8
  body of, 148, 152–154, 275, 299
  as *commentarius,* 18–19
  date, 1, 10, 122–124
  Harleian manuscript, 1
  mnemonic dimension of, 84–86,
    279–280
  and *ratio,* 54
  and rhetoric, 79–81, 140–144
  structure, 25, 42–45, 85–86
Dêmiourgos, 236
Democritus, 26, 131
Diana, 256
Dinocrates, 12, 92–101, 124–129,
    139, 142, 152
Dio Cassius, 28, 226, 298–300
Diodorus Siculus, 131
Diogenes Laertius, 59, 62, 110,
    269

Dionysius of Halicarnassus, 130, 133, 272

Diotogenes, 205

Divination, Etruscan science of, 51, 163, 168–169, 191. *See also* Augury, auspices

Divine mind (*divina mens*), 55, 69–70, 122, 133, 227, 234

Doric order, 43, 220, 222

Doryphoros of Polykleitos, 274
and the Prima Porta statue of Augustus, 264–269

Drawing, 32, 45, 61, 78, 157

Egypt, 94, 124, 131, 239–241

Entasis, 157

Ephesus, 290–291

Epicureanism, 59, 143, 145, 210

Epidaurus, 216

Erechtheion, Athens, 30–31, 295–296

Etruscans. *See* Divination

Etymology, 70–71, 73

Euhemerus of Messene, 131

Eurythmy, 65–66, 79, 198–200, 211

Eurytus, 44

Evander, 113–115, 118, 120, 124

Fabius Maximus, Paulus, 246

Fabius Pictor, Quintus, 118

Fabrica and *ratiocinatio*, 28, 32–33, 38, 44, 60–61, 97, 112
and signifier-signified, 74–75, 78–79

Facundus Novius, 230, 248

Fame, 7–8, 196, 270

Fano, basilica, 217, 291

Fensterbusch, Kurt, 39

Ferri, Silvio, 78

Festus, Sextus Pompeius, 28, 163, 165, 182, 184–185

Fides (Roman god), 33

Fingers, 43–44

Fire, 142–144, 146, 148, 226, 254–256

Firmitas, 199

Flamen of Jupiter, 75

Fleury, Philippe, 3

Florus, Lucius Annaeus, 182, 276–277

Four. *See also Quadrata*; Squares, squaring
as number of cosmic order, 40, 161, 274
relation to ten, 45–46, 274

Frontinus, Sextus Julius, 5, 19, 24–25, 233
De aquis, 20, 25
De limitibus, 169–172

Fulvius Nobilior, 115

Gaius Caesar (grandson of Augustus), 217–218, 270, 291, 295

Galatia (Asia Minor), 285

Galen, 196, 266

Gaul, 22–24, 143, 280
urbanization of, 282–283

Geography, 20, 22

Geometry, 45, 78, 157, 182
and geometrical footprints, 135–139, 154
of the Prima Porta cuirass, 257–261
of Vitruvian man, 156–157

Geryon, 113, 120

Gnomonice (gnomonics, clock construction), 25, 229–250

Gnomons, 137–138, 230, 235–236, 245

Goody, Jack, 16

Grain distribution, 124–125

Greeks, 130, 140, 150

Greek learning, 136, 139–140, 149, 168, 238 (*see also Paideia*)

Grimal, Pierre, 111

Gros, Pierre, 3, 7–8, 141, 174, 217, 291

Halicarnassus, 150

Health, 47, 63

Hêgemonikon (ruling principle), 62

as *mens* in man, 55, 261

sun as, 233–239

Heliopolis, 241

Heraclitus of Ephesus, 88

Heraclitus Homericus, 109

Hercules, 72, 98–110, 145

and Alexander, 98–101

and Augustus, 120–124

as benefactor, 101–102, 109, 130–131, 133–134

and Cacus, 113–115, 118

at the crossroads, 101, 115

Gallic, 103–105, 110, 199

and Mercury, 104–110, 112

and the Muses, 115–118

as Rome's first founder, 113–115

temples of, 113, 115–118, 121, 125

as universal *logos,* 110

as world conqueror, 130–131

Hermes. *See* Mercury

Herodotus, 21

Hexis (habit, trained ability), 61–62, 69, 78

History, knowledge of, 30–31

Homer, 148, 169

Horace (Quintus Horatius Flaccus), 67, 186–187, 189, 193

Horizon, 161

Horologium Augusti (sun clock of Augustus), 230, 244–250

Howe, Thomas Noble, 4

Humanitas, 115, 118, 121, 134–135, 141, 145–146, 149–152, 156, 193

Hut of Romulus

on the Capitol, Rome, 81–82, 143, 146–148

on the Palatine, Rome, 143, 162–163

Hyginus Gromaticus, 282

Iamblichus, 46

Imperator Caesar, 35–36, 38, 85–88, 102, 129, 134, 278

Imperial cult, 178, 240, 284–288, 294–296

Imperialism, Roman, 133–134

and architecture, 12–13, 303

Imperium, 26–27, 128, 277–280, 291, 298

Incorporeals, 77. *See also Lekta*

India, 52

Ionic order, 43, 220, 222

volutes, 157

Isocrates, 101

Jaeger, Mary, 82

Janus, 105, 109–110

Juba, 118

Julius Theon, C., 111

Juno, 24, 202
Jupiter, 24, 261, 277
  temples of, 24, 26, 28–30, 33, 75,
    81–82, 190–193, 301

Kantorowicz, Ernst, 227
Kienast, Dietmar, 276
Kingship, 226–228
Knowledge of the architect, 16–17,
    30–33, 100, 148. *See also Archi-*
    tectura; *Fabrica* and *ratiocinatio*
Kolossos, 75

Language, 60–61, 71–73, 76–77
Left and right, 169–172
Lekta, 58, 86
  and Stoic language theory, 76–77
Leonardo da Vinci, 156–157
Libri fulgurales (lightning books),
    191
Limits, 169–172, 233
Lituus (augural staff), 163, 167,
    177, 209
Livia Drusilla (wife of Augustus),
    34, 250
Livy (Titus Livius), 17, 19, 82, 111,
    232, 272
Locus, 80–81, 84–86, 183, 278. *See*
    also Memory
Logos, 61, 67, 141, 262–264, 273.
    See also Ratio
Long, A. A., 61
Love, 210–212, 224, 270. *See also*
    Venus; *Venustas*
Lucian, 46, 103–105, 110, 199
Lucius Caesar (grandson of Au-
    gustus), 218

Lucretius (Titus Lucretius Carus),
    103, 142–143, 201, 205, 228
Lydus, John, 47, 161
Lysippus, 127, 270

Macedonia, 92, 97
Macrobius, Ambrosius Theodo-
    sius, 239
Maecenas, Gaius, 227
Manilius, Marcus, 111, 160–161
Maps, 20–22
Mars, 31, 67
Marseilles, 143
Materials, 47
Mathematics, Greek, 24, 44–45.
    See also Number
Measurement, 50–53, 273–274
Mechanics, 3, 25, 39, 48, 130–131,
    230
Memory, 17–18, 31, 46, 60, 80–88,
    279–280
Menenius Agrippa, fable of, 272–
    273
Mercury, 67–70, 150, 187
  and Hercules, 104–110, 112
Millar, Fergus, 34, 51, 138
Milo of Croton, 134
Minerva, 24, 202
Moatti, Claudia, 9, 140
Money and measurement, 53. *See*
    also Coinage
Moon, 169, 172
Mos maiorum (custom of the an-
    cestors), 8, 19, 238
Mural painting, 229, 283, 299
Music, 46
Myron, 270

Nature
  and number, 40
  as source of power, 222–224, 234, 238, 262
Nero (Nero Claudius Caesar Drusus Germanicus), 261
Nicomedes of Bithynia, 204
Nikopolis, 168, 285
Numa Pompilius, 109, 232
Number, 49–50. *See also* Four; Mathematics; Seven; Sixteen; Ten; Three
  and nature, 40

Obelisks, 241–248
Octavian, 10. *See also* Augustus
Odeon of Agrippa, Athens, 291, 296
Oedipus, 232
Officium, 19, 58–59
Ogmios, 103–105
Omnes gentes (all peoples), 8, 131–134, 137, 264, 284, 300
Opus quadratum, 163, 193
Orbis doctrinae, 152–154
Ordinatio, 39–40, 54, 65
Ovid (Publius Ovidius Naso), 10, 152, 188, 276, 280
Oxyrhincus, 162

Paideia (Greek learning), 139–140, 149–150, 152–154
Pammenes, 296
Parthenon, Athens, 294–296
Parthia, 256
Parthians, return of standards by (20 B.C.), 251, 262, 270, 275, 294

Pebble diagrams, 44–45
Pensabene, Patrizio, 165
Pergamon, 149
Pericles, 31
Perrault, Claude, 1–2, 6
Phidias, 270, 296
Philanthropia, 101. *See also* Benefits
  and conquest, 130–154
Philip of Macedon, 73, 101, 127
Philodemus, 205
Phrygia, 143
Plato, 24, 26, 46, 131, 134
  Phaedrus, 272
  Timaeus, 48, 236
Pliny the Elder (Gaius Plinius Secundus), 20, 65, 95, 109, 133–134, 200, 205, 230, 248
Plutarch, 96, 100–101, 110, 118, 127, 199
Poggio Bracciolini, Giovanni Francesco, 1
Politics and religion, 183–191
Pollini, John, 262
Pollitt, J. J., 34, 200
Polykleitos
  canon of, 196, 266, 270, 274
  Doryphoros statue, 264–269, 274
Pompey (Gnaeus Pompeius Magnus), 19, 204
Pomponius, Sextus, 57
Pontus, 143, 146
Poplar, sacred to Hercules, 112–113, 120
Posidonius, 62, 144

Power
  body of, 278
  dependence on access to the
    gods, 28–30, 186–188, 238,
    261
  grounding in nature, 222–224,
    234, 238, 262
  localization of, 189, 278
Praetorium, 168
Price, Simon, 294
Prima Porta statue of Augustus,
    250–275, 290
  canonic proportions of, 274
  and the Doryphoros of Poly-
    kleitos, 264–269
  iconography of, 251–261
  and Vitruvian man, 257–261
Primitive hut, 142
Prodicus, 101, 115
Prometheus, 131
Propertius, Sextus, 118
Proportion, 3, 40, 195–197, 200,
    270, 273. *See also* Symmetry
Psammetikos II, 244
Ptolemy II Philadelphus, 216
Pulchritudo, 200
Pythagoras, Pythagoreanism, 24,
    26, 40–42, 46–49, 83, 96, 110,
    118, 131, 134, 161, 169, 274

Quadrata (squared, divided in
    four), 161. *See also Roma
    quadrata*; Squares, squaring
  statues of Polykleitos described
    as, 268–269
Quality (*qualitas*), 54–55, 199
Quantity (*posotês*), 40, 54, 199

Quintilian (Marcus Fabius Quin-
    tilianus), 77–79, 81

Ramses II, 244
Ratio, 54–55, 66–71, 127–128, 238.
    See also Logos
  as agent of coherence in bodies,
    55–56, 196, 261
  and language, 60–61
  and rhetoric, 143–144, 199
Raven, J. E., 274
Religio (Roman religion), 183–198
  inseparability from politics, 184–
    191
  naturalization of, 238
  and temples, 183
  worldliness of, 184
Renewal (*renovatio*), 144, 226,
    284–296
Res publica (the Roman common-
    wealth), 59, 71
Rhetoric, 79–82, 140–144, 272
  and eurythmy, 199
Rhetorica ad Herennium, 81, 132–
    133
Rhodes, 95–97, 135, 149
Ritual, 75, 163, 238. *See also*
    Augury, auspices; Divination
Romano, Elisa, 3
Romanocentricity, 301
Roman world, limits of, 143, 148,
    152–154, 181, 300–301. *See also*
    Rome: empire
Roma quadrata, 162–163, 166,
    268, 290
Rome
  arts of, 151
  calendar, reform of, 239–240

central position of, 64, 133, 137, 238, 245–246
city of (*urbs*), 152
civilizing mission of, 151, 220
colonization by, 138–139, 280–285
empire, 275–276, 302 (*see also Corpus imperii*; Imperialism, Roman; *Imperium*)
monuments and topographical sites (*see also* Rome: temples)
  ara maxima, 113–115, 118
  Ara Pacis Augustae, 213, 244–246
  Aventine, 113, 115
  Campus Martius, 20, 213, 248
  Capitol, 24, 28, 81, 107, 113, 115, 143, 175, 190, 192, 232
  Circus Flaminius, 124, 190
  Circus Maximus, 163, 244
  Citadel (*arx*), 143, 168
  Forum of Augustus, 31, 127
  Forum Boarium, 113–115, 120, 125
  Forum of Caesar, 204
  Forum Romanum, 105, 175, 204, 239, 275
  golden milestone (*miliarium aureum*), 275
  Horologium Augusti (sun clock of Augustus), 230, 244–250
  house of Augustus, 163–165, 192
  Mausoleum of Augustus, 245
  Palatine, 113, 115, 143, 163–165, 192, 244
  Sacra Via, 107
  shrine of Fides, 33

natural supremacy of, 64, 238
origins, 162–163
religion (*see Religio*)
republic, 9
  fall of, 10, 66–67, 140, 226
temples
  Apollo Caelispex, 125
  Apollo Palatinus, 162–165, 190, 244
  Augustan Concord, 105–109, 112
  Divus Julius, 175–179, 190, 205, 209, 239, 290
  Hercules Musarum, 115–118
  Hercules Victor, 113, 116–117, 125
  Jupiter Capitolinus, 24, 26, 28–30, 33, 75, 81–82, 191, 301
  Jupiter Feretrius, 190–191
  Jupiter Tonans, 192–193
  Mars Ultor, 31
  Portunus, 125
  Saturn, 275
  Sol, 244
  Venus Genetrix, 204
  Venus Victrix, 204
Romulus, 31, 120, 163, 175, 191
  Capitoline hut of, 81–82, 143, 146–148
  Palatine hut of, 143, 162–163
Rowland, Ingrid, 4
Rüpke, Jörg, 24
Rykwert, Joseph, 4

Salamis, 30
Samothrace, 216, 235
Schilling, Robert, 202
Scopas *minor*, C., 125

Scrolls (constituting *De architectura*), 11, 39–43, 85, 154
Seneca, Lucius Annaeus, 26, 56–57, 77, 132, 261
Servius (Servius Grammaticus; Maurus Servius Honoratus), 5
Seven, 40, 43
Sextius, Quintus, 26
Sextus Empiricus, 56, 58, 76–77
Scheid, John, 75
Shield of Achilles, 148
Shield of Aeneas, 146–148
Sidonius Apollinaris, 5–6
Signification, 71–88, 98–100, 192–193, 227
Signifier-signified (*quod significat, quod significatur*), 74–79, 98–100
Simonides of Ceos, 149, 269
Sixteen, 50–51, 169
Small, Jocelyn Penny, 80
Sol, 244, 254, 256
Solinus, Gaius Julius, 95–96, 162–163, 165
Sophocles, 97
Speusippus, 46, 49
Sphinx, 122
  riddle of, 232
Squares, squaring, 51, 161–162, 197. *See also* Four; *Quadrata*
  at Athens, 291–296
  and augury, 166–168, 178
  and gnomonics, 230–232, 246
  and the Prima Porta statue of Augustus, 257–261
  and Vitruvian man, 160–183
Stewart, Andrew, 266

Stoicism, 11, 26, 48–49, 55–58, 61–63, 109, 149, 160–161, 233, 236, 261
  Augustan, 111–112
  and the brotherhood of man, 132
  and the formation of cities, 210–212, 269–270
  and language theory, 61, 76–78
Strabo, 22–23, 95–96, 139–140
Suetonius (Gaius Suetonius Tranquillus), 59, 111, 121, 165, 191, 211, 220, 257, 299
Summum templum architecturae, 28–30, 145–148, 301
Sun, 169, 172–177, 209, 233–248, 296
  hegemony of, 233–239, 288
Sundials, 235–250. *See also Gnomonice*
Superstitio, 185
Surveying, 169–172, 232
Syme, Sir Ronald, 278
Symmetry (*symmetria*), 40, 65–66, 199–200. *See also* Proportion
  in the body politic, 272–273
  and the canon of Polykleitos, 266–269
  and coherence in bodies, 195–197
  in public speaking, 272

Tacitus, Cornelius, 28, 151–152, 191, 290
Tarraco, 290
Teleon, 43–44, 274. *See also* Ten
Tempering (*temperatura*), 63–64, 66, 137

Temple of Amon, Karnak, 241
Temple of Apollo, Nikopolis, 168,
     285
Temple of Apollo Epikourios,
     Bassae, 215–216
Temple of Ares, Athens, 291
Temple of Artemis, Ephesus, 96,
     174
Temple of Augustus, Antioch in
     Pisidia, 285–290
Temple of Caesar, Alexandria, 241
Temple of Hercules, Tibur, 121
Temple of Roma and Augustus,
     Athens, 294–296
Temple of Zeus Olympios, Athens,
     216, 220
Temples, 47, 53–54. *See also*
     Rome: temples
  Augustan building of, 187–188,
     190–195
  orientation of, 173–178, 209, 254,
     288
  and power, 186–188
  proportions of, 210
  and Roman religion, 183
  signifying power of, 192–193
  and Vitruvian man, 183
Templum, 166
Ten, 118–120, 128
  circularity of, 161–162
  as *kratos* (power), 96
  as mnemonic frame of *De archi-
     tectura*, 87
  perfection of, 39–54, 274
Tertullian (Quintus Septimius
     Florens Tertullianus), 244
Tetractys, 45–46, 50, 84, 128, 274.
     See also Ten

Theater of Dionysos, Athens, 294–
     295
Theaters, 47–48, 66
Theology
  tripartite (Varro), 49, 51–52, 238
  of Victory, 54
Theon of Smyrna, 24
Three, 22
  as the condition of wholeness, 24
  and structure of *De architectura*,
     25
Thutmosis III, 241
Tiberius (Tiberius Claudius Nero
     Caesar), 105, 254, 276
Time, 47, 228, 232, 234, 239–240,
     248, 300. *See also* Sundials
Tralles, 290
Triumphs, 7, 25–26, 28, 30, 75. *See
     also* Augustus: triple triumph
  and temple building, 186–187
Truth
  of *De architectura*, 2–3
  and the true (*alêtheia* and *to
     alêthes*), 57–58, 97

Utilitas, 199

Varro, Marcus Terentius, 9, 16,
     24–25, 54–55, 67, 79, 95, 103,
     127, 142, 162, 169, 226, 228,
     232, 248
  etymologies, 70–71, 73
  language theory, 71–73
  numerology, 40
  on Polykleitos's statues, 268–269
  tripartite theology, 49, 51–52, 238
  on Venus, 200–201, 224, 254–
     256

Vasaly, Ann, 82
Velitrae, 192
Venus, 31, 34, 200–209, 224. *See also Venustas*
  Anadyomene, 205–209
  binding power of, 200–201, 224, 254–256
  and Caesar, 204
  cosmic dimension of, 201, 209
  felix, 203
  genetrix, 201–202, 204, 209
  as Lucifer (morning star), 209, 254
  and Pompey, 203
  and Roman power, 203–209
  and Sulla, 203
  victrix, 204
Venustas, 12, 199–200, 203, 272. *See also* Beauty; *Pulchritudo*
  and pleasure, 200, 210
  relation to Venus, 200–204, 224
  and the Stoic city, 210–212
  worldliness of, 200
Venusta species (beautiful appearance, eurythmy), 199, 211–212
Vernant, Jean-Pierre, 75
Vestal virgins, 75
Veyne, Paul, 152
Virgil (Publius Vergilius Maro), 67, 83, 111, 113, 118, 120–121, 146–148, 186, 189, 193, 202, 277
Vitruvian man, 156–183, 295
  as the architect's template, 181–183
  and Augustus, 197–198
  coherence of, 196–197

  geometrical attributes of, 160–162
  as a metaphysical proposition, 160–162
  passivity of, 157, 181
  and the Prima Porta statue of Augustus, 257–261
  as a ritual formula, 163–178
  and Roman religion, 183
Vitruvius (Marcus Vitruvius Pollio). *See also De architectura*
  alleged failings, 74, 102, 175, 229, 299
  and Augustus, 1, 8, 10, 35–39, 51, 102, 302
  and Caesar, 10, 25, 28, 35, 38, 167, 218, 301
  date and identity of, 1, 7, 305 (n. 2)
  desire to be of service, 7–8, 131–132
  historicity of, 5, 13
  old age, 1, 102–103
  originality, 7
  reception of, 303
    ancient, 5–6
    modern, 2–4
    Renaissance, 1–2, 6
  and Stoicism, 57, 112
  and writing, 16–17
Vulcan, 146

Wallace-Hadrill, Andrew, 140
Water, 25, 42, 48, 88, 137, 254–256
Weinstock, Stefan, 240
Wesenberg, Burkhardt, 3
Women, 185, 300

Woolf, Greg, 282
Writing, 16–17, 32, 45, 78
  and *auctoritas,* 34, 36
  benefits of, 25–26
  and conquest, 21–22
  cubical, 40–42, 83–84
  and memory, 17–18, 82, 85

Xerxes, 30

Zeno, 109